Multilateralism and the United Nations Security Council

Madeleine O. Hosli · Gabriela M. G. Bueno ·
Katyayni Champawat · Sofia Pires Lopes
Editors

Multilateralism and the United Nations Security Council

Voting, Power, and Coalition-Formation

palgrave
macmillan

Editors
Madeleine O. Hosli
Leiden University
The Hague, The Netherlands

Gabriela M. G. Bueno
Leiden University
The Hague, The Netherlands

Katyayni Champawat
Leiden University
The Hague, The Netherlands

Sofia Pires Lopes
Leiden University
The Hague, The Netherlands

ISBN 978-3-031-85319-7 ISBN 978-3-031-85320-3 (eBook)
https://doi.org/10.1007/978-3-031-85320-3

This Palgrave Macmillan imprint is published by the registered company Springer Nature Switzerland AG
The registered company address is: Gewerbestrasse 11, 6330 Cham, Switzerland

Contents

Notes on Contributors

Viraj Balutkar is a young professional, working as a programme officer for the Netherlands Advisory Board on impact investing. He is a recent graduate with an Advanced MSc in International Relations and Diplomacy from Leiden University. Viraj is passionate about learning and writing on topics related to impact, sustainability, and climate tech and wrote his Master's thesis on the EU's climate security risks mitigation efforts. Professionally, Viraj has held roles in the impact and venture philanthropy sector and likes to volunteer for social activities in his free time. He holds a Bachelor's in economics and hails from the city of Mumbai, India.

Gabriela M. G. Bueno holds a Bachelor's degree in international studies with a minor in anthropology from Flagler College. She is the author of the chapter *COVID-19 in the Americas: Challenges in the Institutionalisation of the Gender Equality Agenda* (Palgrave Macmillan and Springer Nature 2022). Earlier, she pursued her academic career at Korea University in South Korea and Yamanashi Gakuin University in Japan in both social sciences and international relations. She specialised in global governance and cooperation, in special, regional structures of cooperation and integration in Latin America and historical memories as a political tool for diplomacy. She is currently enrolled in a Master's in International Relations, Global Order in Historical Perspective and is a program and research assistant at Leiden University.

Katyayni Champawat recently earned her Master's degree with *cum laude* in International Relations and Diplomacy from Leiden University, following her Bachelor's degree in History from Lady Shri Ram College, Delhi University. During her undergraduate studies, she specialised in gendered Indian history and continued to deepen her engagement with gender theory, feminism, and post-colonial perspectives in her graduate studies. Her Master's thesis, titled "Feminist Foreign Policy for a Greener Tomorrow: Unveiling the Nexus Between Canada's Feminist International Assistance Policy and the Climate Crisis," integrated literature on ecofeminism, feminist foreign policy, poststructuralism, and ontological security. From October 2024 to December 2024, she was interning at United Nations OCHA. Katyayni is passionate about communications, research, and writing.

Breanna N. Cross Hailing from Richmond, Virginia in the United States, Breanna recently graduated *cum laude* with an Advanced Master of Science in International Relations and Diplomacy from Leiden University, where she focused her research on multilateralism and international organisation. During her studies, she completed a year-long internship in atrocity risk and prevention for the U.S. Department of State and worked as a research assistant in counterterrorism and child psychology for the EU-funded PREPARE project. Before pursuing her Master's degree, Breanna worked for almost five years as a trial paralegal in complex defence litigation for an international law firm.

Elise Galy–Jammou–Préfontaine is currently a Master's student in European Affairs, specialising in Europe in the World, at Sciences Po Paris. She completed her Bachelor's degree in Political Science at Paris II Panthéon-Assas in Paris and got the certificate of International General Studies (CIEG) of l'Institut des Hautes Études Internationales (IHEI) of this same university.

Alexandra Hall is a graduate of Leiden University with an Advanced Master's degree in International Relations and Diplomacy. Previously, she graduated *magna cum laude* with a Bachelor's degree in Political Science, complemented by a minor in Justice Studies, from Westminster University located in her home state of Utah. Her academic focus includes areas such as climate change, populism, immigration, and the United Nations, equipping her with a well-rounded understanding of global issues. With a diverse set of interests and a passion for global justice, she has applied her knowledge through her work and volunteer roles with several local grassroots organisations. Driven by this dedication, she continues to strive for a positive impact through her involvement in international relations and advocacy.

Peppi Heinikainen is a doctoral student at Tampere Peace Research Institute (TAPRI). Her doctoral dissertation studies norm contestation and the state of multilateralism in the United Nations Security Council's P5 discussions on the Libyan and Syrian civil wars. She holds an MA degree in International Peace and Security from King's College London and a BA degree in European Studies from Maastricht University. Her prior research has focused on the Finnish security and defence policy identity and the difficulties of peace mediation in Ukraine and Syria. Peppi is based in Helsinki, Finland and works closely with EU, foreign, and defence policy issues.

Tareq Yacoub Helou is a PhD candidate pursuing a double degree in International Relations at the University of São Paulo and King's College London. He holds a Bachelor of Science in Economics from the Federal University of Paraná and a Master of Science in International Administration and Global Governance from the University of Gothenburg. His research focuses on the political economy of multilateral development finance, regional integration, the BRICS, the United Nations Security Council, and EU–Latin America relations.

Madeleine O. Hosli is a professor of International Relations at Leiden University. Her main research interests are in international organisation, international political economy, and European integration. She is the author of *The Euro: A Concise Introduction to European Monetary Integration* (Lynne Rienner, 2004) and *The European Union and the United Nations in Global Governance* (Bristol University Press, 2022). She is the co-editor of *The Changing Global Order* (Springer 2020), *The Future of Multilateralism: Global Cooperation and International Organizations* (Rowman and Littlefield 2021), and *The Global, Regional and Local Politics of Institutional Responses to COVID-19: Implications for Women and Children* (Palgrave Macmillan and Springer Nature 2022). She has published widely in international peer-reviewed journals.

Barney Jansen holds a dual Bachelor's degree in Korean Studies and Public Administration and a Master's degree in International Relations and Diplomacy, both from Leiden University (Netherlands). The combination of Korean Studies and International Relations equips him with a unique perspective on East Asian geopolitics, enabling a deep dive into the intricacies of the Korean Peninsula and its regional impact. His academic journey is marked by a strong focus on international affairs, particularly in Asia, allowing for a comprehensive analysis and understanding of contemporary challenges and opportunities in Asia.

Beatrice Levorato is a graduate of the advanced International Relations and Diplomacy program at Leiden University. She holds a Bachelor's degree in International and Diplomatic Sciences from the University of Trieste and has completed winter courses at The Hague Academy of International Law. She completed an internship in the Political Affairs division at the Organisation for the Prohibition of Chemical Weapons (OPCW) and has collaborated as a junior associate with *The Diplomat Magazine*. Her academic interests include climate security, disaster politics, and risk reduction.

Sofia Pires Lopes holds an Advanced Master of Science in International Relations and Diplomacy from Leiden University, in the Netherlands, and a Bachelor in Political Science and International Relations from Nova University of Lisbon, in Portugal. During her bachelor studies, she spent a semester abroad as part of the Erasmus+ programme at the University of Milan, in Italy. From September 2024 to February 2025, she was an intern at the Education and Events Team at T.M.C Asser Instituut in The Hague. She is also a UK and European Affairs Team member at ITSS Verona and a volunteer at the Platform for Undocumented Migrants (PICUM). Sofia is passionate about Foreign Policy Analysis, Policy Change, and Gender issues.

Rennan Pastich Loureiro has completed a Bachelor's and Master's degree in Political Science and International Relations at the Federal University of Pernambuco (UFPE), Brazil. Research interests include International Relations Theory, Comparative Politics, Democratisation, Global Health Governance, International Organisations, and advanced methodologies such as data analysis and network analysis.

Binghua Lu is a junior Chinese researcher with an academic background in History and International Relations. Her research interests lie in Chinese politics, China and global security, the Belt and Road Initiative and global governance, and China's role in multilateralism under the

UN system. During her Master of Arts in History, she generated interest in Sino-West relations in the modern age by looking into the initiation of the China-Britain-US business-political interactions in Macau, China, before the Opium War in 1840. She holds an Advanced MSc degree in International Relations and Diplomacy from Leiden University. Her experience as an academic researcher and policy consultant underpins her aspiration to integrate academic findings into the process of real-world problem-solving. She is also an entrepreneur, aspiring to facilitate a better connection of business resources between China and Europe while promoting the UN Sustainable Development Goals.

Natalia Luers is a Master's student in International Security Studies at the Sant'Anna School of Advanced Studies in Pisa and the University of Trento. Previously, she obtained her dual Bachelor's degree in International Relations and Political Science at Universidad Empresarial Siglo 21 in Córdoba, Argentina. Her research interests revolve around global and regional governance on disarmament and non-proliferation of Weapons of Mass Destruction.

Guilherme Pucarinho Soares de Oliveira is an Advanced Master's student in International Relations and Diplomacy at Leiden University. Guilherme interned at the Portuguese Mission to the United Nations in New York and worked as an external coordinator for the Portuguese Association of Researchers and Students in the United Kingdom (PARSUK) in London. With PARSUK, he contributed to the PUMP report, which presents the most comprehensive analysis of scientific collaborations between Portugal and the UK. He also represented the organisation at Connects-UK. His academic background includes a Bachelor's in politics and international relations from Queen Mary University of London, where he completed a thesis on implementing sustainable development goals in Brazil. Conversely, he is passionate about Global Affairs and Sustainable Development.

Sahib Rasulov is a junior Azerbaijani researcher with an academic background in International Relations and History. His research interests are foreign policy analysis and security & defence policies, emergence of the modern state, and regional security with focus on the Middle East and South Caucasus. Throughout the Advanced MSc International Relations and Diplomacy at Leiden University, taught in cooperation with the Clingendael Institute (Netherlands), he developed interest in various aspects of security and their impact on negotiations conduct. His graduate thesis focused on analysing the impact of trilateral relations of Türkiye, Russia, and Iran in Azerbaijan's security culture.

Umang Sodhi is a research professional and international relations specialist with an Advanced Master's degree in International Relations and Diplomacy from Leiden University. With a robust background in quantitative research and stakeholder engagement, she has developed expertise in regulatory analysis, funding, security, and global development. Her research experience includes quantitative data analysis using R Studio, SPSS, and Excel, with a published scholarly work on climate migration in the Sage Journal *Political Studies Review*. Professionally, she has worked across diverse sectors, including corporate affairs at a large FMCG company, community development at a local NGO, and as the founder of Level Up Advisory, a research-based consultancy supporting NGOs and enterprises.

Anri Stepanian is a young professional and recent graduate from Leiden University with an Advanced MSc in International Relations and Diplomacy. He has served in the Georgian military and has internship experiences in NGOs in Georgia and The Hague. His expertise lies in the South Caucasus region and he is interested in learning more about climate change and water degradation in the region. Anri has a Bachelor's in International Relations from the Georgian Institute of Public Affairs in Georgia.

Koen van Schijndel holds a Bachelor's degree in European Studies from Maastricht University and an Advanced Master's degree in International Relations and Diplomacy from Leiden University. Although the author's academic background has largely been focused on the European region and the European Union in particular by diving deeper into specific challenges that European countries and the European Union face in current times, the Master's degree enabled the author to expand interests beyond the aforementioned region and into Africa, Asia, and the Middle East.

Abbreviations

AL	Arab League
AOSIS	Alliance of Small Island States
AU	African Union
BRI	Belt and Road Initiative
CFSP	Common Foreign and Security Policy
CICA	Conference on Interaction and Confidence Building Measures in Asia
CPLP	Portuguese-Speaking Language Community
CSRs	Country-Specific Recommendations
DRC	Democratic Republic of the Congo
E10	Non-permanent UNSC member-states
EC	European Community
ECOSOC	United Nations Economic and Social Council
EEAS	European External Action Service
EEG	Eastern European Group
EESC	European Economic and Social Committee
EGD	European Green Deal
EMU	Economic and Monetary Union
EP	European Parliament
EPC	European Political Cooperation
ES	European Semester
ESM	European Stability Mechanism
ESS	European Security Strategy
EU	European Union
EUMS	European Union Member-States
FGM	Female Genital Mutilation

G4	The Group of Four
G77	Group of 77
GCC	Gulf Cooperation Council
GRV	Gender-Related Violence
GVB	Gender-Based Violence
HR	High Representative
IAEA	International Atomic Energy Agency
ICC	International Criminal Court
ICJ	International Court of Justice
ICRC	International Committee of the Red Cross
ICT	Information and Communication Technology
IDA	International Disability Alliance
IGO	Intergovernmental Organizations
IMF	International Monetary Fund
INTERPOL	International Criminal Police Organization
IOs	International Organisations
IR	International Relations
IS	Islamic State
JIM	Joint Investigative Mechanism
LAC	Latin American and Caribbean
LAS	League of Arab States
LEU	Low-Enriched Uranium
MINUJUSTH	United Nations Mission for Justice Support in Haiti
MINURSO	United Nations Mission for the Referendum in Western Sahara
MINUSCA	United Nations Multidimensional Integrated Stabilization Mission in the Central African Republic
NAM	Non-Aligned Movement
NATO	North Atlantic Treaty Organisation
NGEU	NextGenerationEU
NGOs	Non-Governmental Organisations
OAS	Organisation of American States
OECD	Organisation for Economic Co-operation and Development
OHCHR	Office of the High Commissioner for Human Rights
OIC	Organisation of Islamic Cooperation
OPEC	Organisation of the Petroleum Exporting Countries
P2	China and Russia
P3	UK, USA, and France
P5	Permanent UNSC member-states
PA	Principal-agent theory
PSC	Political and Security Committee
R2P	Responsibility to Protect
RRF	Resilience and Recovery Fund

S&E	Small and Emerging Powers
SCO	Shanghai Cooperation Organization
SDGs	Sustainable Development Goals
TEU	Treaty of the European Union
TFEU	Treaty on the Functioning of the European Union
UAE	United Arab Emirates
UK	United Kingdom
UN	United Nations
UNDOF	United Nations Disengagement Observer Force
UNEF II	United Nations Emergency Force II
UNFCCC	United Nations Framework Convention on Climate Change
UNFICYP	United Nations Peacekeeping Force in Cyprus
UNGA	United Nations General Assembly
UNHCR	United Nations High Commissioner for Refugees
UNHRC	United Nations Human Rights Council
UNICEF	United Nations Children's Fund
UNIDIR	United Nations Institute for Disarmament Research
UNIFIL	United Nations Interim Force in Lebanon
UNMIL	United Nations Mission in Liberia
UNMISS	United Nations Mission in South Sudan
UNMOGIP	United Nations Military Observer Group in India and Pakistan
UNODC	United Nations Office on Drugs and Crime
UNOMIG	United Nations Observer Mission in Georgia
UNSC	United Nations Security Council
UNSDGs	United Nations' Sustainable Development Goals
UNTAG	United Nations Transition Assistance Group
US	United States
USA	United States of America
USSR	Union of Soviet Socialist Republics
WEOG	Western Europe and Others Group
WFP	World Food Programme
WHO	World Health Organisation
WMDs	Weapons of Mass Destruction
WMO	World Meteorological Organization
WNA	World Nuclear Association
WPS	Women, Peace and Security

List of Figures

Chapter 5

List of Tables

Chapter 10

CHAPTER 1

Introduction: Challenges to Multilateralism and the United Nations Security Council

Sofia Pires Lopes, Katyayni Champawat, Gabriela M. G. Bueno, and Madeleine O. Hosli

Multilateralism, as a common buzzword within global politics, has proved to be rather elusive. However, without it, pure "power politics" would be likely to reign on the international level. Commonly understood as any effort by multiple states to coordinate activities based on shared and agreed-upon principles, the concept has evolved to reflect the realities of its context (Lavelle 2020). Multilateralism, however, is often seen as the foundation for global rules-based governance (Hosli et al. 2021).

Multilateralism Certainly, multilateralism can be quite tedious when organizations encompass a high number of member states but aim to have consensus between their governments. Nowadays, "minilateralism" is at times seen as an alternative to multilateralism, to create consensus within smaller groups of states, potentially aiming to present solutions achieved to the entire membership thereafter. But "minilateralism" may

S. P. Lopes · K. Champawat · G. M. G. Bueno · M. O. Hosli (✉)
Leiden University, The Hague, The Netherlands
e-mail: m.o.hosli@fgga.leidenuniv.nl

M. O. Hosli et al. (eds.), *Multilateralism and the United Nations Security Council*, https://doi.org/10.1007/978-3-031-85320-3_1

lack legitimacy as agenda-setting and decision-making is then limited to a small group of members within an organization.[1]

The principle of multilateralism is also core to activities of several regional organizations. A prominent example is the European Union (EU), which operates on a daily basis and in a longer-term perspective based on (regional) rules-based governance. Yet, in an increasingly fragmented world, with deep material interdependence, multilateralism is said by some to have reached an impasse: With the rise in regional powers, the increasing global power struggles and related tensions, and the new "non-traditional" threats, it is seen as remaining stuck in its traditions and aligned with allegedly unnecessary bureaucracy such as layers of decision-making and approval, competing interests, and veto powers. The COVID-19 pandemic, in that perspective, only exposed these weaknesses even further (albeit a counter-argument could be that several multilateral institutions managed to cope with the effects of the pandemic rather well albeit being in a challenging situation themselves).[2]

At the heart of frequent criticism along such lines is the United Nations (hereafter referred to as the UN), especially the United Nations Security Council (the UNSC). As a dynamic multilateral organization that notes the membership of virtually every country, the UN presents the stage on which the changing realities of the world are played. The UNSC, as the organ with the most power, presents a microcosm of the same. This book was conceived keeping this changing reality and its reflection within the UNSC in mind. It also demonstrates, however, how many international powers still support multilateralism and the UN as an encompassing global governance institution.

By focusing on the UNSC and multilateralism, we will highlight some crucial aspects of the latter, while providing new insights on the operation and functioning of the former. Analyzing the ways of operation of the UNSC also requires embedding it into a broader context of global governance (and of the institutional structure of the UN itself). There arguably is not much literature yet addressing current trends of decision-making and voting in the UNSC; hence, it is of crucial importance to better understand its ways of operation, challenges faced due to its member

[1] On minilateralism, see for example Anuar and Hussain (2021).

[2] See for example Alhashimi et al. (2021).

state composition and, finally, the actual (voting) behavior of permanent as compared to non-permanent members of the UNSC.

Exploring its operations also implies that its embedding into the current system and the network of international organizations needs to be understood. While this book cannot cover all organizations operating in the complex system of global governance, it will focus on selected ones, and focus on the interaction of some regional organizations—here notably the EU—with the UN and the UNSC. This approach will also be taken in this introduction to the book.

International, intergovernmental, and non-governmental organizations play an important role in the framework of multilateralism, global and regional governance. The League of Nations became the first intergovernmental organization primarily concerned with maintaining peace "via collective security, disarmament, and arbitration" (Trent and Schnurr 2018, 26). The League's timid success, proven by its endeavors in the Balkan refugee crisis in the 1920s and in the challenges related to the end of the Second World War, showed that multilateralism was more than a liberal ideal; it was a realist necessity, calling upon the creation of the United Nations (Trent and Schnurr 2018, 22–32). Reaffirming the need for cooperation and multilateralism, the UN created a stage for countries to rebuild, for war crimes to hold official trials, for the elaboration of plans for eradicating hunger and other humanitarian work to function, and, most importantly, for the creation of an international Charter. The UN Charter is a crucial international treaty to which Members are bound, extending it to the Statute of the International Court of Justice (ICJ), making the Charter the leading instrument in international relations (United Nations n.d.-c).

The United Nations is composed of six central bodies. Given the scope of this book, it is important to understand the internal functioning of the UN's several bodies, agencies, and entities. The General Assembly (UNGA) is the largest body of the UN, comprising all 193 member states, making it the only UN organ with (almost) universal representation (United Nations n.d.-b). It adopts resolutions based on a simple majority voting threshold, whereas some decisions, such as a change of the UN Charter, require a two-thirds majority to pass. This also applies to a (formal) adaptation of the composition of the UNSC, where in addition to this requirement, consent of the P5 and national-level ratification would be needed.

In addition, the UN has the Economic and Social Council (ECOSOC) for coordination, recommendation, policy review, dialogue, and implementation of development goals. This body is the central mechanism for activities in the economic and social spectrum, having a total of 54 members elected by the UNGA (United Nations, n.d.-b). Alongside these two bodies, the UN encompasses the Trusteeship Council—established in the early UN days for the supervision of 11 Trust territories, which have, by now, all achieved self-government—and the Secretariat. The latter comprises the organization's Secretary-General, recognized as the Chief Administrative Officer, overseeing UN's functions and operations, appointed by the UNGA and voted on by the UNSC, and thousands of UN Staff across the world (United Nations n.d.-b). The UN's principal judicial office is the International Court of Justice (ICJ), located in The Hague (Netherlands), which aims to settle legal disputes submitted by the States and functions according to the Charter and Statute (United Nations n.d.-b).

Lastly, the UN has the UNSC to maintain international peace and security. The Council has 15 members: five permanent (P5), consisting of China, France, the Russian Federation, the United Kingdom (UK), and the United States of America (USA), and 10 non-permanent (E10), elected every two years by the UNGA to represent the UN's membership, aiming to discuss in both private and public meetings contentious security conflicts around the world (United Nations, n.d.-b). The UNSC is mostly known for finding peaceful means to resolve complex conflicts by imposing sanctions, deploying missions, agreeing to settlements, and, as a whole, keeping and restoring international peace (United Nations n.d.-b).

For its role in international peace and security, it can be argued that the Council is the most important UN institution. Yet, the UN's work expands far beyond the UNSC and the other five central bodies. It also encompasses an extensive system of various funds, specialized agencies, and programs, all in specific areas of work, which are important in the context of multilateralism and global governance. Some examples include the United Nations High Commissioner for Refugees (UNHCR), the United Nations Children's Fund (UNICEF), UN Women, and the World Food Programme (WFP); and specialized agencies such as the

International Monetary Fund (IMF) and the World Health Organization (WHO).[3]

UNHCR is a UN organization dedicated to assisting vulnerable individuals, including those forced to migrate, and refugees. Men, women, and children can benefit from the UNHCR's efforts. The organization is actively engaged in areas affected by violent conflict, with a recent example being its work in Afghanistan. However, its reach is global, and it operates in various regions worldwide.[4] The United Nations International Children's Emergency Fund (UNICEF) primarily focuses on the protection of children.[5] Its activities often overlap with those of the UNHCR, as UNICEF also addresses the needs of children who are forced to migrate, live in refugee camps, or face threats regarding their access to nutrition, education, clean water, sanitation, health care, and a safe living environment. In contexts of violent conflict, UNICEF plays a critical role in supporting many boys and girls.

Another relevant UN entity is UN Women, which specifically addresses the situations of women and girls. Humanitarian action is a core focus of this organization, as it works to protect women and girls in challenging circumstances, including those characterized by conflict and war. In many parts of the world, fundamental rights for women and girls are not upheld, including the right to political participation and freedom from harmful traditional practices such as female genital mutilation (FGM) and gender-related violence (GRV). Women are often systematically excluded from meaningful and equal participation in society, particularly in representative roles. Consequently, UN Women face the significant challenge of promoting respect for the basic rights of approximately half the world's population.

Given their mandates, the activities of UN Women significantly overlap with those of UNICEF, particularly in protecting and ensuring basic needs for girls, including access to education and health care. This overlap extends to the mission of UNHCR as well; female refugees are often adversely affected by the challenges of forced displacement, such as violent conflict, compounded by gender-specific discrimination, including gender-based violence (GBV). For instance, girls in refugee camps,

[3] See Hosli et al. (2021).

[4] For an overview of the work of the UNHCR, see https://www.unhcr.org/.

[5] On answers of UNICEF to effects of COVID-19, e.g., see Cornia et al. (2020).

including the (former) well-known al-Hawl camp in Syria, frequently face a range of dangers and risks that hinder their personal development, leading to issues like forced child marriage and sexual violence.

There are several other UN agencies and programs that are important to multilateralism and global governance. The World Food Programme (WFP), for example, focuses on supplying emergency relief to conflict and disaster-riddled territories, on supporting the promotion of good nutrition and food systems, and on building resilience against conflict, climate change, displacement, and economic turmoil (World Food Programme, n.d). For its notorious work in conflict settings, the WFP was awarded the Nobel Peace Prize in 2020.

The IMF is a UN-specialized agency dedicated to uphold financial stability through policy advice, capacity development, and financial assistance in diverse topics such as trade, fiscal policy, and sovereign debt. Indeed, the IMF is usually a very much discussed organization in the midst of global financial crises (and COVID-19's economic repercussions were no exception). Similarly, the World Health Organization (WHO) is also a UN-specialized agency, but dedicated to health, connecting public and private entities in promoting health, coordinating worldwide responses to health crises, and upholding healthier lifestyles.

These UN agencies and programs arguably complement the more intergovernmental operating UN institutions such as the UNGA and the UNSC. They largely function through voluntary donations, however, that fund the system as a whole and sometimes assess contributions. The system works in conjunction with the central bodies of the UN, aiming to achieve its many objectives in various thematic areas (United Nations n.d.-b). Generally, each (UN) organization maintains its own mission and priorities, as well as a specific place within the international network of global governance. Their activities are also shaped by their unique histories and management cultures. Recent UN efforts to create a unified approach, known as "one UN," aim to streamline activities and financial flows among various UN entities. While specialized agencies, funds, and programs of the UN often achieve very helpful results in practice and have a clear own organization identity, the "one UN" initiative seeks to reduce fragmentation within the UN system and to align the work of its individual institutions more closely. Fragmentation has arguably been exacerbated by financial pressures; to attract donor support amid limited funding, individual UN organizations may compete with one another, particularly during crises such as the global financial downturn and the COVID-19 pandemic which created increased pressures on national governments and with this, decreased their inclination to fund such organizations.[6]

Arguably, the UN system is complex, delving into many areas of global governance. The UN agencies, funds, and programs mentioned above are central to the current multilateral network of international organizations and collaborate closely with regional and local actors and organizations. There are also strong connections with other intergovernmental and non-governmental organizations. For example, there is daily collaboration between the International Committee of the Red Cross (ICRC), UNHCR, UNICEF, and the non-governmental organization (NGO) Save the Children. With a long history of providing assistance in conflict-affected areas, the ICRC is recognized for its prompt action in emergencies. The organization is committed to the principle of neutrality, ensuring that it is not seen as supporting the goals of any party in conflict. This principle is crucial for the organization's work, as it often allows the ICRC to access areas in need of assistance. It provides essential supplies, including food and clean drinking water, educates local residents to meet their own needs, and intervenes when other sources of support are unavailable. The organization is of core importance and complements the activities of organizations such as the UNGA (or even UNSC).

The NGO Save the Children is a key organization focused on the well-being of children (Orlassino 2022). It naturally has synergies with some UN organizations and with institutions such as the ICRC. Other international NGOs and UN organizations focus specifically on the defense of human rights. For example, Amnesty International actively advocates against political imprisonment, the death penalty, and torture. Founded in 1961, it has become one of the most prominent organizations for international human rights advocacy, often taking positions that challenge the interests of governments involved.

At times paralleling efforts of such NGOs, UN organizations take up similar topics. For example, the United Nations Human Rights Council (UNHRC), established by UNGA Resolution 60/251 on March 15, 2006 and headquartered in Geneva, has as a main purpose to strengthen

[6] Example, see Hosli et al. (2021).

the promotion and protection of human rights globally. It is responsible for both standard-setting and implementation, addressing violations thematically (e.g., torture or freedom of speech) as well as in specific countries (including Afghanistan, the occupied Palestinian territories, Sudan, Syria, and Myanmar).

Accordingly, the UN system maintains close synergies with several intergovernmental and non-governmental organizations, some of which have also received a standing invitation to participate as Permanent Observers in the UNGA sessions and the UN offices. Recent examples include, next to regional organizations such as the African Union (AU) and the EU, the Organisation for Economic Co-operation and Development (OECD), the Organization of American States (OAS), and the International Criminal Police Organization (INTERPOL), among many others (United Nations, n.d.). As observers, these organizations cannot vote, but can access most meetings and documentation (United Nations, n.d.-a).

This practice is also seen in some instances for the United Nations Security Council (UNSC). To facilitate constructive debates, critical actors to the issues on the agenda may be invited to speak in front of the organization. However, just like Observers in the UNGA, they cannot vote (*Arria-formula Meetings: UN Security Council Working Methods: Security Council Report*, n.d.). In the case of the UNSC, a new meeting method has been institutionalized to accommodate non-actors and non-members through including them into informal meeting: The Arria-formula forms the basis of this new approach (*UN Security Council Working Methods: Security Council Report*, n.d.).

Accordingly, current patterns of global multilateralism encompass a wide range of institutions that interact mutually and arguably form the core of global rules-based governance, driven by common global agendas. Nonetheless, multilateralism is torn by the conflicting interests of powerful UN member states; several UN organizations and other (global) institutions are similarly affected by such tensions and conflicting dynamics. Due to its specific structure and member constellation, the UNSC is a powerful, yet arguably non-balanced global institution that may undergo structural changes in terms of membership in the future, but currently operates based on an institutional setup decided upon in the first decades of its existence.

Generally, the UNSC operates based on eight official methods[7]: (1) Executive Director Statements, (2) Penholders and Chairs, (3) the Veto, (4) Procedural Vote, (5) Arria-formula Meetings, (6) Informal Interactive Dialogue, (7) Security Council Visiting Missions, and (8) Security Council Annual Report to the General Assembly (Interactive Handbook | Security Council n.d.). All of these methods are of central importance to the operation of the institution. While the analysis of these approaches cannot be exhaustive, our book, while acknowledging the general context of global multilateral cooperation, focuses on several of them in more detail.

The veto is perhaps the most contentious method of the UNSC, and it is the main procedure distinguishing permanent from non-permanent members (*UN Security Council Working Methods: Security Council Report*, n.d.). According to Article 27 (3) of the UN Charter, to be adopted, all substantive decisions of the UNSC must be made with "the concurring votes of the permanent members," implying a P5 member can vote against a decision; by casting a negative vote, they have the power, for example, to prevent a UNSC resolution from passing. Elected members can cast a negative vote (or abstain). However, a combination of other negative votes is needed to go against the majority passing a decision. This is exemplified in the procedural vote, which is also addressed in Article 27, stating that decisions must be made by "an affirmative vote of nine members" to pass. Thus, a vote can be cast as "yes," "no," or an "abstain." If nine members vote "yes" on a resolution, it passes. Therefore, an elected member's negative vote will only have weight in practice when it carries other members' votes to go against a decision.

Our book will have two parts. The first one addresses the use of veto, abstentions and coalition-formation in the UNSC. Bueno et al. (this volume) explore how the use of abstentions has affected resolutions on peace missions or their extensions over the last decades. It uses newly assembled data to show which countries abstained from voting on given resolutions and which ones voted against them (and in which substantive areas). Based on a theoretical framework linking coalition-formation with

[7] See ("Interactive Handbook | Security Council" n.d.) for a more comprehensive analysis of the methods.

negotiation analysis, it presents outcomes and demonstrates how coalitions formed in the UNSC usually far exceed the number of votes needed to pass a resolution.

Thereafter, Helou et al. (this volume) focus, also based on a newly assembled dataset, on the sponsorship patterns of (draft) resolution in the UNSC. The authors show which (permanent or non-permanent) UNSC members have tended to co-sponsor resolutions together (with this setting the agenda in UNSC deliberations). They also focus on the role of the Western Powers within the UNSC (the P3) compared to the role of China and Russia (the P2), respectively.

Focused on UNSC activity centered on the Syrian civil war, Heinikainen (this volume) explores great power rivalry compared to patterns of multilateral cooperation, with a focus on the role of the United States, China, and Russia. Syria is a clear example of the impasse the UNSC experienced due to power rivalries among the P5 members.

Using a newly assembled collection of UNSC resolution texts, Cross (this volume) analyses whether it is possible to predict veto usage in the UNSC by employing a random forest classification. Her findings allow for a reflection upon the motives behind P5 veto use and how it jeopardise the UNSC's legitimacy.

In the second part of the book, Luers and Galy-Jammou-Préfontaine (this volume) address the role of small and regional powers in the UNSC focusing on non-traditional security threats. This demonstrates both the agency and influence of such powers and the importance of areas paralleling the more traditional threats to (global) security.

Lu et al. (this volume) show how small and emerging powers affect decision-making in the UNSC. They demonstrate the role of non-permanent UNSC membership and the changing context of global governance which provides a new "voice" to UNSC members other than the P5.

The next two chapters focus on the role of a regional organization—the EU—in the UNSC context. Balutkar and Stepanian (this volume) describe the patterns and role of the EU in the UNGA and, notably, the UNSC. They argue that the EU is an actor of considerable importance within the Security Council context, in spite of challenges in terms of internal coherence within this (regional) organization. Similarly, van Schijndel and Jansen (this volume) discuss how three EU member states—Germany, Portugal and Luxembourg—have acted as E10 member states in terms of both voting and co-sponsorship patterns, again basing their analysis on newly collected data on this theme.

Finally, the chapter by Levorato et al. (this volume) embeds activities of the EU as a regional organization into patterns of UN-focused multilateralism more generally, by analyzing how the EU has incorporated the UN Sustainable Development Goals (SDGs) into its overarching financial and fiscal programs, notably the European Semester (ES) and the NextGenerationEU (NGEU) project. The chapter shows how regional organizations are not only important in contexts such as collaboration on the implementation of UN in peace missions, but can also matter considerably to more general multilateral goals and ambitions, such as the funding at national member state levels for the seventeen SDGs.

Based on new insights on the operation of the UNSC and related data, we believe the book makes a novel contribution to a still largely underexplored topic. Generally, as our chapters confirm, discussion to gather support in the UNSC in the context of the drafting of resolutions (or even voting) is often based on informal meetings, including frequent diplomatic exchanges and maneuvering. Informal consultations and dialogues are often cast as Arria-formula meetings, where a member (or members) of the UNSC "to gather information from individuals or organisations with knowledge of developments on the grounds" initiate informal discussions (*Arria-formula Meetings: UN Security Council Working Methods: Security Council Report*, n.d.). Such gatherings are highly confidential, and no record or note on the outcome is taken; this process arguably lacks transparency, but provides a flexible procedural framework for members to be open about their actual concerns (*Arria-formula Meetings: UN Security Council Working Methods: Security Council Report*, n.d.).

Formal voting power allocation very much privileges veto powers in the UNSC. But veto use has not been practiced by some P5 members for several decades, such as France and the UK. In spite of frequent impasses, the UNSC has created a large number of peace missions and settlements, during and even more so after the Cold War (with more impasses having occurred again in the more recent past). Peace missions based on UNSC resolutions are arguably perceived as more legitimate than missions built, for example, by P5 members using external alliances. In spite of the effectiveness of several missions, some authors are critical as regards UNSC functioning. Merril et al. (2015), for example, established that the UNSC's main challenges reside in the divergence of interest among its members, with this divergence letting resolutions negatively affect initiatives such as the crucial Responsibility to Protect (R2P) ideal and the power balance between P5 and E10 members. Nonetheless, the very R2P initiative perhaps derived largely due to E10 agency. Veto power in the UNSC affects not only the operation of this institution, but can also have repercussions on several other aspects of the organization's work, including its membership or executive changes (United Nations, n.d-b).

Upholding multilateralism and rules-based global governance, in general, has been a challenging endeavor. Some have argued that multilateralism is caught in deadlock (Lavelle 2020, 245). Challenges are amplified if nationalist or populist domestic-level parties question its principles and oppose its actual operation. This has been seen even within P5 member states (the first Trump administration in the US from 2016 to 2020, which may again have similar characteristics during the second one, from 2024 to 2028), the UK's choice to leave the EU or Russia's violation of international law principles in the context of the war in Ukraine. Populist sentiments have also been critical of European integration and the EU, a key example of regional integration based on a strongly institutionalized network of transnational collaboration. By attacking multilateral structures verbally or in practice, calling them obsolete, or weaponizing worldwide cross-border challenges, such instances may also jeopardize cooperation between state and non-state actors, or UN institutions and international organizations. The paradox between a need to act at an international level to tackle trans-border challenges and the importance to address opposed domestic demands appears to be growing, also within some of the P5 states. For example, the initial responses to the COVID-19 pandemic reflected nationalist and isolationist calls for action (Cannon 2023, 293). Such challenges are real, but our book will argue that this will not, in fact, mean there is an "end to multilateralism." Multilateralism as a pattern of global governance has a long history and has been affected by processes of reorganization and renegotiation over time. As new threats arise, however, so will the need for new solutions on the global level.

The response to COVID-19 is perhaps the most recent example that may have demonstrated the importance of multilateralism to a larger audience. The pandemic has led to pernicious health, socioeconomic, and geopolitical consequences, which have seriously strained the multilateral response systems, but are also the source of much academic interest

(Cannon 2023, 291). To address the various challenges posed by the COVID-19 pandemic—such as the pressures on healthcare systems and economic activity in all UN member states—many governments have focused primarily on their domestic situations before aiming to address them through the existing network of regional and international organizations (including the UNGA or the EU). This global health crisis has, arguably, led many countries to adopt an "inward-looking" perspective, perceiving the pandemic-related challenges as stemming from external factors and concentrating potential solutions almost exclusively on the national level. This created a paradox, as COVID-19, by nature a health pandemic, transcended borders and presented an international challenge that could only realistically be addressed through collective global efforts and agreements.

However, such trends may also have enhanced the very demand for multilateralism, as a negotiation-based method to address collective challenges. Regional and global power dynamics have frequently hindered coordinated efforts to address the pandemic's effects and to implement unified health policies and remedies on the global level. The World Health Organization (WHO), the foremost international entity dealing with global health, found itself caught in a political crossfire between major rival powers, especially the USA and China. Mutual accusations complicated the organization's work, and since it comprises primarily medical and health experts, it struggled to deliver the political responses that were necessary. Consequently, political considerations occasionally clashed with medical responses to the pandemic's challenges. A similar situation can arguably be seen for the World Trade Organization (WTO), considerably affected by power rivalries on the global level, but being of central importance to rules-based patterns of global trade governance.

As a global protector of human rights and human well-being more generally, the UN had to find ways to move forward despite the numerous challenges posed by COVID-19. By employing innovative approaches to navigate difficulties, the organization sought to motivate stakeholders and enhance efforts to tackle urgent challenges. A prominent example was the early call by UN Secretary-General António Guterres to initiate a global ceasefire in response to the new "collective enemy" (the COVID-19 virus)—a call that, regrettably, was not heeded by various parties engaged in violent conflict, while it complemented actions such as those mandated based on UNSC resolutions.

The pandemic has again highlighted the critical importance of multilateralism and global collaboration in developing common strategies and preventing isolationist national behaviors that ultimately harm a multitude of actors. While the crisis complicated international cooperation in many respects, it also emphasized the need for a broader international coalition to align policies and promote progress toward new global agreements. This, in turn, strengthened calls for multilateralism, even though some of global governance institutions, including the UNSC, are seen as reflecting dated global power constellations.

A good example of intergovernmental cooperation and alignment with the UN is the EU. As one of the most important regional contributors to the UN budget, it has often reasserted its commitment to uphold the rule-based international order (EUISS 2021). The EU arguably shares many principles and core values enshrined in the UN Charter, such as the protection of fundamental human rights, and often aligns its activities with those of UN agencies. Similarly, the AU is of crucial importance to some major UN initiatives, including the Agenda 2035 and its related SDGs. In this sense, while regional organizations may themselves be composed of member states with heterogeneous preferences, they are often operating based on multilateral principles and with this, resemble patterns of operation of the UN and other global governance institutions.

The UN, currently consisting of 193 member states, faces much heterogeneity, encompassing a mix of democratic and more autocratic states. As a result, the UN's modes of operation and decision-making structures are influenced by rivalries among its member states and their systems, and more significantly, by the competition rooted in global power politics. This can be seen most prominently in the context of the UNSC, where stalemate among some of the P5 members—China, France, Russia, the United Kingdom, and the USA—has hindered many initiatives, including those aimed at protecting vulnerable populations in situations of violent domestic conflict, with Syria being a prominent example of this.

Formal UNSC reform has so far proven illusive (not least due to the high threshold for change applicable), but the call to include new members is persisting. This notably refers to underrepresented regions in the UNSC, such as Africa and Latin America. Royeppen (2024) stipulates clear challenges in the UNSC that should be addressed for the functioning of the Council to remain legitimate and robust to tackle current conflicts, which, according to the author, are to consider "more restraint on power politics, minimum criteria approach for membership to improve capacity, and increased representation linked to increased legitimacy" (Royeppen 2024, 6). In 2005, the G4—Germany, Japan, Brazil, and India—came close to acceptance of a draft resolution in the UNGA that would have provided them with permanent UNSC seats; in 2015, the AU, after several earlier initiatives, reinstated the need for reform; in 2023, the BRICS group (Brazil, Russia, India, China, and South Africa) issued a joint statement supporting existing earlier drafts (Amt, n.d.; Jazeera 2024a, b; "Declaração De Joanesburgo II—Sandton, Gauteng, África Do Sul—23 De Agosto De 2023," 2023). This demonstrates that the UNSC's role is still perceived as being of crucial importance to global peace and security internationally, while dissatisfaction with its current setup also continues.

Our chapters demonstrate how many of these structural challenges affect both P5 and E10 roles, and patterns of decision-making within the UN more generally. We intend to contribute to the existing research gap on the UNSC and its embedding into global governance and multilateralism. The various chapters provide new insights into UNSC decision-making, voting, co-sponsorship, and veto patterns, as well as the role of a regional organization such as the EU when facing the new threats to multilateralism. While aiming to describe the broad contours of global-level multilateralism, we also aim to delve into specific hurdles and challenges in this respect, not least those related to the operation of the UNSC.

We believe the analyses presented in this book provide several novel insights for academics working on multilateralism, the UN or the UNSC. It can also be of much interest to students in courses such as those focused on International Organization, Global or Regional Governance, the EU or the UN. It may be captivating to those studying relationships between the UN and other (global) institutions and among UNSC members (both the P5 and the E10). Considering the role of the UNSC as an important peace mechanism in global affairs, the book can also provide more practical insights relevant to academics, students and practitioners interested in themes such as peacekeeping, conflict resolution, and patterns of international negotiation and diplomacy.

With the various contributions to the book, insights are provided on the functioning of multilateralist principles in practice, agenda-setting, and decision-making in the UNSC, global power dynamics as reflected in international institutions and potential responses to the current challenges to multilateralism. With this book, we hope to illustrate both in an academic and a more practical perspective how multilateralism matters, countering voices that might argue otherwise. We also aim to demonstrate the advantages and limitations of the UNSC as a global governance institution. With this, we hope our book might inspire researchers to conduct more analyses related to the UN, the UNSC, and their links with multilateralism more generally, as core institutions in the context of current, and changing, patterns of global governance.

References

"About." *International Monetary Fund*. Accessed December 18, 2024. https://www.imf.org/en/About.

Anuar, Amalina, and Nazia Hussain. *Minilateralism for Multilateralism in the Post-COVID Age*. S. Rajaratnam School of International Studies, 2021.

Alhashimi, Hana, Andres Fiallo, Toni-Shae Freckleton, Mona Khalil Ali, Vahd Mulachela, and Jonathan Viera, eds. *The Future of Diplomacy After COVID-19: Multilateralism and the Global Pandemic*. Abingdon, Oxon and New York, NY: Routledge, 2021.

Amt, A. "Reform of the United Nations Security Council—Questions and Answers." *German Federal Foreign Office*, n.d. Accessed December 18, 2024. https://www.auswaertiges-amt.de/en/aussenpolitik/internationale-organisationen/vereintenationen/reformsr-fragen/231618.

"Arria-formula Meetings: UN Security Council Working Methods." *Security Council Report*, n.d. Accessed December 18, 2024. https://www.securitycouncilreport.org/un-security-council-working-methods/arria-formula-meetings.php.

Blavoukos, Spyros, Dimitrios Bourantonis, and Ioannis Galariotis. "In Quest of a Single European Union Voice in the United Nations General Assembly: The Politics of Resolution 65/276." *Cooperation and Conflict* 52, no. 4 (2017): 451–468.

Cannon, Cecilia. "Chapter 17 The UN at 75: A Political Declaration and a Global Conversation". In *Does the UN Model Still Work? Challenges and Prospects for the Future of Multilateralism*, edited by Kim Fontaine-Skronski, Valeriane Thool, and Norbert Eschborn, 289–303. Brill, 2023.

Cornia, Giovanni Andrea, Richard Jolly, and Frances Stewart. 2020. "COVID-19 and Children, in the North and in the South. UNICEF, Office of Research—Innocenti Discussion Paper DP 2020-02".

"Declaração de Joanesburgo II—Sandton, Gauteng, África do Sul—23 de agosto de 2023." *Ministério Das Relações Exteriores*. August 24, 2023. Accessed

18 December 2024. https://www.gov.br/mre/pt-br/canais_atendimento/imprensa/notas-a-imprensa/declaracao-de-joanesburgo-ii-sandton-gauteng-africa-do-sul-23-de-agosto-de-2023.

De Clercq, Morgane B. "The Multilateral Trading System in a Changing World: The WTO and Current Threats Challenging its Survival." In *The Future of Multilateralism: Global Cooperation and International Organizations*, edited by Madeleine O. Hosli, Taylor Garrett, Sonja Niedecken, and Nicholas Verbeek, 55–71. Rowman and Littlefield, 2021.

Drieskens, Edith, Laura Van Dievel, and Yf Reykers. "The EU's Search for Effective Participation at the UN General Assembly and UN Security Council." In *The EU and Effective Multilateralism*, edited by Edith Drieskens and Louise van Schaik, 33–50. Routledge, 2014.

Felten, Léa. "Recognising the Shadow Pandemic in the Humanitarian Sector: Ending Violence Against Women in the Aftermath of COVID-19." *International Journal of Humanitarian Action* 8, no. 9 (2023): 1–13. https://doi.org/10.1186/s41018-023-00142-5.

Fiott, Daniel, and Marco Zeiss. "Multilateralism." In *Yearbook of European Security: 2021*, 44–57. European Union Institute for Security Studies (EUISS), 2021.

Gottschalk, Keith. "Explainer: The Non-aligned Movement in the 21st Century." *The Conversation*. 28 September 2016. Accessed December 18, 2024. https://theconversation.com/explainer-the-non-aligned-movement-in-the-21st-century-66057.

Han, Yue. "The World Health Organization under COVID-19: Behind the Crisis." In *The Future of Multilateralism: Global Cooperation and International Organizations*, edited by Madeleine O. Hosli, Taylor Garrett, Sonja Niedecken, and Nicholas Verbeek, 39–54. Rowman and Littlefield, 2021.

Heine, J. *The Global South Is on the Rise—But What Exactly Is the Global South?* The Conversation, 2023. https://theconversation.com/the-global-south-is-on-the-rise-but-what-exactly-is-the-global-south-207959.

Hogan, E. *A Closer Look at the Global South*. Carnegie Endowment for International Peace, 2024, May 20. https://carnegieendowment.org/research/2024/05/global-south-colonialism-imperialism?lang=en

Hosli, Madeleine O., Taylor Garrett, Sonja Niedecken, and Nicholas Verbeek, eds. *The Future of Multilateralism: Global Cooperation and International Organizations*. Lanham, MD: Rowman and Littlefield, 2021.

Hosli, Madeleine O. "The United Nations and Challenges to Multilateralism." In *The Future of Multilateralism: Global Cooperation and International Organizations*, edited by Madeleine O. Hosli, Taylor Garrett, Sonja Niedecken, and Nicholas Verbeek, 3–18. Lanham, MD: Rowman and Littlefield, 2021.

Hosli, Madeleine O. *The European Union and the United Nations in Global Governance*. Bristol, UK: Bristol University Press, 2022.

Hosli, Madeleine O., and Thomas Dörfler. "Why Is Change So Slow? Assessing Prospects for United Nations Security Council Reform." *Journal of Economic Policy Reform* 22, no. 1 (2017): 35–50.

Interactive Handbook | Security Council. n.d. https://main.un.org/securitycouncil/en/content/interactivehandbook

Iacovidou, Irini, and Himanshi Sharma. "COVID-19 & the Digital Divide: Responding to the South Asian Digital Divide in the Education Sector." In *The Global, Regional and Local Politics of Institutional Responses to COVID-19: Implications for Women and Children*, edited by Madeleine O. Hosli, Amy Blessing, and Irini Iacovidou, 133–156. Palgrave Macmillan, 2022.

Jazeera, Al. "Officials at UN Security Council Push for a Permanent Seat for Africa." *Al Jazeera*, 12 August 2024. Accessed December 10, 2024. https://www.aljazeera.com/news/2024/8/12/officials-at-un-security-council-push-for-a-permanent-seat-for-africa.

Jazeera, A. Officials at UN Security Council Push for a Permanent Seat for Africa. *Al Jazeera*, 12 August 2024. https://www.aljazeera.com/news/2024/8/12/officials-at-un-security-council-push-for-a-permanent-seat-for-africa.

Lavelle, Kathryn C. *The Challenges of Multilateralism*. Yale University Press, 2020. https://doi.org/10.2307/j.ctvxkn79b.

Makubalo, Nandy, Madeleine O. Hosli, and Michaël Lantmeeters. "The African Union in the United Nations." In *Group Politics in UN Multilateralism*, edited by Katie V. Laatikainen and Karen E. Smith, 76–96. Brill, 2020.

Merrill, J., Sinatra, M., Yasmin, P. N. A., & Institute of Strategic and International Studies. "UNSC Challenges and Opportunities." In *ISIS Focus: March 2015*, 10–13. *Institute of Strategic and International Studies*, 2015. http://www.jstor.org/stable/resrep13524.3.

O'Malley, Alanna. "School's Out Forever? 'The Effect of COVID-19 on Educational Opportunities for Women and Girls in the Global South." In *The Global, Regional and Local Politics of Institutional Responses to COVID-19: Implications for Women and Children*, edited by Madeleine O. Hosli, Amy Blessing, and Irini Iacovidou. 179–195. Palgrave MacMillan, 2022.

Onu Italia. "BRICS Joint Statement Calls for UNSC Reform with Greater Role for India, Brazil, South Africa." 31 August 2023. Accessed November 20, 2024. https://onuitalia.com/2023/08/24/brics-joint-statement-calls-for-unsc-reform-with-greater-role-for-india-brazil-south-africa/.

Orlassino, Chiara. "Preventing a Knock-on Pandemic: How the World's Biggest Children's Charity Responded to the Virus that Doesn't Make Children Sick." In *The Global, Regional and Local Politics of Institutional Responses to COVID-19: Implications for Women and Children*, edited by Madeleine O. Hosli, Amy Blessing and Irini Iacovidou, 89–109. Palgrave MacMillan, 2022.

Panke, Diana. "Speaking with One Voice: Easier Said Than Done? The EU in the UNGA." In *The EU in UN Politics: Actors, Processes and Performances,* edited by Spyros Blavoukos and Dimitris Bourantonis, 27–46. Palgrave Macmillan, 2017.

Patrick, Stewart, and Alexandra Huggins. "The Term 'Global South' Is Surging. It Should Be Retired." *Carnegie Endowment for International Peace*. 15 August 2023. Accessed December 18, 2024. https://carnegieendowment.org/posts/2023/08/the-term-global-south-is-surging-it-should-be-retired?lang=en.

Pesce-Monteiro, Barbara. "Foreword." In *The Future of Multilateralism: Global Cooperation and International Organizations*, edited by Madeleine O. Hosli, Taylor Garrett, Sonja Niedecken and Nicholas Verbeek, vii–ix. Rowman and Littlefield, 2021.

Protopsalti, Dimitra. "UNICEF & UN WOMEN in the Post-COVID-19 Era: How the Pandemic Is Expected to Reshape the Humanitarian Agenda." In *The Future of Multilateralism: Global Cooperation and International Organizations*, edited by Madeleine O. Hosli, Taylor Garrett, Sonja Niedecken, and Nicholas Verbeek, 19–38. Rowman and Littlefield, 2021.

Royeppen, A., ed. "United Nations Security Council Reform." In *United Nations @ 70*, 5–8. Institute for Global Dialogue. Accessed December 18, 2024. http://www.jstor.org/stable/resrep07780.6.

Smith, Karen E. (2020) 'The European Union'. In roup Politics in UN Multilateralism. Diplomatic Studies (16), edited by Karen E. Smith and Katie Verlin Laatikainen, 45–59. Brill Academic Publishers.

Trent, John and Laura Schnurr. *A United Nations Renaissance: What the UN is, and What it Could Be*. Verlag Barbara Budrich, 2018.

UN Women. "COVID-19 and Ending Violence Against Women and Girls." *COVID-19 Brief*. Accessed December 18, 2024. www.unwomen.org/en/digital-library/publications/2020/04/issue-brief-covid-19-and-ending-violence-against-women-and-girls.

"UN Security Council Working Methods." *Security Council Report*. Accessed December 18, 2024. https://www.securitycouncilreport.org/un-security-council-working-methods/.

United Nations. "About Us." *United Nations*. Accessed December 18, 2024. https://www.un.org/en/about-us.

United Nations. "UN Charter." *United Nations*. Accessed December 18, 2024. https://www.un.org/en/about-us/un-charter.

"Who We Are." *World Food Programme*. Accessed December 18, 2024. https://www.wfp.org/who-we-are.

Zumsteeg, Solène. "Increased Domestic Violence in Europe: A Shadow Pandemic." In *The Global, Regional and Local Politics of Institutional Responses to COVID-19: Implications for Women and Children*, edited by Madeleine O. Hosli, Amy Blessing, and Irini Iacovidou, 157–177. Palgrave Macmillan, 2022.

PART I

Voting Behaviour and Co-Sponsorship in the UN Security Council

CHAPTER 2

Coalitions, Peace Missions, and UNSC Decision-Making

Gabriela M. G. Bueno, Madeleine O. Hosli, and Alexandra Hall

1 Introduction

The United Nations Security Council (UNSC) is regarded as one of the most influential institutions responsible for maintaining international peace, security, and cooperation. It determines the existence of threats or acts of aggression and how to resolve them peacefully. The UNSC is charged with creating peace operations and other diplomatic instruments through meetings and resolutions to foster and sustain peace where such threats arise.

However, this chapter demonstrates that institutional structures and geopolitical rivalries often impede the Council's activities. Based on a new data collection of 628 UNSC resolutions authorising peace missions and extensions from 1948 to early 2024, this study explores how the P5 and E10 members make decisions regarding peacekeeping. We analyse their voting behaviours in passing or hindering resolutions and observe patterns

G. M. G. Bueno · M. O. Hosli (✉) · A. Hall
Leiden University, The Hague, The Netherlands
e-mail: m.o.hosli@fgga.leidenuniv.nl

M. O. Hosli et al. (eds.), *Multilateralism and the United Nations Security Council*, https://doi.org/10.1007/978-3-031-85320-3_2

of coalition formation. Voting behaviour within the UNSC is a fairly underexplored topic, with very little updated research conducted that focuses on the area of peacekeeping. Therefore, this study and dataset are an addition to existing literature, aiming to understand how the mechanisms for implementing and extending peace operations can be politicised and how P5 and E10 members vote within the UNSC.

Established in 1946, the UNSC's decisions are binding for all United Nations member states. The composition of the UNSC has been a subject of intense debate, leading to gradual adaptations in working methods rather than formal structural changes. UNSC decisions are made in informal and formal meetings, with informal meetings not being publicised and lacking recorded proceedings (they mainly occur in the form of informal dialogues and consultations), whereas formal meetings can lead to recorded votes and statements. Our analysis, based on the new dataset mentioned, highlights that while nearly all UNSC resolutions pass unanimously, peace mission extensions tend to be more politicised, often resulting in abstentions or condemnatory statements.

Since its establishment, the UNSC has set up about 70 peace operations across Africa, the Americas, Asia, Europe, and the Middle East, making these operations a primary response to global crises. Arguably, peacekeeping operations are a vital mechanism for international stability. Our research collects new information on votes related to peace missions and their extensions, alongside descriptive analyses of related statements, to address the existing literature gap regarding how important decisions and coalitions are made in the UNSC. We propose that coalitions within this institution are influenced by various factors, including institutional constraints, voting weights, national preferences, and the ambition to uphold the organisation's legitimacy and credibility.

Following an increase in membership approved by the United Nations General Assembly (UNGA) in 1965, the UNSC now consists of fifteen members: Five permanent members (the United States, China[1] Russia[2] the United Kingdom, and France) and ten rotating non-permanent members elected by the UNGA for two-year terms to represent different regions of the world. The non-permanent members do not hold veto

[1] The Republic of China until 1971 and mainland China thereafter (see UN Resolution 2758).

[2] Formerly the Union of Soviet Socialist Republics (USSR).

power. The UNSC operates based on draft resolutions submitted by its members in accordance with the agenda, which are carefully considered and debated before being accepted or rejected through a vote.[3] The UNSC requires an affirmative vote of nine members, including the concurring votes of the permanent members, to adopt a resolution (*UN Security Council Working Methods: Security Council Report* n.d.).[4] An abstention is also a viable option, and the vote of a member from the E10 can be crucial in determining the outcome of a resolution (Lu et al. this volume).

Based on previously established approaches, our chapter aims to present an adapted framework to better understand negotiation processes in the UNSC, including member state behaviour, voting, and abstentions. UNSC negotiations are characterised by an imbalance of power among its members, stemming from unequal distributions of resources and influence, reinforced by the possibility of a 'hidden veto' (Nahory 2004): An implicit threat of veto usage by UNSC permanent members during informal consultations. Since nine votes are required for a decision to be made and a resolution to pass, the voting behaviour of each member matters, as it can influence the outcome in various ways. According to Vreeland and Dreher (2014, 35–61), the resolution will fail to pass if even one E10 member defects from a minimal winning coalition. Conversely, if at least one coalition member opposes a resolution and votes affirmatively, it may become a pivotal actor. Such mechanisms increase the leverage of non-permanent member states (Lu et al. this volume; van Schijndel and Jansen this volume). Voting behaviour plays a critical role in determining UNSC outcomes, making the formation of coalitions for unanimity or the defection from winning coalitions an important aspect of the voting procedures. Moreover, UNSC coalitions can be influenced by tactics like vote-buying or leveraging votes as collateral (Vreeland and Dreher 2014, 35–96). In addition, we analyse some speaking notes of (public) UNSC meetings to refine the exploration of voting behaviour and abstentions.

[3] Early literature on the workings of the Security Council includes Bailey (1998), Krasno (2002) and Chan (2003). On UNSC resolution authorship, see Helou et al., this volume.

[4] See Article 27.3: "Decisions of the Security Council on all other matters shall be made by an affirmative vote of nine members including the concurring votes of the permanent members; provided that, in decisions under Chapter VI, and under paragraph 3 of Article 52, a party to a dispute shall abstain from voting."

Our chapter is organised as follows: It begins with a discussion of the UNSC's voting rules and procedures, highlighting the importance of coalitions for the passage of resolutions and their influence on votes. The following section provides an overview of coalition-formation theories and discusses coalition dynamics within international institutions. Based on this, we aim to formulate an approach to how coalitions are formed and decisions made in the UNSC environment, enabling us to assess our data in this light. Following this, we outline our methodological approach to gathering and analysing our new data on peacekeeping operations, present empirical results on UNSC coalitions, and summarise our findings.

2 Coalition Theories and the Security Council

The primary objective of coalition-formation theory is to predict actor behaviour by considering both actor preferences and institutional constraints. These theories are essential for assessing why certain members of an organisation vote in favour of an outcome, which coalition holds greater significance from their perspective, and why. Hence, understanding voting behaviour within an institution is crucial to grasping the rationale behind decision-making and coalitional choices. Our chapter's focus on such approaches serves as a vital tool to understand how the P5 (the five permanent members of the UNSC) and E10 (the ten elected non-permanent members) interact within the UNSC's operational framework.

De Vries and Maria (1999) categorises significant strands of coalition-formation theory into policy-oriented and power-oriented approaches as the major clusters.[5] A fundamental principle of power-oriented coalition-formation theories, or 'policy-blind approaches,' is that actors joining a coalition seek to maximise their individual gains, such as by securing office. Power-oriented approaches represent early iterations of coalition-formation theories, encompassing variants like the minimal winning approach, the minimum size approach, and the bargaining proposition. In the context of many governmental institutions, members typically aim to form coalitions with the fewest members possible to avoid divisiveness,

[5] An application of coalition theories to the UNSC can be found in Moody (2005). For an overview of coalition formation (and social choice approaches more generally) see van Deemen (1997).

which could weaken their power and reduce the need for compromise. Accordingly, a coalition member can exert more influence on the final decision by minimising the number of coalition partners.

In their book, Von Neumann and Morgenstern (1947) developed the minimal winning approach as a fundamental game theory concept: Players strive to form coalitions with as few members as necessary since the value of a winning coalition does not increase with additional members. In fact, a smaller coalition allows for more significant individual payoffs. However, if a coalition consists of only a minimal number of members, the departure of even one player can render the coalition powerless (Von Neumann and Morgenstern 1947, 420–499).

Within the UNSC framework, a coalition adhering to the minimal winning approach would be limited to a maximum of nine members, including the P5, and does not permit abstentions. Conversely, as described by Gamson (1961) and Riker (1962), the minimum size approach shares similarities with the minimal winning approach but introduces further criteria. In a weighted majority voting scenario, a coalition must meet the minimum number of members and the minimum weight requirements. Due to the power disparities between the P5 and the E10, the operation of the UNSC reflects a weighted majority voting game (Brams 2003; Hosli et al. 2011). In practice, a UNSC coalition based on the minimum size approach also comprises nine members, including the P5. However, losing any single member would cause the coalition to collapse.

Leiserson (1968) presented the bargaining proposition, which resembles the minimal winning approach but focuses more on the decision making process of the actors involved. Instead of prioritising the increase of individual power, actors often prefer smaller coalitions for the convenience of negotiation. Thus, in the UNSC context, coalitions typically form with nine members, including the P5.

In contrast, policy-oriented coalition-formation approaches, arguably more suitable to study coalition-formation processes in international organisations, motivate actors to join a coalition by evaluating their policy preferences alongside their goals for power enhancement.[6] Several methods for understanding policy-oriented coalition theories have been identified, including approaches based on conflict of interest, minimal

[6] When assessing their priorities, it is assumed that the conditions of reflexivity, anti-symmetry, completeness, and transitivity are in effect.

range, and policy distance (Sommerer et al. 2022, 816–841). According to the authors, similar voting patterns among members reflect a greater homogeneity in their policy preferences: UNSC members frequently form coalitions with like-minded individuals, which diminishes the need for compromise on policy issues.

According to Axelrod (1970), the conflict of interest approach posits that players with related preferences and ideological goals will likely form stable coalitions. This implies that a successful coalition should comprise ideologically similar members positioned close to one another on an underlying policy scale—meaning they share the same or similar policy preferences, thereby uniting to advance their interests. Additionally, the coalition should be minimal, ensuring the number of members is sufficient to meet the decision threshold. In the context of the UNSC, this approach, alongside its voting regulations, suggests that for a resolution to pass, a coalition should include the mandatory P5 plus at least four E10 members positioned between them based on their policy preferences.

De Swaan (1973) introduced the policy distance approach, which posits that players compare their preferred policies with the expected policy outcomes of a coalition. In his research on European parliaments, he found that players prefer to form coalitions that align most closely with their policy preferences. In the context of international organisations, this implies that players will choose the winning coalition with the smallest distance between a member state's preferred policy and the expected policy outcome.

When exploring international institutions, however, traditional coalition-formation theories may apply in different ways than they do in other decision-making scenarios, such as national-level government formation processes. Member states in international organisations often aim to form inclusive coalitions that involve more members than necessary to reach a decision (Moody 2005), a trend confirmed by Scherzinger (2023) based on interviews with high-ranking P5 and E10 officials, who showed a strong desire for unanimity in UNSC resolutions.

Coalition-formation processes in international organisations can be motivated by multiple factors, including the differing interests of member states, power asymmetries, or geopolitical rivalries. Member states may seek to enhance the legitimacy and credibility of the organisation as a whole, as well as improve their standing within it. Forming a large winning coalition can bolster the organisation's legitimacy and foster a sense of cohesion, reflecting a broad consensus that makes decisions more credible (Scherzinger 2023). Heisenberg (2005), studying decision-making within the Council of the European Union, has referred to this as the 'culture of consensus.'

Moreover, 'good standing' considerations may influence coalition-formation dynamics, as member states often express concerns about their own standing and that of the organisation. These concerns can reflect national interests and influence their choices within the institution.[7] Consequently, accounting for such effects, a coalition must meet two fundamental conditions: It should aim to include as many members as possible to enhance legitimacy, and the assessments of individual member states' gains will play a crucial role in this process. Achieving consensus lends greater credibility to the organisation's decisions, such as UNSC resolution; states will generally only vote against a proposal if they are willing to risk their 'good standing' and potential future influence within the institution. However, national considerations, such as perceived threats to security, will also matter.

Smaller or weaker states with non-permanent seats in international organisations, like the UNSC, may hesitate to disrupt the negotiation environment. For such states, power and influence often stem from forming coalitions aiming to gain international recognition and legitimacy within the organisation. Although they may lack power in unequal negotiation dynamics (see Lu et al. this volume), they can leverage regional or issue-specific authority to gain an advantage in discussions (Van Schijndel and Jansen this volume).

Given the need for adaptations in terms of coalition-formation approaches to study institutions like the UNSC, we examine member behaviour when choosing which coalition to join or leave in the area of resolutions on peace missions. We will present an approach based on three Tiers, aiming to incorporate more traditional coalition-formation approaches and insights from negotiation analysis. Accordingly, as Fig. 1 illustrates, member states in the UNSC must consider three Tiers when deciding to join a coalition.

The first Tier (I) refers to national self-interest, which encompasses the 'parochial interests' of member states—those that directly impact

[7] Although, in the instance of voting on UN peacekeeping's usage of force and enlarging military capacity. Howard and Dayal (2018) argue that behavior is driven by group-preserving dynamics among P-5 members rather than deliberate strategies to enhance peace and security.

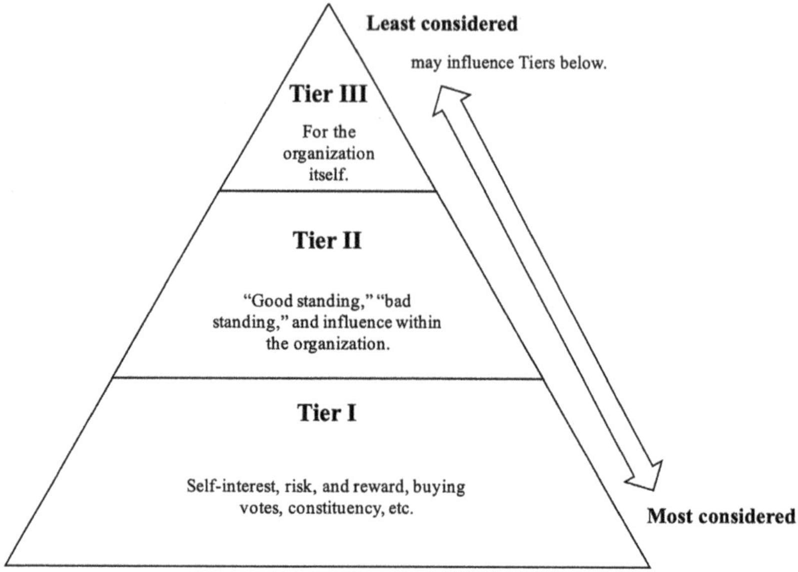

Fig. 1 Coalition-formation in international institutions: three Tiers (*Source* Own compilation based on existing literature and theoretical approaches)

their own countries. Vreeland and Dreher (2014) state that vote-buying typically occurs at this level as member states weigh potential national-level risks and rewards. Scherzinger (2023) discusses factors other than vote-buying that operate at this level (2023).

However, our analysis indicates that most member states are unlikely to overtly defend their national interests by voting 'no' in the UNSC unless a draft resolution poses significant threats to their parochial interests, affects national security, or reflects a broader power struggle. As a result, UNSC coalitions usually consist of members casting affirmative votes (or possibly abstaining); these coalitions tend to be 'oversized,' meaning they exceed the formal majority needed.

Tier II pertains to a member's standing within the organisation. Our analysis of UNSC speaking notes reveals that delegations prefer to avoid being placed in bad standing by casting a veto (or voting 'no,' in the case of the E10). Instead, they tend to abstain when they cannot support a draft resolution. Generally, unless specific national-level risks are involved, members will only vote against a resolution if they are willing to risk losing future influence and potentially being placed in 'bad standing' in exchange for perceived greater gains (Volden and Carruba 2004).

Moreover, non-permanent members who are frequently elected to the UNSC often have more influence within the organisation compared to other E10 members since they have had more opportunities to assert their interests and leave their mark on the UNSC. For example, non-permanent members such as Japan and Germany, which are significant financial contributors to the UN, may have held a UNSC seat often enough to wield more influence within the institution than other member states in their respective geographical regions.

Thus, Tier II holds greater significance for such members. Moreover, UNSC members seeking legitimacy either within or outside the organisation may be less inclined to engage in vote-buying or vote-selling, as discovering such actions could jeopardise their legitimacy (Vreeland and Dreher 2014).

Tier III focuses on maintaining the organisation's standing. For example, the more cohesive the final vote on a UNSC draft resolution, the greater legitimacy and credibility the institution can demonstrate, benefiting all its members (Vreeland and Dreher 2014; Scherzinger 2023). This Tier is often reflected in members' public statements. Nonetheless, caution is advisable, as a member can exploit Tier III to obscure a parochial national interest, framing their vote as being for the institution's broader legitimacy while serving their interests.

The 'oversized' nature of UNSC winning coalitions is partly due to the diverse interests that influence their formation. UNSC states appear to be motivated by a desire to pursue their own national interests—similar to perspectives derived from power-oriented coalition-formation approaches—while also seeking to enhance the institution's legitimacy and achieve unanimity, all while avoiding potential loss of standing within the organisation due to audience costs. Additionally, they respond to global power struggles and dynamics while attempting to uphold the organisation's reputation. In practice, however, the importance of each Tier can vary during the negotiation process. For instance, if an actor perceives risks associated with Tiers I and III (such as the organisation failing to pass a resolution unanimously while the draft resolution threatens the member's parochial interests), they will likely prioritise Tier I over Tier III.

3 Methodological Approaches

By exploring peace operations and their extensions, we will now assess how coalitions in the UNSC have formed in practice. Our newly compiled data allows for a basic quantitative analysis of votes alongside a more qualitative assessment of statements made by UNSC members.

To achieve this, we focus on the relatively rare instances in which resolutions in the UNSC were contested, leading to abstentions or even negative votes. Thus, the coalitions examined are based on voting patterns that deviate from the default option of unanimity (Vreeland and Dreher 2014; Scherzinger 2023). Abstentions are particularly noteworthy as they are infrequently explored in existing literature despite their potential to convey discontent without undermining a peacekeeping operation. We will demonstrate that, although abstentions are seldom acknowledged for their significance, they represent an essential means for a country to express its interests and the rationale behind its decision.

Additionally, although rarely stated explicitly, the default voting bloc traditionally includes powers that represent Western (hegemonic) ideology. Non-Western powers often cast votes that oppose a unanimous affirmative outcome (see Table 1). According to Vreeland and Dreher (2014), unanimous voting has historically been influenced by the United States, which has pressured elected members of the E10 to cast 'favourable' votes (138). Moreover, P5 members can exert pressure on elected members of opposing coalitions or attempt to draw them into their own coalitions (Dreher et al. 2009). Conversely, voting decisions—especially by P5 members—can be influenced by or affect international power dynamics, and these dynamics likely extend to actions taken by other powers (Moody 2005).

An analysis of the P5 members' speaking notes during public meetings indicates that veto power is typically employed only when a permanent member feels threatened or is inclined to create a hostile environment. This suggests that P5 members often prefer to abstain rather than veto resolutions, thereby expressing their discontent within the UNSC. However, members may resort to negotiation and sometimes even vote-buying to prevent P5 members from casting a negative vote (Vreeland and Dreher 2014, 35–96).

The examples considered in our analysis focus on specific (well-known) UN missions, including the United Nations Military Observer Group in India and Pakistan (UNMOGIP) from 1948 to the present, the United

Table 1 Abstentions by P5 members on peace mission initiation and extensions, United Nations Security Council (January 1948–April 2024)

P5 Member	*Target Regions*	*Total Abstentions*
China	Africa (11), Americas (3), Europe (1), Middle East (28)	43
Russian Federation	Africa (22), Americas (4), Europe (1), Middle East (1)	28
USSR	Africa (1), Asia (5), Middle East (4)	10
United Kingdom	Africa (3)	3
United States	Africa (3)	3
France	Africa (2)	2
	Total	89

Source Own data collection based on UN Digital Library

Nations Mission for the Referendum in Western Sahara (MINURSO) from 1991, which is still ongoing, and the United Nations Mission in South Sudan (UNMISS) from 2011 to the present. Also included are the United Nations Multidimensional Integrated Stabilization Mission in the Central African Republic (MINUSCA) from 2014 to 2021 and the United Nations Mission for Justice Support in Haiti (MINUJUSTH) from 2017 to 2019.

Table 1, based on our data collection, offers an overview of all P5 abstentions in the UNSC concerning peace operations and resolutions extending their mandates between 1948 and April 2024. Due to the importance of peace mission operations as a mechanism for maintaining peace based on UNSC resolutions, respective data were collected based on the UN Digital Library. Generally, the United States, the United Kingdom, and France rarely join a dissenting coalition in the UNSC.[8] Two primary coalitions are identified: A default coalition and a dissenting coalition, the latter including those who abstained or voted 'no.'

The dataset explored includes all resolutions voted on in this area in the UNSC from 1948 to April 2024, covering both terminated peace missions and those still in effect (628 in total). However, it excludes UNSC resolutions that pertain exclusively to sanctions or

[8] The US government uses assessments for 'coincidence voting' to evaluate this 'default option': If over 50 per cent of a member's votes align with that of the United States, they are typically considered part of the default UNSC coalition.

mission enhancements, to maintain comparability across cases. After their establishment, most peace operations resulted in extension resolutions approved by the UNSC. Generally, a failure to pass a UNSC resolution for mission extension can lead to the termination of a UN peace operation. The dataset organises resolutions by region, year, and resolution number and records how each member voted ('yes,' 'no,' and 'abstention.') during its years of UNSC membership.

To analyse patterns of coalition formation, however, we focus solely on contested UNSC votes—those that generated at least one abstention or 'no' vote—since these cases reflect a departure from the typical expectation of UNSC unanimity. For example, out of the 628 resolutions collected, only 74 had at least one abstention, indicating that the majority of UNSC decisions achieved unanimity. Consequently, a departure from unanimous support has important implications.

After analysing the data, we qualitatively explored selected missions that were notable, particularly those that resulted in several abstentions or 'no' votes. This analysis includes a qualitative assessment of public statements, UNSC meeting records specific to these missions, and news articles and other related documents, aiming to gain additional insights into the motivations for dissent, political visions, and perspectives at the time of the respective UNSC votes.

4 Negotiations in the Security Council: Three Tiers

Since 1946, there have been almost 250 vetoes or 'no' votes in the UNSC, with only 23 directly related to peace missions. Remarkably, only one of these vetoes has resulted in the complete termination of a peace operation: The Russian veto in 2009 concerning a two-week extension of the United Nations Observer Mission in Georgia (UNOMIG). This veto was influenced by the Russo-Georgian War, which occurred in 2008 and reflected Russian national interests (Dickinson 2021). The vetoed resolution was sponsored by members of the North Atlantic Treaty Organisation (NATO),[9] including Austria, Croatia, France, Germany, Turkey, the United Kingdom, and the United States, who had declared

[9] Draft sponsors were Austria, Croatia, France, Germany, Turkey, the United Kingdom, and the United States.

Georgia to be a future member of NATO six months prior to the Russian invasion (Dickinson 2021). The Russian delegate in the UNSC argued that the veto was necessary to prevent what they viewed as interference by 'Western partners' in the region (S/PV.6143, 2–3).

According to Saner (2008), and encapsulated in Tier I of the three-Tier approach, UNSC members, like participants in any international institution, have their own parochial national interests that shape the negotiation process. This, in turn, influences potential areas of agreement. Consequently, we can observe that actors may join a dissenting coalition by abstaining if a draft resolution is perceived as directly impacting their national interests. This pattern likely holds true more broadly when UNSC members face significant perceived risks or rewards. For instance, the 2016 UNSC vote on the West-Saharan peace mission MINURSO was very much influenced by the national interests of the involved actors and was highly contested, as Table 2 illustrates.

For instance, New Zealand typically supported the 'default' coalition, meaning it voted with the United States more than 50% of the time. Therefore, its decision to abstain from voting on the 2016 MINURSO resolution was noteworthy. E10 membership in 2016 comprised Angola, Egypt, Japan, Malaysia, New Zealand, Senegal, Spain, Ukraine, Uruguay and Venezuela. New Zealand's abstention, moreover, contrasted with the dissenting votes of two other E10 members, Uruguay and Venezuela. This was an uncommon occurrence, indicating that the 2016 vote on the MINURSO resolution was highly contentious.

Moreover, the outcome encompassed an abstention by a P5 member (Russia) and two E10 member states (Angola and New Zealand). Consequently, the winning coalition on the resolution consisted of ten UNSC members, including four P5 states, exceeding the minimum winning

Table 2 Abstentions by permanent and non-permanent Security Council Members on MINURSO (S/RES/2285), 2016

UNSC Member	Abstention	No
Uruguay	0	1
Venezuela	0	1
Angola	1	0
New Zealand	1	0
Russian Federation	1	0
Total	3	2

Source Own data collection based on UN Digital Library

requirement by just one vote. This is one of the rare cases where predictions based on power-oriented coalition approaches get some empirical support.

In another case, concerning the United Nations Transition Assistance Group (UNTAG) in Namibia, the three Western P5 members (the 'P3) cast a veto. UNTAG was established in 1978 based on UNSC Resolution 435, but its implementation faced significant obstacles in the 1980s due to Western vetoes and South Africa's refusal to cooperate (Berat 1990). The political environment in Namibia was hostile; the Cold War conditions and tensions had led to the deployment of Cuban troops and Western allies, forming the Western Contact Group to support Namibia's independence. Additionally, there were efforts by the US government to overthrow the Angolan government, which was in a coalition with South Africa at the time.

A 'no' vote from a P5 member constitutes a veto, but as Table 3 shows, negative votes cast by E10 members related to peace missions are also uncommon.

Table 3 Opposing votes ("No") by non-permanent members on peace missions or their extensions, United Nations Security Council (January 1948 to April 2024)

Year	Total 'No' votes	UNSC Resolution	Peace Operation	UNSC Member voting 'no'
2000	1	S/RES/ 1301(2000)	MINURSO	Namibia
2009	2	S/RES/ 1873(2009) S/RES/ 1898(2009)	UNFICYP	Turkey
2010	2	S/RES/ 1930(2010) S/RES/ 1953(2010)	UNFICYP	Turkey
2016	1	S/RES/ 2285(2016)	MINURSO	Uruguay
2016	1	S/RES/ 2285(2016)	MINURSO	Venezuela

Source: Own data collection based on UN Digital Library

In the 2016 UNSC vote about extending the MINURSO mission in Western Sahara, Venezuela and Angola expressed unease about potential favouritism towards Morocco,[10] citing political and economic ties with influential countries and historical opposition to their own UNSC membership aspirations. Uruguay voted 'no' alongside Venezuela: Uruguay's decision to support Venezuela was influenced by political ties, with Uruguay's left-leaning government publicly endorsing Venezuelan President Nicolás Maduro. Latin American and Caribbean (LAC) E10 states explicitly voted against the default UNSC majority, with LAC's opposition notably based on the alleged lack of impartiality in respective resolution drafts.

However, Jamaica was the first LAC state to change the 'default' as a UNSC non-permanent member in 2000, voting on resolution S/RES/1301. It then abstained for the first and only time on a peace mission expansion resolution, claiming that 'there are doubts within the Security Council' and that the resolution would not be 'following its mandated procedure' by ignoring essential reports from the mission's envoy (S/PV.4149, 2–3).

It is hard to claim, however, that LAC countries abstained only based on Tier I motives during their UNSC tenure, given geopolitical concerns, rivalries, and MINURSO's highly controversial history since its creation, especially as 'Western Sahara is Africa's longest-running territorial dispute and an issue of continental and international law and diplomatic controversy' (Lulie 2016). Although LAC countries' decisions to move away from the majority can be explained based on the three interlinked negotiation Tiers (the revealed self-interest of Uruguay and Venezuela included), another instance may showcase the relevance of Tier II more clearly.

For the 2017–2018 term, it was the first time in more than 30 years that Bolivia had regained its non-permanent seat on the Security Council. Bolivia's UN Ambassador stated that Bolivia's membership would focus on tackling the 'root causes of conflict' (Fillion 2018). The statement made by Bolivia in 2018 highlighted the country's commitment to 'defending multilateralism' and upholding the principles outlined in the UN Charter. In relation to resolution S/2018/901, Bolivia requested a

[10] Lulie (2016) even claimed "the council, pressured by the Morocco lobby, was unable to support the Secretary-General, or condemn Morocco's response." Allegedly, Morocco was a known ally to many Western UN member states, particularly the United States and France at the time.

meeting to discuss the agenda item: 'Maintenance of International Peace and Security: Root Causes of Conflict—The Role of Natural Resources.' Throughout its voting and speeches, the Bolivian delegation emphasised its opposition to what it perceived as unilateral and politically biased actions within the UN Security Council (UNSC) (Letter S/2018/901, 1–3).

Bolivia's position in the UNSC seemed closely tied to Tiers I and II. Notably, the Bolivian delegation took steps to assert its importance within the UNSC. Bolivia's national priorities were exemplified by its abstention from the 2018 MINURSO resolution (S/RES/2440), aligning with the LAC stance on upholding the principle of self-determination. This example challenges the assumption that non-permanent members, or E10, typically refrain from opposing winning UNSC resolutions. Instead, it illustrates a non-permanent member's pursuit of legitimacy and advocacy for its national principles, demonstrating a link between organisational legitimacy and its position within the institution.

In the context of Tier II dynamics, Russia abstained from the MINURSO Resolution 2440, citing its significance for regional stability: Its delegation stated that it supported the extension of 'the mandate of the United Nations Mission for the Referendum in Western Sahara (MINURSO) [as it] is important for regional stability' (S/PV.8387, 5). This decision reflected Russia's reluctance to oppose the extension of the mission while demonstrating it remained committed to its principles.

As permanent UNSC members, both China and Russia have often abstained, generally avoiding a veto on peace mission resolutions unless the content directly contradicted their national interests or historical positions within the UNSC. For P5 members, abstaining on such resolutions, in line with Tier II negotiation dynamics, arguably carries more weight than for E10 members, as a 'no' vote could effectively block the continuation of a peace mission, with this posing a greater risk to their own standing compared to that of E10 member states.

Fig 2 presents an overview of the proportion of individual P5 member abstentions in the total number of P5 abstentions on peace mission initiation and extensions between January 1948 and April 2024.

According to Fig. 2, China had the highest proportion of P5 member abstentions, at 47.7%, followed closely by the USSR (later Russia) at 43.2%. In contrast, the United States and the United Kingdom combined accounted for just under 10%, while France had a mere 2.3%.

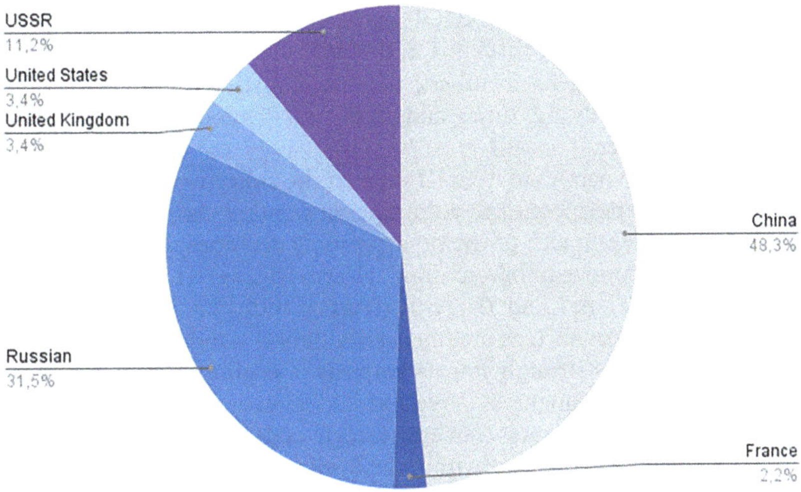

Fig. 2 Shares of abstentions by P5 states: initiation and extensions of peace missions (United Nations Security Council, January 1948–April 2024) (*Source* Own data collection based on UN Digital Library)

Additionally, China has the highest number of abstentions when voting alongside another member. Out of a total of 47 joint abstentions (see Table 4), China abstained in unison with another member 30 times. The Chinese delegation voted together with Iraq eight times—the most frequently a member has voted 'with' China—regarding the United Nations Disengagement Observer Force (UNDOF) peacekeeping operation, which has monitored the Israeli-Syrian tensions since 1974 (Background 2023). They shared the same vote on three resolutions in 1974 and five in 1975. Notably, after Iraq's E10 mandate concluded, China continued to abstain alongside another member of the Middle East group until 1977, when the Libyan Arab Jamahiriya joined them in abstaining. In these eight instances, both China and Iraq expressed opposition to military presence in the Middle East, particularly from significant superpowers. China asserted that the aggression in the region stemmed from 'the contention between the superpowers for hegemony in their selfish interest,' which, according to its delegation, created interference and contributed to conflict (S/PV.1774, 3). China was vocal about its position, particularly in calling out the self-interests of other members during the early UNDOF mandate, aligning with Tier II and III reflections. While both China and Russia have the highest number of abstentions among P5 members, they have abstained together on the same resolution only 12 times and have never vetoed a peacekeeping resolution together.

Negotiation dynamics in Tier III refer to the collective benefits for the organisation: A more cohesive voting pattern within the UNSC is likely to enhance the legitimacy of the organisation's decisions, especially when its reputation is under public scrutiny. However, Tier III is arguably less influential than Tiers I and II are in terms of individual member states' motivations: Factors such as member states' 'good standing' and national interest calculations strongly impact patterns of coalition formation. This aligns with the assessment by Vreeland and Dreher (2014), who argue that powerful UNSC states can use foreign aid to E10 members as a mechanism to garner support within the institution and bolster credibility for their decisions.

Our qualitative analysis of some statements and related documents reveals a consistent rhetoric among dissenters and members of the 'default' coalition over time, although this may be less apparent in the statements from the latter group. For instance, during the 2016 MINURSO vote, both Uruguay and Venezuela criticised the 'default' coalition for allegedly granting excessive leeway to Morocco due to

Table 4 Permanent members (P5) abstaining together with another member on the same resolution by region on peace mission initiations and extensions, UNSC (January 1948–April 2024)

P5 member	*Target regions*	*Total joint abstentions per member*
China	Africa (11), Americas (2), Middle East (17)	30
France	Africa (2)	2
Russian Federation	Africa (18), Americas (3), Middle East (1)	22
United Kingdom	Africa (3)	3
United States	Africa (1)	1
USSR	Africa (1), Asia (3), Middle East (4)	8

Source Own data collection based on UN Digital Library.

pre-existing political ties. They argued that the resolution was drafted under questionable conditions, thereby jeopardising its legitimacy (S/RES2285). However, given that both countries also had self-interested goals, these accusations—which were framed as being in the best interest of the mission and the UNSC as a whole—may be interpreted as a tactic to lend more credibility to their statements. Accordingly, Tier III is frequently invoked to justify actions by either coalition, while the true self-interested motivations remain obscured within the coalition-formation process.

Moreover, Tier III can help define or reaffirm the Security Council's role as an international actor by referencing the organisation's values, rules, or even the UN Charter. For example, in 2016, South Sudan asserted that 'the adoption of the resolution goes against a basic principle of United Nations peacekeeping operations, which is the consent of the main parties to the conflict, and against the Charter of the United Nations, which urges Members to respect the sovereignty, territorial integrity, and political independence of other States' (S/PV.7754, 12). Such statements underscore that universal values support the organisation's operations and are often invoked—albeit superficially—affecting the evaluations and voting decisions of UNSC members.

In analysing the voting patterns related to peace missions at the UNSC, it becomes clear that specific missions have experienced notably high rates of abstention. This is shown graphically in Fig. 3. For example, the UNDOF and the United Nations Emergency Force II (UNEF II) faced relatively high contestation. In the Middle East, the United Nations Interim Force in Lebanon (UNIFIL) also contributed significantly to the overall abstention rates.

Furthermore, peace missions in Africa—such as MINURSO and UNMISS, as well as missions like UNTAG and the United Nations Mission in Liberia (UNMIL)—have shown a considerable share of abstentions, thereby influencing regional abstention trends. Additionally, missions located in Asia, the Americas, and Europe, including UNMOGIP, MINUJUSTH, and the United Nations Peacekeeping Force in Cyprus (UNFICYP), have also recorded notable rates of disagreement reflected by abstentions.

Regarding member states sharing abstentions (see Fig. 4), both E10 and P5 members at times align by voting together against a default

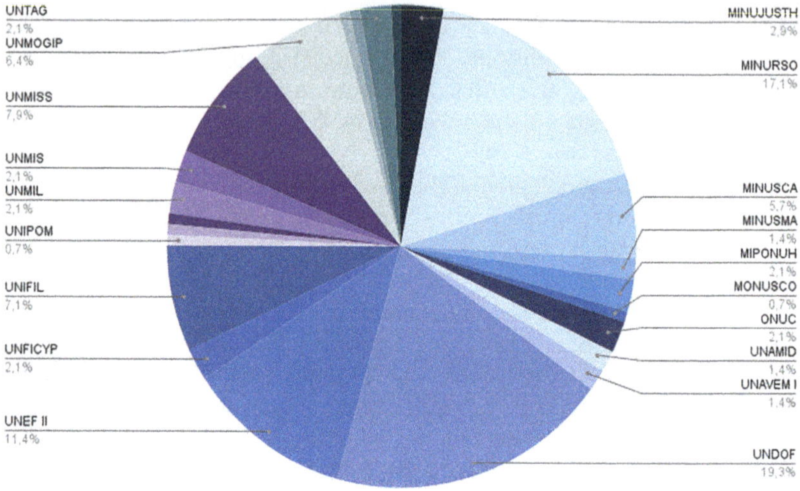

Fig. 3 Abstentions on initiation and extensions of peace missions, UNSC January 1948–April 2024 (*Source* Own data collection based on UN Digital Library)

position. For instance, China and Iraq have abstained from UNDOF resolutions eight times, while China and Russia have abstained from multiple resolutions seven times in total.[11]

The P5 Western powers (the P3) also tend to abstain together, as Fig. 4 shows. For example, the United Kingdom and the United States voted together on S/RES/566, China, France, and the United Kingdom on S/RES/143, and finally, France, Russia, and the United Kingdom on S/RES/2333. Rarely does a P3 member vote against the default; however, particularly against the United States, they use abstention to express discontent. It is noteworthy that the United States has vetoed 11 peacekeeping extension resolutions and sponsored 537 out of 628, whereas Russia and China have vetoed 5 and 2 resolutions, with 327 and 333 sponsorships, respectively.[12]

[11] This concerns resolutions on Africa, S/RES/2448, S/RES/2605, S/RES/2625, S/RES/2640, S/RES/2677, and on the Americas: S/RES/1212, S/RES/2410.

[12] On patterns of UNSC resolution sponsorship more generally, see Helou et al., this volume.

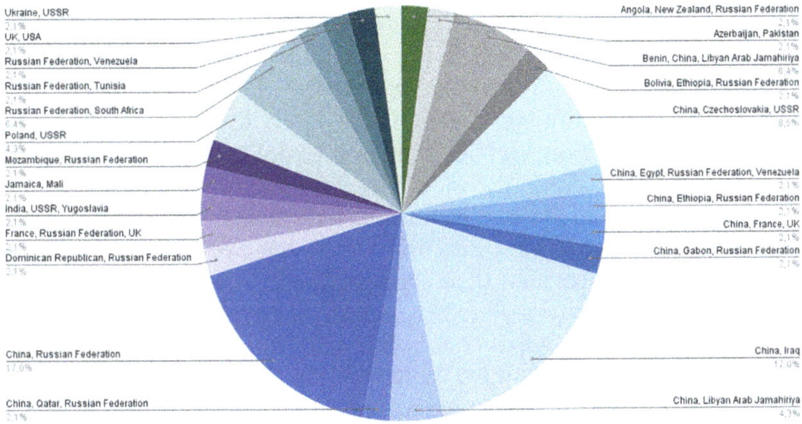

Fig. 4 Groups of member states abstaining together on the same resolution on initiations and extensions of peace missions, UNSC January 1948–April 2024 (*Source* Own data collection based on UN Digital Library)

China and Iraq have abstained together related to UNDOF resolutions, and China and Russia have abstained in 12 different cases, eight of which involved only the two of them abstaining. Moreover, Jamaica and Mali abstained together on S/RES/1303, and Azerbaijan and Pakistan on S/RES/2058. Our exploration suggests that for a P5 member to lead a coalition against the default winning coalition, there must be a significant contention in the draft resolution or a strong conflict with an E10 member's national beliefs and interests (Tier I).

Moreover, even when a P5 member leads, it is rare that members go against the winning coalition aiming to affect the voting results unless a P5 veto is involved. The closest instance may have been the 2016 MINURSO vote; however, it still did not defeat the default. This suggests that when a member votes in a way that breaks unanimity, examining the Tiers is crucial to understanding the decision-making process and the impact of this member's vote on the UNSC and the member's domestic environment.

International institutions like the UNSC have clear incentives to seek consensus and minimise opposing votes or abstentions on draft resolutions, with a preference for unanimous adoption. While the majority of resolutions pass without negative votes or abstentions, some contestations do occur, revealing underlying policy preferences. The formation of winning coalitions in the UNSC is linked to these policy preferences. However, minimal winning coalitions are rarely formed, which distinguishes this context from conflict of interest or policy distance approaches in more standard coalition theories.

The data collected on peace mission votes demonstrate that UNSC resolutions can face opposition, with some members voting 'no' or abstaining while others lend their support. Nonetheless, such opposition remains rare. Our analysis aimed to identify the driving forces that lead UNSC states to either support a coalition by voting 'yes' or oppose it, often accompanied by issuing a statement. In this context, abstentions serve as a milder form of opposition, signalling clear resistance against a draft resolution.

Over time, insights drawn from UNSC voting patterns on peace missions reveal that the 'default' winning coalition comprises all fifteen Security Council member states, reinforcing the goals outlined in negotiation Tier III. In contrast, voting 'no' or abstaining relates to Tier I, while Tier II imposes constraints based on considerations related to Tier III. However, our examination of statements and political dynamics surrounding opposing votes underscores the relevance of all three negotiation Tiers. Comparatively, traditional coalition theories are less applicable, as winning coalitions in the UNSC tend to be much larger than either power-oriented or policy-oriented approaches would predict.

5 Conclusions

Our analysis has confirmed that winning UNSC coalitions often exceed the minimum requirements for resolutions to pass. These coalitions are interconnected based on the policy priorities of member states. We have shown that member state priorities are influenced by various layers of international negotiations, which differ from the principles applicable to coalition formation in national governments. The formation of coalitions in the UNSC involves dynamics based on both power-related and policy-related considerations. Still, unlike in national-level coalition-formation processes, UNSC coalitions are not solely formed to enhance a party's power or minimise conflicts of interest. Instead, the primary objective is to achieve broad consensus—ideally, unanimity—to enhance the legitimacy of Security Council resolutions.

Our chapter explores member-state voting behaviour on resolutions regarding peace missions and their extensions in the UNSC based on new data. We study how the UNSC operates and what drives member-state voting behaviour during actual votes. With this, we also focus on the role of the E10 members, alongside the P5, in coalition formation, which is influenced by considerations based on negotiation Tiers I to III.

Consensus or unanimity is the norm for making decisions in the UNSC, publicly demonstrating unity among its members. This aim, while arguably less prevalent than considerations related to Tiers I and II, still influences motivations regarding coalition formation. Empirically, negative votes on peace missions or their extensions are rare in the UNSC; the same holds for abstentions.

Member states of the UNSC, including the P5 and E10, carefully evaluate the consequences of their voting decisions concerning their standing within the organisation. While a negative vote from an E10 member may have less impact on a resolution than a negative vote by a P5 member (which constitutes a veto), as it does not necessarily lead to the failure of establishing or continuing a UN peace operation, it is still rarely used in practice.

Based on newly assembled data on UNSC voting and descriptive information on member behaviour related to selected peace missions and their extensions, our analysis corroborates how coalition formation in the UNSC differs from government formation processes. It sheds light on the complex dynamics underlying coalition formation and decision-making in international institutions such as the UNSC, which remains relatively underexplored, given its significance in global affairs.

Future research can use such data compilations to conduct additional quantitative or qualitative analyses of the UNSC's voting and coalition-formation processes. Researchers can also explore the extent to which specific peace missions were contested, how dissenting votes related to a mission's geographical focus, or how the specific composition of the E10 during a Security Council term affected UNSC decision outcomes.

In many international institutions, traditional incentives for actors to join coalitions based on power-seeking motives appear to matter less, while policy-oriented motives may be more relevant. However, as our exploration shows, members often join winning coalitions based on national policy preferences and priorities while keeping legitimacy concerns about the institution they represent in mind. The interconnections among national interests, the desire to avoid negative standing within an organisation, and efforts to uphold the institution's collective legitimacy are the primary drivers of voting behaviour in the UNSC. This also holds for UNSC votes on peace missions or their extensions, generally resulting in oversized coalitions where only a few members openly oppose a given resolution.

References

Axelrod, Robert. *Conflict of Interest: A Theory of Divergent Goals with Applications to Politics*. Markham Pub. Co., 1970.

Background. "UNDOF." *United Nations Disengagement Observer Force*, February 20, 2023. https://undof.unmissions.org/background.

Bailey, Sydney D. "New Light on Abstentions in the UN Security Council." *International Affairs (Royal Institute of International Affairs 1944–)* 50, no. 4 (October 1974): 554–573. https://doi.org/10.2307/2615923.

Berat, Lynn. "Namibia: The Road to Independence and the Problem of Succession of States." *Journal of Political Science* 18, no. 1 (1990): Article 10. https://digitalcommons.coastal.edu/jops/vol18/iss1/10.

Binder, Martin, and Jonathan Golub. "Civil Conflict and Agenda-Setting Speed in the United Nations Security Council." *International Studies Quarterly* 64, no. 2 (2020): 419–430. https://doi.org/10.1093/isq/sqaa017.

Bohemen, Gerard van. "UN Security Council: Brief: United Nations Peacekeeping Operations." Speech transcript. https://www.mfat.govt.nz/en/media-and-resources/un-security-council-brief-united-nations-peacekeeping-operations/.

Bohemen, Gerard van. "UN Security Council: The Situation Concerning Western Sahara." Speech transcript, 2016a. https://www.mfat.govt.nz/en/media-and-resources/un-security-council-the-situation-concerning-western-sahara/.

Bohemen, Gerard van. "UN Security Council Open Debate: Protection of Civilians." Speech transcript, 2016b. https://www.mfat.govt.nz/en/media-and-resources/un-security-council-open-debate-protection-of-civilians-2/.

Brams, Steven J. *Negotiation Games: Applying Game Theory to Bargaining and Arbitration*. New York: Routledge, 2003

De Swaan, Abram. *Coalition Theories and Cabinet Formations: A Study of Formal Theories of Coalition Formation Applied to Nine European Parliaments After 1918*. Amsterdam: Elsevier, 1973.

de Swaan, Abram. *Coalition Theories and Cabinet Formations*. PhD diss., University of Amsterdam, 1973.

De Vries and Miranda Wilhelmina Maria. *Governing With Your Closest Neighbour: An Assessment of Spatial Coalition Formation Theories*. Diss.,

Radboud University, 1999. https://repository.ubn.ru.nl/bitstream/handle/2066/18833/18833_govewiyoc.pdf.

Dickinson, Peter. "The 2008 Russo-Georgian War: Putin's Green Light." *Atlantic Council*, August 7, 2021. https://www.atlanticcouncil.org/blogs/ukrainealert/the-2008-russo-georgian-war-putins-green-light/.

Dreher, Axel, Jan-Egbert Sturm, and James Raymond Vreeland. "Development Aid and International Politics: Does Membership on the UN Security Council Influence World Bank Decisions?" *Journal of Development Economics* 88 (2009): 1–18. https://doi.org/10.1016/j.jdeveco.2008.02.003.

Ekengren, Ann-Marie, Fredrik D. Hjorthen, and Ulrika Möller. "A Nonpermanent Seat in the United Nations Security Council: Why Bother?" *Global Governance: A Review of Multilateralism and International Organisations* 26, no. 1 (2020): 21–45. https://doi.org/10.1163/19426720-02601007

Fillion, Stéphanie. "Bolivia's Priority in the UN Security Council: Why Conflicts Begin." *PassBlue*, October 10, 2018. https://www.passblue.com/2018/10/01/bolivias-priority-in-the-un-security-council-why-conflicts-begin/.

Gamson, William A. "A Theory of Coalition Formation." *American Sociological Review* 26 (1961): 157–171.

Gross, Leo. "Voting in the Security Council: Abstention from Voting and Absence from Meetings." *The Yale Law Journal* 60, no. 2 (1951): 209–257. https://doi.org/10.2307/793412

Heisenberg, Dorothee. The institution of 'consensus' in the European Union: formal versus informal decision-making in the council. *European Journal of Political Research* 44, no. 1 (2005): 65–90. https://doi.org/10.1111/j.1475-6765.2005.00219.x

Hosli, Madeleine O., Rebecca Moody, Bryan O'Donovan, Serguei Kaniovski, and Anna. C. H. Little. "Squaring the Circle? Distributive and Collective Effects of Security Council Reform." *Review of International Organisations* 6, no. 2 (2011): 163–187. https://doi.org/10.1007/s11558-011-9113-1.

Hosli, Madeleine O., and Thomas Dörfler. "Why Is Change so Slow? Assessing Prospects for United Nations Security Council Reform." *Journal of Economic Policy Reform* 22, no. 1 (2017): 35–50. https://doi.org/10.1080/17487870.2017.1280301

Howard, Lise Morjé, and Anjali Kaushlesh Dayal. "The Use of Force in UN Peacekeeping." *International Organization* 72, no. 1 (2017): 71–103. https://doi.org/10.1017/s0020818317000431.

Junn, Robert. S., and Tong-Whan Park. "Calculus of Voting Power in the U.N. Security Council." *Social Science Quarterly* 58, no. 1 (1977): 104–110. http://www.jstor.org/stable/42859752.

Karns, Margaret. P., Tana Johnson, and Karen A. Mingst. *International Organisations: The Politics and Processes of Global Governance*. 2nd ed. Boulder, CO: Lynne Rienner Publishers, 2010.

Keating, Colin. “Power Dynamics between Permanent and Elected Members.” In *The UN Security Council in the 21st Century*, edited by Sebastian von Einsiedel, David M. Malone, and Bruno Stagno Ugarte, 77–94. Boulder, CO: Lynne Rienner, 2016.

Landry, Carole. “Divided UN Council Votes to Bring Back Full Western Sahara Mission.” *Middle East Eye*, April 29, 2016. https://www.middleeasteye.net/news/divided-un-council-votes-bring-back-full-western-sahara-mission.

Leiserson, Michael. *Coalitions in Politics: A Theoretical and Empirical Study*. Yale University Press, 1966.

Leiserson, Michael. “Factions and Coalitions in One-Party Japan: An Interpretation Based on the Theory of Games.” *American Political Science Review* 62, no. 3 (1968): 770–787. https://doi.org/10.2307/1953429

Lulie, Hallelujah. “The Word that Reignited the Western Sahara Debate.” *Institute of Security Studies Africa*, April 26, 2016. https://issafrica.org/iss-today/the-word-that-reignited-the-western-sahara-debate.

“Maduro at the U.N. Security Council.” *Human Rights Watch*, February 15, 2016. https://www.hrw.org/news/2016/02/15/maduro-un-security-council.

McCully, Murray. “New Zealand Takes UN Security Council Seat.” *Speech Transcript*, November 10, 2015. https://www.beehive.govt.nz/release/new-zealand-takes-un-security-council-seat.

Miranda, Boris. “O Plano de Putin e Evo Morales para Construir a Usina Nuclear Mais Alta do Mundo na Bolívia.” *BBC News Brasil*, July 2019. https://www.bbc.com/portuguese/internacional-48967932.

Moody, Rebecca. *Coalition formation strategies in the United Nations Security Council*. Thesis, Leiden University, 2005.

Nahory, Céline. “The Hidden Veto.” *Global Policy Forum*, May 2004. https://archive.globalpolicy.org/security-council/42656-the-hidden-veto.html.

Neumann, John Von, and Oskar Morgenstern. *Theory of Games and Economic Behaviour*. Princeton: Princeton University Press, 1947.

O’Dell, Hope. “How the US Has Used Its Power in the UN to Support Israel for Decades.” *Global Affairs*, February 22, 2024. https://globalaffairs.org/bluemarble/how-us-has-used-its-power-un-support-israel-decades.

Osorio, Christian Garzon. “Beyond the Structural Asymmetry of the UNSC: A Bargaining Power-Analysis of Resolutions 2220 and 2216.” Master’s Thesis, University of Oslo, 2016. https://www.duo.uio.no/handle/10852/58355.

Power, Samantha. “Statement by the U.S. Ambassador to the UN on the Newly Elected Members of the Security Council.” *Speech Transcript*, October 17, 2014. https://geneva.usmission.gov/2014/10/17/statement-by-the-u-s-ambassador-to-the-un-on-the-newly-elected-members-of-the-security-council/.

Peace and Security Council Report (PSC Report). "New Developments around Western Sahara Could Create an Opportunity for Africa to Assert its Position." *Institute for Security Studies*, 2016. https://issafrica.org/pscreport/psc-insights/a-new-opportunity-to-assert-africas-role-in-western-sahara.

Riker, William H. *The Theory of Political Coalitions*. Westport: Greenwood Press Publishers, 1962.

"Role of the Security Council." *United Nations Peacekeeping*. n.d. https://peacekeeping.un.org/en/role-of-security-council.

Security Council, 7th year: 611th meeting. UNSC Doc S/PV.8510 (23 December 1952). Available from https://digitallibrary.un.org/record/3800240?ln=en.

Security Council, 29th year: 1774th meeting. UNSC Doc S/PV.1774 (31 May 1974). Available from https://digitallibrary.un.org/record/54806?ln=en&v=pdf.

Security Council, 55th year: 4149th meeting. UNSC Doc S/PV.4149 (31 May 2000). Available from https://digitallibrary.un.org/record/415201?ln=en.

Security Council, 57th year: 4563rd meeting. UNSC Doc S/PV.4563 (30 June 2002). Available from https://digitallibrary.un.org/record/468013?ln=en&v=pdf.

Security Council, 64th year: 6143rd meeting. UNSC Doc S/PV.6143 (15 June 2009). Available from https://digitallibrary.un.org/record/657911?ln=fr&v=pdf.

Security Council, 71st Year: 7684th Meeting. UNSC Doc S/PV.7684 (29 April 2016). Available from https://digitallibrary.un.org/record/827602?ln=en.

Security Council, 71st Year: 7754th Meeting. UNSC Doc S/PV.7754 (12 August 2016). Available from https://digitallibrary.un.org/record/837150?ln=en.

Security Council, 73rd Year: 8387th Meeting. UNSC Doc S/PV.8387 (31 October 2018). Available from https://digitallibrary.un.org/record/1651129?ln=fr.

Security Council, 73rd Year: 8422nd Meeting. UNSC Doc S/PV.8422 (13 December 2018). Available from https://digitallibrary.un.org/record/1656180?ln=en.

Security Council, 74th Year: 8510th Meeting. UNSC Doc S/PV.8510 (12 April 2019). Available from https://digitallibrary.un.org/record/3800240?ln=en.

Saner, Raymond. *The Expert Negotiator: Strategy, Tactics, Motivation, Behaviour, Leadership*. 3rd ed. Martinus Nijhoff, 2008.

Scherzinger, Johannes. *Searching for Themes in a Chamber full of Noise? How Language Affects United Nations' Actions and Decisions*. PhD diss., University of Zurich, 2023.

Sommerer, Thomas, Squatrito, Theresa, Tallberg, Jonas. et al. Decision-making in international organizations: Institutional design and performance. *Review of International Organizations* 17 (2022), 815–845. https://doi.org/10.1007/s11558-021-09445-x.

Stavropoulos, Constantin A. "The Practice of Voluntary Abstentions by Permanent Members of the Security Council Under Article 27, Paragraph 3, of the Charter of the United Nations." *The American Journal of International Law* 61, no. 3 (1967): 737–752. https://doi.org/10.2307/2197464.

Taylor, Adam. "Analysis at Trump's U.N. Security Council Meeting, Bolivia's Leftist Leader Could Play Foil." *The Washington Post*, September 25, 2018. https://www.washingtonpost.com/world/2018/09/25/trumps-security-council-meeting-bolivias-leftist-leader-could-play-foil/.

Theofilopoulou, Anna. "The United States Institute of Peace Special Report: The United Nations and Western Sahara, a Never-Ending Affair." *USIP*, July 2016. https://www.usip.org/sites/default/files/sr166.pdf.

Volden, Craig, and Clifford Carrubba. "The Formation of Oversized Coalitions in Parliamentary Democracies." *American Journal of Political Science* 48 (2004): 521–537. https://doi.org/10.1111/j.0092-5853.2004.00085.x.

"UN Security Council Working Methods: Security Council Report." n.d. https://www.securitycouncilreport.org/un-security-council-working-methods/.

United Nations. "About Us | United Nations." n.d. https://www.un.org/en/about-us.

United Nations. "UN Security Council Meetings & Outcomes Tables." *United Nations Digital Library—Veto List*. n.d. https://research.un.org/en/docs/sc/quick.

United Nations, Department of Public Information. "Security Council Extends Mandate of United Nations Mission for Referendum in Western Sahara by 10 Votes in Favour, 2 Against, with 2 Abstentions, SC/12346, April 2016." https://www.un.org/press/en/2016/sc12346.doc.htm.

United Nations, Department of Public Information. "Double Veto Prevents Security Council from Adopting Draft Resolution Intended to Impose Sanctions for Use of Chemical Weapons in Syria, SC/12737, February 2017." https://reliefweb.int/report/syrian-arab-republic/double-veto-prevents-security-council-adopting-draft-resolution-intended.

United Nations General Assembly Resolution 1991 (XVIII). "Question of Equitable Representation on the Security Council and the Economic and Social Council [1963] UNGA 112; A/RES/1991 (XVIII), 17 December 1963." http://www.worldlii.org/int/other/UNGA/1963/112.pdf.

United Nations Security Council Resolution 1301 (S/RES/1301), "On Extension of the Mandate of the UN Mission for the Referendum in Western Sahara (MINURSO)," 31 May 2000. https://digitallibrary.un.org/record/415205?ln=zh_CN.

United Nations Security Council Draft Resolution S/2009/310, *On a Two-Week Extension of UNOMIG's Mandate to Allow More Time for Negotiations on a*

New Security Regime in the Region (14 June 2009). https://www.securitycouncilreport.org/un-documents/document/georgia-s-2009-310.php

United Nations Security Council Resolution 2285 (S/RES/2285), *On extension of the mandate of the UN Mission for the Referendum in Western Sahara (MINURSO)* (30 April 2017). https://digitallibrary.un.org/record/827561

United van Nations Security Council Resolution 2440 (S/RES/2440), *On extension of the mandate of the UN Mission for the Referendum in Western Sahara (MINURSO)* (30 April 2018). https://digitallibrary.un.org/record/1650912?ln=fr

United Nations, Security Council, *Letter dated 9 October 2018 from the Permanent Representative of the Plurinational State of Bolivia to the United Nations addressed to the Secretary-General* S/2018/901. https://www.securitycouncilreport.org/un-documents/document/s2018901.php

Uruguayan Presidencia. "Uruguay Cancela Su Deuda por Petróleo con Venezuela en 262 Millones de Dólares." *Uruguay Presidencia Comunicación*, June 7, 2015. https://www.gub.uy/presidencia/comunicacion/noticias/uruguay-cancela-su-deuda-petroleo-venezuela-262-millones-dolares.

U.S. Department of State, Bureau of International Organization Affairs. *Voting Practices in the United Nations 2015.* 2016. https://2009-2017.state.gov/p/io/rls/rpt/2015/practices/index.htm.

Vreeland, James Raymond, and Axel Dreher. *The Political Economy of the United Nations Security Council.* Cambridge University Press, 2014. https://doi.org/10.1017/CBO9781139027755.

"Venezuela Elected to UN Security Council." *The Guardian*, n.d. https://www.theguardian.com/world/2014/oct/16/venezuela-united-nations-security-council.

"Western Sahara: Arria-Formula Meeting, Consultations and MINURSO Adoption." *Security Council Report,* April 26, 2016. https://www.securitycouncilreport.org/whatsinblue/2016/04/western-sahara-arria-formula-meeting-consultations-and-minurso-adoption.php

"Western Sahara: Mission Mandate Extended for 12 Months." *Security Council Report*, April 29, 2016. https://www.securitycouncilreport.org/whatsinblue/2016/04/western-sahara-mandate-extended-for-12-months.php.

Van Deemen, Adrian M. A. *Coalition Formation and Social Choice.* Kluwer Academic Publishers, 1997.

CHAPTER 3

Coalition Formation and Co-sponsorship in the United Nations Security Council

Tareq Yacoub Helou, Madeleine O. Hosli, and Rennan Pastich Loureiro

1 Introduction

The United Nations Security Council (UNSC) is the only international organisation authorised to sanction the use of force by sovereign nations. Given its authority, the UNSC plays a central role in global affairs. Our chapter examines how UNSC members have shaped the agenda by (co-)sponsoring resolutions from 2011 to 2023, focusing on collaboration patterns among permanent (P5) and non-permanent members (E10)

T. Y. Helou (✉)
Institute of International Relations, University of São Paulo, São Paulo, Brazil
e-mail: tareq@usp.br

M. O. Hosli
Leiden University, The Hague, The Netherlands
e-mail: m.o.hosli@fgga.leidenuniv.nl

R. P. Loureiro
Federal University of Pernambuco, Recife, Brazil
e-mail: rennan.loureiro@ufpe.br

M. O. Hosli et al. (eds.), *Multilateralism and the United Nations Security Council*, https://doi.org/10.1007/978-3-031-85320-3_3

using newly collected data. Additionally, we compare these patterns with co-sponsorship data for the United Nations General Assembly (UNGA) to determine if similar coalition behaviours emerge in both arenas.

Research on co-sponsorship of UNSC resolutions is not extensive, but several studies have focused on resolution co-sponsoring in the General Assembly instead (Finke, 2021; Dijkhuizen and Onderco 2019; Lee and Stek 2016; Seabra and Mesquita 2022a, b). Recent attention has been given to the speed with which internal conflicts are brought to the UNSC agenda, considering political, economic, or geographic connections between target states and UNSC members (Binder and Golub 2020). This builds on earlier research that examined why some conflicts are formally addressed by the Security Council while others are not (Brecher and Wilkenfeld 1997; Iwanami 2011).

Adaptation of coalition models to study behaviour in international organisations has often involved the analysis of voting records. Voting patterns have been utilised to identify coalitional behaviour in organisations such as the European Union (Häge 2013), the UNGA (Voeten 2000, 2013; Bailey et al. 2015), and the International Criminal Court (ICC) (Welch and Watkins 2011). Additionally, scholarly literature has explored mechanisms such as 'vote buying', where UNSC voting support is exchanged for foreign aid (Vreeland and Dreher 2014), and 'issue linkage', where concessions in one area are used to gain advantages in another. Although voting generally pertains to the most contentious political decisions—while many others are adopted by consensus or unanimity (Vreeland and Dreher 2014)—it still reveals some coalitional behaviour among member states.

The UNSC's voting practices are complex due to its exclusive membership of fifteen countries—which is very different from the 193-member UNGA. The P5 hold veto power, while the E10 serve two-year terms without immediate re-election. Although there have been proposals to reform the UNSC, significant institutional obstacles have prevented formal changes, leading to adaptations in operating procedures instead (Hosli and Dörfler 2019). Given the latest trends in multilateralist institutional cooperation, global security governance, and the political (re-) emergence of larger global powers, as well as the emergence of new humanitarian challenges in recent years, it is worth exploring how coalitional behaviour has been changing within the UN. This assessment may involve evaluating opposition to a perceived 'dominating coalition' in the

UNSC or assessing the consequences triggered by relying on this institution to manage international security issues. Furthermore, it is of interest to investigate whether coalitional behaviour in the UNSC aligns with the one observed for the UNGA.

Exploring co-sponsorship of resolutions and coalition formation from 2011 to 2023 in the UNSC, using newly collected data, we observe a trend towards greater authorship independence by the P3—France, UK and USA—which persisted in the wake of Brexit. By comparison, Russia and China have shown increased alignment[1] in UNSC authorship and the use of vetoes. However, they are less active setting the agenda in the UNSC in general compared to their P3 counterparts (a trend that the practice of 'penholdership' in the UNSC further confirms). In this chapter, we compare these results with new data on co-sponsorship in the UNGA to ascertain if similar patterns of behaviour and coalition formation exist among the P5 in both arenas.

The subsequent section focuses on evaluating coalition behaviour in international institutions from a theoretical perspective. Section three outlines our methodological approach for assessing coalition formation and sponsorship in the UNSC and the UNGA. Section four analyses UNGA sponsorship data and compares them with findings for the UNSC. Thereafter, section five presents our analysis and results on coalition behaviour based on the two co-authorship data collections. Section six delves into the practical use and consequences of vetoes by P5 member states. Lastly, the final section summarises the main findings of our analysis and concludes our chapter.

2 Coalitional Behaviour in the United Nations Security Council

Limited research exists on agenda-setting and coalition behaviour among the UNSC's 15 member states. Factors impacting the UNSC's decision to discuss and vote on a particular issue have been explored, however,

[1] The term 'alignment' is employed in this context as the practice of co-sponsorship signifies a more pronounced and deliberate stance compared to the mere convergence of interests typically observed in voting patterns. Furthermore, this type of interaction often exhibits a tendency towards inertia or 'stickiness,' wherein countries that co-sponsor a resolution are likely to continue co-sponsoring subsequent resolutions, thereby reinforcing their alignment.

indicating P5 individual priorities, preferences of the delegation proposing the agenda, and 'public accountability costs'.[2]

Our study emphasises the characteristics of draft resolutions, sponsorship, and co-sponsorship, as crucial for analysing coalition formation in UNSC decision-making, procedures, and outcomes. Sponsorship and co-sponsorship data from UNSC draft resolutions provide insights into a member's intentions and solidify a country's stance on relevant global issues and preferred measures to be taken. It also has to be kept in mind that the 'penholdership practice', where a (permanent) UNSC member chairs negotiations and initiates a draft resolution, is of crucial importance to Security Council operations (Helou and Hosli 2025).

Phenomena such as private, closed-door consultations, penholding practices, and the influence of elected UNSC members demonstrate the relevance of routine informal consultations among UNSC members. Countries vie for a seat on the UNSC to access these consultations (Malone 2006), a mechanism still valid today despite adaptations of UNSC working methods. These consultations, especially among the P5, and more specifically the P3 (USA, UK, and France), have been in place for decades. Typically, draft resolutions are only voted on after being discussed informally, leading to the formation of coalitions based on common understanding and compromise (Prantl 2005). While assessing these consultations is difficult due to their secrecy, they reveal the underlying dynamics of power and the motivations behind coalition-building.

Nico Krisch (2008) examined the dynamics within the P5 as developments in the 'Great Powers Club'. He demonstrated that P5 members often reach a consensus on resolutions that contradict their interests due to side deals or vague language in resolutions. The author noted that the P3 had greater influence and more opportunities to bypass the Council compared to Russia and China. However, outside options have also allowed these two countries to negotiate for more favourable votes, albeit at a cost (Krisch 2008, 141).

Recent literature also focused on the role of smaller states in the UNSC.[3] Krisch (2008) argues that while the Great Powers (P5) significantly influence the Council, non-permanent members also impact its functioning (Krisch 2008, 136). Moreover, the pursuit of unanimous

[2] Also see Bueno et al., this volume.

[3] For small and emerging powers in the UNSC, also see Lu et al., this volume.

votes suggests that all members strive to represent the international community (Krisch 2008, 139; Bueno et al., this volume). This trend is also evident today, with the Council's operations hindered by power rivalries and geopolitical competition, yet all members, including the P5, aim to present themselves as representatives of the global community.

The aim to achieve unanimity provides an opportunity for smaller states, as the P5 will try to get as many votes as possible within UNSC procedures. However, Hosli and Dörfler claim that the process of getting support from non-permanent members can be fairly complex; seeking support will largely be based on the substantive focus and the position of the composition of the E10 at the time (next to bilateral relations between a veto power and the remaining ten Council members) (Hosli and Dörfler 2019, 46).

Additional literature on smaller states focuses on identifying factors enabling them to impact the UNSC, and their self-perception as non-permanent members. Baldur Thorhallsson (2012) explored power dynamics in the Council from a perspective of administrative competencies, ranging from initiatives taken and knowledge acquired, to skills such as strong leadership and an ability to build coalitions (Thorhallsson 2012, 140) As such, these are some of the most essential factors determining both whether a small country may be elected to the Council for two years (as a non-permanent member) by the UNGA and whether it will be influential.

But what are some of the main reasons to be engaged in the tough competition for a non-permanent UNSC seat? Ann-Marie Ekengren et al. (2020) identify three power-enhancing benefits: Influencing decision-making, expanding networks, and preserving status (Ekengren et al. 2020, 23). These benefits highlight that coalition formation in the UNSC is not limited to the P5; smaller countries, especially non-permanent members, also play a significant role in decision-making dynamics.[4]

Prantl (2005) examined the interplay between informal state coalitions, including those formed within the UNGA, and the Security Council, positing that these groups emerged due to systemic power shifts and have influenced the UNSC's decision-making. He argued that informal alliances act as agents of incremental change, complement UNSC efforts, and compete for governance authority. Using a case-study approach and

[4] For an analysis of EU non-permanent UNSC member states, see van Schijndel and Jansen, this volume.

unpublished archival sources, Prantl highlighted the significant role of informal coalitions in shaping UNSC decisions and their implications for global governance.

Recently, an initiative taken by Luxembourg and presented on behalf of the Benelux countries has aimed to enhance the accountability of the UNSC towards the UNGA: The use of veto will need to be justified in front of the General Assembly.[5] This initiative may further increase accountability for veto use and enhance pressures on the P5 to refrain from using their veto power.

However, research on UNSC member states regarding agenda-setting and coalition behaviour is limited. Susan Hannah Allen and Amy Yuen explored why the UNSC addresses some issues but not others. Their findings show that several factors, including P5 priorities, the proposing delegation's preferences, and the costs associated with public accountability, influence the UNSC's decision-making process (Allen and Yuen 2022, 8). Moreover, they argue that the UNSC's decision to address an issue depends on its potential to pass through the Council (Allen and Yuen 2022, 11).

While formal UNSC decision-making procedures are well understood, penholding arguably affects them. In the UNSC, members are 'assigned' drafts by area or topic—France generally handles Francophone Africa, while the UK focuses on former colonies like Cyprus or Somalia. Penholding can include UNSC non-permanent members too, alone or together with a permanent member. Loiselle (2020) notes that elected members' influence in the UNSC has been limited by the dominance of permanent members and the practice of penholdership, primarily by the P3. Penholding likely reduces transparency and participation for elected members, despite some recent assertive roles by non-permanent members. While increasing elected members' roles may enhance support for the rule of law, inclusivity, and transparency, the asymmetry of influence between permanent and non-permanent UNSC members remains (Loiselle 2020). Monteleone and Oksamytna (2020) argue that penholdership has partly replaced coalitions, with most conflict-specific issues managed by the P3. Ralph et al. (2020), however, suggest that penholdership is a pragmatic approach due to the P3's active engagement in international security.

[5] See https://press.un.org/en/2022/ga12417.doc.htm.

Arguably, however, penholding can strongly affect patterns of coalitional formation in the Council.

To explore how coalitions might form that influence the agenda in the UNSC, it can be of much interest to study the characteristics of draft resolutions. Who sponsored them? Which states co-sponsored resolutions that are then discussed in the UNSC? Can patterns of collaboration be discerned in this context over time?

The sponsorship of draft resolutions[6] by UNSC members can shed light on the sponsors' motives. There are numerous reasons why a member might want to sponsor a draft, including gaining policy advantages. Introducing a draft also allows the sponsor to shape the context in which the issue is debated (Todd 1969). Given that Security Council resolutions are binding for all UN members and often address pressing international issues, they likely are more impactful than UNGA resolutions, which are non-binding and generally deal with less urgent topics (Monteleone 2015).

By co-sponsoring a draft, the authors show a firm stance on issues and preferred measures. Member states valuing certain principles and aiming to highlight them often use co-sponsorship to address international stability threats. Thus, sponsorship data from UNSC draft resolutions are crucial to analyse formation, with this complementing earlier studies on UNSC procedures and outcomes. We build on such earlier studies, while employing new data.

3 Analysing Authorship of UN Security Council Resolutions

For the UNSC, we compiled 796 draft resolutions submitted to the Council from 2011 to 2023, using data from the United Nations Digital Library.[7] Each draft resolution contains detailed information, including on its sponsors, themes, target regions, missions, and outcomes. Drafts without sponsors are excluded from the analysis, but those that were voted on and failed—whether due to insufficient support or a veto—are

[6] The works of authors such as Todd (1969) and Monteleone (2015) have been essential to research UNSC behaviour. More recent sponsorship information can add to such earlier analyses and help understand what seems to be essential to processes of UNSC decision-making.

[7] The data were compiled by Tareq Helou; also see Helou and Hosli (2025).

included.[8] For each year, the dataset tracks the number of drafts sponsored or co-sponsored by individual countries or groups. Categories were created to reflect different sponsorship patterns, offering insights into the dynamics of UNSC draft resolutions.

For instance, drafts exclusively authored by a single country are labelled with 'only', such as 'UK only', indicating drafts authored solely by the UK without co-sponsorship. Other categories capture collaborations, such as 'UK + EU', for drafts co-sponsored by the UK and at least one (other) member of the EU (be they France or an elected UNSC member), or 'UK + non-EU', for drafts co-sponsored by the UK and at least one non-EU country. Finally, 'Non-Permanent EU' contains drafts sponsored exclusively by elected members who are also members of the EU.

These categories often overlap, as a single draft can have multiple member state sponsors belonging to different groups. This overlap is intentional, allowing the study to track alignments within and across member state groups. Generally, P3 members have increasingly taken a leading role in drafting resolutions on routine security issues within the UNSC (notably due to the practice of penholdership). Yet, P5 members seem to prefer acting independently when drafting resolutions in their assigned areas, with little inclination to co-sponsor with other members, whether permanent or elected. These findings align with the insights offered by Loiselle (2020) and Monteleone and Oksamytna (2020).

As Table 1 demonstrates, between 2011 and 2023, 796 draft resolutions were submitted to the UNSC, averaging around 60 per year. The P5 played a significant role in authoring or co-authoring drafts, given that their approval is necessary to avoid a veto. Comparing P5 member state engagement, the UK, France, and the USA were the most active in authoring drafts, either independently or in cooperation with EU states or other non-permanent members. By comparison, China and Russia were much less active in authoring drafts than their Western counterparts.

Focusing on the proportion of submissions drafted independently per member state in the period 2011 to 2023, a trend can be seen of increasingly independent drafting by the P3 (further finetuning reveals that Germany, as a non-permanent member, notably engaged in co-sponsored submissions). The USA, UK, and France started to submit more drafts

[8] This methodology is derived from Monteleone's (2015) investigation into the UNSC but updated with more recent data.

Table 1 Authorship of United Nations Security Council Resolutions, P5 and EU Non-Permanent Members (2011–2023)

Authorship of Drafts	*2011*	*2012*	*2013*	*2014*	*2015*	*2016*	*2017*	*2018*	*2019*	*2020*	*2021*	*2022*	*2023*
UK only	2	5	1	0	6	11	12	14	12	14	16	15	18
UK + EU	27	25	26	44	34	22	17	9	6	8	8	1	1
UK + Non-EU	27	24	30	46	28	23	18	6	3	8	1	2	2
UK + USA	25	21	27	44	33	22	15	7	3	2	8	1	1
UK total	29	31	31	46	41	34	29	23	18	22	24	17	20
USA only	7	7	3	6	8	19	14	17	15	14	14	7	9
USA + EU	30	26	31	47	34	21	16	7	4	2	8	2	1
USA + Non-EU	26	19	30	42	28	26	18	9	6	5	12	7	6
U.S. total	40	34	35	54	43	45	32	26	21	19	26	15	15
France only	5	1	1	2	7	8	8	8	9	8	9	8	6
France + EU	32	29	26	45	30	21	17	6	6	3	0	0	0
France + Non-EU	35	29	29	47	25	23	18	8	6	3	9	4	3
France + USA	30	25	28	44	28	21	16	7	4	2	7	2	1
France Total	41	32	30	49	37	31	26	16	15	12	19	12	9
Non-permanent EU	10	3	1	1	2	3	3	2	6	6	2	5	5
Russia	13	5	5	8	5	7	4	7	5	8	8	4	11
China	5	1	0	2	1	2	1	0	1	2	6	0	1
Total Drafts	67	54	48	66	63	80	67	60	57	64	59	50	61

individually after 2014, possibly influenced by differing political priorities and events such as Brexit.

Figure 1 gives information on the proportion of draft resolutions submitted independently over the total of draft resolutions P3 members were engaged in. It demonstrates that France has shifted to more independent drafting from 2015 onwards, and the USA also showed an increase in independently authored drafts starting in about the same year. These developments possibly reflect the impact of specific political events and changing policy priorities, such as the initiation of the Trump administration in 2017 accompanied by more individualistic political behaviour by the USA and respective reverberations among the rest of the P3.

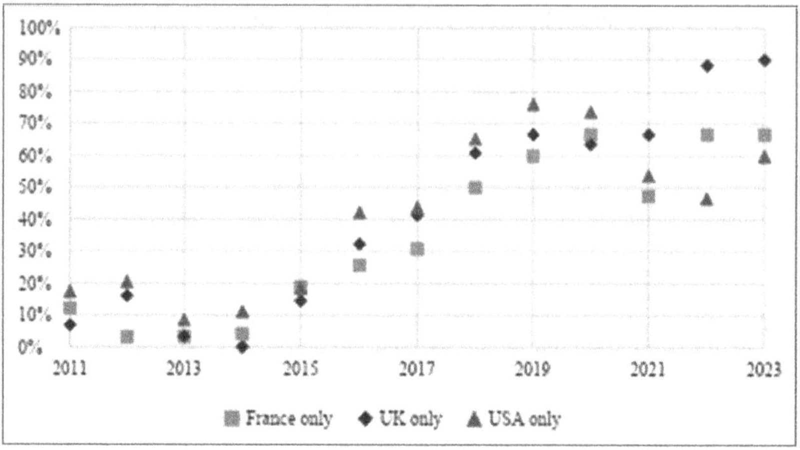

Fig. 1 Proportion of Independently Drafted Submissions to the UNSC (in Per cent of Total per Member State) for the UK, France and the USA, 2011 to 2023

As Fig. 1 confirms, the proportion of UNSC draft resolutions submitted independently by the UK, France, and the USA has risen over time. For the USA, this proportion increased from less than 30% in mid-2015 to over 70% by 2020. It decreased again thereafter—under the Biden administration—ending at about 60% in 2023. The UK saw an even steeper rise, with no individual submissions in 2014 but reaching 90% by 2023. This increase in recent years is certainly also due to Brexit. France followed a similar pattern, with a slight decrease in individual resolution sponsorship between 2011 and 2013, but then an increasing share to just below 70% by 2020, dipping in 2021 but returning to almost 70% in 2023. While these countries exhibit a tendency towards a more individualistic stance, this does not exclude the prospect of continued collaboration within coalitions. However, the data indicates that these coalitions are increasingly marked by some fragility.

4 A Comparison with Co-Sponsorship in the United Nations General Assembly

Compared to the UNSC, the UNGA arguably represents a more inclusive international arena, comprising 193 member states where all resolutions are voted on without individual veto power, based on the principle of 'one country, one vote'. Comparing these two institutions provides a good understanding of how states form coalitions and align their policies in different institutional contexts within the UN system.

To obtain co-sponsorship data for the UNGA, we utilise the database compiled by Seabra and Mesquita (2022a, b),[9] which includes co-sponsorship information for all General Assembly resolutions from 2000 to 2019.[10] This database provides an advantage regarding the extended timeframe, as the UNSC data does not extend to the first decade of the new millennium. However, it also presents a disadvantage as the UNGA data only goes up to 2020, missing recent developments such as the Ukraine war and the COVID-19 pandemic, which may have influenced member state priorities and coalition formation within the UN.

Additionally, the structural differences between the UNSC and UNGA are crucial. The UNGA not only includes all 193 UN member states (each with one vote and no veto power), but its resolutions are generally also non-binding, albeit reflective of 'global opinion'. In contrast, the UNSC comprises 15 members—the P5 and E10—and issues binding resolutions, often including enforcement measures. The political dynamics also differ: the UNGA has been influenced by alliances and regional blocs like the G77 and the Non-Aligned Movement (NAM), while the UNSC is largely dominated by the strategic interests of its permanent members. Given these differences, a comparative analysis of state behaviour in these two crucial UN bodies as revealed by resolution co-sponsorship can provide insights into decision-making processes and it can help determine whether observed behaviours are institution-specific or reflective of more general global trends.

The co-sponsorship data were used to analyse the coalitional behaviour of the P5 members in the UNGA and to compare it with priorities

[9] Available at https://dataverse.harvard.edu/dataset.xhtml?persistentId=doi:10.7910/DVN/MPQUE2.

[10] The database has data up to 2020, but, as there was no data for the entire legislative year of the Assembly, we opted to remove 2020 from our analysis.

revealed based on UNSC co-sponsorship information. Of notable interest is whether member state behaviour aligns with the one observed within the UNSC.

Figure 2 presents the trends in co-sponsorship of UNGA resolutions by the P3 countries. There is a noticeable downward trend in the number of resolutions co-sponsored by all three Western countries over the years, with two important declining phases, one in 2007 and another starting in 2015 and continuing until the end of the observed period. This decline may indicate a reduction in joint coordination among the three countries, especially after the mid-2010s, reflecting how changes in national priorities were likely influenced by events such as Brexit and the start of the (first) Trump administration in the USA. It can also be reflective, however, of the practice of 'penholdership', assigning P3 members chair positions in terms of negotiations and the initiation of draft resolutions.

As Fig. 2 demonstrates, the extent of joint co-sponsorship in the UNGA by the P3 has decreased over time. However, there is a notable increase in co-sponsorship between France and the UK, indicating that the USA is the outlier in this context. Assessing resolutions sponsored separately by each P3 member, a certain consistency over the years is discernible, with a significant peak in 2018, suggesting a change in the political landscape. This pattern differs from the UNSC co-sponsorship data, where there is a stronger trend towards individual sponsorships.

Figure 3 illustrates the co-sponsorship trends of UNGA resolutions for the P2 (China and Russia) and their interactions with the P3 (France, UK, USA) between 2000 and 2019. There is a noticeable increase in the number of UNGA resolutions co-sponsored by China and Russia over time, particularly from 2010 onwards. Co-sponsoring of Russia with the P3 was relatively extensive in the early 2000s, declined thereafter, increased slightly by about 2010, before dropping to low levels by 2018. Co-sponsorship between China and the P3, by comparison, remained relatively low during the time assessed. The P2 co-sponsorship trend, however, intensified between 2010 and 2015 and, after a slight dip in 2016, increased again until the end of the decade.

In reviewing the co-sponsorship information for Russia and China (P2) alongside the P3, a downward trend is apparent: Starting in 2015, there is a notable decline in the level of co-sponsorship by the P2 with the P3, a trend continuing until the end of the decade, reflecting a widening divergence in the strategic and political priorities between China and Russia, on the one hand, and the P3 countries, on the other hand. Taken together,

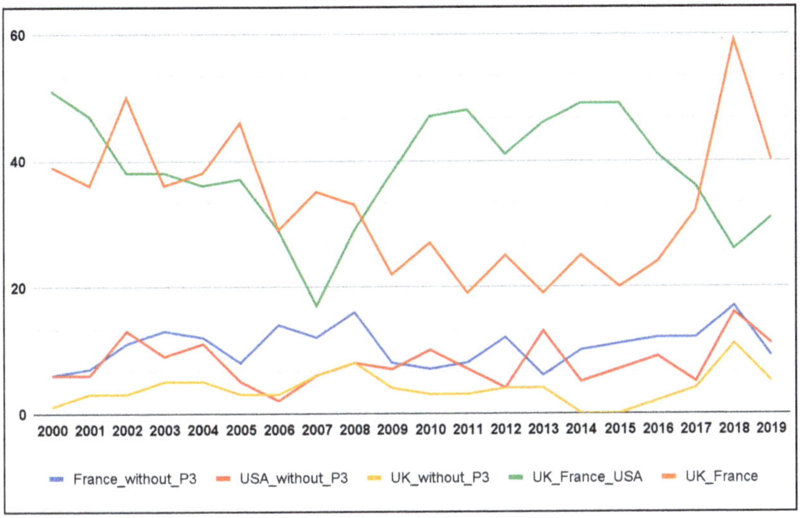

Fig. 2 Trends in Co-Sponsorship Among P3 Members in the UNGA (2000–2019). *Notes* The figure only includes resolutions sponsored by UNGA member states that were permanent members of the UNSC (non-permanent members are excluded). France_without_P3 represents resolutions co-sponsored by France alone, without the USA and UK. USA_without_P3 captures resolutions sponsored by the USA individually, without France and the UK. UK_without_P3 indicates resolutions sponsored by the UK alone, without France and the USA. UK_France, whereas USA tracks resolutions co-sponsored by all three P3 countries (France, UK, and USA). The UK_France line represents resolutions co-sponsored by the UK and France, but without the USA

these patterns highlight how geopolitical shifts and evolving alliances are increasingly reflected in co-sponsorship behavior across both the UNSC and the UNGA.

The comparative examination of co-sponsorship data for the UNSC and the UNGA demonstrates distinct patterns of cooperation and non-cooperation among the P5. The analysis affirms that the alignment between China and Russia has intensified in both the UNSC and the UNGA in terms of resolution co-sponsoring, although individual sponsorships may be considered less politically significant in the UNGA than in the UNSC and their level of sponsorship within the Security Council remained relatively low. Moreover, our analysis reveals a decrease in

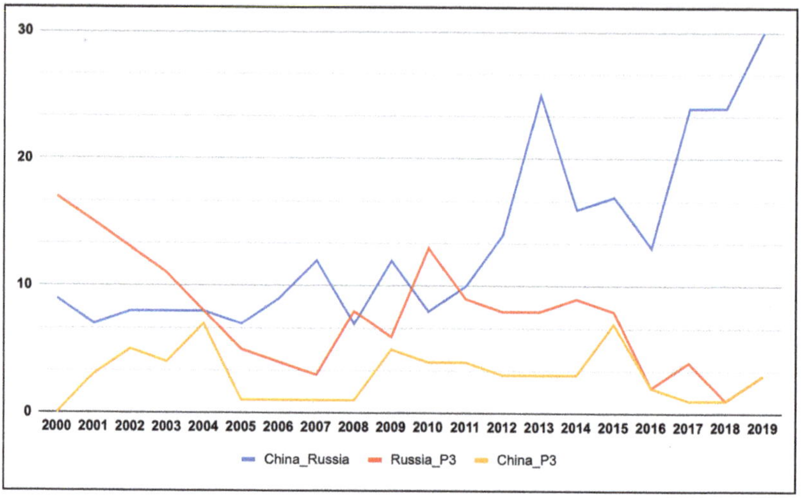

Fig. 3 Trends in Co-Sponsorship Between Russia and China in the UNGA (2000–2019). *Notes* China_Russia represents resolutions co-sponsored by China and Russia, whereas Russia_P3 shows resolutions co-sponsored by Russia and the P3 countries (France, UK, USA). China_P3, by comparison, captures resolutions co-sponsored by China and the P3 countries (France, UK, USA)

general P3 collaboration, while alignment between the UK and France in the UNGA, despite Brexit, was clearly strengthened.

The alignment between Russia and China in terms of co-sponsorship may reflect a growing convergence in their security perspectives, particularly in opposition to Western security interests. As Korolev (2020) notes, while the military alliance between Moscow and Beijing remains relatively limited, a broader strategic partnership can be discerned. The co-sponsorship patterns analyzed here may reflect this trend: in the UNSC, a 'high politics' arena, Russia and China's alignment remains relatively low but is gradually increasing, whereas in the UNGA, a broader political arena encompassing multiple themes and interests, the geopolitical alignment of these two powers seems much stronger.

As for the P3 countries, the divergence of the USA from France and the UK in the UNGA is not surprising, as cohesion among Western allies has declined since the first Trump administration (Mosler and Potrafke 2020). However, the strong convergence between France and the UK in the UNGA, even after Brexit, is particularly noteworthy. It warrants further investigation into the underlying mechanisms, especially given that data for the Security Council show a decline in co-sponsorship between the UK and EU member states after 2016.

5 Substantive Contents of Draft Resolutions and Decision Outcomes

Returning to analysing dynamics within the UNSC, it is helpful to categorise draft resolutions into broader thematic areas to explore the issues addressed. Drafts submitted to the Security Council can vary significantly in terms of content, scope, wording, urgency, and substantive range: Some draft resolutions are highly controversial and often experience vetoes due to a single contentious article, while others, particularly those addressing procedural issues, are typically concise and much less disputed.

We use agenda-setting terminology from the UNSC to classify draft resolutions into the following categories: Peacekeeping, Human Rights, Internal Security, Monitoring, Sanctions, and Others. Peacekeeping involves activities related to the maintenance of peace and security, including troop deployment, stabilisation missions, support missions, and ceasefires. Human Rights cover issues addressing human rights, human trafficking, humanitarian assistance, child protection, and safeguarding the rights of women in vulnerable areas.[11] Internal Security encompasses initiatives strengthening national police, capacity-building programmes, the training of military personnel, and security-related governance. Monitoring involves truce supervision, codes of conduct, establishing panels of experts, addressing political violence, weapons of mass destruction (WMDs), and nuclear non-proliferation. Sanctions cover economic sanctions, arms embargoes, sanction monitoring, travel restrictions, and asset freezes. The Others category, by comparison, includes topics not covered in the previous categories (albeit often relevant to them), such as appointments, measures against piracy, or international counter-terrorism.

Figure 4 provides an overview of how these categories were reflected in UNSC draft resolutions authored by P5 and (non-permanent) EU member states between 2011 and 2023. As Fig. 4 shows, the highest

[11] On how such themes see the Introduction of this volume.

share of draft resolution authoring by P5 members concerned the area of peacekeeping, with the USA, the UK and France all at 47%, Russia at 39%, and China at 35% of their total. China's relatively low share in peacekeeping resolutions compared to other substantive categories likely reflects its hesitancy to interfere in what it considers to constitute member state internal affairs. Non-permanent EU members, similarly, had a 35% share in peacekeeping resolutions in the total of draft resolutions in which they participated (but a relatively high share of 23% in the area of human rights).

Sanctions as a topic seem to be frequently emphasised by France and the USA as a share in their total, with 16% each, and by the UK with 15%. In the meantime, Russia addressed this topic in only 4% of all cases, and non-permanent EU Security Council members in 6% of their cases. This may be due to resolutions on sanctions often being more controversial and context-dependent than other substantive categories (Hosli and Dörfler 2019).

Human rights were extensively focused on by non-permanent EU member states (23%) and much less by Russia (16%). Curiously enough, the USA focused on human rights in only 10% of all cases, while China did so in 13%.

In the category Internal Security, some general trends can also be observed. Firstly, when such resolutions are supported by only one member state, often France or the USA, they usually concern former colonies or areas of geopolitical interest. Such practice is enhanced based on the use of penholderships inside the Council, which often lead to repeated resolutions on similar themes. Likewise, there are instances where permanent UNSC members supported the adoption of sanctions, but non-permanent members did not, reflecting diverse coalitions over time, largely due to the biennial rotation of the non-permanent membership. Russia and China often did not support draft proposals on sanctions, highlighting the varying stances within the UNSC on this theme. Table 2 provides an overview of the total number of UNSC draft resolutions for the respective categories from 2011 to 2023.

As Table 2 shows, Peacekeeping as a category has been at the forefront of UNSC activity: Between 2011 and 2023, out of a total of 792 UNSC

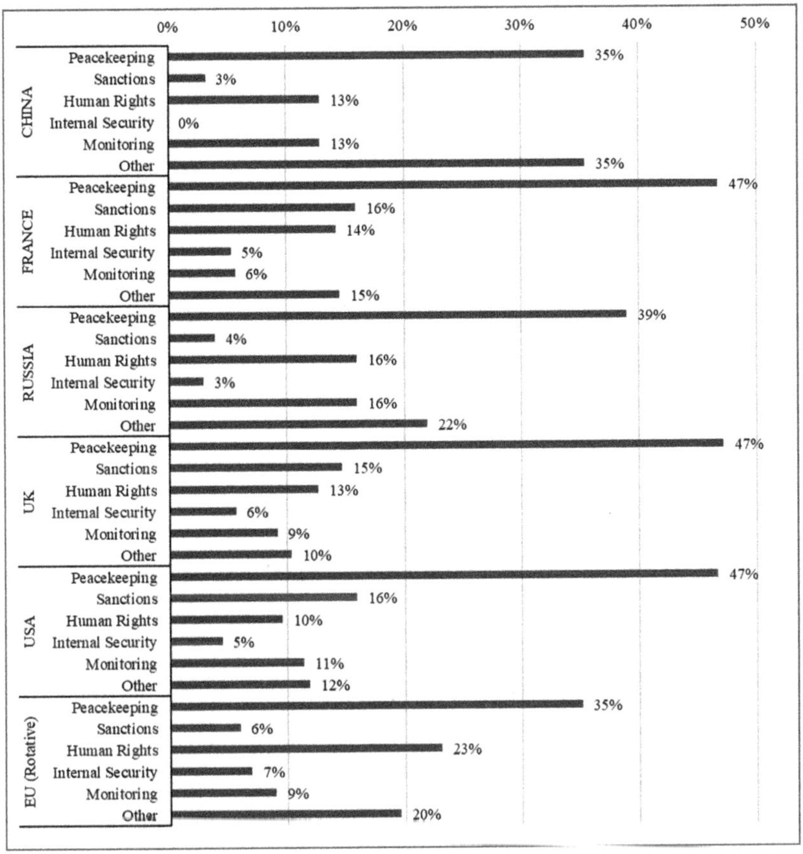

Fig. 4 Draft Resolutions in the United Nations Security Council 2011–2023 by Substantive Categories (in Percent of a Member State's Total Participation in Resolution Drafting)

resolutions, almost one-half (360) concerned peacekeeping.[12] Sanctions were also a frequent topic, with 139 drafts proposed, most of which were penned by the UK and the USA. Human rights comes in third,

[12] On UNSC resolutions on peace mission establishment and extension, see Bueno et al., this volume.

Table 2 Number of Draft Resolutions by Substantive Category (2011–2023)

	2011	*2012*	*2013*	*2014*	*2015*	*2016*	*2017*	*2018*	*2019*	*2020*	*2021*	*2022*	*2023*	*Total*
Peacekeeping	27	14	30	35	33	42	29	33	27	29	30	17	14	360
Sanctions	11	7	4	11	8	14	13	11	10	12	11	12	15	139
Human Rights	4	6	3	5	8	8	3	9	7	8	4	7	17	89
Internal Security	5	13	0	1	2	1	1	0	4	1	3	4	0	35
Monitoring	7	8	4	0	7	7	10	5	6	7	6	4	10	81
Other	13	6	7	14	5	8	11	2	3	7	5	5	2	88
Total	67	54	48	66	63	80	67	60	57	64	59	49	58	792

with 89 instances, followed by the category of Monitoring, with 81 draft resolutions.

6 Coalition Formation and Vetoes in the Security Council

The use of vetoes is a defining characteristic of the UNSC and a major source of contention regarding its current *modus operandi*. Despite controversy related to its use, veto power remains a significant tool within the UNSC. While France and the UK have abstained from using their vetoes for decades, the USA, Russia and China have continued to use this power quite regularly.

Yet, vetoing is not necessarily the sole means by which a draft resolution can be prevented from being accepted. Although a clear majority of submissions pass each year, some fail due to insufficient supporting votes. While France and the UK may not have the perceived legitimacy to assert a veto and generally aim to prevent its use, they may still be influential in terms of aligning with non-permanent members to block submissions to the UNSC.

As previously observed in co-sponsorship patterns, the P3's 'transatlantic coalition' seems increasingly less united in terms of their coalition formation (although France and the UK have aligned more often in the UNGA). In the UNSC, co-drafting behaviour is less frequent for China and Russia overall, while data from the UNGA resolution context show a growing alignment between the two in recent years. Vetoing in the

UNSC, however, is more frequent for China and Russia. Table 3 demonstrates the total number of vetoes cast by China, Russia and the USA between 2011 and 2023.

Among the P3, France and the UK have both refrained from employing their veto powers since 1989. Mahbubani (2013) describes them as 'yesterday's powers', possessing smaller geopolitical capabilities than some countries in the Global South have today, according to the author. As such, should either exercise their veto, the author contends, there would likely be an uproar by the international community (although, arguably, they still have considerable agenda-setting power).

Analysing UNSC co-sponsorship data together with veto records provides some further insights. Understanding co-sponsorship as agenda-setting reveals which activities are being prioritised in the UNSC. Moreover, by examining the substantive categories we can identify the issues that have been addressed compared to those left out of formal UNSC discussions.

Table 4 provides an overview of vetoes employed throughout the time of our analysis (2011 to 2023), in conjunction with the targeted region/country and the substantive category of a draft resolution. Between 2011 and 2023, 33 draft resolutions were vetoed in the UNSC. The majority of these vetoes, 28 in total, were cast by Russia (five in 2017 alone). China vetoed 12 draft resolutions (all in conjunction with Russia), and the United States six, five of which concerned resolutions focused on Israel/Palestine.

As Table 4 demonstrates, the situation in Syria has been a highly contentious topic in the framework of UNSC deliberations. With its strategic interests in the region, Russia has been cautious about UN-sanctioned interference, notably since the Libyan mission was established based on Resolution S/2011/1973, sponsored by the USA (despite

Table 3 Number of Vetoes by China, Russia and the United States in the United Nations Security Council, 2011 to 2023

Vetoes	*2011*	*2012*	*2013*	*2014*	*2015*	*2016*	*2017*	*2018*	*2019*	*2020*	*2021*	*2022*	*2023*	*Total*
China	1	1		1		1	1		3	2		1	1	12
Russia	1	1		2	2	2	5	2	3	2	1	4	3	28
USA	1						1	1		1			2	6

Table 4 Vetoed Draft Resolutions in the Security Council, by Substantive Focus and Target Region, 2011–2023

Draft	*Veto Caster*	*Target*	*Topic*
S/2011/24	USA	Israel/Palestine	Human Rights
S/2011/612	China, Russia	Syria	Human Rights
S/2012/77	China, Russia	Syria	Human Rights
S/2014/348	China, Russia	Syria	Human Rights
S/2015/508	Russia	Bosnia and Herzegovina	Human Rights
S/2018/516	USA	Israel/Palestine	Human Rights
S/2019/961	China, Russia	Syria	Human Rights
S/2020/654	China, Russia	Syria	Human Rights
S/2022/155	Russia	Ukraine	Human Rights
S/2022/538	Russia	Syria	Human Rights
S/2023/506	Russia	Syria	Human Rights
S/2023/773	USA	Israel/Palestine	Human Rights
S/2023/792	China, Russia	Israel/Palestine	Human Rights
S/2023/970	USA	Israel/Palestine	Internal Security
S/2012/538	China, Russia	Syria	Monitoring
S/2015/562	Russia	Ukraine	Monitoring
S/2017/172	China, Russia	Syria	Monitoring
S/2017/315	Russia	Syria	Monitoring
S/2017/884	Russia	Syria	Monitoring
S/2017/962	Russia	Syria	Monitoring
S/2017/970	Russia	Syria	Monitoring
S/2014/189	Russia	Ukraine	Other
S/2017/1060	USA	Israel/Palestine	Other
S/2018/321	Russia	Syria	Other
S/2019/186	China, Russia	Venezuela	Other
S/2020/852	USA	Indonesia	Other
S/2016/1026	China, Russia	Syria	Peacekeeping
S/2016/846	Russia	Syria	Peacekeeping
S/2019/756	China, Russia	Syria	Peacekeeping
S/2022/720	Russia	Ukraine	Peacekeeping
S/2018/156	Russia	Yemen	Sanctions
S/2021/990	Russia	n/a	Sanctions
S/2022/431	China, Russia	North Korea	Sanctions
S/2023/638	Russia	Mali	Sanctions

Russia initially giving its consent). Out of the 28 vetoed UNSC draft resolutions, 17 concerned Syria, with most being co-vetoed by Russia and China, and occasionally by Russia acting individually. The joint opposition of Russia and China was largely due to the language used in the resolutions regarding monitoring bodies and humanitarian missions. After vetoing these resolutions, Russia did not propose its own drafts, however, and subsequent drafts often failed to secure enough votes in the UNSC. Russia's stance on vetoing resolutions related to Syria aimed to prevent any member from proposing actions that did not align with its own terms, regardless of the proposal's origins. The P5's division over Syria has arguably paralysed the UNSC (Gifkins 2012, 390)[13]; However, it is possible to speculate that the Syrian regime change that took place in December 2024 will likely decrease UNSC's attention to this specific case.

Successfully adopting a UNSC resolution depends on P5 preferences, their interpretations of respective challenges, as well as their ability to act outside the Council. The case of Syria exemplifies this: While outside options could have achieved desired outcomes for the P3, they would likely have created long-term negative perceptions by a wider audience, while UNSC approval reflects international support for the use of force (Allen and Yuen 2022, 104). Thus, the P3 generally prefer acting within the UNSC framework instead of based on 'outside arrangements'. Nonetheless, shifting global power dynamics and Chinese and Russian efforts to gain support in the Global South have likely reduced the feasibility of outside options that the P3 traditionally possessed, although P3 influence arguably remains strong.

As permanent UNSC members, Russia and China interact regularly with the three 'Western powers' in the P5 context; yet, in spite of their patterns of collaboration, they also show different perceptions and behaviours within the UNSC. As Ferdinand (2013) claims, Post-Soviet Russia aims to regain influence globally as a superpower, but has become more defensive over time due to limited resources and a desire to avoid antagonising other permanent UNSC members. Conversely, China's increased UNSC engagement, albeit passive in terms of resolution co-sponsoring, aligns with its economic rise and a shift towards a more active foreign policy behaviour. Russia's defensive posture and China's assertiveness have complicated their common position: While Russia often paralyses the UNSC, China maintains some degree of cooperation (Gowan 2021). Both countries resist isolation but are limited in their capacities in terms of introducing and passing (contested) resolutions.

[13] See Heinikainen, this volume, for further insights on the matter of great power rivalries and its impact on UNSC decision-making, also in the context of Syria.

Both P2 members tend to prioritise non-interference and sovereignty, although supporting a multipolar world with the UNSC as a key institution within it (Purushothaman and Unnikrishnan 2015). This shared vision of the role of the UNSC has led to coordination, especially since the Arab Spring, to avoid isolation and present an alternative international narrative. However, the P2 also differ on issues like Russia's stance on Europe, with China being more cautious than Russia is (not least due to economic interests and considerations).

P3 countries actively set UNSC agendas, strengthened by the penholdership practice, and co-sponsor resolutions; in this, they are often supported by non-permanent UNSC members. Russia has been less active in terms of resolution co-sponsorship, with China even less involved, whereas these two P5 members have cast the most vetoes between 2011 and 2023. The UK and France, while reluctant to use their veto power, have rather actively sponsored or co-sponsored resolutions on the Council's agenda.

7 Conclusions

The influence of resolution co-sponsorship on the activities of the UNSC and the inclination of certain members to veto draft resolutions are important to understanding patterns of decision-making in this institution. Exploring trends of cooperation and estrangement among the P5 countries is core to an analysis of coalition formation and decision outcomes in the UNSC.

Generally, the involvement of the P5 members seems to strongly influence the inclusion of items in the UNSC agenda, particularly when they focus on civil wars or non-democratic states. For instance, Russia and the USA brought the Syrian conflict onto the UNSC agenda more than 50 times, with 17 resolutions vetoed during this period.

Our analysis of co-sponsorship information sheds light on the active participation of the P3 and some non-permanent UNSC members in terms of setting the UNSC agenda. In contrast, Russia and China, while less involved in drafting individual or co-sponsored resolutions, have shown a trend towards increased collaboration among each other, a trend corroborated by UNGA co-sponsorship patterns.

Until 2014, France, the UK and the USA collaborated on nearly every UNSC draft resolution submitted. However, they shifted to initiating more individual drafts in subsequent years. This change may be linked to differing priorities under the (first) Trump administration and the impact of Brexit on UK-France coordination in the UNSC. Nevertheless, the shift towards more individualised behaviour in drafting UNSC resolutions contrasts with aligned patterns in the recent past in terms of UNGA resolutions' co-sponsorship by these two states. In 2014, the UK co-sponsored all 46 of its submissions with at least one other UNSC member state. In contrast, by 2019, roughly two-thirds of the UK's submissions were individual, and by 2023, almost all of them (90%) were individually authored.

Our analysis shows that P3 members have increasingly embraced individualised strategies in drafting UNSC resolutions with a gradually higher proportion of individual sponsorship observed between 2011 and 2023. The decline of P3 collaboration suggests a gradual division between the Western permanent members of the UNSC, but is also due to the very practice of penholdership, where a P3 member tends to be the main initiator of a Security Council draft resolution, often on a recurrent theme.

The categorisation of draft resolutions into substantive categories reveals that peacekeeping missions were prevalent for all P5 members, while sanctions featured significantly for the P3 and, to a lesser extent, Russia. Resolutions on human rights issues, in relative terms, were less frequently addressed in terms of sponsorship by the USA, and even less so by Russia and China. However, 'Monitoring' emerged as an important area, in terms of shares in total sponsorship of resolutions, for both Russia and China.

Comparing P5 co-sponsorship behaviour in the UNSC and the UNGA, it is possible to find alignment among the P2 members, on the one hand, and between France and the UK, on the other hand, in the UNGA context. While P3 alignment with a P2 member was relatively common in the early 2000s in terms of UNGA resolution sponsorship (notably in the case of Russia), this trend decreased in the decades thereafter. Exploring the underlying reasons behind these alignment patterns and linking historical events in foreign policy to the evolution of co-sponsorship mechanisms lies beyond the scope of this chapter. However, developments such as Brexit, shifts in Middle East and North Africa security policies, and the (first) Trump administration offer key insights into the P3's increasingly individualised approach. Meanwhile, the partnership between Beijing and Moscow, driven by seemingly shared perceptions of the USA as a potential geopolitical threat and bolstered by some increased economic and military cooperation, reflects a tendency towards greater co-sponsorship in the UNGA context (while co-sponsorship of the P2 in the UNSC remains modest). Such dynamics warrant further exploration in future research, particularly regarding the role of the P3 and the P2 (and their collaboration with non-permanent UNSC members).

Our analysis also confirms patterns of coalition formation among the P5 through actual voting on UNSC resolutions, affirming P3 and P2 adhesion when focusing on veto use. Our explorations emphasise the informal dynamics occurring in the UNSC and call for future research to delve deeper into patterns of coalition formation on draft resolutions, collaboration of P5 members with the E10, and to extend the analysis beyond the years included in our study. Based on our study of resolution co-sponsoring, however, we aim to help fill a crucial gap in terms of research focused on UNSC coalition formation and decision-making.

References

Allen, Susan, and Amy Yuen. *Bargaining in the UN Security Council: Setting the Global Agenda*. Oxford University Press, 2022.

Bailey, Michael A. "Is Today's Court the Most Conservative in Sixty Years? Challenges and Opportunities in Measuring Judicial Preferences." *Journal of Politics* 75, no. 3 (2013): 821–834.

Bailey, Michael A., Anton Strezhnev, and Erik Voeten. "Estimating Dynamic State Preferences from United Nations Voting Data." *Journal of Conflict Resolution* 61, no. 2 (2015): 430–456.

Bailey, Sidney D., and Sam Daws. *The Procedure of the UN Security Council*. 3rd ed. Oxford University Press, 1998.

Bearce, David H., and Stacy Bondanella. "Intergovernmental Organizations, Socialization, and Member-State Interest Convergence." *International Organization* 61 (2007): 703–733.

Binder, Martin, and Jonathan Golub. "Civil Conflict and Agenda-Setting Speed in the United Nations Security Council." *International Studies Quarterly* 64, no. 2 (2020): 419–430. https://doi.org/10.1093/isq/sqaa017.

Brecher, Michael, and Jonathan Wilkenfeld. *A Study of Crisis*. University of Michigan Press, 1997.

Dijkhuizen, Frederieke, and Michal Onderco. "Sponsorship Behaviour of the BRICS in the United Nations General Assembly." *Third World Quarterly* 40, no. 11 (2019): 2035–2051.

Dörfler, Thomas. *Security Council Sanctions Governance: The Power and Limits of Rules*. Routledge, 2019.

Ekengren, Ann-Marie, Fredrik Dybfest Hjorthen, and Ulrika Möller. "A Non-Permanent Seat in the United Nations Security Council: Why Bother?" *Global Governance* 26 (2020): 21–45.

Falk, Richard. 2016. "The UN in the Middle East and the Arab Awakening." In *Interventions in Conflict*, edited by Rami George Khouri, Karim Makdisi, and Martin Wählisch, 77–88. Palgrave Macmillan. https://doi.org/10.1057/978 1137530820_6.

Feurle, Loie. "Informal Consultation: A Mechanism in Security Council Decision-making." *NYU Journal of International Law and Politics* 18, no. 1 (1985).

Ferdinand, Peter. "The Positions of Russia and China at the UN Security Council in the Light of Recent Crises." *European Parliament Briefing Paper*, Directorate-General for External Policies of the Union, Directorate B, 2013. https://data.europa.eu/doi/10.2861/13655.

Gifkins, Jess. "The UN Security Council Divided: Syria in Crisis." *Global Responsibility to Protect* 4, no. 3 (2021): 377–393. https://doi.org/10.1163/187 5984X-00403009.

Gowan, Richard. "Minimum Order: The Role of the Security Council in an Era of Major Power Competition." *United Nations University Centre for Policy Research*. November 2021. Accessed 20 November 2024. https://cpr.unu.edu/research/projects/minimum-order.html#outline.

Grant, Charles. *Russia, China and Global Governance*. Centre for European Reform, 2012.

Häge, Frank M. "Coalition Building and Consensus in the Council of the European Union." *British Journal of Political Science* 43, no. 3 (2013): 481–504. https://doi.org/10.1017/S0007123412000439.

Helou, Tareq Yacoub. "The EU in the United Nations Security Council: Trends from the United Kingdom and France." *Policy Brief* 7, UNU-CRIS, Bruges, 2019.

Helou, Tareq Yacoub, and Madeleine. O. Hosli. "Dynamics of Coalition Formation in the United Nations Security Council 2009 to 2023." Paper presented at the 62nd Annual Meeting of the Public Choice Society, March 6–8, 2025, Louisville, Kentucky.

Helou, Tareq Yacoub and Madeleine O. Hosli. "Resolution Co-Sponsorship in the United Nations Security Council 2011 to 2023." Paper presented at the 66th Annual Convention of the International Studies Association (ISA), March 2–5, 2025, Chicago, IL

Hosli, Madeleine O., and Thomas Dörfler. "Why is Change So Slow? Assessing Prospects for United Nations Security Council Reform." *Journal of Economic Policy Reform* 22, no. 1 (2019): 35–50. https://doi.org/10.1080/174 87870.2017.1305903.

Iwanami, Yukari. "Setting the Agenda of the UN Security Council." *SSRN Scholarly Paper* No. 1919942. 2011. https://doi.org/10.2139/ssrn.1919942.

Jowitt, Ken. *New World Disorder*. Centre for European Reform, 1995.

Koenders, Bart. "Statement during the Election of Non-Permanent Members for the UN Security Council." *Government.nl*. June 28, 2016. Accessed December 12, 2024. https://www.government.nl/documents/media-articles/2016/06/28/statement-during-the-election-of-non-permanent-members-for-the-un-security-council.

Korolev, Alexander. "How closely aligned are China and Russia? Measuring strategic cooperation in IR." *International Politics* 57.5 (2020): 760–789.

Krisch, Nico. "The Security Council and the Great Powers." *SSRN Scholarly Paper* No. 2440758, 2008. https://papers.ssrn.com/abstract=2440758.

Krastev, Ivan. "The Unravelling of the Post-1989 Order." *Journal of Democracy* 27, no. 4 (2016): 88–98.

Lee, Eugene, and Peter E. Stek. "Shifting Alliances in International Organizations: A Social Networks Analysis of Co-Sponsorship of UN GA Resolutions, 1976–2012." *Journal of Contemporary Eastern Asia* 15, no. 2 (2016).

Loiselle, Marie-Eve. "The Penholder System and the Rule of Law in the Security Council Decision-Making: Setback or Improvement?" *Leiden Journal of International Law* 33, no. 1 (2020): 139–156. https://doi.org/10.1017/s0922156519000621.

Mahbubani, Kishore. *The Great Convergence: Asia, the West, and the Logic of One World*. Public Affairs, 2013.

Malone, David M. *The International Struggle over Iraq: Politics in the UN Security Council, 1980–2005*. Oxford University Press, 2006.

Marchesi, Daniele. "The EU Common Foreign and Security Policy in the UN Security Council: Between Representation and Coordination." *European Foreign Affairs Review* 15 (2010): 97–114.

Mikulaschek, Christoph. "Issue Linkage Across International Organizations: Does European Countries' Temporary Membership in the UN Security Council Increase Their Receipts from the EU Budget?" *The Review of International Organizations* 13, no. 4 (2018): 491–518.

Monteleone, Carla. "Coalition Building in the UN Security Council." *International Relations* 29, no. 1 (2015): 45–68. https://doi.org/10.1177/0047117814552140.

Monteleone, Carla, and Kseniya Oksamytna. 2020. "Liberal Institutionalism." In *United Nations Peace Operations and International Relations Theory*, edited by Kseniya Oksamytna and John Karlsrud, 8. Manchester University Press. https://doi.org/10.7765/9781526148889.00008.

Mosler, Martin, and Niklas Potrafke. "International Political Alignment during the Trump Presidency: Voting at the UN General Assembly." *International Interactions* 46.3 (2020): 481–497.

Nahory, Céline. *The Hidden Veto.* Global Policy Forum, United Nations Security Council, 2004.

Prantl, Jochen. "Informal Groups of States and the UN Security Council." *International Organization* 59, no. 3 (2005): 559–592. https://doi.org/10.1017/S0020818305050204.

Purushothaman, Uma, and Nandan Unnikrishnan. *Trends in Russia-China Relations: Implications for India.* Observer Research Foundation, 2015.

Ralph, Jason, Jess Gifkins, and Samuel Jarvis. "The United Kingdom's Special Responsibilities at the United Nations: Diplomatic Practice in Normative Context." *The British Journal of Politics and International Relations* 22, no. 2 (2020): 164–181. https://doi.org/10.1177/1369148119887317.

Riker, William. *The Theory of Political Coalitions.* Yale University, 1962.

Seabra, Pedro, and Rafael Mesquita. "Beyond Roll-Call Voting: Sponsorship Dynamics at the UN General Assembly." *International Studies Quarterly* 66, no. 2 (2022a): https://doi.org/10.1093/isq/sqac008.

Seabra, Pedro, and Rafael Mesquita. "UN General Assembly Sponsorship Dataset." *Harvard Dataverse*, V3. 2022b. https://doi.org/10.7910/DVN/MPQUE2.

Smith, Courtney B. *Politics and Process at the United Nations: The Global Dance*, 2006.

Thorhallsson, Baldur. "Small States in the UN Security Council: Means of Influence?" *The Hague Journal of Diplomacy* 7, no. 2 (2012): 135–160. https://doi.org/10.1163/187119112X628454.

Todd, James. "An Analysis of Security Council Voting Behavior." *The Western Political Quarterly* 22, no. 1 (1969): 61–78.

Van Deemen, Ad M. A. *Coalition Formation and Social Choice.* Kluwer Academic Publishers, 1997.

Voeten, Erik. "Clashes in the Assembly." *International Organization* 54, no. 2 (2000): 185–215.

Voeten, Erik. Data and Analyses of Voting in the United Nations: General Assembly. In *Routledge Handbook of International Organization*, edited by Bob Reinalda, 54–66. Routledge, 2013.

Vreeland, James Raymond, and Axel Dreher. *The Political Economy of the United Nations Security Council: Money and Influence.* Cambridge University Press, 2014.

Welch, Claude E., and Ashley F. Watkins. "Extending enforcement: The Coalition for the International Criminal Court." *Human Rights Quarterly* 33 no. 4, (2011): 927–1031. https://doi.org/10.1353/hrq.2011.0055

CHAPTER 4

Multilateral Cooperation and Great Power Rivalry in the UNSC: An Analysis of UNSC Discussions Between China, Russia, and the United States on the Syrian Civil War in 2011, 2016, and 2021

Peppi Heinikainen

1 Introduction

After the Union of Soviet Socialist Republic (USSR) collapsed in 1991, the United States of America (USA) achieved hegemony in global politics after the years of the Cold War's bipolar rivalries with the USSR. Consequently, the United Nations Security Council (UNSC) began to increasingly adopt more resolutions as its permanent members (P5)—China, France, Russia, the United Kingdom (UK), and the USA—did not feel the need to use their veto power as much as they did during the Cold War due to the improving relations (Hageboutros 2016). However,

P. Heinikainen (✉)
Tampere Peace Research Institute (TAPRI), Tampere, Finland
e-mail: peppi.heinikainen@tuni.fi

M. O. Hosli et al. (eds.), *Multilateralism and the United Nations Security Council*, https://doi.org/10.1007/978-3-031-85320-3_4

in Russian President Vladimir Putin's (2007) Munich speech, there were signs that Russia intended to challenge the USA's hegemony. Since then, the dynamics have become increasingly contentious, and great power rivalry has returned. The 2022 illegal Russian aggression against Ukraine has shown that the era of great power politics is not over and that rivalry has intensified. Nevertheless, China, Russia, and the USA regularly sit together in the UNSC. The discussions held there give insight into how great power rivalry is reflected in the countries' rhetoric and what this tells about the state of multilateral cooperation between these states.

This chapter's purpose is to better understand the great power rivalry in China's, Russia's, and the USA's rhetoric in the UNSC. The great powers are seen here as countries with significant political, economic, and military power relative to other countries. Additionally, they share a permanent membership in the UNSC and possess nuclear weapons. According to Von Einsiedel, Malone, and Stagno Ugarte, the crisis in Libya, Syria, and Ukraine has shown that the deterioration of relations between great powers has complicated the decision-making of the UNSC (Von Einsiedel et al. 2015, 2). They believe that the struggle between China, Russia, and the USA could pose the greatest threat to the relevance of the UNSC as this could cripple the UNSC's operationality (Von Einsiedel et al. 2015, 2). Thus, analysing the great power rivalry in the UNSC, especially from a rhetorical perspective, is imperative. By focusing on UNSC meetings and decision-making related to the Syrian civil war in the years 2011, 2016, and 2021, this chapter analyses the three powers in three different years and draws conclusions regarding the visibility of great power competition in the UNSC and its impact on multilateral cooperation.

The Syrian civil war began in March 2011 as the Arab Spring-inspired uprising turned into a civil war. The war has claimed over 300,000 civilians' lives in over ten years (UN Human Rights Office 2022). The conflict's root causes are multifaceted, including lack of political freedom, oppression, corruption, and unemployment (BBC 2023). Growing dissatisfaction led to violently suppressed protests in March 2011 (BBC 2023). By June 2011, armed opposition had formed, and the civil war erupted fully (Laub 2023). The Syrian civil war has been complicated by external involvement. Moreover, the conflict has strengthened numerous jihadist groups, especially in its early years (Byman 2018). Western powers have publicly predominantly supported the opposition, while Russia has been the strongest supporter of the regime. Russia succeeded in turning the tide of the conflict in 2015 by supporting the government with airstrikes (Doucet 2015). Furthermore, Russia has been one of the most active negotiators in the conflict. Over the years, with Russia's support, the government has managed to regain control of most areas. However, in December 2024, the rebels, led by the Hayat Tahrir al-Sham (HTS), managed to capture Damascus and topple the al-Assad regime (Michaelson 2024).

Numerous attempts at peace in Syria have largely failed, and the UNSC is considered to have failed in its tasks (McGreal 2015; Dempsey 2023; Lederer 2023), with China and Russia voting against many proposals. The veto's active use is explained by Russia's support for the Syrian government and by Resolution 1973 (2011) on the first Libyan civil war. On 17 March 2011, the UNSC adopted Resolution 1973, which authorised all necessary measures to protect civilians in Libya (S/RES/1973 2011). China and Russia abstained, alongside Brazil, Germany, and India. The resolution allowed for military action led by the North Atlantic Treaty Organization (NATO) and the operation eventually led to Muammar Gaddafi's death in October (Charbonneau 2011). The first Libyan civil war ended in October 2011 with a regime change. Thus, China and Russia saw that regime change was possible through military intervention permitted by the UNSC, having thereafter sought to prevent the UNSC from enabling anything similar in Syria or elsewhere. This has led to difficulties in UNSC decision-making and is reflected in the rhetoric analysed here.

2 Great Power Rivalry Between China, Russia, and the USA

The late 1990s and early 2000s were relatively peaceful times in great power relations, with the USA enjoying long-standing hegemonic dominance (Brands 2017, 1). Great power rivalry, however, began to increase again as China's and Russia's increasingly authoritarian leaders perceived democratisation as a threat to their power and the West thus failed to integrate them into the liberal order (Brands 2022). Moreover, as the 2000s progressed, the balance of power leaned towards China and Russia, and their economic and military capabilities developed and began to better match those of the USA (Brands 2022). By the end of the 2000s, tensions had escalated. President Vladimir Putin's speech at the Munich Security Conference in 2007 marked a clear turning point, reflecting

Russia's changing attitude towards the West. In this speech, President Putin addressed the expanding use of military force in international relations, accused the NATO of expansionism, and questioned the motives behind NATO expansion (Putin 2007). The speech indicated the deteriorating relations and the growing confrontation between Russia and the West. In 2014, Russia illegally annexed the Crimean Peninsula (Lee Myers and Barry 2014), which, according to Trenin, restarted the rivalry between Russia and the USA (Trenin 2014, 1). The rivalry has been primarily economic and political, but military aspects have been included. For Russia, the competition is about remaining a power in international order and "holding on to the remnants of the Russian empire" (Marcus 2018). The rivalry has since intensified, especially with Russia's invasion of Ukraine in 2022.

While Russia, previously the USSR, has been a traditional challenger to the USA due to the Cold War, China emerged as a threat in the 2000s after the lull of the Cold War and has since surpassed Russia (Lam and Silver 2023). In 2006, the US Quadrennial Defense Review Report stated that "China has the greatest potential to compete militarily with the United States" (US Department of Defense 2006, 29). While China's actions are not as hostile as Russia's, there are concerns over the security situation in the South China Sea, where China has sought to claim new territories, and in Taiwan. Moreover, China has skilfully used soft power in Africa as well as in Europe, where many economies are dependent on China's investment in critical infrastructure (Visala 2022; Saarinen 2022). Hence, while cutting ties with Russia has been relatively easy in the aftermath of February 2022, it would be very difficult to do so with China (Saarinen 2022). This makes China's role even more important, and the possibility of conflict between China and the West is worrisome.

Bekkevold (2018) has highlighted that the great power competition is between China, Russia, and the USA, presenting that the relationship between these countries is better characterised by competition than cooperation (Bekkevold 2018, 141). As rivalry increasingly defines the relationships between the three countries, it naturally reflects in the UNSC, where countries should collaborate to make international peace and security decisions. Decision-making has become more difficult, especially in conflicts like Syria and Israel-Palestine, where the great powers have strong interests. According to Gowan (2018), China, Russia, and the USA increasingly behave in ways reminiscent of the Cold War, and their hostility affects the UNSC's diplomacy (Gowan 2018, 1). Despite the deteriorating relations, the UNSC likely remains a central venue for discussions among these countries, as none of them want conflicts to be completely unregulated (Gowan 2018, 14). Therefore, while great power rivalry exists, it does not endanger multilateral cooperation as it is in the interest of the three countries to engage multilaterally in matters of peace and security.

3 Analysing Great Power Rhetoric

The UNSC is the highest platform for international cooperation and decision-making among the great powers which makes it an excellent place to analyse great power politics and understand their rhetoric. Analysing rhetoric helps to understand how great powers manifest their ideas and perspectives in the UNSC, as the rhetorical choices and tones of speeches show how they speak to each other. Through this, it is possible to develop an understanding of whether tense relations are conveyed in UNSC speeches or whether countries can still act constructively and diplomatically. This chapter analyses UNSC meeting minutes on the Syrian civil war from 2011, 2016, and 2021. The data is gathered from meetings with votes, for this gives us an insight into decision-making and multilateral cooperation. The Syrian civil war was chosen as a case as it is one of the most significant civil wars with outside involvement in the twenty-first century, and the great powers have been involved there. The years have been chosen five years apart to analyse possible changes in dynamics over time. The year 2011 was a natural starting point as the year when the conflict began.

The chapter analyses eight meetings, focusing on recurring rhetorical choices and tone. Via rhetorical analysis, it can be seen what kind of arguments the states make about their relations with each other and how they seek to persuade others to support their point of view and narratives. Rhetoric is classically defined by the Greek philosopher Aristotle as "the power of finding available means of persuasion" (Garver 2009, 10). Hence, rhetoric is about how a speaker employs language and arguments in trying to persuade others. This analysis focuses on rhetorical context, arguments, and narratives. Rhetorical context is used to understand where the speech is situated. This is done by analysing the conflict situation in Syria and the place of the speech, here the UNSC, which creates expectations for the speakers. At the UNSC, the language and rhetoric are more diplomatic than in some other forums and there are rules and procedures to be followed. An analysis of rhetorical arguments allows for a deeper understanding of what the three powers are conveying, whereas analysis of tones can tell about the state of rivalry. This examination focuses on what kind of arguments the states have about great power rivalry and multilateral cooperation. The arguments can give evidence about great power rivalry as the states present certain narratives through their arguments that they want the audiences to accept. Finally, arguments showcase how the states view multilateral cooperation at the UNSC.

To analyse the tone, the notions of Rank (1980) are used. Rank suggests that rhetoric involves claims, accusations (direct and indirect), and promises and threats (Rank 1980, 39–41). Rank's work is used as an analysis technique to examine whether the rhetoric of the great powers includes these elements. Rhetoric is categorised into three types:

1. *Positive rhetoric*: The speaker expresses gratitude, makes positive promises, or supports other participants.
2. *Negative rhetoric*: The speaker is hostile, threatening, accusatory, or uses hostile language towards other participants.
3. *Neutral rhetoric*: The speaker takes a stance on the issue without significantly reacting to other participants.

In addition to these rhetorical tones, the analysis delves into narratives by exploring if there are repetitive narratives in the meetings, which reflect great power rivalry. Perelman has highlighted the importance of repeating stories, as it clarifies issues, identifies enemies, and offers solutions (in Kuusisto 1996, 273). Therefore, the purpose is to examine the narratives presented by China, Russia, and the USA in these meetings and understand what they reveal about the great power rivalry in the UNSC. It should be noted that in addition to the official discussions at the UNSC meetings, the members engage in back-channel talks and informal discussions before and during the meetings. These can have an impact on the outcomes of the meetings as well as on the relations between the states. However, as these discussions are not publicly available, they could not be accounted for in this study.

4 Great Power Rivalry in the UNSC in 2011, 2016, and 2021

The following sections present the key contents, rhetoric, and narratives presented in the meetings regarding Syria in 2011, 2016, and 2021 and illustrate how great power rivalry is reflected in the UNSC meetings.

4.1 2011

By the time the UNSC convened first to vote on Syria on 4 October 2011, the war had already caused significant civilian casualties and displacement. The international community was divided on how to respond. While the West advocated for pressuring the regime, Russia and China were wary of external interference, citing the precedent of NATO's intervention in Libya. During the vote, a draft resolution proposed by the West aimed to condemn Assad's regime and hinted at potential sanctions. Both Russia and China voted against the draft. This marked a significant moment in UNSC dynamics, as the veto deepened divisions and escalated negative rhetoric, which this chapter now examines.

For Russia, the veto was a broader defence of its geopolitical interests, given its support to the Syrian government and fears of regime change. Russian UN Representative Vitaly Churkin criticised the draft resolution as unbalanced, arguing it targeted the regime while ignoring violence by opposition groups (S/PV.6627 2011, 3). This statement highlighted the Russian support for the regime. Representative Churkin stressed that Russia would only cooperate if attempts at regime change were abandoned (S/PV.6627 2011, 3). The fear of regime change seems to be influenced by Russia's experience in Libya, which was brought up by Representative Churkin, who linked the two conflicts together (S/PV.6627 2011, 5). For Russia, the experience in Libya set a dangerous precedent that regime change could happen through UNSC authorisation, and it has since sought to block similar efforts in the UNSC. Representative Churkin appeared to generalise Russian opinion onto the entire international community by mentioning that the whole community is concerned that NATO might act again to implement the Responsibility to Protect (S/PV.6627 2011, 4). This statement highlights Russia's criticism of the West and NATO members and shows its opposition to past actions.

The American rhetoric showed the USA's opposition to the actions of the Chinese and Russians. The USA argued that Syrians can apprehend from the voting those who support human rights and those who do not (S/PV.6627 2011, 8), essentially accusing both China and Russia of being against human rights. In response to Russia's accusations of attempts at regime change, the USA's UN Representative Susan Rice stated that this is not about military intervention or Libya, and these allegations are a "cheap ruse" from those who sell weapons to the government instead of supporting the people (S/PV.6627 2011, 8). These statements show that the USA posits itself on a morally higher ground by saying that they support human rights and do not sell weapons to the Syrian government.

China's rhetoric was more neutral, yet it reflected reservations. Like Russia, China's UN Representative Li Baodong noted that the draft resolution could complicate matters as it included a threat of sanctions (S/PV.6627 2011, 5). Representative Li stated that China could not vote in favour of the draft as it focused "on exerting pressure on Syria, even threatening to impose sanctions" (S/PV.6627 2011, 5). Hence, China is more aligned with Russia than the USA. China expressed concerns over Syrian sovereignty by noting that any UNSC action must comply with the UN Charter and the principle of non-interference (S/PV.6627 2011, 5). China's position, while less confrontational, mirrored Russia's in opposing measures perceived as coercive or interventionist, reflecting a shared apprehension about the implications of the Libyan experience.

The rhetoric exposes a disparity in how the conflict is being approached. China and Russia centred their discourse on the ideas of non-interference and sovereignty, with Russia taking a more direct accusatory stance. Instead, the USA placed a strong emphasis on human rights and worked to counter China's and Russia's stances based on human rights. The rhetoric and different stances indicated great power rivalry, particularly between Russia and the USA, with China playing a more cautious yet aligned role with Russia. There were important ramifications for UNSC multilateral cooperation. The veto highlighted how difficult it is to reach an agreement in a split UNSC. According to the USA, the final draft was "watered-down" to appease the Chinese and Russian delegations, yet it was still unable to win their support (S/PV.6627 2011, 8). Notwithstanding these obstacles, the UNSC's meeting and subsequent attempt at negotiations demonstrated a continued, if fragile, commitment to multilateralism. Nonetheless, the confrontational rhetoric foreshadowed challenges in subsequent decision-making and concerns about the UNSC's capacity to effectively handle the deteriorating situation in Syria due to the growing rivalry between major powers and their conflicting agendas. In the end, the vote was a reflection of deeper rifts in international diplomacy.

4.2 2016

The civil war in Syria intensified between 2011 and 2016. In 2013, chemical attacks were used, and the terrorist organisation Islamic State (IS) emerged (Loft et al. 2022, 3). In 2014, the US-led coalition began to fight against the organisation. In 2015, Russia started a military campaign in Syria by participating in airstrikes, which is widely seen as a turning point in favour of the Syrian government (Loft et al. 2022, 4). This could explain negative stances between Russia and the USA in 2016. By 2016, the situation in Syria had worsened, especially for the opposition and the civilians, due to the airstrikes and the strengthening of ISIS (UNICEF 2017; CPA 2024). Parallel to the worsening situation on the ground, there is an evident change to worse in the analysed rhetoric, especially between Russia and the USA. In 2016, the UNSC convened to vote on Syria six times (on February 26th, October 8th, October 31st, November 17th, December 5th, and December 31st). The analysis shows that rhetoric is more on the negative side, while multilateral cooperation continues.

During the first vote of 2016, on February 26th, the UNSC unanimously approved Resolution 2268 on the cessation of hostilities and the entry of humanitarian workers into Syria (S/RES/2268 2016). This agreement was likely motivated by the escalating humanitarian crisis on the ground, as Syria faced ongoing violence, destroyed infrastructure, and increased civilian casualties. Despite the unanimity of the draft and the fact that it was a joint proposal by Russia and the USA, the rhetoric of the USA was confrontational.

Representative Samantha Power's rhetoric was particularly critical, mirroring the broader scepticism about Russia's dedication to the ceasefire. While she recognised the importance of the resolution, Representative Power accused Russia, and the Assad regime of intensifying military operations against opposition forces just before the cessation of hostilities was to begin. She stated, "it is hard to seem serious and sincere about ceasing hostilities when you ramp up fighting right up to the minute the cessation of hostilities is to take effect" (S/PV.7634 2016, 6). This criticism underscored the USA's distrust of Russia's motives and its broader discontent with the discrepancies between diplomatic agreements and real actions on the ground. From Washington's perspective, Russia's behaviour—characterised by indiscriminate bombings and an emphasis on bolstering the Assad regime—threatened the resolution's humanitarian and political aims. Representative Power's confrontational style reflected a growing rift between the USA and Russia, both in the UNSC and in broader international relations. Although ostensibly unified in the need for a ceasefire, the USA viewed Russia's actions as worsening the humanitarian crisis and increasing civilian casualties.

Interestingly, despite the rather negative language by the USA, Russia chose not to respond to the criticism. Representative Gennedy Gatilow commended the resolution as a vital step towards a political resolution and stressed common objectives, such as decreasing violence, fighting terrorism, and enhancing humanitarian conditions (S/PV.7634 2016, 7–8). Russia's rhetoric is notoriously different from the American one as it is more constructive and does not attack the USA. The rhetoric seems to portray Russia as a collaborative partner in multilateral diplomacy, casting itself as essential in brokering the resolution. Nonetheless, Representative Gatilow indirectly criticised external influences—likely Western nations—for undermining Syria's sovereignty as he noted that external forces should stop the ongoing violations of Syria's sovereignty (S/PV.7634 2016, 8). This statement aligns with Moscow's narrative of countering perceived Western interventionism. Although Russia avoided directly addressing the American allegations, its rhetoric deflected attention from its ground activities, where Russian airstrikes were frequently connected to considerable civilian harm and targeting of opposition-held territories. Russia's strategy emphasised its dual approach: Presenting itself as a stabilising agent in the conflict while portraying Western actions as destabilising interference. By invoking the subject of sovereignty and territorial integrity, Russia attempted to divert the focus from its military operations to a critique of Western policies in Syria and the larger Middle East.

China's rhetoric was mainly neutral and focused on implementing a ceasefire and the resolution (S/PV.7634 2016, 10–11). The speech started positively as China welcomed Russia's and the USA's joint agreement (S/PV.7634 2016, 10). China's approach seems to position itself as an impartial mediator and on a higher moral ground as Representative

Liu Jieyi pointed out that “major countries in the region should stop their mutual finger-pointing—and play a constructive role in the forthcoming implementation of the cessation of hostilities” (S/PV.7634 2016, 11). China seems to depict itself as a responsible and stabilising agent, calling for unity and pragmatic cooperation within the UNSC.

Resolution 2268 demonstrated the UNSC’s capability for cooperation in tackling urgent humanitarian issues, yet the differing rhetorical approaches of its members exposed persistent divisions. The USA’s negative stance reflected its frustration with Russia’s actions and their impact on civilians. At the same time, Russia’s cautiously positive rhetoric concealed its military goals under the pretext of sovereignty and counterterrorism. China’s neutral position aimed to establish it as a mediator. These interactions illuminate the intricacies of multilateral cooperation concerning the Syrian conflict. Even during moments of superficial agreement, the UNSC remained polarised, mirroring broader geopolitical conflicts and competing ideas about global governance.

The next meeting on October 8th marked one of the most confrontational ones and witnessed votes on two draft resolutions (S/PV.7785 2016). Before the meeting, the situation on the ground had deteriorated, and the UN Special Envoy Staffan de Mistura implored the USA and Russia to improve the situation (UN News 2016a). Russia and Venezuela voted against the first draft while China abstained, and the Western countries along with many others, rejected the second draft. The polarised voting underscored the absence of consensus among key players and set the scene for intense rhetorical disputes.

The meeting’s rhetoric was confrontational from the beginning. Russian Representative Churkin highlighted how everyone was aware of the background of the Syrian civil war: “After destroying Libya and deeming it a great success, the troika of the three Western permanent members of the Security Council turned on Syria” (S/PV.7785 2016, 4). The statement is highly accusatory and hostile towards Western countries. Representative Churkin seems to imply that the Syrian civil war is purely the fault of Western countries, disregarding entirely the internal Syrian situation. Representative Churkin uses the strong term “destroying” regarding Libya and accuses the USA, together with France and the UK of seeking “an opportunistic invasion” (S/PV.7634 2016, 4). This accusatory language likely aimed to shift focus away from Russia’s contentious military actions in Syria, which included comprehensive airstrikes on opposition-controlled areas, while presenting the West as the main antagonist in destabilising the region. Representative Churkin said that Russia's draft was sensible, yet he understood that it would not receive votes because of some countries' opposition to Russia and others' lack of courage (S/PV.7634 2016, 4). Thus, Representative Churkin posited that the Western opposition to Russia's draft resolution stemmed from a bias against Moscow and the draft was opposed simply because it originates from Russia, regardless of its content.

The American rhetoric is no less severe than that of Russia, for Representative David Pressman issued a harsh condemnation of Russia's involvement in the Syrian conflict and accused Russia of seeking to take eastern Aleppo. Representative Pressman stated that Russia ensured in the vote that the Syrian regime was strengthened, costing the lives of 275,000 Syrians (S/PV.7634 2016, 8). Representative Pressman openly accused Russia of killing Syrians and stated that many would describe Russia's actions as war crimes, claiming Russia to be one of the worst perpetrators terrorising Aleppo. Representative Pressman even said that Russia should stop starving and killing Aleppo's children (S/PV.7634 2016, 8–9). Such phrasing underscored the moral aspect of the American argument, depicting Russia's actions as not only strategically detrimental but fundamentally inhumane. These harsh allegations highlighted the USA's frustration with Moscow's backing of the Assad regime and the human cost of this.

Compared to Russia and the USA, China's speech was again more neutral. Representative Liu highlighted that the French-Spanish draft proposal, while containing important elements, did not fully respect the sovereignty, independence, and territorial integrity of Syria, and China had to abstain (S/PV.7634, 2016, p. 14). China pointed out that Russia's draft reflected these and was "complete, comprehensive and balanced out" and China regretted that it did not pass (S/PV.7634 2016, 15). Hence, China sided with Russia. China even seemed to put forth the narrative that China and Russia are more interested in Syrian sovereignty, territorial integrity, and independence than the West. This could be done to remind others of what happened in Libya and that China and Russia are opposed to something similar occurring again. This positioning resonated with Beijing's foreign policy principles, which predominantly favour state sovereignty over humanitarian interventions, reflecting its caution regarding resolutions that could facilitate external interference. Even though Russia and the USA are openly engaging in negative rhetoric, China remained diplomatic and neutral. During the meeting,

China called for UNSC unity and a "positive and constructive role" in Syria (S/PV.7634 2016, 15), which plays into the way how China posits itself as a neutral party.

After the Chinese speech, Russia continued its attack on the USA and the UK by noting that they used provocative rhetoric (S/PV.7634 2016, 16). Representative Churkin created the impression that Russia behaves better than the Western countries and does not engage in provocation. Ironically, Russia immediately attacked both countries by responding to Britain's plea to end suffering:

> Indeed, how about it? How about immediately putting an end to supporting various thugs around the world—terrorists, extremists and all the other amateurs exacerbating the situation in one country or another? How about putting an end to interfering in the affairs of other sovereign States? Just give up these colonial customs and leave the world in peace. The situation would improve in a great many parts of the world. (S/PV.7634 2016, 16)

The statement contains many interesting elements as Russia directly challenged the role of the West in the world, accusing them of interfering in the affairs of sovereign states. Representative Churkin presents the issue as if Western countries support "thugs", although the USA feels that Russia itself does so in Syria (CBS 2017). Herein, Russia evokes the (neo)colonial narrative to oppose the possible interventionist implications. This helps Russia to seek support from other postcolonial member states. Thus, Representative Churkin directly challenged the Western-dominated world order.

The meeting highlighted the growing divide between Russia and the USA. Russia positioned itself as a stabilising entity countering Western interventions while accusing the USA and its allies of violating Syrian sovereignty. In contrast, the USA depicted Russia as a principal supporter of the Assad regime's violence, holding Moscow accountable for war crimes and humanitarian disasters. This clash mirrored larger geopolitical tensions, with each side striving to legitimise its actions and undermine the other. China steered clear of provocative language and framed its views in terms of neutrality and constructive diplomacy. This stance probably sought to bolster Beijing's reputation as a responsible player within the UNSC. The meeting revealed the splits within the UNSC and showcased the shortcomings of multilateral cooperation in addressing the Syrian crisis. The conflicting narratives of Russia, the USA, and China reflected the wider geopolitical tensions influencing the UNSC's discussions.

The second meeting of October, on the 31st, was significantly more polite, and the UNSC unanimously adopted Resolution 2314, extending the mandate of the Joint Investigative Mechanism (JIM) (S/RES/2314 2016). This represented a significant turn from the confrontational language of the previous meeting, indicating that increased tensions in one session do not necessarily persist. Nevertheless, the situation in Aleppo and Idlib continued to worsen between these meetings, with assaults on civilians and schools highlighting the pressing need for a solution.

China's statement was again neutral and focused on finding a political solution and respecting Syrian sovereignty (S/PV. 7798 2016, 5). This consistent posture allowed China to sidestep direct involvement in the conflict between the USA and Russia that typically takes place in the meetings, positioning itself as a mediator focused on overarching principles rather than assigning blame. The rhetoric from the USA was neutral, with Representative Michele Sison employing emotional appeals, mentioning the plight of children impacted by chemical weapons, a strategy that highlighted the human toll of inaction (S/PV.7798 2016, 2–3). While Representative Sison avoided direct accusations towards Russia, she made a remark questioning why the UNSC would not want to identify the individuals responsible for chemical weapons attacks—a likely indirect critique of Russia's support for the Syrian government (S/PV.7798 2016, 3). This tactic combined emotional appeal with a gentle rhetorical challenge to Russian viewpoints, emphasising the USA's ongoing scepticism of the Assad regime and Russia. Russia's statement began with a positive tone as Representative Churkin thanked the others for understanding Russia's position (S/PV. 7798 2016, 3). Nonetheless, Representative Churkin did not completely refrain from criticism, warning that the JIM should not be treated as a toy to criticise the Syrian government (S/PV.7798 2016, 3). This statement implicitly seems to suggest that the USA and its partners were unfairly targeting Damascus, reflecting Russia's wider narrative of protecting Syrian sovereignty from foreign interference. Despite these veiled criticisms, the overall atmosphere of the meeting remained rather neutral, illustrating the UNSC's capacity to pass resolutions despite existing tensions and engage in multilateral cooperation with pressing matters, such as the use of chemical weapons the use of which the JIM investigates.

In the next vote, on November 17th, the UNSC unanimously approved another extension of the JIM's mandate with Resolution 2319 (S/RES/2319 2016). China's statements adhered to its typical approach, emphasising the need to honour Syrian sovereignty and avoid provocative language (S/PV.7815 2016, 3). This consistent stance reinforced China's image as a pragmatic and non-aggressive player within the UNSC. The USA commenced positively with Representative Power expressing thanks to everyone for the mandate's extension and particularly thanking Russia for continuing negotiations long enough (S/PV.7815 2016, 2). However, Representative Power pointed out that Russia's involvement in Syria since 2015 had granted the Syrian government a significant advantage on the battlefield (S/PV.7815 2016, 3). While articulated diplomatically, this observation underscored ongoing American apprehensions about Russia's influence in extending the conflict.

Russia's rhetoric was quite neutral, although Representative Vladimir Safronkov remarked that it is sad to hear statements against the Syrian government and direct accusations from the USA (S/PV.7815 2016, 4). Mostly, Representative Safronkov focused on terrorism and how Russia has been trying to draw attention to evidence of terrorists using chemical weapons (S/PV.7815 2016, 4). Representative Safronkov said that Russia has been trying to prompt action, but unfortunately, its efforts had been thwarted, and the result was only now becoming evident (S/PV.7815 2016, 4). While Representative Safronkov did not directly reference the West, his comments seem to subtly position Western nations as partially responsible for the use of chemical weapons due to their opposition to Russia's proposed measures.

The resolution's unanimous adoption likely played a role in the more neutral language. Although the underlying tensions between the USA and Russia were still apparent through discreet comments and indirect critiques, the overall atmosphere was more constructive. This change highlights a trend within the UNSC: Even with significant geopolitical divides, the UNSC possesses the ability for multilateral cooperation where a consensus can be reached.

The next meeting on December 5th heralded a notable increase in confrontational language, signalling deepening rifts among its members. One factor for this could be the USA's presidential elections held in November 2016, which led to the election of Donald Trump and created uncertainties about the upcoming American policies towards China and Russia. The draft resolution was not adopted, as China, Russia, and Venezuela opposed it, while Angola abstained (S/PV.7825 2016). The meeting was marked by mutual blame, especially between the USA and Russia, and indicated a significant shift in China's tone as it adopted a more confrontational position.

Russia's Representative Churkin launched a forceful critique of the Western permanent members, alleging that they were applying excessive pressure on other nations to vote on the draft resolution (S/PV.7825 2016, 2). Representative Churkin accused the West of provoking tensions both within the UNSC and in the Syrian conflict. Tensions between the USA and Russia became highly accusatory. The USA claimed that Russia falsely said it was close to an agreement with the USA (S/PV.7825 2016, 3). Russia noted that such a statement undermined the work done by Secretary of State Kerry and Foreign Minister Lavrov, and it was regrettable that agreements were reached, and then it was said that there was no agreement (S/PV.7825 2016, 3). The statement likely referred to the bilateral attempts by Kerry and Lavrov to come up with a ceasefire solution in August, September, and October 2016 (Browne and Labott 2016; Borger 2016; France24 2016). Additionally, during the UNSC meeting, the USA accused Russia of empty promises and killing civilians (S/PV.7825 2016, 3), while Russia demanded that the USA take responsibility for "resolving the problem in Syria" (S/PV.7825 2016, 3). Representative Churkin openly stated that there is no unity between the countries (S/PV.7825 2016, 3), which showed a negative picture of the state of multilateral cooperation

Representative Sison's comments also extended to China, marking a significant shift in American discourse, which had previously concentrated more on Russia. Representative Sison said that Russia prefers to continue killing people with its ally al-Assad, and history will remember that Russia, China, and Venezuela prevented the UNSC from acting (S/PV.7825 2016, 10–11). While the USA's critique of China was not as harsh as that aimed at Russia, it still conveyed exasperation over Beijing's ongoing alignment with Moscow.

China's Representative, Liu, initially adopted a characteristically diplomatic and neutral stance, stressing the necessity for a political resolution and promoting additional negotiations within the UNSC to reach an agreement (S/PV.7825 2016, 8). Representative Liu appeared to side with Russia in the dispute between the USA and Russia by stating that the USA and Russia have made diplomatic efforts (S/PV.7825 2016, 8). Interestingly, for the first time, China responded assertively to criticism. Representative Liu challenged the USA's allegations by probing into the roots of the Syrian conflict and the broader destabilisation of the Middle East, suggesting that the USA held historical accountability for these issues:

> With regard to the statement made by the United States representative, I would like to emphasize one point. How did the situation in Syria come about, and how did the problems that other countries in the Middle East are dealing with reach the point where they are today? Where did they begin, and why? What has been the role played by the various countries concerned? The historical record is very clear. Every member of the Council is very well aware of that. It cannot be changed by distorting the positions of some countries on the Council. (S/PV.7825 2016, 13)

This remark mirrored a rhetorical strategy often used by Russia, positioning the USA as the main destabilising influence in the area and as a culprit for the situation in the Middle East. China, moreover, seemed to be generalising that the whole UNSC knows this. The USA responded to the accusation by stating that the conflict in Syria started with protests against al-Assad and that the accusations against the USA in this matter were absurd (S/PV.7825 2016, 14).

The language used in this meeting highlighted the widening rift between the USA and Russia. Both nations levelled direct charges against each other, with Russia directly attacking Representative Sison, saying that it was unfortunate that she was "so aggressive" in seeking to disavow the initiative of Secretary of State Kerry with Minister Lavrov in Geneva by saying that they were not close to an agreement (S/PV.7825 2016, 13). The Russian representative said that he hoped that Kerry would find "the strength to pursue this initiative, because it could lead to an effective and lasting solution" (S/PV.7825 2016, 13), indicating a willingness to work with Kerry. The statement is interesting because it seems to drive a wedge between the Americans, making it seem like Russia wants to find a common solution with Secretary Kerry while the American UN delegation is against it.

The meeting exposed the UNSC's fragmentation as rising tensions and confrontational language prevailed throughout the meeting. Russia persisted with its narrative of Western provocation, blaming the USA for hindering multilateral efforts. The USA's rhetoric remained critical of Russia and expanded to China, attributing blame to both for obstructing progress regarding the humanitarian crisis in Syria. While the USA continued to concentrate mainly on Russia, its rivalry with China became more apparent. China's unusually straightforward critique of the USA pointed to a growing rivalry between the two countries, reflecting increased tensions between them and showing China openly challenging the USA. This change illustrates Beijing's readiness to confront American accusations more directly. Consequently, the meeting signified a low point for UNSC unity, with the rejected resolution and mutual accusations mirroring the larger geopolitical rivalries that obstructed multilateral action on Syria.

In the last meeting of 2016, on December 31st, the UNSC unanimously adopted Resolution 2336 regarding the ceasefire agreement (S/RES/2336 2016). Before the meeting, the UNSC had been warned by the UN humanitarian officials about the almost catastrophic situation on the ground, and the opposition and government agreed on a ceasefire (UN News 2016b, 2016c), which was brokered by Russia and Turkey (Walker and Shaheen 2016). The rhetoric is quite benign, with short and rather superficial statements. The USA briefly stated that it welcomed Russia's and Turkey's actions in Syria (S/PV. 7855 2016, 2). Representative Sison said that they could support the resolution, although they were concerned that not all information was available (S/PV. 7855 2016, 2). This cautious endorsement demonstrated the USA's emphasis on preserving unity within the UNSC, considering the severe humanitarian conditions present. The USA avoided direct criticism or confrontational language, indicating a more restrained stance compared to earlier meetings. China adopted a neutral and constructive approach, emphasising principles that are key to its foreign policy, with Representative Wu Haitao talking about issues such as sovereignty, independence, and territorial integrity (S/PV. 7855 2016, 6), emphasising China's role regarding these. China noted that it approved "the positive result" that Russia and Turkey achieved (S/PV. 7855 2016, 6). Contrary to the USA, China did not voice any concerns about the process. Moreover, China discussed how a political solution is the only way and that the whole international community should seize the opportunity to advance this (S/PV. 7855 2016, 6). China did not make any comments towards the USA or the West, and there is no negativity in the Chinese statements. The rhetoric can even be seen to be positive, as China appreciated the positive efforts of Russia and Turkey.

Russia's Representative Churkin started with a more positive tone by thanking everyone (S/PV. 7855 2016, 7). However, the tone grew more accusatory, though not explicitly confrontational, as Representative Churkin brought up how meetings between Foreign Minister Lavrov and Secretary Kerry always lead "to serious agreements that—unfortunately remained unfulfilled" (S/PV. 7855 2016, 8), thus continuing the discussion that took place at the beginning of December, albeit in a less aggressive manner than in the earlier meeting. Representative Churkin stated that if certain UNSC members cannot or do not want to support the efforts of Russia and Turkey, they should not complicate matters (S/PV. 7855 2016, 8). The statement was likely directed at the USA and other Western permanent members. Furthermore, Representative Churkin asked these members not to repeat clichés that achieve nothing (S/PV. 7855 2016, 8), likely referring to the Western statements against Russia and the Syrian government. While not directly naming the USA or other Western members, these statements reflected ongoing frustrations with Western positions on Syria and the regime.

In 2016, the great power relations became more apparent based on the increasingly negative rhetoric. The negative rhetoric and rivalry could be due to the changes in the state of conflict in Syria, with the regime and Russia gaining the upper hand. Towards the end of the year, the upcoming change in the White House might have increased tensions, given the uncertainties about the future American policies. The difference between the unanimous meetings and the ones with vetoes shows that cooperation varies from meeting to meeting depending on the situation on the ground and the content of the draft resolutions. Tensions were, however, apparent in all meetings, and the more confrontational meetings did not paint a very positive picture of multilateral cooperation. The ability to cooperate was, however, highlighted in how Russia and the USA worked together on a draft resolution in February 2016. Hence, collaboration remained operational at large while facing great difficulties in the more confrontational meetings. Thus, it seems that, while great power rivalry exists, it does not hinder the multilateral cooperation at the UNSC from taking place, albeit the results of the meetings vary.

4.3 2021

In 2021, ten years after the start of the civil war, the UNSC convened to vote on Syria only once. From 2016 to 2021, numerous mediation attempts took place, such as those between Russia, Turkey, and Iran in Astana in 2017, yet no lasting peace was obtained. Chemical attacks continued in 2017 and 2018, leading to airstrikes by the US, the UK, and France in 2018. From 2018 to 2019, the US began withdrawing from Syria, considering ISIS defeated. The ceasefire signed in March 2020 largely held, and by 2021, the government's position had once again solidified, despite the ongoing conflict (Loft et al. 2022, 6).

The UNSC unanimously adopted Resolution 2585 on coordinating and distributing aid on 9 July 2021 (S/RES/2585 2021). Compared to 2016, the rhetoric was more neutral and even positive between the USA and Russia. The USA spoke of how the two worked together to initiate humanitarian aid, showing that cooperation was possible (S/PV.8817 2021, 2). In its statement, Russia expressed gratitude to the USA, stating that they were witnessing a historic moment as Russia and the USA had successfully reached an agreement for the first time and even drafted a resolution everyone supported (S/PV.8817 2021, 3). The positive rhetoric was likely a result of the efforts of the USA and Russia in 2021 to improve their relations, as they agreed on diplomatic actions and bilateral strategic stability dialogues in Geneva in June (Biden 2021). In 2021, hopes were expressed that bilateral relations could improve under the Biden administration. Baklitskiy (2021) notes that the Biden administration's foreign policy centred on managing competition with China and addressing global challenges (Baklitskiy 2021). For the USA, Russia in 2021 had an important role in solving conflicts around the globe (Baklitskiy 2021). Moreover, the focus on China could have led the USA to want to avoid conflict with Russia, and it was believed that Russia could be less confrontational towards the USA when there was less pressure towards it from Washington (Baklitskiy 2021). In 2021, Russia and the USA jointly promoted solutions to problems at the UN and submitted a resolution to the UN General Assembly (UNGA) together, which led to hopes that such cooperation might continue (Baklitskiy 2021). All of this could explain the more positive rhetoric between Russia and the USA in this meeting.

At the same time, the American focus on China instead of Russia created a more negative stand between China and the USA. During the meeting, China noted that there was still much room for improvement in the resolution (S/PV.8817 2021, 4). This may be a sign that US-China relations began to deteriorate in the late 2010s. In 2020, there were diplomatic tensions between China and the USA, whereas in 2021, the USA, for example, accused China of the genocide of the Uyghurs and the Biden administration kept in place the Trump administration's tariffs (CFR, n.d.). In June 2021, the USA got NATO to declare China as a security threat (CFR n.d.). In 2020, China moreover switched to the so-called wolf warrior diplomacy, which was markedly different from "the famously bland" Chinese diplomacy as the diplomats now started to directly go against any criticism towards China (Westcott and Jiang 2020). All these could explain the increased tensions in 2021.

The meeting in 2021 was more neutral and even positive compared to the meetings in 2011 and 2016. There were signs of rivalry between China and the USA. Based on the rhetoric, one could assume some positive developments in the US-Russia relationship. Nonetheless, the efforts to improve relations with Russia were outlived by February 2022 when Russia began its illegal war against Ukraine. Baklitskiy rightfully noted in 2021 that the US-Russia relationship "is troubled and could deteriorate further at any moment" (Baklitskiy 2021). Hence, while great powers have sometimes shown an interest in improving their relations, the political landscape might change quickly, leading to new realities. At the same time, great power rivalry does not mean the end of multilateral cooperation. While especially the US-Russia relations have been tense, they have still engaged in multilateral and bilateral cooperation and managed to pass UNSC resolutions, even unanimously and by co-authoring draft resolutions. Great power rivalry creates challenges for cooperation as it becomes more confrontational when tensions are running high. However, the fact that the UNSC can be a decision-maker shows that rivalry does not oppose multilateral cooperation.

5 Conclusion

The analysis of the meetings shows that there are tensions between great powers, especially between Russia and the USA. Discussions between these two are sometimes highly confrontational, with Russia showing open hostility towards Western countries in 2016. At the same time, multilateral cooperation continued amidst the difficulties, and there were even unanimous resolutions.

The American and Russian rhetoric is characterised by mostly negative tones. Russia's strongest element in its rhetoric is blaming the West. Russia often brings up various accusations, such as seeking a regime change, anti-Russian sentiment, interference in the affairs of sovereign states, and starting the situation in Syria. Thus, Russia actively challenges the Western-led liberal order and creates a narrative of the West, and especially the USA, as antagonistic forces.

Similarly, the USA's rhetoric is often accusatory. During these meetings, the USA accused Russia several times of killing civilians and supporting al-Assad. Accusations sometimes extend to China. Great power rivalry is visible between the USA and Russia. However, the analysed unanimous meetings show that Russia and the USA can discuss more neutrally and express gratitude to each other. In general, it can be stated that the rhetoric in unanimous meetings is significantly more neutral than in meetings where the veto is used.

Although the great power rivalry is intensifying between China and the USA, it is not as evident in meeting rhetoric before 2021. This somewhat less clear Sino-American rivalry supports the observation that Russia is a more aggressive opponent to the USA than China. While China is a larger military and economic threat to the USA, so far, it has not acted as aggressively in international politics compared to Russia, which has illegally annexed parts of Ukraine and wages war there. The overall tone of rhetoric throughout these analysed years shows that Russia is rhetorically more aggressive than China.

China's rhetoric is the most diplomatic and neutral. However, its alignment with Russia's positions is noticeable. China rarely responds to accusations unless they are directly and harshly targeted, and when it does, responses tend to be more diplomatic. China often highlights sovereignty, territorial integrity, and political settlement and emphasises the role of the UN. It often emphasises its own actions by stating how constructively it has acted in negotiations.

Thus, great power rivalry is somewhat evident in the analysed meetings. It is clear how Russia challenges the USA and the USA's role in the world. China also challenges USA leadership but not as explicitly while aligning itself with Russia's positions. In conclusion, the great power rivalry is visible in the rhetoric used in the UNSC. Chapter 3 mentioned how such rivalries can paralyse the UNSC and we do find evidence for the same. However, the UNSC was not paralysed in an absolute sense; instead, it was still able to make decisions, which shows that great powers can still cooperate. Multilateral cooperation is nonetheless becoming more difficult, given the global challenges. The conflicts, for example, in Ukraine and Gaza, tend to create challenges for the UNSC (Tarquinio 2024). Yet, the UNSC still regularly comes together to try to seek out solutions and oftentimes still succeeds with conflicts with less external involvement. This shows that multilateral cooperation can remain functional, albeit its nature is becoming increasingly confrontational. The great powers still have an interest in coming together to decide on security issues as global security impacts them all. However, decision-making is increasingly limited to issues on which countries can agree, such as conflicts where they have no clear interests. It remains to be seen how the UNSC's effectiveness will change in the coming years, but at present, it still provides a functional multilateral platform for the great powers.

Given that this research focused on certain years and a certain conflict, there is room for future research on the subject. At the time of writing, the Syrian regime has just been toppled by the rebels. Later research could focus on these developments. Different conflicts and years could be addressed to see whether the research yields similar results on the rhetoric and relations between China, Russia, and the USA. Moreover, research could focus on all meetings instead of just those with a vote to see whether there are rhetorical differences.

References

Baklitskiy, Andrey. *Small Victories: Why US-Russia Relations Could Improve Under Biden*. European Council on Foreign Relations, 2021. Accessed August 1, 2024. https://ecfr.eu/article/small-victories-why-us-russia-relations-could-improve-under-biden/.

BBC. "Why Has the Syrian War Lasted 12 Years?" *BBC News*, 2023. Accessed July 31, 2024. https://www.bbc.com/news/world-middle-east-35806229.

Biden, Joe. "Remarks by President Biden in Press Conference, June 16, 2021." *The White House*, 2021. Accessed June 23, 2024. https://www.whitehouse.gov/briefing-room/speeches-remarks/2021/06/16/remarks-by-president-biden-in-press-conference-4/.

Bekkevold, Jo Inge. "China, Russia, and the Great Power Contest in the Middle East." In *Sino-Russian Relations in the 21st Century*, edited by Jo Inge Bekkevold and Bobo Lo, 141–166. London: Palgrave Macmillan, 2018.

Borger, Julian. "John Kerry Lands in Geneva for Syria Peace Talks with Russia's Sergey Lavrov." *The Guardian*, September 8, 2016. Accessed July

21, 2024. https://www.theguardian.com/world/2016/sep/08/syria-peace-talks-geneva-john-kerry-sergey-lavrov.

Brands, Hal. "Six Propositions about Great Power Competition and Revisionism in the 21st Century." *University of Pennsylvania Global Order Papers*, 2017. Accessed July 29, 2024. https://global.upenn.edu/sites/default/files/go-papers-all.original.pdf.

Brands, Hal. "America's War for Global Order Is a Marathon." *Foreign Policy Magazine*, February 25, 2022. Accessed June 1, 2024. https://foreignpolicy.com/2022/01/25/americas-war-for-global-order-is-a-marathon/.

Browne, Ryan, and Elise Labott. "Kerry Announces US-Russia Deal on Syrian Ceasefire." *CNN*, September 9, 2016. Accessed July 21, 2024. https://edition.cnn.com/2016/09/09/politics/syria-ceasefire-kerry-lavrov/index.html.

Byman, Daniel L. "6 Counterterrorism Lessons from the Syrian Civil War." *Brookings Institution*, 2018. Accessed July 20, 2024. https://www.brookings.edu/articles/6-counterterrorism-lessons-from-the-syrian-civil-war/.

CBS. "Former U.S. Ambassador Talks Russia Tensions, Calls Syrian President 'a Thug'." *CBS News*, June 28, 2017. Accessed May 31, 2024. https://www.cbsnews.com/video/former-us-ambassador-talks-russia-tensions-calls-syrian-president-a-thug/.

Council on Foreign Relations (CFR). "U.S.-China Relations." Accessed July 23, 2024. https://www.cfr.org/timeline/us-china-relations.

Charbonneau, Louis. "U.N. Ends Mandate for NATO Operations in Libya." *Reuters*, October 27, 2011. Accessed July 31, 2024. https://www.reuters.com/article/world/un-ends-mandate-for-nato-operations-in-libya-idUSTRE79P6EC/.

CNN. "2011 Libya Civil War Fast Facts." *CNN*, March 28, 2022. Accessed June 9, 2024. https://edition.cnn.com/2013/09/20/world/libya-civil-war-fast-facts/index.html.

Council on Foreign Relations (CPA). "Conflict in Syria." Accessed July 28, 2024. https://www.cfr.org/global-conflict-tracker/conflict/conflict-syria.

Dempsey, Judy. "Judy Asks: Is the United Nations Still Fit for Purpose?" *Carnegie Endowment for International Peace*, September 2023. Accessed July 30, 2024. https://carnegieendowment.org/europe/strategic-europe/2023/09/judy-asks-is-the-united-nations-still-fit-for-purpose?lang=en.

Doucet, Lyse. "New Confidence in Damascus as Russian Strikes Turn the Tide." *BBC News*, December 16, 2015. Accessed June 14, 2024. https://www.bbc.com/news/world-middle-east-35108994.

Fong, Clara, and Lindsay Maizland. "China and Russia: Exploring Ties Between Two Authoritarian Powers." *Council on Foreign Relations*, 2024. Accessed July 23, 2024. https://www.cfr.org/backgrounder/china-russia-relationship-xi-putin-taiwan-ukraine#chapter-title-0-3.

France24. "Syria Talks Resume in Lausanne with Little Hope of Breakthrough." *France24*, October 15, 2016. Accessed July 21, 2024. https://www.france24.com/en/20161015-us-syria-talks-truce-failure-kerry-lavrov-russia-usa-turkey-iran-qatar-egypt-saudi-jordan.

Garver, Eugene. "Aristotle on the Kinds of Rhetoric." *Rhetorica: Journal of the History of Rhetoric* 27, no. 1 (2009): 1–18.

Gowan, Richard. *Minimum Order: The Role of the Security Council in an Era of Major Power Competition*. Centre for Policy Research at United Nations University, 2018. Accessed June 18, 2024. http://collections.unu.edu/eserv/UNU:6677/UNU-Minimum-Order-FINAL.pdf.

Gritten, David. "Earthquake-Hit Syria to Open Two More Border Crossings for Aid Delivery—UN." *BBC News*, February 15, 2023. Accessed June 26, 2024. https://www.bbc.com/news/world-middle-east-64632877.

Hageboutros, Joelle. "The Evolving Role of the Security Council in the Post-Cold War Period." *Swarthmore International Relations Journal*, 2016. Accessed July 30, 2024. https://works.swarthmore.edu/cgi/viewcontent.cgi?article=1005&context=swarthmoreirjournal.

Kuusisto, Riikka. "Sodan Retoriikasta: Persianlahden ja Bosnian Konfliktit Läntisten Suurvaltajohtajien Lausunnoissa." In *Pelkkää Retoriikkaa: Tutkimuksen ja Politiikan Retoriikat*, edited by Kari Palonen and Hannele Summa, 267–291. Tampere: Vastapaino, 1996.

Marcus, Jonathan. "Russia v the West: Is This a New Cold War?" *BBC News*, 2018. Accessed July 23, 2024. https://www.bbc.com/news/world-europe-43581449.

McGreal, Chris. "UN Security Council Is Failing Syria, Ban Ki-moon Admits." *The Guardian*, September 7, 2015. Accessed July 20, 2024. https://www.theguardian.com/world/2015/sep/07/un-security-council-is-failing-syria-ban-ki-moon.

Michaelson, Ruth. "Bashar al-Assad Reported to Have Fled Syria as Rebels Say They Have Captured Damascus." *The Guardian*, December 8, 2024. Accessed December 9, 2024. https://www.theguardian.com/world/2024/dec/08/bashar-al-assad-reported-to-have-fled-syria-as-rebels-say-they-have-captured-damascus.

Lam, Nam, and Laura Silver. *Americans Name China as the Country Posing the Greatest Threat to the U.S.* Pew Research Center, 2023. https://www.pewresearch.org/short-reads/2023/07/27/americans-name-china-as-the-country-posing-the-greatest-threat-to-the-us/.

Laub, Zachary. *Syria's Civil War: The Descent Into Horror.* Council on Foreign Relations, 2023. https://www.cfr.org/article/syrias-civil-war.

Lee Myers, Stephan, and Ellen Barry. "Putin Reclaims Crimea for Russia and Bitterly Denounces the West." *The New York Times*, March 19, 2014. https://www.nytimes.com/2014/03/19/world/europe/ukraine.html.

Lederer, Edith M. "UN Security Council Fails Again to Address Israel-Hamas War, Rejecting US and Russian Resolutions." *AP News*, August 2, 2023. https://apnews.com/article/un-israel-hamas-war-resolutions-russia-us-546b4b7867e3db3e769775c9e93685dc.

Loft, Philip, and Esme Kirk-Wade. *The Syrian Civil War: Timeline and Statistics.* House of Commons Library, 2022. https://researchbriefings.files.parliament.uk/documents/CBP-9381/CBP-9381.pdf.

Putin, Vladimir. "Speech at the Munich Security Conference 2007." February 10, 2007. http://en.kremlin.ru/events/president/transcripts/copy/24034.

Rank, Hugh. "Analyzing Political Rhetoric." *The English Journal* 69, no. 9 (1980): 38–43.

Saarinen, Merja. "Näin Kiina Otti Niskalenkin Euroopasta." *Helsingin Sanomat*, August 4, 2022. https://www.hs.fi/visio/art-2000009098766.html.

S/PV.6627. 6627th meeting of the UNSC. 2011. https://www.securitycouncilreport.org/un-documents/document/golan-heights-s-pv-6627.php.

S/PV.7634. 7634th meeting of the UNSC. 2016. https://www.securitycouncilreport.org/un-documents/document/spv7634-1.php.

S/PV.7785. 7785th meeting of the UNSC. 2016. https://www.securitycouncilreport.org/un-documents/document/spv7785.php.

S/PV.7798. 7798th meeting of the UNSC. 2016. https://daccess-ods.un.org/tmp/1972833.87184143.html.

S/PV.7815. 7815th meeting of the UNSC. 2016. https://www.securitycouncilreport.org/un-documents/document/spv7815.php.

S/PV.7825. 7825th meeting of the UNSC. 2016. https://www.securitycouncilreport.org/un-documents/document/spv7825.php.

S/PV.7855. 7855th meeting of the UNSC. 2016. https://daccess-ods.un.org/tmp/9413997.53093719.html.

S/PV.8817. 8817th meeting of the UNSC. 2021. https://documents-dds-ny.un.org/doc/UNDOC/GEN/N21/184/35/PDF/N2118435.pdf?OpenElement.

S/RES/1973. UNSC resolution 1973. 2011. https://www.un.org/securitycouncil/s/res/1973-%282011%29.

S/RES/2268. UNSC resolution 2268. 2011 https://documents.un.org/doc/undoc/gen/n16/053/63/pdf/n1605363.pdf.

S/RES/2314. UNSC resolution 2314. 2016. https://documents.un.org/doc/undoc/gen/n16/352/05/pdf/n1635205.pdf.

S/RES/2319. UNSC resolution 2319. 2016 https://documents.un.org/doc/undoc/gen/n16/392/13/pdf/n1639213.pdf.

S/RES/2336. UNSC resolution 2336. 2016. https://documents.un.org/doc/undoc/gen/n17/000/38/pdf/n1700038.pdf.

S/RES/2585. UNSC resolution 2585. 2021. https://documents.un.org/doc/undoc/gen/n21/186/72/pdf/n2118672.pdf.

Tarquinio, J. Alex. “The U.N. Security Council’s Default Is Deadlock.” *Foreign Policy*. Retrieved August 14, 2024. https://foreignpolicy.com/2024/04/02/un-security-council-deadlock-gaza-cease-fire-ukraine-russia/.

Trenin, Dmitri. *The Ukraine Crisis and the Resumption of Great-Power Rivalry*. Carnegie Moscow Center, 2014. https://carnegieendowment.org/files/ukraine_great_power_rivalry2014.pdf.

UN Human Rights Office. “UN Human Rights Office Estimates More Than 306,000 Civilians Were Killed Over 10 Years in Syria Conflict.” June 28, 2022. https://www.ohchr.org/en/press-releases/2022/06/un-human-rights-office-estimates-more-306000-civilians-were-killed-over-10.

UNICEF. “Hitting Rock Bottom: Children’s Suffering in Syria at Its Worst.” 2017. https://www.unicef.org/armenia/en/node/296.

UN News. “Security Council Fails to Adopt Resolutions on Ending Violence in War-Torn Syria’s Eastern Aleppo.” October 8, 2016. https://news.un.org/en/story/2016/10/542262.

UN News. “At Security Council, UN Humanitarian Official Flags ‘Catastrophic’ Situation in Syria Despite Eastern Aleppo Evacuations.” December 23, 2016. https://news.un.org/en/story/2016/12/548502-security-council-un-humanitarian-official-flags-catastrophic-situation-syria.

UN News. “Syria: UN Envoy Welcomes New Ceasefire Between Government and Opposition Groups.” December 29, 2016. https://news.un.org/en/story/2016/12/548652.

United Nations Security Council. “What Is the Security Council?” n.d. https://www.un.org/securitycouncil/content/what-security-council.

US Department of Defense. *Quadrennial Defense Review Report*. 2006. https://history.defense.gov/Portals/70/Documents/quadrennial/QDR2006.pdf?ver=2014-06-25-111017-150.

Visala, Hanna. “Kiinalla On Uusi Taktiikka Afrikassa: Lainoja Annetaan Anteeksi 17 Maalle ja Velkoja Kuitataan Tietulleilla.” *YLE*. 2022. https://yle.fi/a/3-12597013.

Von Einsiedel, Sebastian, Malone, David M. Malone, and Bruno Stagno Ugarte. *The UN Security Council in an Age of Great Power Rivalry*. United Nations University Working Paper Series 4 (2015): 1–25.

Walker, Shaun. “Syria Ceasefire Appears to Hold After Rivals Sign Russia-Backed Deal.” *The Guardian*, December 29, 2016. https://www.theguardian.com/world/2016/dec/29/syrian-government-and-rebels-have-signed-ceasefire-agreement-says-putin.

Westcott, Ben, and Steven Jiang. “China Is Embracing a New Brand of Foreign Policy. Here’s What Wolf Warrior Diplomacy Means.” *CNN*, May 28, 2020. https://edition.cnn.com/2020/05/28/asia/china-wolf-warrior-diplomacy-intl-hnk/index.htm.

The White House. *National Security Strategy of the United States of America*, 2017. https://trumpwhitehouse.archives.gov/wp-content/uploads/2017/12/NSS-Final-12-18-2017-0905.pdf.

CHAPTER 5

A Crystal Ball for Great Power Plays? Predicting Council Vetoes Through Machine Learning

Breanna N. Cross

1 Introduction

While the United Nations (UN) is a direct reflection of liberal internationalist aspirations, the veto survives as a mechanism for achieving the realist aspirations of the five permanent members (the "P5"). The veto has the dual ability to enable the establishment and maintenance of international peace and security *and* block any meaningful or effective action in pursuit of the same. However, while it is one of the most criticised aspects of the Security Council (UNSC), there has been limited research dedicated to investigating any regularities related to the use of the veto, or in other words, whether the prediction of the veto follows previously observed patterns. Specifically, researchers have yet to fully

B. N. Cross (✉)
Universiteit Leiden, Leiden, The Netherlands
e-mail: b.n.cross@fgga.leidenuniv.nl

M. O. Hosli et al. (eds.), *Multilateralism and the United Nations Security Council*, https://doi.org/10.1007/978-3-031-85320-3_5

explore whether there are inherent characteristics related to (1) the resolutions themselves, (2) the states[1] that are the subject of the resolution, or (3) these topic states' bilateral relations with the P5 that may serve as powerful predictors for whether the veto is exercised. There are several obvious case studies related to the use of the veto, such as the relationship between the United States ("U.S.") and Israel, which has garnered intense speculation and criticism (O'Dell, 2023). However, not all resolutions related to Israel have been vetoed by the U.S., which calls into question what are the predictors for the use of the veto, if it is not simply based upon the state(s) in question within a resolution. Thus, the extent to which the use of the veto within the UNSC could be predicted was investigated.

A predictive modelling approach can reveal the differing factors or issues that each permanent member considers when utilising its veto. Permanent members may consider a multitude of factors or, alternatively, they may give similar weight to the same factors as each other when utilizing the veto. Therefore, while a single predictive model applying to the entire P5 could be beneficial, a more thorough and insightful approach should comprise the creation of a predictive model for *each* permanent member. This allows the models to be tailored to any specific cultural, political, economic, and geographic considerations that may affect each member's veto. For this specific approach, the U.S. and Russia, who constitute the two permanent members most divergent in their voting patterns and worldviews, were modelled. Creating separate models enables the identification and comparison of the predictors (and their weights) between the members, providing insight into whether these predictors potentially overlap or diverge. It was surmised that if permanent members operate upon an objective evaluation when considering the utilisation of their veto, the predictors within both models should be (close to) identical in both type and strength. However, if members utilise the veto to protect, "block", or stall measures that may be detrimental to their national interests or allies as critics suggest, the predictors should widely vary in type and strength between models, highlighting the diverging interests and considerations that each member prioritises. Thus, widely diverging predictor types and weights would have negative

[1] The states that are the subject of the resolutions are referred to as "topic states". They are either addressed directly within a resolution's title or body or are the subject of a directive within a resolution by the Council.

implications for the current functioning of the UNSC, indicating that the P5 fail to act cohesively and objectively when utilising their veto, thus providing support for current criticisms towards the actions of the permanent members and immediate calls for reform.

2 The Veto's Divisiveness

To appease the major power players, the creators of the UN, in seeking to establish a new liberal world order, were required to adopt mechanisms within their idealist and liberal institutional framework that are inherently realist in nature, and which allow the P5 to pursue their competitive interests at the risk of undermining the institution's purpose. Thus, to pursue liberalist aspirations, aspects of realism needed to remain, and the UNSC reflects the aspects of these competing international traditions through the existence of the veto (Derviş, 2005, p. 58; Fidler, 1996, p. 415). Unbeknownst at the time, the creators of the UN also established the institution with a rigid and unrealistic threshold for its decision-making processes, including those related to institutional change (Hosli & Dörfler, 2017, p. 38). For example, amendments to the Charter require concurrent vetoes from all five permanent members (United Nations art. 108), an extremely high threshold for change in a period of highly polarized politics. In alignment with path-dependency theory, and in seeking to preserve the institution's purpose and its creators' preferences (i.e., their superior positioning), this high threshold for change now acts as a blockade to implementing institutional transformations that are required for the UN to achieve its stated goals in an ever-changing international environment (Hosli & Dörfler, 2017, p. 38). The P5 successfully cemented their political advantage within the UNSC's framework along with a means of protection (the veto) to prevent their institutional position from ever waning, resulting in the current dilemma where they are free to pursue their ends if they wish, much to the frustration of other UN member states. This has resulted in heavy criticism related to the domination of P5 national interests within the UNSC, and the prevalence of realist aspirations of the P5 over the liberal ideals of the UN when it comes to approved (or vetoed) Council measures (Wouters & Rhys, 2005, pp. 14; 18).

Unsurprisingly, the veto has remained one of the most critical topics during discussions on UNSC reform and is the subject of criticism from governments, civil societies, and academia alike. While earlier critics argued for complete abolishment, efforts have shifted to urging voluntary restraint by the P5 on issues related to atrocity crimes, such as genocide and crimes against humanity (Rashkow, 2022, pp. 441–445). Rather than arguing for veto renouncement simply based on ethical principles, recent efforts have focused on framing the issue of veto restraint not just through the framework of the UN Charter, but also customary international law, the 1949 Geneva Conventions, and other international treaties (Rashkow, 2022, pp. 444–445). In line with the realist assumptions of state behaviour, the P5 have either renounced, brushed over, or avoided discussions related to the abolishment or voluntary restraint. Contrary to the spirit of liberalism, they have expressed little interest in relinquishing their ability to pursue their national interests at the expense of the UN's liberal internationalist goals and their mandate as permanent members of the UNSC, albeit through politically acceptable phrasing (Rashkow, 2022, pp. 441; 443; *General Assembly Debates Security Council's Rising Veto Use*, 2024).

Another common critique is the veto's inherent undemocratic structure in relation to the total number of UN member states (193 total member states) and the proportion of states that hold the veto relative to this number (five permanent members) (Strand & Rapkin, 2010, p. 773). Nevertheless, the permanent membership structure and current procedural rules governing possession and of the veto power have remained unchanged since the institution's inception. It is extremely unlikely that the P5's attitudes will change in the near future, as they have remained opposed to the idea of veto reform for almost eighty years, and the argument for restraint has been accepted only slightly better (Rashkow, 2022, pp. 441). Additionally, the idea of permanent member expansion has been tentatively discussed, with the permanent members cautioning that an overexpansion of permanent membership would undermine Council "efficiency and effectiveness", increasing the potential for deadlock (Rashkow, 2022, pp. 439–440). Furthermore, UNSC expansion would still need the consent of all five permanent members. Thus, any efforts to reform the veto power framework regarding the number of wielders, its usage, or its mere existence will likely be met with unyielding opposition from those who currently benefit from it.

Criticisms of the UNSC's structure have resulted in a large consensus that it is losing legitimacy, and drastic reforms are needed to remedy this decline (Derviş, 2005, p. 59; Hosli & Dörfler, 2017, p. 35; Strand & Rapkin, 2010, p. 773). Critics question permanent members' abilities to see beyond their own national interests, and effectively act in a timely manner on issues that do not directly benefit or threaten those interests. However, the most recent attempt to reform the UNSC occurred under the leadership of Secretary-General Kofi Annan (1997–2006). The two proposed reform models completely excluded any alteration to the veto power (Soderberg, 2015, p. 42). To implement UNSC reform, a majority consisting of two-thirds of member states and the consent of all permanent members are required (United Nations art. 108). And while the desirability for reform is not lacking, there has never been a proposal that has come close to garnering enough votes (Hosli & Dörfler, 2017, p. 36; Soderberg, 2015, p. 42). For example, the strong opposition by African states towards prior proposals has been rooted in their position that effective reform would either eliminate the veto entirely or new permanent members would possess the veto; the current arrangement would not suffice (Soderberg, 2015, p. 42). Since this push for reform under Annan, there has been no meaningful movement on the issue of the veto or UNSC reform in general, and the status quo remains.

3 Conceptualising National Interest(s)

Certain predictors included within the models potentially reflect various manifestations of the "national interest(s)" of a permanent member. There is an inherent tension between permanent members' responsibility to execute their mandate and the potential use of the veto to protect their own "national interest(s)" at the expense of their mandate. Thus, the P5 are faced with a unique dilemma: At their core, they are individual states, but they possess a unique position within the international order which, at times, must be prioritised over their own domestic interests. However, the P5 have not always prioritised their mandate. The use of the veto to protect their "national interest(s)" is a common criticism of the UNSC (Wouters & Rhys, 2005, pp. 14–15), and there are clear historical examples where the veto has been utilised to prioritise national interests and alliances, as well as shield permanent members from effective action (Wouters & Rhys, 2005, pp. 14–17).

Even still, how a state's "national interests" manifest materially, politically, or otherwise depends on the state itself and the historical and political context of the period in which the state exists. "National interest(s)" can manifest in various forms (economic, military, political, cultural, etc.) depending on what the state defines as their "national interest(s)" at a particular moment. Additionally, given the interconnected nature of the state system in the twenty-first century through technological advancements and globalisation, it is not surprising that preserving national interests is now intertwined with a state's success in other areas, such as its foreign policy objectives. For example, Russia outlined their national interests in 2023 which focuses on (1) preventing growing influence from Western states (namely, the U.S.), (2) preserving its sovereignty and territorial integrity as well as the sovereignty and territorial integrity of *other* states, and (3) providing "assistance to Russian allies and partners" regardless of recognition or inclusion in international organisations, among many others (The Ministry of Foreign Affairs for the Russian Federation, 2023). Similarly, the U.S. outlined its national interest objectives under the Biden administration in 2022, focusing on (1) the promotion of democratic values both domestically and internationally, (2) challenging authoritarian governments who possess revisionist foreign policy agendas, (3) deepening economic partnerships with emerging economies, and (4) strengthening its bilateral treaty and NATO alliances, among many others (President of the United States, 2022, pp. 8; 15; 17; 44).

4 Predictive Modelling in Political Science

While predictive modelling has been utilised extensively in the economic, medical, and financial industries to predict phenomena such as fraud detection, credit card risk, and biomarker identification (IBM, n.d.), the political science community has been less enthusiastic towards its adoption. The majority of political empirical research utilises model-based associations to explain phenomena (Druckman et al. 2006, as cited in Cranmer & Desmarais, 2017, p. 145). In inferential modelling, a theoretical model is operationalised into a statistical model with the coefficients being the most important element for model and hypothesis evaluation (Cranmer & Desmarais, 2017, p. 146). Conversely, predictive modelling focuses solely on the performance of the model in question rather than the parameters surrounding the choice of predictors included (Cranmer & Desmarais, 2017, p. 146). Rather than investigating theoretical assumptions about the relationship between variables, it utilises machine learning to identify patterns between predictors and outcomes through computation (Hegelich, 2016, p. 99). Utilising predictive models as a complementary approach to inferential studies enables researchers to potentially discover previously unknown patterns within complex data that would not be possible through traditional inferential modelling on its own (Cranmer & Desmarais, 2017, p. 148), possibly revealing new avenues for research. While inferential approaches may introduce bias due to the investigative process being driven by the interests of the researcher (such as the inclusion or exclusion of specific data), machine learning takes a more practical approach, with the data taken as a "given" without any assumptions (Hegelich, 2016, p. 99). Nevertheless, bias still may exist within the data itself, potentially leading to unreliable and inaccurate predictions as well as feedback loops that reinforce this bias (Rogers & Jonker, n.d.). Machine learning might also reveal patterns within the data that are "nonintuitive" or potentially overlooked when utilising inferential methodologies (Hegelich, 2016, p. 99). Additionally, predictive modelling allows the researcher to understand the weight of each variable's contribution to the model's performance (Cranmer & Desmarais, 2017, p. 149) which is not possible in inferential approaches.

5 Methodology

The data constituted 2800 draft resolutions voted upon between January 1, 1960, and December 31, 2023. The time period encompasses over six decades and covers various political alliances, shifting power relations, and multiple interstate and intra-state conflicts that directly relate to the Council's mandate to maintain "international peace and security". Predictive models for the U.S. and Russia were developed, as these states reflect the strongest divisions in ideologies within the P5, especially with regard to issues such as state sovereignty and territorial integrity, foreign intervention, human rights, and humanitarian aid, among others. The selected predictors (totalling 4,428) comprise both "internal" and "external" predictors. "Internal" predictors are inherent to the resolutions as a product of the Council, such as their text, date, and authorship. "External" predictors fall into two categories: (1) characteristics of the topic state(s) within a resolution; and (2) the bilateral relations between the topic state and the permanent member. These "external" predictors may influence the use of the veto from outside the Council, such as when a permanent exercises its veto power to potentially shield a political or economic ally from punishment. The predictors selected are listed below.

- Resolution Decade (*Resolution_Decade*)
- Authorship by One or Multiple Permanent Members (P5_Author)
- Number of Permanent Member Authors (P5_Number)
- Resolution Authorship by a Specific Permanent Member
    - Resolution Authorship by the U.S. (*US_Author*)
    - Resolution Authorship by the U.K. (*UK_Author*)
    - Resolution Authorship by France (*France_Author*)
    - Resolution Authorship by China (*China_Author*)
    - Resolution Authorship by Russia (*Russia_Author*)
- Resolution Text (Individual Terms)
- Topic State in Resolution (*Topic_State*)
- Topic State's Total Population (*Population*)
- Topic State's Total Geographic Area (*Land_Area*)
- Topic State's Geographic Location
    - Topic State Continent (*Continent*)
    - Topic State Sub-Region (*Sub_Region*)
- Topic State's Total Military Personnel (*Military_Personnel*)
- Topic State's Total Military Expenditure (*Military_Expenditure*)
- Topic State's Energy Commodities (*Energy*)
- Topic State's Iron and Steel Production (*Iron_Steel*)
- Topic State's Political Regime (*Political_Regime*)
- Topic State's Terrorism Prevalence (*Terrorist_Attacks*)
- Topic State's Gross Domestic Product (*GDP*)
- Level of Imports to Permanent Member from Topic State (*US_Import* and *Russia_Import*)
- Level of Exports to Topic State from Permanent Member (*US_Export* and *Russia_Export*)
- Diplomatic Relations Between a Permanent Member and the Topic State
    - Type of Diplomatic Focus of a Permanent Member in Topic States (*US_Diplomatic_Focus* and *Russia_Diplomatic_Focus*)
    - Type of Diplomatic Mission of Permanent Member in Topic State
    - (*US_Embassy_Presence* and *Russia_Embassy_Presence*)
    - Level of Diplomatic Representation of Permanent Member in Topic State

  - (*US_Representation_Score* and *Russia_Representation_Score*)

- Presence of Formal Alliance Between Permanent Member and Topic State
  - Entente (*US_FA_Entente* and *Russia_FA_Entente*)
  - Non-Aggression Pact (*US_FA_Nonaggression* and *Russia_FA_Nonaggression*)
  - Formal Defence Agreement (*US_FA_Defense* and *Russia_FA_Defense*)
  - Neutrality Agreement (*US_FA_Neutrality* and *Russia_FA_Neutrality*).

All "internal" predictors (resolution text, authorship, and decade) were sourced from the UN Digital Library. The resolution texts were collected manually which entailed transferring the text directly into the dataset from the corresponding online PDF. The majority of resolutions underwent optical character recognition ("OCR") to permit machine readability when loaded into the Digital Library, allowing for a direct transfer into the dataset. However, due to low image quality, the process of direct text transference was complemented by manual text entry for numerous resolutions, and a manual review and correction phase of all 2800 resolutions to correct any misspellings and formatting issues, and to remove non-text characters. Finally, due to low image quality, portions of the text for numerous resolutions could not be clearly read, as the text was erased or very faint, excluding direct text transference. Therefore, data imputation was conducted on these resolutions through manual entry of the resolution text. For the 21 predictors that reflect topic state characteristics and bilateral relations between the resolutions' topic state(s) and the U.S. or Russia, the data was collected from various public and private institutions, including the International Monetary Fund (IMF), the World Bank, and the UN, among others.[2]

[2] These sources can be found in the chart located in Appendix.

6 A Brief Overview of P5 Voting in the Council (1960–2023)

Between January 1, 1960 and December 31, 2023, 2800 draft resolutions were voted upon by the UNSC. These resolutions were: (1) adopted unanimously, (2) adopted via a majority, (3) vetoed, (4) adopted without a vote, or (5) failed to be adopted due to an insufficient number of votes. The overall voting positions for the U.S. (Fig. 1) and Russia (Fig. 2) are displayed below. Voting positions within the Council can take six forms: (1) abstain; (2) non-vote; (3) yes; (4) no (or against); (5) veto; and (6) without a vote. Note that the voting position of "no (or against)" is different from the veto, with the former serving as a form of public disagreement without blocking the resolution itself. Both the U.S. and Russia have overwhelmingly approved the majority of draft resolutions. However, the voting position prevalence concerning the other voting options varies, yet all remain low compared to resolution approval.

For voting agreement, the U.S. possesses the highest rate of voting agreement with the U.K. at 95.1%. France is second at 93.2%, and China is third at 84.8%, while Russia possesses the lowest level of voting agreement at 83.6% (Fig. 3). Conversely, Russia's voting agreement percentages were the *exact opposite*. Russia's voting agreement with China is 89.9%, its voting agreement with France is 87.1%, its voting agreement with the U.K. is 86.1%, and its voting agreement with the U.S. is 83.6% (Fig. 4). While disagreement surely exists among the P5, there is a moderately high level of voting agreement among even the most polarised members. With a voting agreement of 83.6%, the U.S. and Russia have voted similarly on 2341 draft resolutions. The remaining 459 draft resolutions were subject to different voting positions between the two members, although this does not automatically imply the veto was used. These differing positions could take a variety of forms and combinations (such as "yes" and "abstain", or "non-vote" and "abstain"), and do not necessarily imply complete polarisation on the subject(s) of these resolutions.

7 The Veto at a Glance

During this period, the P5 exercised their veto power on 152 draft resolutions, equating to an overall veto usage rate of 5.42% (see Fig. 5). The U.S. was the highest user of the veto at 84 instances (3% of all drafts).

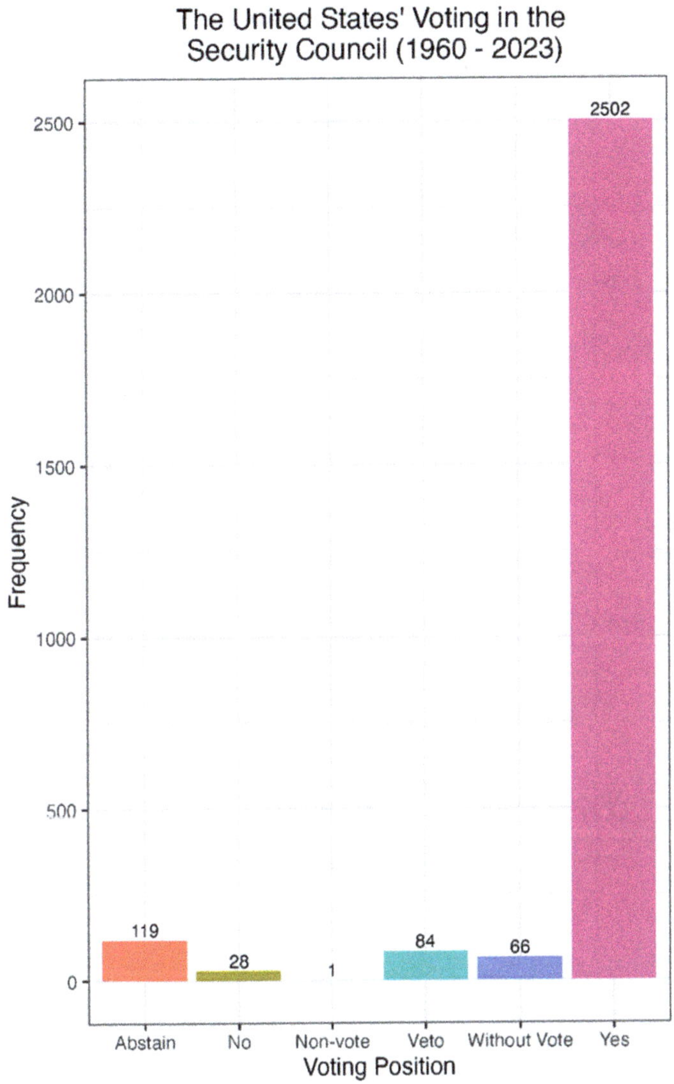

Fig. 1 Bar graph showing the voting position distribution for the United States from January 1, 1960 to December 31, 2023

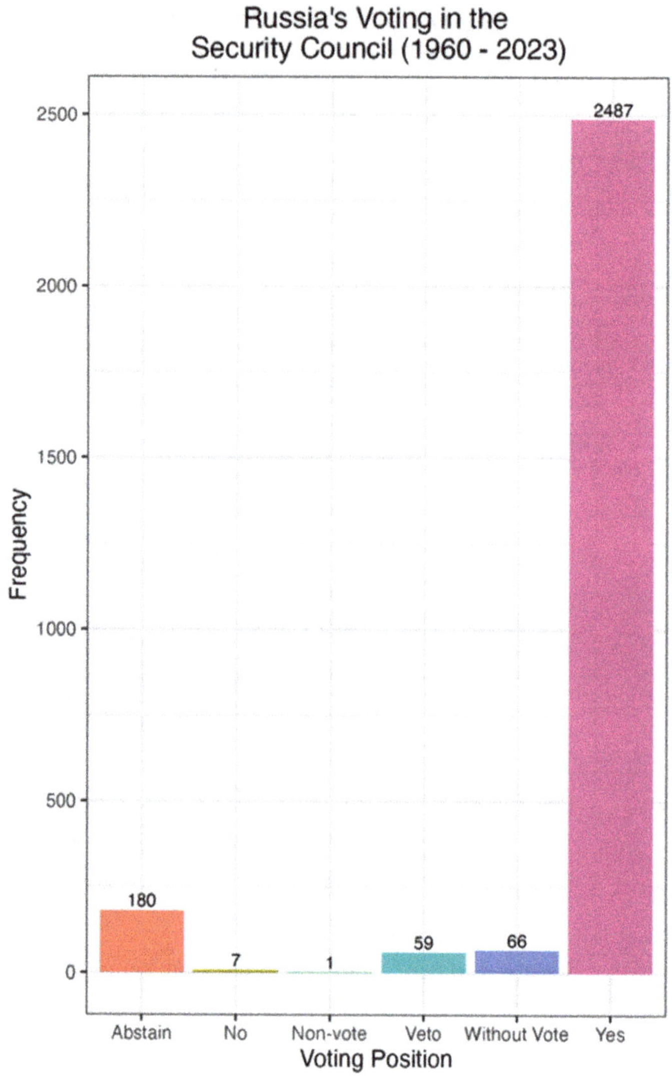

Fig. 2 Bar graph showing the voting position distribution for Russia from January 1, 1960 to December 31, 2023

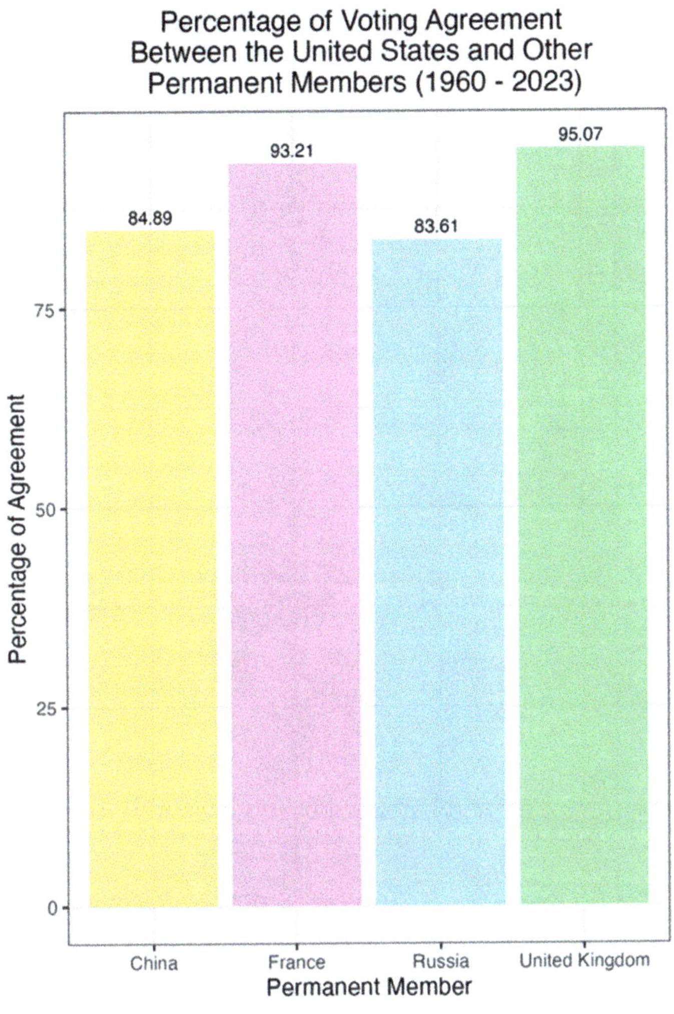

Fig. 3 Bar graph displaying the percentages of voting agreement (i.e., instances where the two members voted the same) between the United States and other permanent members from January 1, 1960 to December 31, 2023

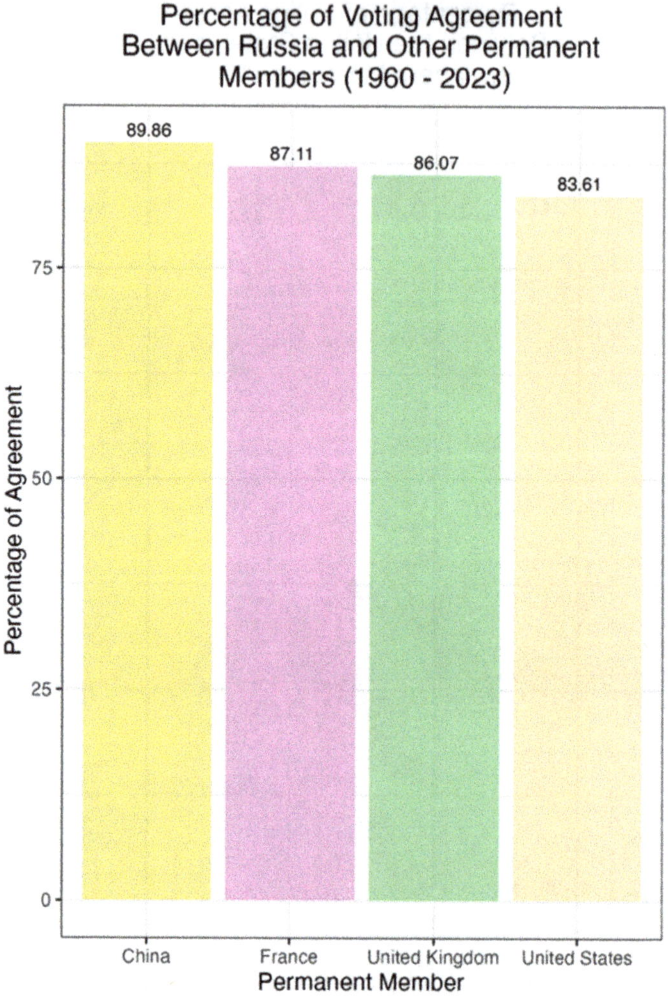

Fig. 4 Bar graph displaying the percentages of voting agreement (i.e., instances where the two members voted the same) between the Russia and other permanent members from January 1, 1960 to December 31, 2023

Russia was the second-highest user at 59 instances (2.1% of all drafts). The U.K. was the third-highest user at 27 instances (0.96% of all drafts), and China was the fourth-highest user at 18 instances (0.64% of all draft resolutions). France is the permanent member that utilised the veto power the least at 14 instances (0.5% of all drafts). The use of the veto by each permanent member is displayed in Fig. 6.

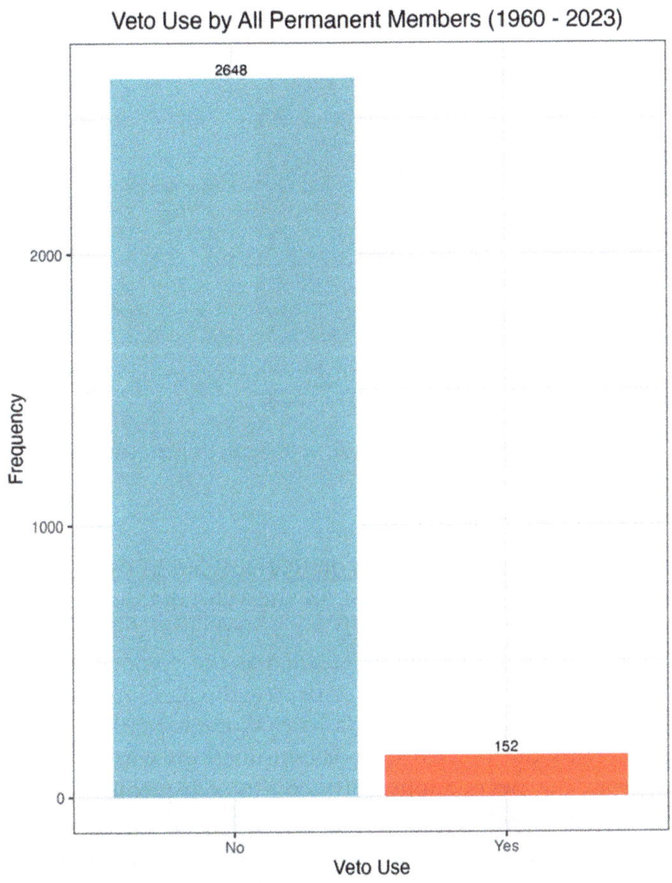

Fig. 5 Bar graph showing all resolutions vetoed by a permanent member from January 1, 1960 to December 31, 2023. This does not reflect the use of the veto by individual members or the occurrences of double- or triple-vetoes

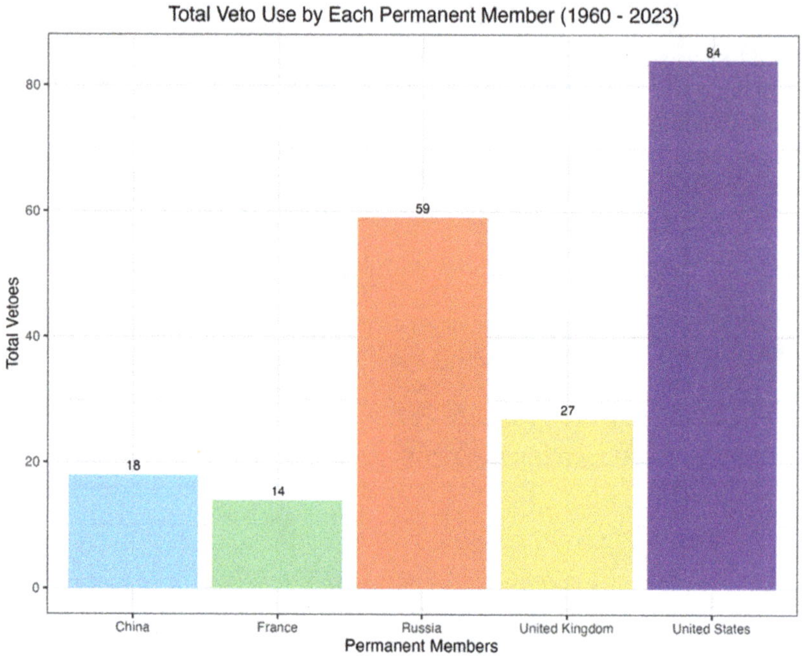

Fig. 6 Bar graph showing the use of the veto by each permanent member from January 1, 1960 to December 31, 2023

Although the veto's prevalence is quite low at 5.42% over 63 years, the data only reflects the affirmative use of the veto and does not consider incidents where a draft resolution was not voted upon due to its susceptibility to a veto. This phenomenon, labelled as the "hidden veto", occurs when a permanent member implies or overtly threatens to utilise the veto on a draft resolution if presented for a vote (Wouters & Rhys, 2005, p. 9). This often occurs during closed-door consultations where the public is excluded from the negotiations between Council members. The "hidden" veto is not an affirmative use of the veto and therefore, instances of this phenomenon are not officially recorded through the UN Digital Library or any other UN organ (Nahory, 2004). Additionally, due to a lack of data on the prevalence of this phenomenon during closed-door consultations and private back-channel discussions which are not subject to documentation, it has been difficult to ascertain the true effects of the "hidden veto" on the efficiency of the Council (Wouters & Rhys, 2005, p. 9). Thus, only affirmative cases of the veto were considered.

It should be noted that Russia and the U.S. have never engaged in a double-veto. A double-veto (or in the rare instance, a triple-veto) occurs when more than one permanent member vetoes the same draft resolution. Given that one veto effectively "kills" a resolution, the occurrences of a double- or triple-veto are rare and often serve to symbolise extreme disapproval of a draft resolution's subject matter. The U.S. has only ever engaged in a double- or triple-veto with the U.K. (26.2% of vetoes) and France (15.5% of vetoes) (Fig. 7). Likewise, Russia has only engaged in a double-veto with China (25.4% of vetoes) (Fig. 8). While the absolute percentages for both the U.S. and Russia are relatively low, it should be noted that vetoes constitute a rare event (Chan, 2003, p. 348), with only 152 vetoes in 64 years. Therefore, the percentage levels displayed in Figs 7 and 8 indicate a relatively high level of veto agreement when engaging in the double-veto.

The data displayed in Figs. 5, 6, 7, and 8 support the rationale behind selecting the U.S. and Russia for predictive modelling. The data reveals that there are two clear "voting blocs" within the P5 configuration, reflecting the heavily documented division between the traditional "Western powers" comprising the U.S., France, and the U.K., and the "non-Western powers" comprising Russia and China. However, the data also reveals that while there is disagreement among the P5, the veto has been used sparingly. Over 64 years of activity, there have been 2800 draft resolutions, with an average of approximately 44 draft resolutions per year voted upon. The veto has been exercised 152 times during this period, averaging approximately two vetoes per year among *all* permanent members since 1960.

Over differing decades spanning 1960 to 2023, we see different patterns in the exercise of the veto by the U.S. (Fig. 9) and Russia (Fig. 10). The majority of vetoes exercised by the U.S. are clustered in 1970–1979 and 1980–1989, while the majority of Russia's vetoes are clustered in 1960–1969, 2010–2019, and 2020–2023. This variation could be due to a variety of reasons, including ongoing issues that both states deemed worthy of the veto or changes in outlook within each state's government regarding the veto. However, the highest decades for veto use by Russia and the U.S. do not overlap. Additionally, the decade for 2020–2023 only contains four years but accounts for a combined 13 vetoes between the two members. If this pattern continues, over 30

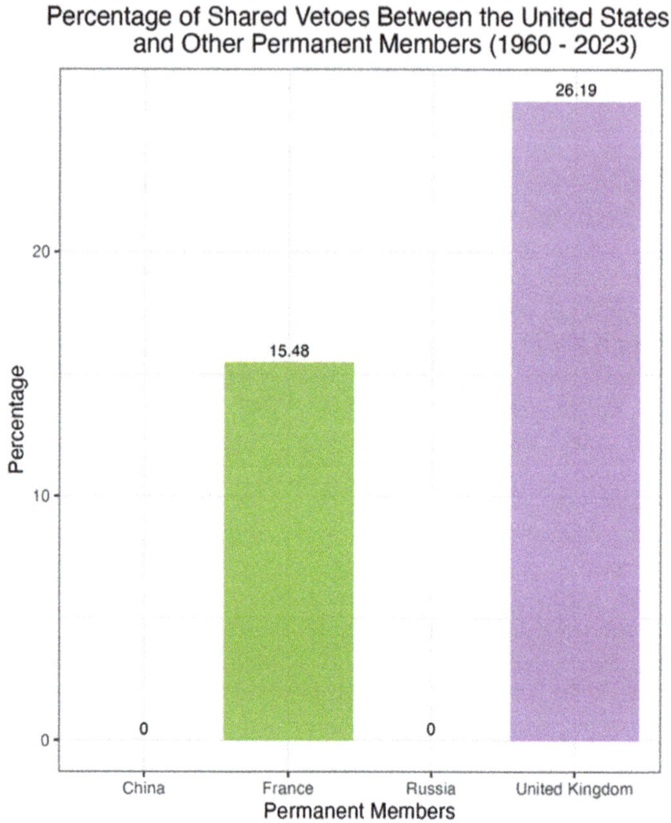

Fig. 7 Bar graph displaying the percentage of shared veto positions (i.e., instances of the double-veto or triple-veto phenomenon) between the United States and other permanent members from January 1, 1960 to December 31, 2023

vetoes will have been utilised in ten years, resulting in a veto prevalence that has not been observed since 1980–1989, which was overwhelmingly driven by Cold War politics, thus highlighting the growing divisions over the most recent issues placed before the UNSC and ideological divisions between these two permanent members.

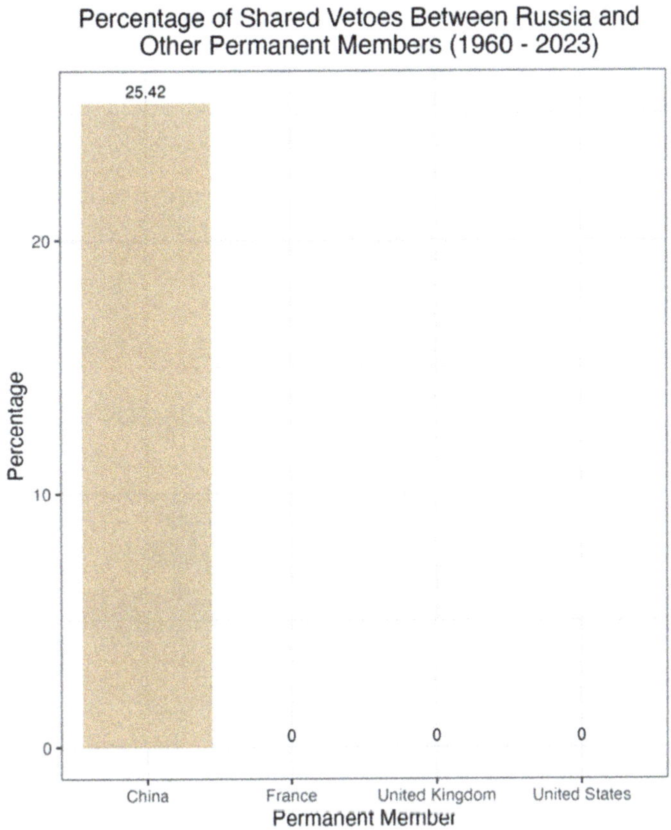

Fig. 8 Bar graph displaying the percentage of shared veto positions (i.e., instances of the double-veto phenomenon) between Russia and other permanent members from January 1, 1960 to December 31, 2023

Regarding authorship, Russia has never vetoed a resolution authored by China. Conversely, 54.2% of Russia's vetoes have applied to U.S.-authored resolutions, 47.5% of vetoes have applied to U.K.-authored resolutions, and 35.6% of vetoes have applied to France-authored resolutions (Fig. 11). This pattern aligns with the previous findings displayed in Fig. 4 (voting agreement) and Fig. 9 (shared vetoes) for Russia. Russia most often aligns ideologically and politically with China, then France and the U.K., and finally the U.S., providing support for the previously

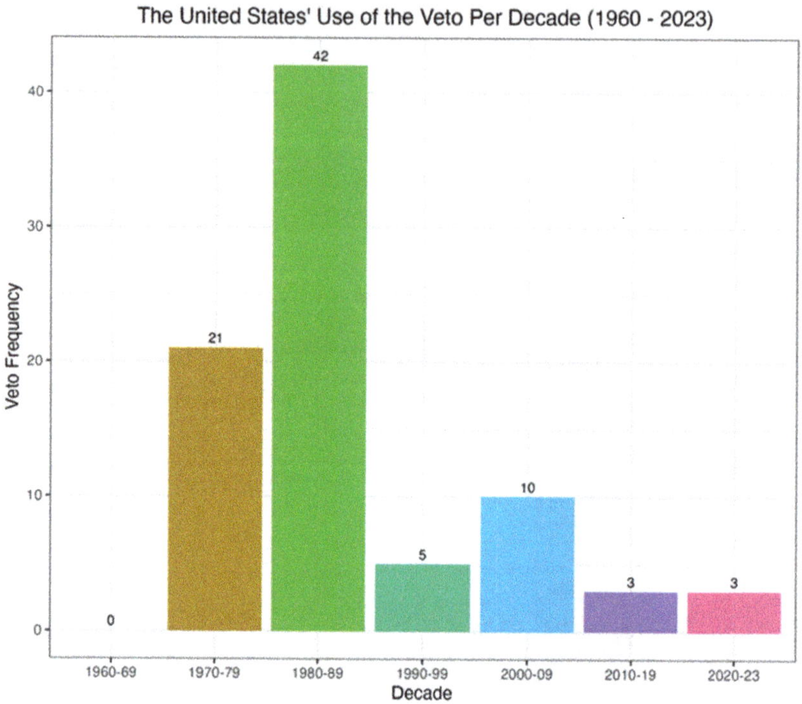

Fig. 9 Bar graph showing the frequency of the veto exercised by the United States per decade between January 1, 1960 and December 31, 2023

discussed divisions within the UNSC. Differing from Russia, the U.S. has utilised the veto on resolutions authored or co-authored by all permanent members (excluding the U.S. itself), but the percentages for each P5 author are relatively low (roughly 10% or less prevalence) (Fig. 12). The U.S. veto follows the same pattern revealed in Fig. 3 (voting agreement), with 10.7% of vetoes utilised against Russian-authored resolutions, 7.14% utilised against Chinese-authored resolutions, 3.57% utilised against France-authored resolutions, and 2.38% utilised against U.K.-authored resolutions. The findings imply that the U.S. will not avoid utilising the veto against a permanent member it considers itself to be ideologically, politically, and culturally aligned, but its veto behaviour in relation to authorship nevertheless aligns with its overall voting agreement behaviour.

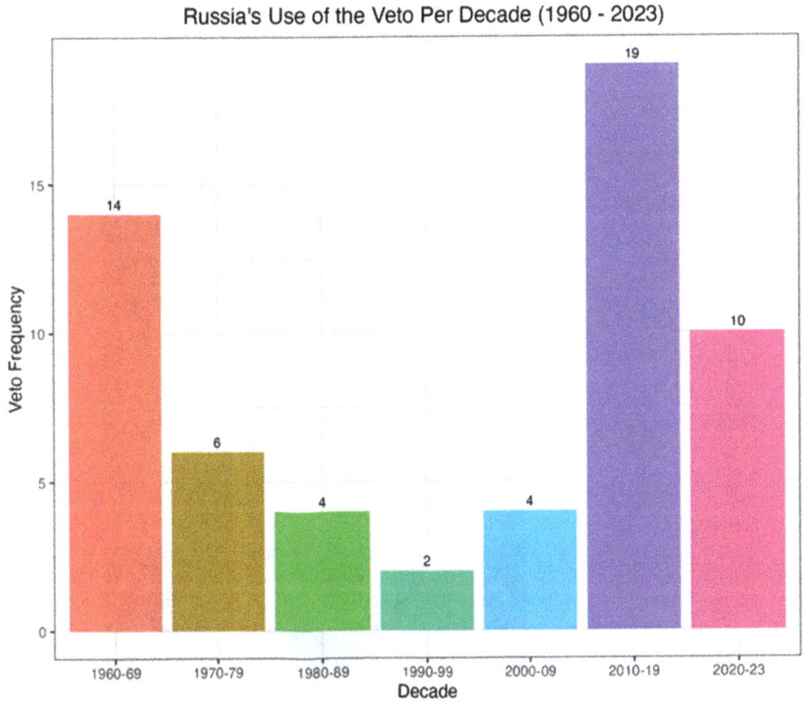

Fig. 10 Bar graph showing the frequency of the veto exercised by the Russia per decade between January 1, 1960 and December 31, 2023

8 Overview of the Predictive Modelling Approach

Random forest classification was conducted through the use of R and R Studio Version 2023.12.1 + 402. Random forest is a machine learning algorithm that utilises the outputs from numerous decision trees to create a single predictive model (IBM, n.d.). Decision trees are a suitable approach for rare event studies (such as the use of the veto in the Council) but are commonly prone to overfitting, which occurs when a model begins to follow the "noise" within the data, providing accurate predictions even when the data points deviate randomly (Frohwein & Lambert, 2000, as cited in Hegelich, 2016, pp. 105; 108; Silver, 2012, as cited in Hegelich, 2016, p. 100). In simpler terms, decision trees are

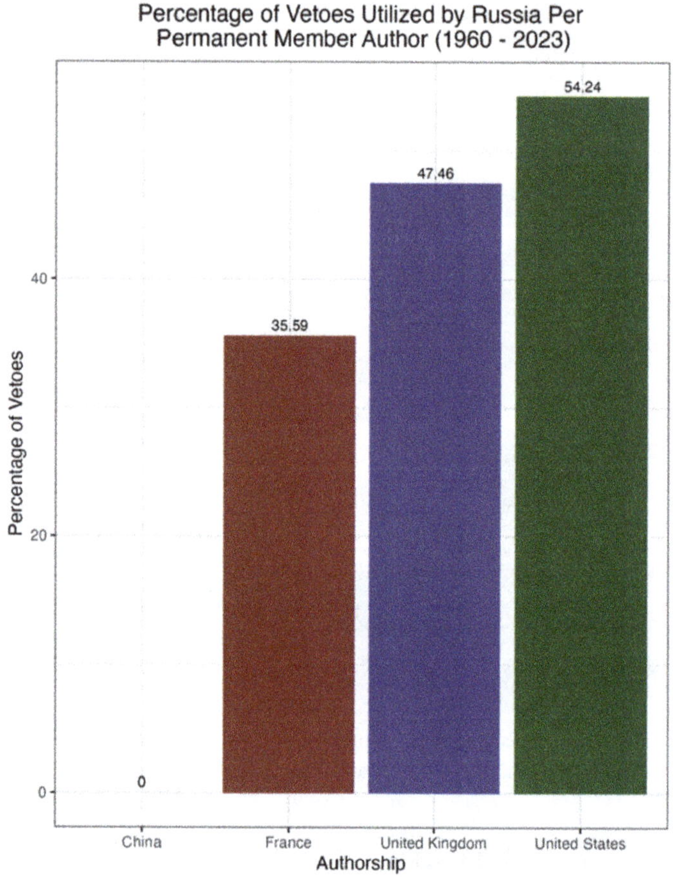

Fig. 11 Bar graph displaying the percentage of resolutions authored per permanent member that were the subject of Russia's veto between January 1, 1960 to December 31, 2023

prone to memorizing the exact training data provided, rather than general patterns within the data, resulting in issues with predictive quality when applied to new data. Random forest, which combines the outputs from a large number of individual decision trees, overcomes this shortcoming (Hegelich, 2016, p. 108). Additionally, hold-out cross-validation, which entails randomly splitting the dataset into a training set and testing set,

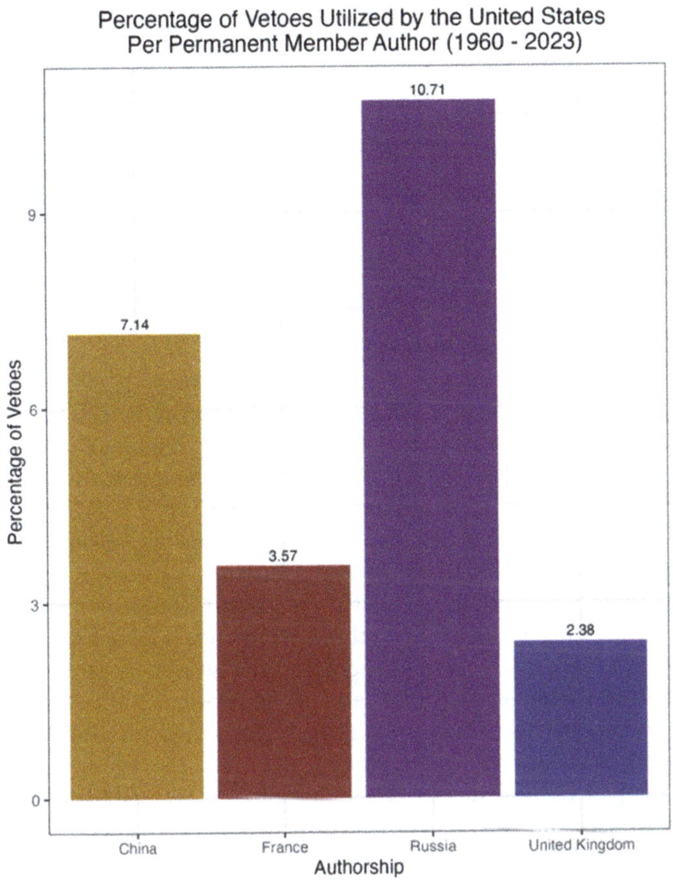

Fig. 12 Bar graph displaying the percentage of resolutions authored per permanent member that were the subject of the Unied States' veto between January 1, 1960 to December 31, 2023

was also implemented to prevent overfitting. The splitting of the dataset follows the empirically verified ratio of setting aside 70% of the data for training, with the remaining 30% used for testing; this ratio has repeatedly provided valid accuracy measures and minimal approximation errors (Gholamy et al., 2018, p. 2). Random forest *classification* was chosen due to the outcome variable—the use of the veto—being categorical and binary ("yes" or "no") (Hegelich, 2016, p. 100). Finally, the analysis was conducted in three separate stages: (1) resolution text-only predictive modelling; (2) predictive modelling using selected non-text predictors reflecting bilateral relations, state characteristics, and resolution characteristics; and (3) a "merged" predictive modelling approach combining the first and second approaches.

9 Model Hyperparameters and Evaluation Metrics

Machine learning algorithms often require the tuning of hyperparameters to optimise performance (Weerts et al., 2020, p. 1). While current software packages provide a default set of hyperparameters for random forest classification, manually tuning the hyperparameters of a model can drastically improve performance depending on the dataset's characteristics (Probst et al., 2019, p. 1; Weerts et al., 2020, p. 1). For all models, a tuneGrid of four values for three specific parameters (*mtry*, *ntree*, and *nodesize*) was pre-selected. The tuneGrid function instructs R to test each specified value for each parameter for the most effective combination to improve overall performance. The three parameters selected are central to model performance and were chosen for their sensitivity to the number of predictors within each model and to improve complexity. Furthermore, model evaluation was conducted using several metrics, including (1) predictive accuracy; (2) recall; (3) precision; (4) F1-score; and (5) Cohen's kappa coefficient (κ). These metrics are calculated through the creation of a confusion matrix, which provides a simplified overview of the "correct and false predictions versus the actual observations" (Dankers et al., 2019, p. 109). These evaluation measures were selected due to their universality when evaluating the basic performance functions in predictive modelling, and their usefulness when evaluating models that are trained and tested on highly imbalanced datasets.

10 The Text-Only Predictive Models

The first approach utilised the individual terms of the resolutions to predict the veto. This resulted in 4,400 text predictors. Language stabilisation through a manual transformation was conducted due to a change from American English to British English during the observation period, ensuring the consistency of text predictors over time. For example, the word "labor" was transformed to "labour", and the word "fulfill" was transformed to "fulfil." However, the list of terms was not exhaustive, as the words selected for transformation were collected during manual review. Because the text data is "internal" to the resolution, the data was not affected by missingness.[3] The text data was also pre-processed through:

1. The exclusion of certain forms of punctuation;
2. The exclusion of terms that appear within the dataset less than five times;
3. The exclusion of unnecessary white space;
4. The transformation of terms to lowercase;
5. The exclusion of numbers; and
6. The exclusion of stop words.

The prediction accuracy for the U.S. text-only model is 0.987, indicating an extremely high level of accuracy (a value of 1.00 is equivalent perfect accuracy). The model's recall measured 1.00, indicating that the model successfully avoided predicting false negatives. However, only 32 of 46 positive veto cases were predicted accurately, indicating the model performed fairly well, but not very well in its prediction of the veto. The model's F1-score measured 0.99, indicating that the model was reliable in its overall predictions. However, this level of accuracy and reliability is highly skewed, as the model was most accurate at predicting *negative* cases of the veto (i.e., the absence of a veto), and only succeeded in predicting 70% of positive cases, indicating strong predictive strength. Consistent with the interpretation method formulated by McHugh (2012), Cohen's kappa coefficient (κ) measured 0.81, indicating the model performed strongly when compared to random chance.

The accuracy for the Russian model measured 0.98, indicating a high level of predictive accuracy. The model's recall measured 1.00, indicating that the model is perfect at avoiding false negatives. The model's F1-score also measured 0.99, indicating that the model is very reliable. However, similar to the model for the U.S., the Russian model's predictive success heavily rests on its accuracy in predicting *negative* cases of

[3] Some of the annexes to the resolutions were not included in the text data. This decision was based upon the annexes' lack of applicability to the substance of the main body of the resolution.

the veto, as it only accurately predicted approximately 8 of 25 positive cases (approximately 30%), indicating poor predictive strength. Cohen's kappa coefficient (κ) measured 0.47, indicating that the model performed weakly when compared to random chance.

Figures 13 and 14 show the thirty highest-weighted terms for the U.S. and Russia, respectively. The higher the mean decrease in the Gini coefficient for a predictor, the more important a predictor is within the model. The highest-weighted terms completely differ between the U.S. and Russia. However, the terms themselves are expected for both states and conform to historically observed patterns for these two permanent members. While terms such as "*Israeli*", "*occupied*", and "*Jerusalem*" serve as strong predictors for the U.S., terms such as "*Syria*", "*Russian*", "*Ukraine*", and "*cross-line*" (a term associated with cross-border aid assistance) serve as strong predictors for Russia. Most notably, they do not share *any* highly weighted text predictors. This finding reveals that there is a complete divergence between the U.S. and Russia when considering the use of the veto, indicating that each member's deliberations are strongly driven by each permanent member's subjective interpretation of the issue before them, as well as their own political, economic, and cultural ideologies. These findings reveal a complete lack of consensus on *how* the veto should be utilised and *what for*, providing further evidence that the long-standing divisions within the UNSC have resulted in the complete absence of common ground between two of the largest power players in the international arena in relation to the most powerful mechanism within the arsenal of a permanent member.

11 The Non-Text Predictor Models

For each model, the number of predictors totalled 28 and encompassed the predictors related to bilateral relations, topic state characteristics, and resolution characteristics. The predictors for *US_Author* and *Russia_Author* were excluded from their respective state's models, as it is assumed a permanent member will not exercise their veto on their own resolution. The non-text predictor model for the U.S. performed poorly compared to its text-only counterpart. The measure for overall accuracy remained extremely high at 0.96. However, the accuracy reflects the model's ability to correctly predict negative cases, as the model correctly predicted only 3 of 46 positive cases, indicating extremely weak predictive strength. Cohen's kappa coefficient (κ) measured 0.11, indicating the performance

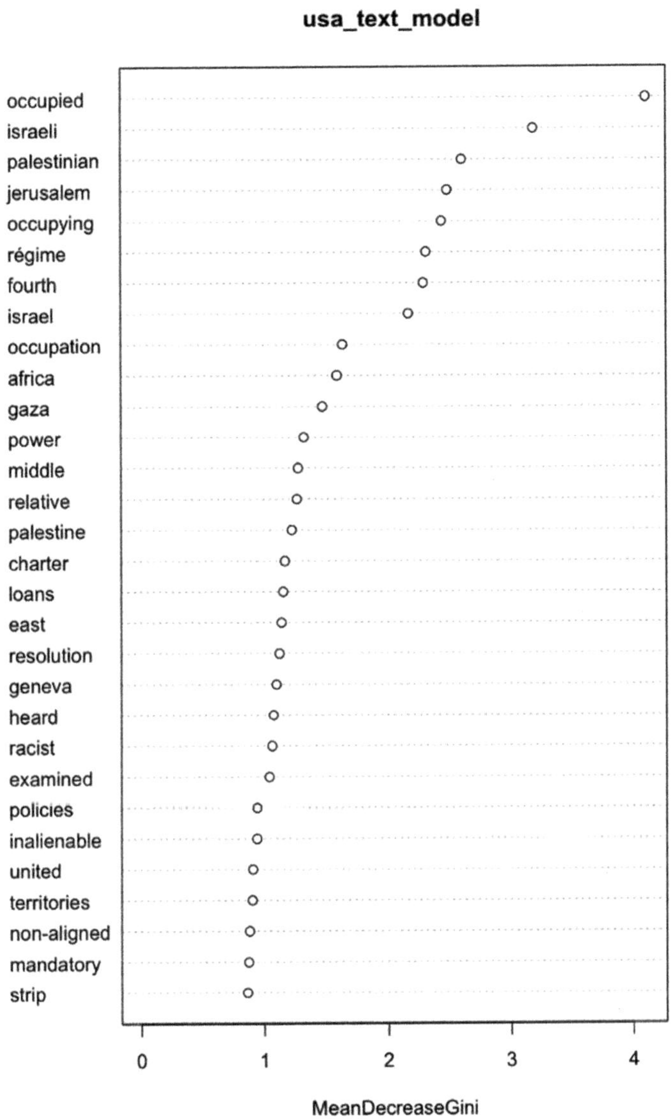

Fig. 13 Plot of thirty highest-weighted terms within the text-only predictive model for the United States

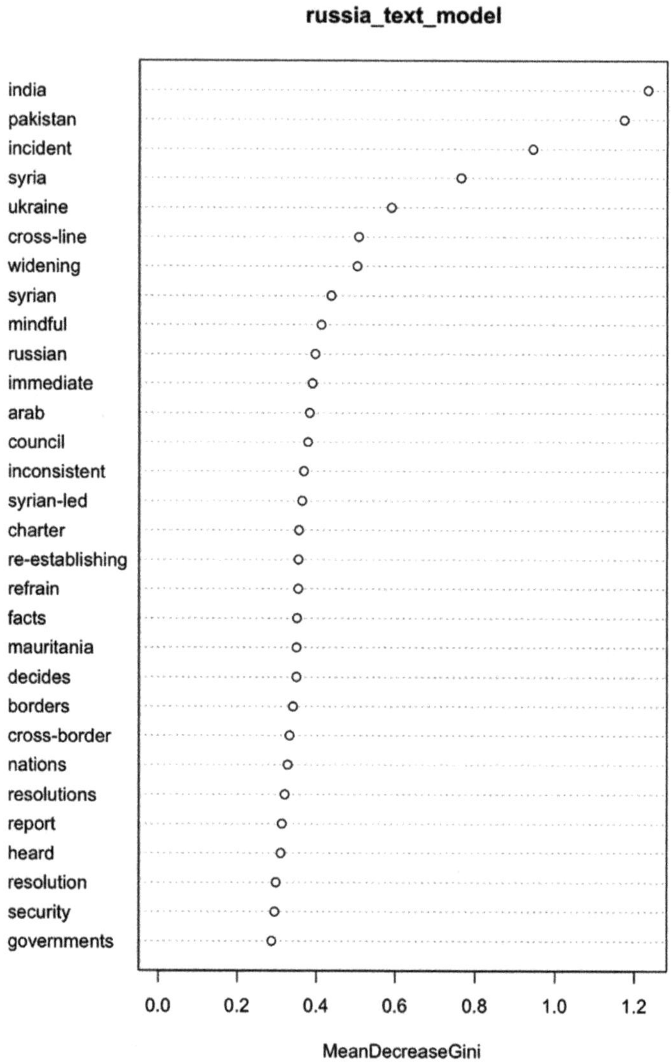

Fig. 14 Plot of thirty highest-weighted terms within the text-only predictive model for Russia

is not much better than if the model's results were generated through random chance. The non-text predictor model for Russia performed even more poorly. With an overall accuracy of 0.97, the model was perfectly accurate (100%) at predicting negative cases of the veto. However, the model did not predict *any* positive cases correctly, while predicting 25 false positives. Additionally, Cohen's kappa coefficient (κ) is equal to 0.00, indicating the model performs no better than random chance in its predictions. Overall, both models are inadequate for predicting the veto.

12 The "Merged" Predictive Models

The "merged" models for the U.S. and Russia (Figs 15 and 16, respectively) combine both text and non-text predictors that were utilised in the first and second modelling phases. For each model, the number of predictors totalled 4428. For the U.S. "merged" model the prediction accuracy for the model is 0.99, indicating an extremely high level of predictive accuracy. The model performed perfectly when predicting negative cases of the veto and quite well when predicting positive cases of the veto, with an accuracy level of roughly 73% (33 of 45 cases). However, the extremely high level of accuracy (0.99) is misleading, given that the model was perfectly accurate at predicting *negative* cases but could only correctly predict 73% of positive cases. Thus, as displayed in all mentioned models thus far, the imbalance in positive and negative cases within the data set for a rare event such as the veto strongly skews the evaluation metric for accuracy. Finally, Cohen's kappa coefficient (κ) measured 0.84, indicating that the "merged" model performed strongly compared to random chance. Overall, the inclusion of text and non-text predictors resulted in a strong predictive model.

Conversely, including text and non-text predictors for Russia resulted in no significant improvement compared to the text-only model. The predictive accuracy remained relatively high at 0.98. Again, this is heavily due to the model's perfect accuracy in predicting negative cases. However, the model only correctly predicted 32% of positive cases (10 of 31 cases). Thus, the accuracy in relation to positive cases is still quite low. Cohen's kappa coefficient (κ) measured 0.48, indicating that the model performed moderately well compared to random chance. Overall, the inclusion of non-text predictors did not improve the text-only predictive model for Russia, and the model remained moderately weak.

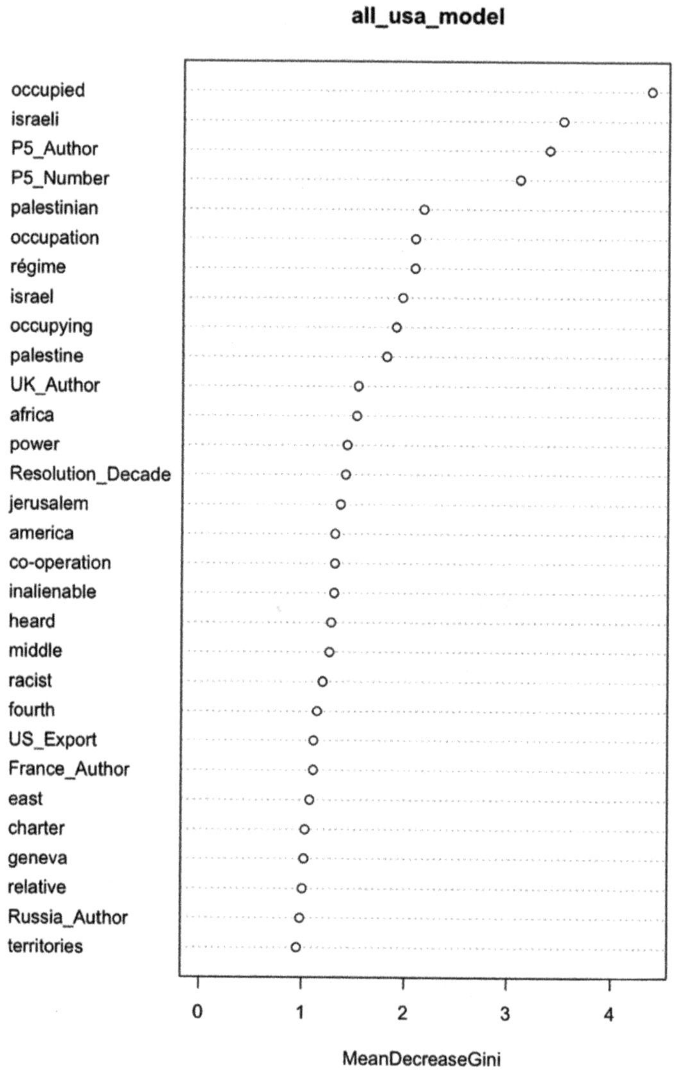

Fig. 15 Plot of thirty highest-weighted predictors within the merged predictive model for the United States

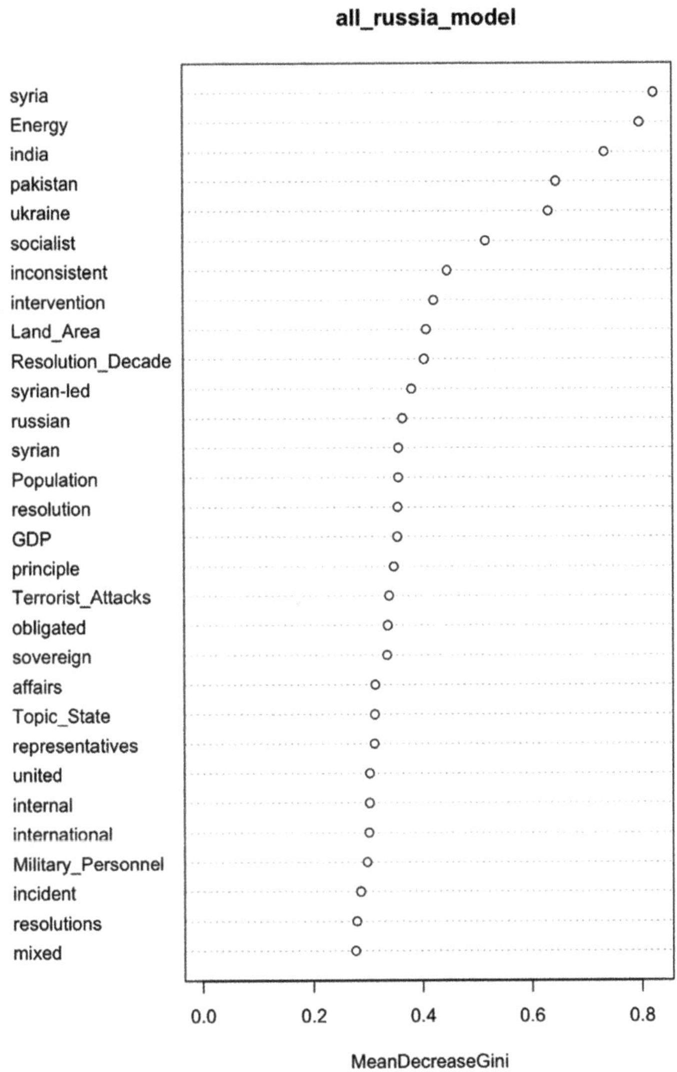

Fig. 16 Plot of thirty highest-weighted predictors within the merged predictive model for Russia

For both "merged" models, non-text or "external" predictors were assigned high Gini values even though they only incrementally improved the U.S. model and failed to improve the Russian model. The highly weighted non-text predictors for the U.S. include "*P5_Author*" and "*P5_Number*" (Fig. 15), indicating that whether a resolution possesses a permanent member author and how many authors possess permanent membership are strong predictors of the U.S. veto. Consistent with the text-only model, terms such as "*Israeli*", "*occupied*", and "*Palestinian*" remain strong predictors of the U.S. veto, supporting the historically observed patterns of behaviour concerning the use of the veto to block resolutions on intervention or proposed condemnation targeting Israel or its actions.

The same could be said for Russia's merged model (Fig. 16).

Consistent with the text-only model, terms such as "*Ukraine*" and "*Syria*" remain strong predictors of the veto for Russia. The term "intervention" also appears, indicating that the Russian veto may be driven by its desire to block interventionist measures that undermine the sovereignty and territorial integrity of existing states. Indeed, Russia has consistently verbalised its opposition to the same. However, non-text predictors, such as "*Energy*" (indicating the level of energy commodities that a topic state possesses) and "*Land_Area*" (indicating the geographic size of a topic state) possess strong positions in the predictor power ranking. The presence of "*Energy*" implies that Russia may consistently utilise its veto to protect states in which it may have a vested interest regarding energy resources. Similarly, the presence of "*Land_Area*" indicates that Russia consistently vetoes UNSC action in larger states which may be due to concerns over the feasibility (or potential effectiveness) of these measures in such a large territory. The predictors related to permanent member authorship (both in name, number, and overall presence) were noticeably absent in the model for Russia, indicating that resolution authorship is not a strong predictor for Russia's veto. Moreover, it should be noted that in the models for both, the U.S. and Russia, the terms "*America*" and "*Russian*" are present, respectively. This supports critics' arguments that the P5 consistently utilises the veto in disproportionate amounts in relation to resolutions where they are the subject of the resolution. However, the term "*America*" could also refer to North or South America (or Central America), indicating that the U.S. utilises the veto with regard to issues within the Western hemisphere, supporting criticisms that allege the P5 utilise the veto to protect their spheres of influence.

Upon comparison, there is only *one* predictor that falls within the strongest thirty predictors for both models—*Resolution_Decade.* The predictor for a resolution's decade (*Resolution_Decade)* possesses a Gini score of approximately 1.2 within the U.S. model (ranking 14 out of 30) and approximately 0.45 within the Russian model (ranking 10 out of 30). This predictor's presence indicates that a resolution's decade is a strong predictor of the veto for both permanent members. This predictor implies that, over decades, permanent members' attitudes towards the utilisation of the veto have transformed. This could be due to the current issues placed before the Council within specific decades, the internal power dynamics and relations within the Council during specific decades, or the nature of the permanent member governments and their varying attitudes towards the utilisation of the veto power during specific decades.

As discussed earlier, the presence of overlapping or completely identical predictors within the models implies that Russia and the U.S. utilise the veto through an objective lens based on their shared principles and mandate in the UNSC and under the Charter. However, the findings reveal that the most ideologically divided members consider extremely diverging factors in their decision-making processes, as only one predictor is shared between the models. Thus, the utilisation of the veto is deeply skewed towards each permanent member's national interests, political ideology, and national alliances. This can be seen in the overwhelming presence of terms related to Israel and the U.S. in Fig. 15 and the overwhelming presence of terms related to Syria, Russia, energy, and international aid in Fig. 16. This directly contradicts the original purpose of the veto, as the mechanism was created as an *objective* tool to prevent potential overreach by the UN as a whole, *not* a tool to protect the individual interests of the P5. The "merged" models ultimately support the historically observed patterns related to the veto and the overwhelming criticisms aimed at its exploitation to protect national interests at the expense of the Council's mandate. Namely, the veto power is being utilised in a highly subjective manner to promote the interests of the few over the many while undermining multilateral efforts to reach a consensus that is agreeable to the UNSC in its entirety.

13 Study Limitations and Possible Improvements

There were multiple predictors subject to missingness, whose data did not span the entirety of the observation time period or were missing multiple data points within the observation time period. Most datasets did not span the entire observation time period, often stopping at 2022 or before. The predictors most affected by these limitations reflected state characteristics and the bilateral relations between the topic state(s) and the permanent member. Overall, the limited availability of political and economic data for numerous states and territories, especially newer and smaller states, resulted in a prominent level of missingness within both datasets.

Second, due to the extent of missingness, data imputation was not conducted. Data imputation entails the replacement of missing data points with actual values (Dankers et al., 2019, p. 82). Specifically, the process utilises "regression models based on other covariates that are used to estimate a likely value" for each missing data point (Dankers et al., 2019, p. 83), but this was not possible due to limitations in the software's computational power. Future predictive models could utilise more powerful software to enable multiple imputations, possibly resulting in more accurate and robust models. Third, a hold-out cross-validation method was used for model creation. However, given the imbalanced nature of the data and the number of predictors (4,428), future approaches should use a *k*-fold cross-validation method. This method requires more computational power and longer computational times but is preferable to the hold-out method due to the model being trained on ***multiple*** test-training splits (represented by *k)*, further minimising overfitting and improving model complexity and accuracy (Allibhai, 2018).

Finally, all datasets related to the veto are highly imbalanced. A perfectly balanced dataset contains equal negative and positive cases, reflected through a prevalence measure of 0.5 or 50% for each group (Dankers et al., 2019, p. 109). The use of the veto from January 1, 1960, to December 31, 2023, has a positive veto prevalence of 5.43%. The datasets used for the U.S. and Russia have even lower positive veto prevalence rates, at 3% and 2.1%, respectively. As machine learning algorithms for classification are developed on the assumption that positive and negative cases within a dataset are nearly or perfectly balanced, the algorithm struggles to locate the "proverbial needle in the haystack" when one class of cases rarely occurs (Hasanin et al., 2019, p. 2). Future models could utilise random under-sampling (which entails balancing the negative and positive cases through the random exclusion of cases from the majority group), random over-sampling (which entails balancing the negative and positive cases through a random replication of cases within the minority group), or more advanced algorithm-based methods such as cost-sensitive learning (Kotsiantis et al., 2006, pp. 2–6) to improve model accuracy and robustness.

14 Implications and Conclusion

While the results of this predictive methodology align with prior analyses aimed at understanding veto use, the use of machine learning to apply this methodology allowed for the inclusion of tens of additional potential predictors that may not be routinely considered when investigating veto use, such as energy production in a topic state and economic exports by the permanent member to a topic state. While more "objective" in its analysis, the predictive methodology allowed for a more holistic view of who or what predicts the use of the veto through the inclusion of over 4,428 potential predictors, compared to traditional methods, which are often limited to a handful of selected variables. Another strength of this methodology lies in its ability to assign predictor weights (see Figs. 13–16). Not only does this methodology reveal what the predictors are for veto use by the U.S. and Russia, but which predictors are more influential within their respective models, providing insight into not just which predictors are influential but also *how* influential they are. Finally, this methodology leaves room for the future inclusion of numerous additional predictors that the researcher believes could improve the models based on further data collection and research, thus allowing the models to be continuously refined to improve overall performance.

While many of the models possessed high accuracy rates, the extremely imbalanced nature of the data undermined the models' efficacy in predicting positive cases of veto utilisation by both the U.S. and Russia. Due to the rareness of positive cases of the veto, the models proved extremely accurate in their predictions of *negative* cases (i.e., absence of the veto). Still, they struggled to predict the rare positive cases accurately. This is a common issue for predictive approaches that seek to solve practical issues within the real world that may be considered "rare" events. Similar to other phenomena researchers have sought to predict, predicting an atypical political event often results in extremely imbalanced datasets, requiring researchers to artificially balance the dataset while trying to minimise any increase in bias.

Nevertheless, this modelling approach proved to be moderately effective in predicting the use of the veto for the U.S., with the "merged" model being the strongest. The model's performance is due to much more than random chance, indicating that the strongest predictors included within the model are given significant consideration when the U.S. utilises its veto. The nature of the predictors that possessed the most weight for the U.S. was not unexpected but are still enlightening. Terminology relating to Israel, Palestine, the occupied territories in the Middle East, as well as the Western hemisphere, were strong predictors of the veto for the U.S., keeping in line with historically observed patterns of behaviour for this permanent member. Additionally, multiple predictors reflecting permanent member authorship possessed a high weight, indicating that the U.S. strongly considers *who* among the P5 is authoring the resolution and *how many* of them are authors. This indicates that the U.S. considers the internal political dynamics within the Council and around the draft resolution when utilising the veto. Finally, the positive case accuracy of 73% indicates that the U.S. has consistently considered the same (or similar) predictors over time when determining whether it should utilise its veto and remains relatively stable in its thought process. In other words, a veto by the U.S. is quite predictable.

Conversely, the models for Russia performed relatively poorly, with accuracy never reaching above 32% for positive cases. This could be due to a larger amount of missing data points within the dataset for Russia. Alternatively, the difference in performance between the "merged" models, considering all but nine predictors were identical between both datasets, could be due to Russia being less consistent over time with its veto and, therefore, less predictable. Another possibility could be that the strongest predictors for a Russian veto were not included in this modelling approach, resulting in poor performance. If true, this would indicate that Russia's decision-making process on veto utilisation involves the consideration of less obvious interests or predictors rather than the state's most basic economic, diplomatic, and material national interests or even the politics within the UNSC itself. It raises the question of what truly drives Russia, as a permanent member, to blockade Council action and whether its rationale towards this controversial tool is systematic or simply ad hoc. Nevertheless, the Russian models possessed numerous text predictors—such as "*sovereignty*", "*cross-border*", "*Russian*", and "*Syria*"—that were expected and historically observed patterns of Russian behaviour when utilising its veto. They indicate that when considering the veto, Russia may consider its ability to access or sell energy commodities to the topic state(s) while also blocking action that it believes may jeopardise the sovereignty of the topic state(s) in question, such as foreign intervention in the form of international aid.

A comparison of the predictor weights between the models reveals a complete divergence from one another. For the "merged" models, only one predictor (*Resolution_Decade*) was present in the top thirty weighted predictors for both permanent members. The near-complete absence of any shared predictors indicates that utilisation of the veto is nearly (if not completely) subjective based upon the individual political, economic, and cultural ideologies of the permanent members. This indicates that criticisms of the veto's exploitation for pursuing competitive national interests are well founded, at least in the case of the U.S. and Russia, and its utilisation is no longer aligned through the fundamental shared principles that dictate their mandate within the Council. These findings provide further support for current criticisms of the UNSC that allege abuse of the veto power and the undermining of the liberal framework upon which the UNSC is founded. Additionally, these findings support current calls for reform aimed at lessening the veto's negative impact on the multilateral negotiations within the UNSC.

However, these findings also shed light on the potential ineffectiveness of proposed reforms aimed at *enlarging* the number of veto power wielders within the UNSC, as suggested by some member states. The findings demonstrate that due to ideological divisions between existing permanent members, the veto has become a tool to advance national visions of how international security should be achieved and maintained, rather than engaging in international multilateral cooperation that seeks to advance the views of the collective majority which benefit the international community as a whole. Thus, it would be counterproductive to reform the UNSC in ways that enlarge the veto power's presence instead of minimising it. If history were to repeat itself, the creation of more veto wielders, regardless of permanent membership status, would only result in additional deadlock and less collective agreement, thus aggravating the existing ideological divisions that have plagued the UNSC for decades. Rather, veto reform should be aimed at reducing the veto's influence, either through new (mandatory) legal restrictions through the Charter or its complete abolishment. However, this can only be achieved with the consent of all five permanent members, which are the direct beneficiaries of the veto and have repeatedly refused or ignored calls for veto reform. Additionally, there are multiple states within the international system that both directly and indirectly benefit from the veto through their alliances with a permanent member, and these states may seek to undermine any processes within the UN to abolish or restrict the veto power. Thus, it is undeniable that as long as the veto remains an integral part of the UNSC, it will possess the potential to realise a state's national interests and foreign policy objectives at the expense of the liberal internationalist objectives the UN has pursued since its creation. This leads to a continuation of the current (and highly problematic) status quo wherein multilateral efforts are undermined by the few at the expense of the majority.

Appendix

Predictor	*Code*	*Predictor Type*	*Measurement*	*Time Period*	*Source*	*Data Entry*
Topic State within a Resolution	*Topic_State*	Categorical	State	1960–2023	Manual Review of Security Council Resolutions	Manual
Gross Domestic Product (GDP)[4]	*GDP*	Numerical (Discrete)	U.S. Dollars	1960–2023	World Bank[5] International Monetary Fund[6]	Existing
Geographic Region	*Sub_Region*	Categorical	United Nation's M49 Standard	1960–2023	United Nations[7]	Manual
Geographic Continent	*Continent*	Categorical	United Nation's M49 Standard	1960–2023	United Nations[8]	Manual

[4] For the predictor reflecting GDP (*GDP*), the data for the period spanning 1960 to 2022 was sourced from the World Bank's open data portal, while the data for 2023 was sourced from the International Monetary Fund (IMF). Additionally, GDP for the Western Sahara for the period spanning 1960 to 2023 was sourced from the International Monetary Fund.

[5] World Bank National Accounts and OECD National Accounts (2023).

[6] International Monetary Fund (2024).

[7] United Nations Statistics Division (2021).

[8] United Nations Statistics Division (2021).

(continued)

Predictor	*Code*	*Predictor Type*	*Measurement*	*Time Period*	*Source*	*Data Entry*
Geographic Land Area[9]	***Land_Area***	Numerical (Continuous)	Square kilometres	1961–2021	World Bank[10] BBC News[11] Britannica[12]	Existing
Total Population[13]	***Population***	Numerical (Discrete)	Per individual	1960–2023	World Bank[14] United Nations Population Division[15]	Existing
Political Regime Type[16]	***Political_Regime***	Numerical (Ordinal)	0, 1, 2 or 3	1960–2022	V-Dem via Our World in Data[17]	Existing

(continued)

[9] For the predictor reflecting total land area (square kilometres) (***Land_Area***), the data for the period spanning 1961 to 2022 was sourced from the World Bank's open data portal. However, the data for the Federal Republic of Yugoslavia (1992 to 2003) was sourced from BBC News. Additionally, the data for the territory of Western Sahara was sourced from Britannica.

[10] United Nations Food and Agriculture Organization (2023).

[11] BBC Monitoring (2006).

[12] The Editors of Encyclopaedia Britannica (2024).

[13] For the predictor reflecting a state or territory's total population (***Population***), the data for the period spanning 1960 to 2022 was sourced from the World Bank's open data portal, while the data for 2023 was sourced from the United Nations Data Portal: Population Division.

[14] United Nations Population Division et al. (2023).

[15] United Nations Department of Economic and Social Affairs, Population Division (2024).

[16] For the predictor reflecting a state or territory's political regime (***Political_Regime***), the data for Yugoslavia during the time period of 1991 to 1995 was manually coded in accordance with the protocol adopted in the V-Dem dataset.

[17] V-Dem (2023).

(continued)

Predictor	*Code*	*Predictor Type*	*Measurement*	*Time Period*	*Source*	*Data Entry*
Prevalence of Terrorism	*Terrorist_Attacks*	Numerical (Discrete)	Number of terrorist attacks in a given year	1970–2021	Global Terrorism Database via Our World in Data[18]	Existing
Energy Commodities	*Primary_Energy_Commodities*	Numerical (Continuous)	Per 1,000 coal-ton equivalents	1960–2012	Correlates of War National Military Capabilities v.6[19]	Existing
Iron and Steel Production	*Iron_Steel*	Numerical (Continuous)	Per 1,000 tons	1960–2012	Correlates of War National Military Capabilities v.6[20]	Existing
Number of Military Personnel	*Military_Personnel*	Numerical (Discrete)	Per 1,000 people	1960–2012	Correlates of War National Military Capabilities v.6[21]	Existing
Military Expenditure	*Military_Expenditure*	Numerical (Discrete)	Per 1,000 USD ($)	1960–2012	Correlates of War National Military Capabilities v.6[22]	Existing

18 Global Terrorism Database (2022).

19 Correlates of War (2021).

20 Correlates of War (2021).

21 Correlates of War (2021).

22 Correlates of War (2021).

(continued)

Predictor	*Code*	*Predictor Type*	*Measurement*	*Time Period*	*Source*	*Data Entry*
Topic State Exports to Permanent Member[23]	*US_Export* *Russia_Export*	Numerical (Continuous)	U.S. Dollars ($)	1960–2023 (for U.S.) 1960–2021 (for Russia)	Correlates of War Trade Dataset[24] UN Comtrade[25]	Existing
Topic State Imports from Permanent Member[26]	*US_Import* *Russia_Import*	Numerical (Continuous)	U.S. Dollars ($)	1960–2023	Correlates of War Trade Dataset[27] UN Comtrade[28]	Existing

(continued)

23 Due to data limitations, the data for *US_Export* and *US_Import* was obtained from the Correlates of War *Trade* (v4.0) dataset for the period of 1960 to 1980, while the data for the period from 1981 to 2023 was obtained from the United Nations Comtrade database. Similarly, due to data limitations, the data for *Russia_Export* and *Russia_Import* was obtained from the Correlates of War *Trade (v4.0)* dataset for the period of 1960 to 1995, while the data for the period from 1996 to 2021 was obtained from the United Nations Comtrade database.

24 Barbieri and Keshk (2016) and Barbieri, Keshk, & Pollins (2009).

25 United Nations Statistics Division (2024).

26 See footnote 23 for caveats.

27 Barbieri and Keshk (2016) and Barbieri, Keshk, & Pollins (2009).

28 United Nations Statistics Division (2024).

(continued)

Predictor	*Code*	*Predictor Type*	*Measurement*	*Time Period*	*Source*	*Data Entry*
Embassy Presence of Permanent Member in Topic State[29]	*US_Embassy_Presence* *Russia_Embassy_Presence*	Numerical (Ordinal)	1–6	1960–2022	Frederick S. Pardee Institute's Diplometrics Diplomatic Representation (DDR) Program[30]	Existing
Diplomatic Focus of Permanent Member in Topic State	*US_Diplomatic_Focus* *Russia_Diplomatic_Focus*	Numerical (Ordinal)	1–3	1960–2022	Frederick S. Pardee Institute's Diplometrics Diplomatic Representation (DDR) Program[31]	Existing
Diplomatic Representation Level of Permanent Member in Topic State	*US_Representation_Score* *Russia_Representation_Score*	Numerical (Ordinal)	0.00–1.00	1960–2022	Frederick S. Pardee Institute's Diplometrics Diplomatic Representation (DDR) Program[32]	Existing

(continued)

29 For the predictors indicating the presence of a diplomatic relationship (representation score, diplomatic focus, and embassy presence), "0" was manually coded for all three predictors if there was an absence of any mention of a diplomatic relationship for the given time period between the topic state and permanent member. This was implemented after consultation with the hosting institute to ensure accuracy.

30 Diplometrics Program (2022) and Moyer et al. (2021).

31 Diplometrics Program (2022).

32 Diplometrics Program (2022).

(continued)

Predictor	*Code*	*Predictor Type*	*Measurement*	*Time Period*	*Source*	*Data Entry*
Presence of Entente Between Permanent Member and Topic State[33]	*US_FA_Entente* *Russia_FA_Entente*	Numerical (Binary)	0 ("No") or 1 ("Yes)	1960–2012	Correlates of War Formal Alliance Data Set[34]	Existing
Presence of Non-aggression Pact Between Permanent Member and Topic State	*Russia_FA_Nonaggression* *US_FA_Nonaggression*	Numerical (Binary)	0 ("No") or 1 ("Yes)	1960–2012	Correlates of War Formal Alliance Data Set[35]	Existing
Presence of Neutrality Agreement Between Permanent Member and Topic State	*US_FA_Neutrality* *Russia_FA_Neutrality*	Numerical (Binary)	0 ("No") or 1 ("Yes)	1960–2012	Correlates of War Formal Alliance Data Set[36]	Existing
Presence of Mutual Defense Agreement Between Permanent Member and Topic State	*US_FA_Defense* *Russia_FA_Defense*	Numerical (Binary)	0 ("No") or 1 ("Yes)	1960–2012	Correlates of War Formal Alliance Data Set[37]	Existing

33 For the predictors indicating the presence of a formal alliance (entente, nonaggression pact, neutrality pact, and mutual defence agreement), "0" was manually coded for all four predictors if there was an absence of any mention of a formal alliance for the given time period between the topic state and permanent member. This was implemented after consultation with the hosting institute to ensure accuracy.

34 Correlates of War (2013) and Gibler (2009).

35 Correlates of War (2013).

36 Correlates of War (2013).

37 Correlates of War, *Formal Alliances (v4.1)*.

References

Allibhai, J. (2018). *Hold-out vs. cross-validation in machine learning*. Medium. https://medium.com/@jaz1/holdout-vs-cross-validation-in-machine-learning-7637112d3f8f.

Barbieri, K., & Keshk, O. (2016). *Correlates of War Project Trade Data Set Codebook* (v4.0). Correlates of War Project. https://correlatesofwar.org.

Barbieri, K., Keshk, O. M. G., & Pollins, B. (2009). TRADING DATA: Evaluating our assumptions and coding rules. *Conflict Management and Peace Science*, 26(5), 471–491. https://www.jstor.org/stable/26275199.

BBC Monitoring. (2006, June 5). *Profile: Serbia and Montenegro*. BBC News. http://news.bbc.co.uk/2/hi/europe/country_profiles/1039269.stm.

Chan, S. (2003). Power, satisfaction and popularity: A poisson analysis of UN Security Council vetoes. *Cooperation and Conflict*, 38(4), 339-359. https://www.jstor.org/stable/45084091.

Correlates of War. (2021). *National Military Capabilities* (v6.0). [Data set]. Correlates of War Project. https://correlatesofwar.org/data-sets/national-material-capabilities/.

Correlates of War. (2013) *Formal Alliances* (v4.1). [Data set]. Correlates of War Project. https://correlatesofwar.org/data-sets/formal-alliances/.

Cranmer, S., & Desmarais, B. (2017). What can we learn from predictive modeling? *Political Analysis*, 25(2), 145–166. https://doi.org/10.1017/pan.2017.3.

Dankers, F., Traverso, A., Wee, L. , & van Kuijk, S. (2019). Chapter 8: Prediction modeling methodology. In P. Kubben, M. Dumontier, & A Dekker (Eds.), *Fundamentals of Clinical Data Science* (pp. 101–120). Springer Publishing. https://doi.org/10.1007/978-3-319-99713-1.

Derviş, K., & Özer, C. (2005). *A better globalization: Legitimacy, governance, and reform*. Center for Global Development. https://www.cgdev.org/sites/default/files/9780815717638-Dervis-better-globalization.pdf.

Diplometrics Program. (2022). *Diplometrics Diplomatic Representation (DDR) Dataset*. [Data set]. Frederick S. Pardee Institute for International Futures. https://korbel.du.edu/pardee/content/diplomatic-representation.

Fidler, D. (1996). Caught between traditions: The Security Council in philosophical conundrum. *Michigan Journal of International Law*, 17(3), 411–453. https://repository.law.umich.edu/mjil/vol17/iss2/7/.

Gibler, D. (2009). *International military alliances, 1648–2008*. [Data set]. CQ Press. https://correlatesofwar.org/data-sets/formal-alliances/.

Global Terrorism Database. (2022). *Number of Terrorist Attacks*. [Data set]. Our World in Data. Retrieved March 1, 2024 from https://ourworldindata.org/grapher/terrorist-attacks.

Gholamy, A., Kreinovich, V., & Kosheleva, O. (2018, February). Why 70/30 or 80/20 relation between training and testing sets: A pedagogical explanation. *University of Texas at El Paso.* https://scholarworks.utep.edu/cs_techrep/1209.

Hasanin, T., Khoshgoftaar, T., Leevy, J., & Seliya, N. (2019). Examining characteristics of predictive models with imbalanced big data. *Journal of Big Data*, 6(1), 1–21. https://doi.org/10.1186/s40537-019-0231-2.

Hegelich, S. (2016). Decision trees and random forests: Machine learning techniques to classify rare events. *European Policy Analysis*, 2(1), 98–120. https://doi.org/10.18278/epa.2.1.7.

Hosli, M., & Dörfler, T. (2017). Why is change so slow? Assessing prospects for United Nations Security Council reform. *Journal of Economic Policy Reform*, 22(1), 35–50. https://doi.org/10.1080/17487870.2017.1305903.

IBM. (n.d.). *What is random forest?* https://www.ibm.com/topics/random-forest.

International Monetary Fund. (2024). *GDP, current prices.* [Data set]. Retrieved April 29, 2024. https://www.imf.org/external/datamapper/NGDPD@WEO/WEOWORLD.

Kotsiantis, S., Kanellopoulos, D., & Pintelas, P. (2006). Handling imbalanced datasets: A review. *GESTS International Transactions on Computer Science and Engineering*, 30(1), 25–36. ISSN: 1738-6438.

McHugh, M. (2012). Interrater reliability: The kappa statistic. *Biochemia Medica*, 22(3), 276–282. https://www.ncbi.nlm.nih.gov/pmc/articles/PMC3900052/.

Moyer, J., Turner, S., & Meisel, C. (2021). What are the drivers of diplomacy? Introducing and testing new annual dyadic data measuring diplomatic exchange. *Journal of Peace Research*, 58(6), 1300–1310. https://doi.org/10.1177/0022343320929740.

Nahory, C. (2004, May). *The hidden veto.* Global Policy Forum. https://archive.globalpolicy.org/security-council/42656-the-hidden-veto.html.

O'Dell, H. (2023, December 18). *How the US has used its power in the UN to support Israel for decades.* Bluemarble. https://globalaffairs.org/bluemarble/how-us-has-used-its-power-un-support-israel-decades.

President of the United States. (2022, October). *National security strategy.* Executive Branch of the United States. https://www.whitehouse.gov/wp-content/uploads/2022/10/Biden-Harris-Administrations-National-Security-Strategy-10.2022.pdf.

Probst, P., Wright, M., & Boulesteix, A. (2019). Hyperparameters and tuning strategies for random forest. *Data Mining and Knowledge Discovery*, 9(3), 1–19. https://doi.org/10.1002/widm.1301.

Rashkow, B. (2022). The United Nations Security Council in the 21st century: Where are we now and where are we heading? *Southwestern Journal of International Law*, 28(2), 430–450. https://www.swlaw.edu/sites/default/files/2023-05/10%20-%20Rashkow.pdf.

Rogers, J., & Jonker, A. (n.d.). *What is data bias?* IBM. https://www.ibm.com/think/topics/data-bias.

Singer, J. D. (1987). Reconstructing the Correlates of War dataset on material capabilities of states, 1816–1985. *International Interactions*, 14, 115–132. https://doi.org/10.1080/03050628808434695.

Soderberg, N. (2015). Time to bring the United Nations Security Council into the 21st century. *Georgetown Journal of International Affairs*, 16(2), 39–46. https://www.jstor.org/stable/43773694..

Strand, J., & Rapkin, D. (2010). Weighted voting in the United Nations Security Council. *Simulation & Gaming*, 42(6), 772–802. https://doi.org/10.1177/1046878110365514.

The Editors of Encyclopaedia Britannica. (2024). *Western Sahara*. Britannica. Retrieved April 1, 2024 from https://www.britannica.com/place/Western-Sahara.

The Ministry of Foreign Affairs for the Russian Federation. (2023, March 31). *The concept of the foreign policy of the Russian Federation*. https://mid.ru/en/foreign_policy/fundamental_documents/1860586/.

UN News. (2024, April 23). *General Assembly debates Security Council's rising veto use*. https://news.un.org/en/story/2024/04/1148896.

United Nations. (1945). *Charter of the United Nations and Statute of the International Court of Justice*. https://treaties.un.org/doc/publication/ctc/uncharter.pdf.

United Nations Department of Economic and Social Affairs Population Division. (2024). *Total population, by sex*. [Data set]. United Nations. Retrieved March 1, 2024 from https://population.un.org/dataportal/data/.

United Nations Food and Agriculture Organization. (2024). *Land area (sq. km)* (AG.LND.TOTL.K2). [Data set]. *World Bank Open Data*. Retrieved March 1, 2024 from https://data.worldbank.org/indicator/AG.LND.TOTL.K2.

United Nations Population Division, United States Census Bureau, Eurostat: Demographics Statistics, & United Nations Statistics Division. (2024). *Population, total* (SP.POP.TOTL). [Data set]. World Bank Open Data. Retrieved March 1, 2024 from https://data.worldbank.org/indicator/SP.POP.TOTL.

United Nations Statistics Division. (2021). *Methodology: standard country or area codes for statistical use (M49)*. United Nations. Retrieved February 28, 2024 from https://unstats.un.org/unsd/methodology/m49/.

United Nations Statistics Division. (2024). *United Nations comtrade database*. [Data set]. United Nations. Retrieved April 15, 2024 from https://comtradeplus.un.org.

V-Dem. (2023). *Political Regime*. [Data set]. Our World in Data. Retrieved March 1, 2024 from https://ourworldindata.org/grapher/political-regime.

Weerts, H., Müller, A., & Vanschoren, J. (2020, July 15). *Importance of tuning hyperparameters of machine learning algorithms*. Eindhoven University of Technology. https://research.tue.nl/en/publications/importance-of-tuning-hyperparameters-of-machine-learning-algorith.

World Bank National Accounts, & OECD National Accounts. (2024). *GDP (current US$)* (NY.GDP.MKTP.CD). [Data set]. World Bank Open Data. Retrieved March 1, 2024 from https://data.worldbank.org/indicator/NY.GDP.MKTP.CD.

Wouters, J., & Rhys, T. (2005, August). *Security Council reform: A new veto for a new century?* (Egmont Paper 9). Royal Institute for International Relations. https://aei.pitt.edu/8980/1/ep9.pdf.

PART II

Multilateralism: Regional Actors, United Nations Agencies, and Member States

CHAPTER 6

The Small and Regional Powers Claim for Agency: A Strategic Usage of Non-traditional Threats Through Arria Meetings

Natalia Luers and Elise Galy-Jammou-Préfontaine

1 Introduction

The contributions to this book have highlighted the increasing necessity to provide more space for debate regarding the United Nations Security Council's (UNSC) architecture. Formally, the composition of the UNSC, addressed in the UN Charter and its additional rules, determines which states have a seat at the Council and voice their national and regional

N. Luers (✉)
University of Trento, Trento, Italy
e-mail: natalia.luers@studenti.unitn.it

E. Galy-Jammou-Préfontaine
Sciences Po, Paris, France
e-mail: elise.galyjammouprefontaine@sciencespo.fr

M. O. Hosli et al. (eds.), *Multilateralism and the United Nations Security Council*, https://doi.org/10.1007/978-3-031-85320-3_6

foreign policy concerns. UNSC's dual composition of fifteen states—five permanent (P5) and ten non-permanent (E10)—defines which and for how long these members are allowed to undertake this diplomatic role (United Nations 1945). Thus, the non-permanent members also denomin the elected members, hold a significant role in representing the stakes of the remaining 188 UN member states.

According to Article 24 of the Charter of the Organisation of the United Nations, the Security Council is responsible for maintaining international peace and security (United Nations 1945). This body is tasked to determine the existence of threats and define the priority challenges to be discussed to prevent further global dissemination. A 1992 emergent informal institutional venue, named the Arria Meetings, provides an additional forum to listen to non-UN-belonging opinions on international peace and security-related issues. The UN Secretariat defines Arria meetings as "very informal, confidential gatherings which enable Security Council members to have a frank and private exchange of views, within a flexible procedural framework with persons whom the inviting member or members of the Council (who also act as the facilitators or conveners) believe it would be beneficial to hear and/or to whom they may wish to convey a message" (Security Council Report 2020). Therefore, if the UNSC's main role is to pinpoint threats to peace and security at the international level, it is necessary to address: What are traditional and non-traditional threats? How do they emerge? How are they conceived in international relations? How are they framed in the international security arena?

The multilateral instrumentalisation of non-traditional threats by the UNSC's elected members remains largely undiscovered in academia, as well as the role of small and regional powers as rotating members in launching discussions on these threats. Consequently, this chapter aims at answering the following research question: What role do small and regional powers play when serving as non-permanent UNSC members in shaping the discussions on non-traditional emergent threats? This question is significant for small and regional states when serving as the E10 in the potential employment of Arria encounters to perform as debate conveners, having more weight in the decision-making of international threat designation.

Traditionally, state survival is defined by an issue which poses an existential threat to the state as the designated referent object. Yet, the Copenhagen School widened the traditional understanding of security and threats building upon the emergence of new non-military sources of threat (Buzan et al. 1998). By broadening the security agenda beyond the state-centred view, this school acknowledged security status for both, issues and referent objects, in the economic, environmental, and societal sectors (Buzan et al. 1998). Nevertheless, when the United Nations and its organs were established, there was no such consideration of threats other than warfare. It was not until the 1990s that non-traditional components were considered by the international community. They can be defined as "challenges to the survival and well-being of peoples and states that arise primarily out of non-military sources [...]. These dangers are often transnational in scope, defying unilateral remedies and requiring comprehensive—political, economic, social—responses, as well as humanitarian use of military force" (NTS-Asia, Caballero-Anthony 2006, 6). A few examples are natural disasters, financial and economic crises, terrorism, widespread diseases, cyberattacks, and many others that appear to endanger individuals, local communities, national societies, and the whole international community (Buzan et al. 1998). Inevitably, this concerned the entire UNSC, challenging their threats designation capacity, hence, the framework used up to the date to address them.

Significantly, climate change accelerated by humankind activities and threats emanating from cyberspace have become leading existential threats to the international community. The World Meteorological Organization (WMO) labelled the 2011–2020 period as the "Decade of Acceleration" (WMO 2023) in which the Antarctic continental ice lost almost 75% more ice than in 2001–2010, warning of the negative impact of the incoming sea level increase on low-lying coastal regions and states. Simultaneously, the International Monetary Fund (IMF) warns that, since the COVID-19 pandemic, malicious cyber incidents have more than doubled, heightening economic firms' losses (Natalucci et al. 2024). Likewise, the World Nuclear Association (WNA) asserts that, since 2003, there have been numerous worldwide cyberattacks on nuclear facilities originating from state and non-state actors (WNA 2022).

All these negative developments weaken UN members and their populations, including those members of the UNSC. Regional powers are another element within the UNSC's composition based on size, political ambition, peer recognition, and international expectations which allow them to occupy a leadership role surpassing their neighbours (Brosig and Lecki 2023). Similarly, small powers encompass those states lacking material-based power and are in a weaker position in the geopolitical, historical, and geographical context (Reire 2021). Several authors have analysed small states' behaviour towards great powers (Efremova 2019) and how they employ their agency to gain influence and pursue international political goals (Long 2017). A recent contribution (Gailišs 2024) discerns how small powers can become active international actors leveraging their mandate as non-permanent members at the UNSC, while current trends depict behavioural changes of regional powers (Nolte and Schenoni 2021). On E10s' role, its cruciality lies in their bridge-building role between the UNSC and the other 188 member states (Martin 2020).

At the beginning of the twenty-first century, international law perspectives (Wellens 2003) unveiled UNSC's role and position on new threats. Academic contributions (Goodwin 2022) discussed the UNSC's incapacity to manage unconventional threats such as climate change, while others (Pobjie 2020) emphasised the role of Article 24 of the UN Charter in delimiting the UNSC's mandate and power to engage with pandemics and climate crises. Regarding the Arria-formula meetings, most of the academic work refers to gatherings on the use of drones by terrorist groups (Rogers 2022), its utility as a means to engage the UNSC on a response to the Rwandan genocide (Oksamytna 2017), and NGOs' use of an Arria meeting on the gendered experiences during war (Hill et al. 2003). The Mexican strategic usage (Modirzadeh and Olabuenaga 2021) of this kind of reunion to circumvent the agenda-setting struggle reveals a robust argument for the non-permanent members' use of these institutionalised encounters. Some contributions have studied the role of small and regional powers in addressing climate change in the UNSC, illustrating the usefulness of Arria-formula meetings in this process (Maertens 2018, 2021).

This chapter relies on a documentary research approach of primary international organisations' and states' reports and documents. Secondary sources from previous academic contributions on the topic were also consulted to understand the role(s) adopted by small and regional powers when serving as elected members of the UNSC, particularly, in agenda-setting initiatives on the growing importance of non-traditional threats among the international community. To substantiate our arguments throughout the chapter, two case studies of the most acute international threats are combined. The choice on the topics of climate change and cybersecurity is motivated by several reasons. Climate change has been a recurring issue in international current events, which has consequently generated a global focus aimed at addressing this complex governance challenge translating into several debates and other strategies to include it into the UNSC's mandate. Cybersecurity, on the other hand, has been a recent surfacing topic at the UNSC thanks to small and regional powers through their political strategies and agenda-setting abilities. This chapter thus spotlights a complementary channel for the elected members to influence the UNSC agenda by including various state and non-state actors' views.

Firstly, this chapter explores the treatment of non-traditional threats at the UNSC. Secondly, it engages with the interests of small and regional powers and how they are reflected in the UNSC. Thirdly, it delves into the existing institutional tools and roles these states can have at the Council to incorporate non-traditional threats as political priorities. Finally, it examines how elected members use the informal meetings' format to address these cybersecurity and environmental threats.

2 Non-traditional Threats: Falling into the Cracks of the UNSC

Non-traditional threats were neither addressed nor considered when the United Nations was created in 1945. The UN Charter was designed to tackle what we now call traditional threats—armed conflicts and disputes—as illustrated in its Preamble. This focus is shown through Chapters VI and VII, which present the methods and tools available for the UNSC for resolving such issues (United Nations 1945). Yet, these measures seem inadequate in confronting emerging issues that are not caused by states or designated actors. This emphasis on military threats can be explained by the historical context of its drafting as it was shaped by the priorities outlined at the 1945 San Francisco Conference (Rychnovská 2015). Participating nations were predominantly concerned with preventing conflicts and escalations that would lead to warfare.

This narrow interpretation of security, which originates from an institutional and territorial sovereignty perspective, has been increasingly challenged as, since the end of the Cold War, the UN's framework has evolved to address emerging threats that have raised worldwide attention. These new challenges in the security realm are being inherently transnational, highly complex, and interconnected, making it impossible for states to deal with these threats on their own (Jones et al. 2009, 37). This has gradually broadened the international community's competencies and understanding of peace and security. Therefore, the intervention of the United Nations and other international organisations has become imperative.

In this regard, Article 24 of the UN Charter, which does not limit the UNSC's mandate to specific topics of concern (United Nations 1945), has been increasingly expanded through practices to address these issues collectively (Caballero-Anthony 2006; Rychnovská 2015). Article 34 further states that the UNSC can "investigate [...] any situation" (United Nations 1945) to fulfil its responsibility. This widened approach was explicitly put in place in 1992 through the adoption of a Note S/23500 by the President of the Security Council, David Hannay, which states that "non-military sources of instability in the economic, social, humanitarian, and ecological fields have become threats to peace and security" (UNSC 1992, 3). This signalled not only an institutional acknowledgement of the notion of human security for the first time ever, but also an emphasis that "the United Nations membership as a whole, working through appropriate bodies, need to give the highest priority to the solution of these matters" (UNSC 1992, 34).

The increasing number of resolutions taken since this note highlights the recognition on the part of the international community that institutional stability within a State does not guarantee that it is immune from any threats and risks for itself and its population (Eriksen et al. 2022). Indeed, external factors to institutional stability or state aggression can also impede peace and security in a country or region. Climate change is a significant factor, as it can disrupt food chains, provoke mass migration flows, and raise sea levels, putting many populations at risk. Moreover, it is deeply linked with traditional security considerations as it can aggravate conflicts (IPCC 2014) or be a threat multiplier (Hardt 2017). The Global Adaptation Initiative Country Index of the University of Notre Dame reveals that the countries in conflicts, such as the Democratic Republic of Congo, Sudan, or Yemen, considered to be most politically fragile, are also the most vulnerable countries to climate change (University of Notre Dame 2021).

Despite this recognition, the UNSC failed in efficiently addressing such threats due to the multiplicity and complexity of the questions these threats pose, bringing varied points of view and potential solutions that clash with the national interests of different countries. Non-traditional threats such as climate change, cyberspace, and the COVID-19 pandemic have greatly exacerbated the rivalries between the permanent member states of the Security Council (Charbonneau 2021; Tikk and Kerttunen 2020). There has been an extensive debate during open debates at the UNSC on whether these emergent issues can be considered threats, whether the UNSC is legitimate in tackling these problems, and what type of international norm or decision needs to be established to ensure international peace and security (S/PV.5663, 2007; S/PV.6587, 2011).

As surprising as it may seem, some non-traditional threats have never been brought up by the P5 at the UNSC, with the most blatant case being related to cyberspace, despite their seriousness at an international level. Indeed, "most cyber incidents with known or suspected state involvement have occurred under the explicit or implicit endorsement of the permanent members of the UNSC" (Tikk and Schia 2020, p.7). This dynamic is contrary to the one present at the United Nations General Assembly (UNGA), which passed a Resolution on the Developments in the Field of Information and Telecommunication in the Context of International Security on the 5th of December 2016 (A/RES/73/27, 2016), or the declarations of the Secretary-General of the UN António Guterres in 2017 which considers cyber war as being "more and more able to disrupt relations among States and destroy some of the structures and systems of modern life" (Guterres 2017).

These rivalries block any progress because of the structural functioning of the Security Council. Article 27 of the UN Charter awards the five permanent members the ability to "veto" a Resolution if it does not correspond to the countries' aspirations (United Nations 1945). It is not the case for the elected members, whose vote against a Resolution wouldn't impede it from being approved (United Nations 1945). Consequently, even though the principles of the UN assert that all countries are equal, some countries are more equal than others in the United Nations. This implies that decisions can only be made in the goodwill of the permanent members, which has become increasingly difficult as they have conflicting points of views and interests.

Climate change and cyberspace have shown particularly stark perspectives. On climate change, China and Russia have different interpretations of it and what it implies compared to other permanent members such as France and the United Kingdom (UK), while the United States of America (USA) has had an evolving position on the topic as it is greatly influenced by national politics (Briggs 2023, 331; Selby 2019; Hulme 2009). China has had a tradition of disregarding international environment policies and prioritising its economic growth at the expense of the climate (Vuori 2023). This is justified by the industrialised/developing nation dichotomy (Vuori 2023) which many countries from the South also support. During the open debates of 2007 and 2011 on climate change, the country argued that the UNSC did not have legitimacy to address this topic, considering it a development issue rather than an international threat to security and peace. Hence, it advocated that the United Nations Framework Convention on Climate Change (UNFCCC) is the right institution to tackle this issue. Russia has adopted a strong and comparable position, originating from a lack of recognition from national politics of the security threat of climate change as well as a certain enthusiasm at the opportunities and developing benefits it generates for the Arctic Russian regions (Stepanov 2023; Putin 2017). China's position has nevertheless slightly changed, since the UNSC's 8451st meeting that took place on the 25th of January 2019, by acknowledging that climate change is an international threat to security and peace (S/PV.8451, 2019, 15), although its position on the legitimacy of the UNSC hasn't changed since.

On the other hand, certain permanent members of the UNSC such as the UK and France have advocated for an increased consideration of security threats in the UNSC caused by climate change. Their contribution is substantial as illustrated by the organisation of the UK of the first open debate at the UNSC on this specific topic in April 2007 (S/PV.5663 2007). Similarly, France convened the organisation of the Arria meeting of April 2020 which has emerged from this initiative and, for the first time, with the contribution of ten members of the UNSC, an initiative to address climate-related security risks (Permanent Mission of France to the United Nations in New York 2020).

Moreover, the USA has had evolving stances on the issue, leading to a change of position at the UNSC. It has come out of its sort of neutral position in order to support more progress on the matter at the Council due to its own interests regarding the rise of sea levels (Briggs 2023). Nevertheless, the country showed hostility in addressing the topic at the UN when Trump in power in 2016 (Selby 2019; Hulme 2009).

The threat of abusive use of the veto and the conflicting views of the permanent members led to a certain paralysis of the agenda-setting on many non-traditional threats between 2011 and 2018 (Hardt et al. 2023). No open debate or other formal format was organised during that period specifically on the topic of climate change until international social movements corroborated alarming conclusions of the Intergovernmental Panel on Climate Change (IPCC) report, which made agenda-setting inevitable. The Security Council remained divided on the subject, with Russia vetoing the drafted resolution of December 2021 on Integrating Climate-Related Security Risk into Conflict-Prevention Strategies (S/2021/990 2021; United Nations 2021). Consequently, small and regional powers appear to have, at first sight, no leverage in the UNSC as any progress is directly linked to the goodwill of the P5. In this sense, critical literature regarding the daily malfunctioning of the Security Council raises concerns about its "deficit of democracy" (Gordanić 2021), which translates into the flawed consideration of non-traditional threats within the institution. As Richard Haas expresses, "The major powers get the UN they want, not the one the world needs" (Haass 2020).

3 Transcending Borders: the Particular Interests of Elected Powers in Addressing Non-traditional Threats at the UNSC

The division between the permanent members of the Security Council is not the only internal division seen in the institution. Small and regional powers are not a homogeneous group in the international scene when it comes to addressing non-traditional threats. These divisions are visible at the UNGA, where states have different views and interests depending on the issue at stake. The Group of 77 (G77) is a par excellence illustration of these differences. This coalition was created as the Non-Alignment group in the context of the Cold War to enhance its influence and negotiating capacity in the different areas of the UN. Now, it consists of 130 member states—small and regional powers representing the Global South—and it is one of the biggest coalitions in the UNGA. This does not mean that they have unanimous views on a myriad of topics. For instance, regarding climate change, the G77 has been divided on the question on whether the UNSC is competent in tackling this issue or not.

These tensions have been particularly seen through the different open debates of 2007 and 2011. It has been the case with the debate in April 2007 in which countries among the coalition had divergent views. Pakistan, representing the G77 at the time, expressed how "The ever-increasing encroachment by the UNSC on the roles and responsibilities of other principal organs of the United Nations represents a distortion of the principles and purposes of the Charter; it also infringes on their authority and compromises the rights of the general membership of the United Nations" (S/PV.5663 2007, 24). The country voiced concerns over the UNSC's illegitimate appropriation of this issue when there are other frameworks dedicated to it. During its speech, Pakistan underlined its view that climate change is a development issue, and not a threat to international peace and security, an opinion which was shared by other members of the coalition like Indonesia, South Africa, and China (S/PV.5663 2007).

Nevertheless, other states, like Papua New Guinea, who spoke on behalf of the Pacific Islands Forum, and also members of the G77, did not share the view put forward by Pakistan, revealing the tensions in the group regarding climate change. The country underlined how climate change is a threat to peace and security: "The dangers that small islands and their populations face are no less serious than those faced by nations and peoples threatened by guns and bombs. The effects on our populations are as likely to cause massive dislocations of people as past and present wars" (S/PV.5663 2007, 28). Therefore, the Security Council "[...] is the paramount international forum available" for these countries (S/PV.5663 2007, 29). In the open debate of 2011, the President of Nauru, speaking on behalf of the Alliance of Small Island States (AOSIS), emphasised this point of view by imploring the UNSC to "seize this opportunity to lead" the efforts in tackling climate change (UNSC 2011b). These tensions, which are also asserted within the Organisation of the Petroleum Exporting Countries (OPEC), as some countries' economies rely on petroleum export, reveal not only the "slowly eroding of the common identity" of the G77 (Vihma et al. 2011), but also the complexity and multiplicity of climate security and its implications at an international level.

Nonetheless, the issue of non-traditional threats has become overtime a pressing issue for small and regional powers. The multiplication of scientific research on the urgency of the issue, as well as the growing pressure of nations and Non-Governmental Organisations (NGOs) to act upon it, has led to an increasing consciousness of the consequences of non-traditional threats, namely its security implications. This can be seen on the subject of climate change (IPCC 2007, 2014, 2023), which now will be addressed first, followed by a focus on cybersecurity threats, despite the lack of academic literature on the latter (Tikk and Schia 2020).

Climate change's direct ramifications on the Alliance of Small Island States (AOSIS) and other countries have contributed to pressuring the international community to address this issue (S/PV.5663 2017, 28; Maertens 2018). Its devastating effects, already evident in these countries through displacement and economic repercussions, are considerably prominent in international news. This rise of awareness is further amplified by the expanding concerns of international organisations and populations, leading to large-scale worldwide environmental protests since 2018 (Laux 2021). The rising visibility since 2018 has led to a multiplication of debates and other formats of discussions in the UNSC on the topic (directly or indirectly). Moreover, it strongly impacted the positions of certain P5 members, such as the USA's positioning during the Obama administration (2009–2017), while the USA, prior to this administration, had a neutral position on the topic and on the UNSC's competencies regarding it (Briggs 2023, 332).

In addition, resorting to the UNSC generated added value since it is a legally binding body, counteracting global governance's attempts (and failures) in concluding agreements on the topic (Maertens 2021). UNSC's binding nature has been leveraged by countries to categorise climate change as a non-traditional threat and to reply to challenges to contemporary multilateralism with tools and mechanisms available in the international scene. It can be seen, above all, as a call for action by the international community.

Despite not having as much leverage as the P5, small and regional powers have developed the capacity of agenda-setting in the UNSC to more accurately address non-traditional threats. Through a variety of strategies later explored, these powers have managed to enable a process of climatisation, meaning "a process [...] which other domains of world politics are framed through a climate lens and transformed as a result of such a translation" (Maertens 2021), as the securitisation of climate change has seen a certain resistance from some permanent members. Hence, by doing so, there has been a process for establishing a systematic approach by the UNSC to take into consideration the risks caused by climate change (Maertens 2021).

Through this ability of agenda-setting in the UNSC, some countries have found it strategic to address non-traditional threats as a means to gain agency to secure a seat as a non-permanent member. This was the case of Saint-Vincent and the Grenadines which capitalised on the impact of climate change on their territory during their election campaign (Gonsalves 2019). Other countries have also used niche diplomacy to take advantage of such issues. It is the case of Switzerland for the 2023–2024 mandate (Eriksen et al. 2022), as well as Estonia for the 2020–2021 mandate (Loik and Jürgenson 2023). Estonia has put climate change as well as cyberspace as top priorities for the UNSC (Ministry of Foreign Affairs 2020; Loik and Jürgenson 2023), with the clear objective of agenda-setting these subjects, as demonstrated through its two-year mandate. Pushing to address these issues allows small and regional powers to "put pressure on the most polluting states—so that they reduce their emissions—and the most developed States—so that they finance adaptation policies" (Maertens 2021), potentially influencing the permanent members' perspectives on non-traditional threats.

4 Balancing the Global Power Scale: Tools and Roles of Small and Regional Powers as Elected Members Towards Non-traditional Threats

UNSC's elected members face various hardships in leveraging their perspectives and in influencing the course of decisions. The short-term duration of the mandate—consisting of two years—hinders the proper development and accumulation of institutional memory (Nick Pay and Postolski 2021). Likewise, the lack of human, material, and economic resources affects African and Asia-Pacific Groups (see Appendix), impeding them from taking part in diplomatic tasks and attending all kinds of meetings. Hence, these countries need to employ alternative tools and strategies to circumvent their inferior starting point. Among these, chairing Council subsidiary bodies matters, fulfilling the presidency's proceedings responsibilities before and during its tenure, and attending all forms of meetings, of public and private character, informal consultations, and dialogues held with non-Council members and bodies (both informal and Arria-formula meetings), are fundamental approaches.

Throughout the years, the UNSC has made adjustments to its working methods, responding to the worldwide request for its structural reform and its members' multilateral involvement. These were mainly geared to the P5 share of tasks on procedural matters with the E10, foretelling new roles for the small and regional powers as members of the Council, and inevitably conceding them a larger portion of agency in formal and informal decision-making processes (Nick Pay and Postolski 2021). Some of these adjustments and strategies in working methods are discussed later in this chapter. The principal organisational tools in the UNSC are the penholdership, the transitory presidency, and the legitimate coalition-building strategies. These tools often overlap within one elected member period, balancing the scale of power distribution within the Security Council. In consequence, the E10 have at their disposal three ways to alter UNSC outcomes: as (co)penholders, as threat identifiers, and/or as decision influencers.

Contemplated as a complementary option for any Council member to lead proceedings, the pen-holding rule (Security Council Report 2024) consists of an informal arrangement in which one or more members launch and chair documents' drafting amidst Council deadlocks. In other words, they head informal drafting processes of UNSC resolutions, presidential statements, and press statements. Then, they take these drafts to discussion with the other Council members in informal consultations. This strategy is highly important for small and regional powers when holding a non-permanent seat at the UNSC because it allows them to play an active role as agenda-setters and/or to build up thematic and political momentum for future resolutions. The Socialist Republic of Vietnam viewed this role as an extra opportunity dually beneficial for burden-sharing among the 15 members and having a proactive role in holding emergency meetings, organising open debates, and leading visiting missions (VIET LAM 2020). In 2023, the United Arab Emirates (UAE) employed the pen-holding rule in a joint statement with Japan on Afghanistan (Permanent Mission of the United Arab Emirates to the United Nations 2023) to explain the Council voting on two resolutions, one related to the mandate extension of the UN Assistance Mission and another to acknowledge the dire security situation in the country.

On the same note, the rotating presidency incorporated in the Provisional Rules of Procedure gives the President of the Council the power of representing the entire body and of presiding over the meeting for a month, as stipulated in Rule 18 (Rule 18, United Nations Security Council 2023). Each presidency's expected monthly assessment allows an additional role as a threat identifier. This document contains a summary of the Council events during that month, leaving some free space to bring identified threats under the attention of the international community.

Another key tool is the formation of coalitions within the UNSC bloc. Coalitions are conceived as an enabler for E10 to be positioned as power brokers within the Security Council (Nick Pay and Postolski 2021). The diverse combinations of countries that might come together to set a certain agenda allow states to play the multilateral game and counterbalance well-established groups such as the P3, formed by the

UK, France, and the USA. During South Africa's last tenure, in 2019–2020, the country spoke on behalf of the A3 +1 (Niger, South Africa, Tunisia + St Vincent, and the Grenadines) and called for the implementation of the strategic approach to conflict resolution and peacebuilding in the Democratic Republic of the Congo (DRC) (Department of International Relations and Cooperation Republic of South Africa 2020). A recent trend indicates that the coalition P3 monopolises the penholding on most country files on the humanitarian situation in Syria, West Africa, and the Sahel (Security Council Report 2024). Similarly, China and the Russian Federation, which compose the P2 group, stand in solidarity with the Global South states, particularly with small and regional powers (Cai et al. 2024). They underline their belonging to the UN-external grouping of the BRICS, which includes the P2 plus India, Brazil, and South Africa, countries that aspire a permanent seat in a future reformed Council (Cai et al. 2024). The solidarity approach is emulated in the P2 voting patterns supporting the A3 (Niger, South Africa, and Tunisia) (Cai et al. 2024).

Council members have also employed alternative unofficial instruments. Among them, a collective brainstorming session known as the Annual Retreat very much matters (Security Council Report 2019), which brings together the senior diplomats of the 15 UNSC members and the UN Secretariat staff in a countryside location. These sessions are a crucial informal setting to further discuss specific topics of interest. In 2019, Guyana, a non-permanent member, took advantage of that year's theme being the evolving nature of conflicts to raise alarm on contemporary and new emerging threats, with an explicit reference to the risk of terrorism in the Caribbean (Permanent Mission of the Cooperative Republic of Guyana to the United Nations 2019).

Regarding the two non-traditional threats under study, non-permanent members have used these tools and strategies to bring climate change and cybersecurity into the Security Council's realm. Climate change was included in 2013 when Portugal, acting as the Council President, convened an official session on *New Challenges to International Peace and Security and Conflict Prevention* (Maertens 2018). This topic was again featured in 2015, with New Zealand's debate on "Small Island Developing States Facing Threats to Peace and Security" (New Zealand Ministry of Foreign Affairs and Trade 2015). In 2016, the Senegalese presidency held a continuation session on "Water, Peace, and Security" of an Arria meeting previously hosted, where delegates pointed out the security implications of climate change (Security Council Report 2018). Lastly, during sessions devoted to the Sahel in 2016 and 2017, climate threats were mentioned a handful of times, with the UN Secretary-General stressing that "The situation in the Sahel concerns us all. Poverty, underdevelopment, and climate change have contributed to humanitarian and security crises" (Maertens 2018, 112). Although these debates illustrated the rising concerns around climate change as a threat, they were not enough to overcome the Council's institutional obstacles and for elected members to acquire a prominent role in setting its agenda.

Finally, the so-called Arria-formula meetings are another flexible institutional practice, recalling the Security Council's dominion over its own procedure. We dedicate the next subsection to this topic. To adequately reflect its growing adoption, we argue that it opens a new chapter for the E10 in terms of agency in decision-making dynamics. Some authors find in the reform of the Council's working methods and the incorporation of several diverse civil society representatives an opportunity for the E10 to become norm entrepreneurs and a possible factor for future structural reform (Nick Pay and Postolski 2021).

At the same time, Arria meetings offer another item of analysis of world politics. They serve as an informal and contemporary platform for delegations and civil society to raise their versions of changing world political dynamics.

Great powers are already using Arria meetings as a geopolitical tool to deploy their own narrative amidst international warfare in the UN diplomatic environment. First, in May 2022, the Russian Federation held an Arria encounter on the "Systematic and mass grave violations of the international humanitarian law as well as other war crimes committed by the Ukrainian military personnel and militia and discovered in the course of ongoing special military operation of the Russian armed forces" (Security Council Report 2022). Later, in July, the same delegation organised an Arria encounter on the "Neo-Nazism and radical nationalism: exploring root causes of the crisis in Ukraine" envisioning to disseminate what they considered the history and current status of Nazism in Ukraine (Security Council Report 2022). Recently, the Permanent Mission of the Russian Federation to the United Nations brought together the UN Member States, Permanent Observers, UN entities, civil society organisations, and press to address the "Crimes of the Ukrainian Armed Forces and the nationalist battalions" (Permanent Mission of the Russian Federation to the United Nations 2024) to further attempt to demonstrate evidence of the Ukrainian violation of international humanitarian law. The strategic political use of the Arria meetings within UN diplomacy becomes a clear sign of the great utility these meetings contain, especially when the goal is to balance the global power scale by convincing wider audiences. Great powers have exploited this diplomatic tool to continue to build up their alliances even in times of war; it is a matter of time—and praxis—before the elected members realise its powerful use to start walking the same path.

5 Elected 10's Manoeuvre: Arria-Formula Meetings for Non-traditional Threats

The Arria-Formula Meetings date back to 1992 (United Nations 2002), when Venezuelan Ambassador Diego Arria, at the time the President of the Council, accepted to hear the testimonial experience from Fra Joko Zovko (Security Council Report 2020), a Croatian priest, on the violence perpetrated in Bosnia and Herzegovina in the UN delegate's lounge. Ambassador Arria invited the Council members to meet with him as well, triggering Arria to institutionalise the innovative format during the Venezuelan mandate as an elected member. Later on, the meetings moved from the lounge to a UN conference room supported by interpretation, expanding the practice to the six UN official languages and creating a new practice that soon came to be cast by the 15 Council members on different topics and with varying frequency (Security Council Report 2020). It is in note 507 by the 2017 President of the Security Council (United Nations 2017) that Arria meetings were first described as a flexible and informal forum for enhancing UNSC members' deliberations, thus marking that year as the beginning of their UN institutionalisation.

Throughout its development, some customary practices became the backbone of the Arria forums. There is no steering function in these meetings; instead, the convening member(s) chair them while acting as moderators. This procedure differs from regular consultations on many aspects. Firstly, Arria meetings are convened by a UNSC member or members so they are not recognised as an activity of the Council. Secondly, attendance is not mandatory, although Members of the Secretariat are obliged to attend if they are invited; interpreters and a Conference Officer are expected to attend. Thirdly, they take place in a conference room. Fourthly, organiser(s) send out a written invitation where date, time, place, and stakeholders' briefers are indicated; and, finally, these meetings are not announced in the daily UN Journal (United Nations 2002). Besides, these forums have been placed in a dedicated "research tool" section on the Security Council website segment. The UN Arria Meetings Dashboard is an interactive research tool created by the Security Council Affairs Division keeping the record of the reunions held since 1992, along with their subject and the organiser(s). Yet, if further information on attending stakeholders and arguments exchanged is expected, intervening members' and other entities' websites contain this information.

As discussed before, Arria meetings offer an optional diplomatic platform for all UN members and civil society to speak up on world political affairs related to international peace and security. Thus, they are not of minor importance since they pose a political UN institutionalised extra channel to change the rules of the game, or at least, to start discussions on how to possibly change them. Through this way, some delegations may handle the Arria sessions for ulterior aims of persuading larger audiences and its representatives and forging alliances that could enhance their power projection beyond the UN settings.

The highest number of Arria meetings held was in 2021 (32 meetings), mostly addressing terrorism, counterterrorism, technology, COVID-19, and Ukraine (see Arria-Formula Meetings Dashboard). Throughout 2023, the 22 meetings convened primarily touched on Ukraine, children and armed conflict, Protection of Civilians (PoC), the Women, Peace, and Security (WPS) agenda, technology, and conflict prevention. The Dashboard portrays that the countries convening most of these types of meetings are France, the UK, the USA, Germany, Estonia, the Russian Federation, Belgium, Ireland, Norway, and Kenya.

Looking closer into the subjects of the Arria gatherings, both non-traditional threats under consideration—climate change and cyber threats—were discussed (United Nations Department of Political and Peacebuilding Affairs 2024). On the same note, particular attention is paid to the Council members' organisers. Climate change has been a topic of these meetings seven times, being first discussed in 2013 under the prompt "*Security Dimensions of Climate Change*" organised by Pakistan and the UK (United Nations Department of Political and Peacebuilding Affairs 2024). In 2015, Spain and Malaysia convened a meeting to examine climate change's role as a threat multiplier for global security (United Nations Department of Political and Peacebuilding Affairs 2024). In 2017, Ukraine called for a meeting on the security implications of sea level rising due to climate change (United Nations Department of Political and Peacebuilding Affairs 2024). In the same year, France, Germany, Italy, Japan, the Maldives, the Netherlands, Peru, Sweden, and the UK had a meeting on "Climate Change: Preparing for Security Implications of Rising Temperatures" (United Nations Department of Political and Peacebuilding Affairs 2024). In 2020, Belgium, France, the Dominican Republic, Estonia, Germany, Niger, Saint Vincent and the Grenadines, Tunisia, the UK, and Vietnam set up a reunion to analyse the latest data on climate and security risks (United Nations Department of Political and Peacebuilding Affairs 2024). In the beginning of 2022, the United Arab Emirates held an Arria-formula event related to climate finance for upholding peace and security (United Nations Department of Political and Peacebuilding Affairs 2024); at the end of the same year, Kenya and Norway, together with Albania, France, Gabon, Ghana, Germany, Ireland, Japan, Malta, Mozambique, Nauru, Switzerland, the UAE, the UK, and the USA, met to debate the climate, peace, and security opportunities for the UN Peace and Security Architecture.

Cybersecurity and international peace and security were an issue at stake under the Arria format for the first time in 2016. Through a joint Spain-Senegal effort, an encounter was pioneered to discuss a secure and reliable international cyberspace that respects human rights, promoting the harmonisation of national legislation and further developing international cooperation on cyber defence (Ministro de Asuntos Exteriores, Unión Europea y de Cooperación 2017). In this meeting, the guest ICT4Peace Foundation (ICT4Peace Foundation 2016) urged the states to engage in conflict prevention in cyberspace by prioritising its peaceful uses and requested states to commit to protecting critical civilian infrastructure from malicious activity by both state and non-state actors. During the same occasion, transnational anti-crime networks emphasised that the Council's primary focus in the area of cybercrime should be the use of Information and Communication Technology (ICT) in terrorist activities (Global Initiative against Transnational Organised Crime 2019). In 2017, Ukraine organised an Arria session on "Hybrid wars as a threat to international peace and security, Ukraine" to demand the international community to prevent, and implement measures against, acts of hybrid warfare, to protect the rights and interests of victims, and hold accountable the responsible while insisting on the necessity to elaborate a universal definition of hybrid warfare (Permanent Mission of Ukraine to the United Nations 2017). Ukraine, a then-elected member of the Security Council, illustrates the strategic political use of the Arria meetings within UN diplomacy while trying not only to provide its own definition of a new phenomenon known as hybrid warfare but also embracing the new political window within the UNSC to identify a threat.

In 2020, Estonia, Belgium, the Dominican Republic, Indonesia, and Kenya zoomed in on cyber stability, conflict prevention, and capacity building (United Nations Department of Political and Peacebuilding Affairs 2024). A couple of months later, Indonesia, Belgium, Estonia, Vietnam, and the International Committee of the Red Cross (ICRC) convened an Arria gathering specifically on cyberattacks against critical infrastructure (United Nations Department of Political and Peacebuilding Affairs 2024). A year later, Estonia and the UK targeted the prevention of malicious cyber activities' impact on civilians through this informal setting. In 2023, Albania and the USA delved into the responsibility and responsiveness of states to prevent cyberattacks on critical infrastructure. In 2024, in a meeting initiated by the Republic of Korea and co-hosted by Japan and the USA, the Arria encounter reviewed the evolving cyber threat landscape and its implications for the maintenance of international peace and security (United Nations Department of Political and Peacebuilding Affairs 2024).

Between 2020 and 2024, five other Arria events were convened on cybersecurity's different dimensions of threats (United Nations Department of Political and Peacebuilding Affairs 2024). Although Estonia showed an impressive agenda-setting role (Permanent Mission of Estonia at the United Nations 2024), other elected members started increasingly co-organising these reunions too, with the participation of the ICRC as a non-Council member. In April 2024, the Republic of Korea, the USA, and Japan hosted an Arria discussion on the "Evolving Cyber Threat Landscape and Its Implications for The Maintenance of International

Peace And Security", including technical briefings from the Deputy to the High Representative for Disarmament Affairs, the United Nations Institute for Disarmament Research (UNIDIR)'s Director, Dr. Robin Geiss, and the Director of blockchain analysis at Chainalysis, Valeria Kennedy (UNIDIR 2024). This meeting aimed at raising awareness among UN members on developing cyber issues, at promoting a better understanding of cybercrime and how it is a threat to international peace and security, and at providing recommendations on how the UNSC addresses these threats and how the response ought to complement ongoing work at the UNGA (UNIDIR 2024). The various facets of cybercrime—ransomware attacks, cryptocurrency heists, and cyber-mercenaries—were examined, and the cruciality of cooperation in such a "grey area" highlighted (UNIDIR 2024).

Three preliminary observations can be extracted from the development of this informal non-Security Council activity. The increasing forum-convening trend aligns with deeper debates on each threat-related theme and the growing E10 convening agency. Besides, the Arria meeting formula is a soft diplomacy format that encourages openness on the part of UNSC's elected and non-elected members, bolstering multilateralism amidst an era of contested legitimacy of international organisations. In this regard, the organisation of Arria-formula meetings is one of the six performance indicators to measure the influence (Brosig and Lecki 2023) of regional powers at the UNSC. These authors found that regional powers organise a relatively small number of such forums compared to the E10 and P5. It is possible to argue that, via calling for Arria meetings, elected UNSC members may set an informal agenda on novel issues that are not handled as threats to international peace and security. E10 members also take advantage of the flexibility that these meetings entail: apart from the obligation of following some guidelines to conduct them properly, rotating members can organise or co-organise with other UN members an event of such dimensions on issues and areas that suit their and/or the general public's interests.

The rationale behind convening these meetings can also vary. The UNSC members may host these gatherings to prevent some threats from reaching an international scale or from co-existing with other threats, such as armed conflict, worsening the situation and creating unmanageable crises. Joint UK-Pakistan efforts to address the security dimensions of climate change in 2013 marked the first multilateral effort in considering the latter as a potential threat to the former (Security Council Report 2013). This subsequently generated political, policy, and academic reactions, opening up a new debate beyond the two inviting countries. The G77 + China statement (Permanent Representation of Fiji to the United Nations 2013) backlash acquired a denouncing tone on the UNSC′s expansion over the roles and responsibilities of other UN organs (S/PV.5663 2007). Particularly, by recalling the bodies and instruments already tackling climate-related challenges, it warned about the potential of this initiative to sediment precedents. Thus, this evidenced the powerful impact of modifying the agenda-setting rules and practices. Hence, the elected UNSC member Pakistan put climate change on the multilateral agenda, changing the long-term P5 perspective on the necessity to address its security aspects.

In addition, both the format and the multifaceted nature of these non-traditional threats allow the UNSC's elected members to informally bring these concerns to the Council agenda. More importantly, through the soft diplomacy's character of the Arria Meetings, the E10 can push the P5 to discuss them in the framework of more formal Council venues (Boutellis 2022). A Mexican diplomat denotes the importance of the post-meeting document creation:

> After we organised this 'Arria-formula', we produced the Chair Summary of the meeting, and we attached to it all the interventions that we received in this 'Arria-formula' and then submitted it both to the Council and the Secretary-General requesting it to be circulated to all Council and UN members respectively. We did that because, even though the meeting was an informal one, the document became an official document once it was distributed to the Council, and the document itself will now find its way to the Repertoire. So there's something there in writing in terms of registry and record. Now the meeting is somehow on record to show that at least there was this discussion with these opinions being expressed. (Modirzadeh and Olabuenaga 2021, 309)

In terms of the Council's working methods, the diplomat stressed that more states participated in the Mexican-convened gathering than those submitting "Article 51 letters". These letters are the materialisation of

Article 51 of the UN Charter. Article 51 (United Nations 1945) recognises the UN Charter signatories 'states' right to self-defence and allows them to resort to it, with the duty to report this immediately to the Security Council. Hence, these letters are the result of those states recurring to their right, composing significant documents on the development of diplomatic international relations.

From a diplomatic angle, the Arria format has considerable advantages: it represents an opportunity for states to give their opinion in a comfortable atmosphere on certain themes "from a more abstract and general point of view", avoiding compromising their bilateral relationships or alliances with powerful countries (Modirzadeh and Olabuenaga 2021, 332). This way, through Arria gatherings, rotating members can build momentum for Council resolutions and capture political demands beyond the UN bubble.

Arria discussions were foundational in the adoption of Resolution 2475 on the protection of persons with disabilities in armed conflict (S/RES/2475 2019) and of Resolution 2493 on Women, Peace, and Security (WPS) (S/RES/2493 2019). In 2018, Poland co-convened this encounter with Côte d'Ivoire, Germany, Kuwait, and Peru on the situation of persons with disabilities in armed conflict, enjoying the support of the United Nations Children's Fund (UNICEF), the Office of the High Commissioner for Human Rights (OHCHR), and the International Disability Alliance (IDA) (United Nations Department of Political and Peacebuilding Affairs 2024). The unanimous adoption of Resolution 2475—"calling upon member states and parties to armed conflict to protect persons with disabilities in conflict situations and to ensure they have access to justice, basic services, and unimpeded humanitarian assistance" (United Nations 2019a)—confirms the transcendental success of the Arria meeting formula which aimed to "present concrete actions the Security Council can consider to assist, protect" (International Disability Alliance 2018).

Also in 2018, South Africa hosted an Arria reunion with Bolivia, France, Germany, and Poland to address the protection of children born of sexual violence in conflict zones (United Nations Department of Political and Peacebuilding Affairs 2024). Besides, it arranged a validation forum envisioning (United Nations 2019b) the country's adoption of its own national action plan on Women, Peace, and Security, and closely interacted with other stakeholders such as NGOs, civil society, and specialised third-party organisations (Nick Pay and Postolski 2021). Through Resolution 2493 (S/RES/2493 2019), the elected members managed to create an international consensus to recommit to its WPS agenda.

Specifically, regarding climate change (Maertens 2018), E10 members built momentum, especially during the period 2013–2018. Throughout this time, no open debates were organised by members of the UNSC solely on the topic of climate change. However, instead, four Arria meetings were organised during the same period. The use of Arria meetings has been a strategic way for some of the members who wish to push forward the topic of climate change at the UNSC, despite the inability to do this through official procedures such as open debates. It is due to the divisions on the matter by the P5 that progression through official procedures is impeded, as well as public opinion that diverted attention to other threats than climate change during that same period (Hardt et al. 2023).

Considering recent discursive and institutional developments on cyber threats and the previous example of how Arria meetings are a strategic tool to build momentum for the organisation of official procedures such as drafted resolutions and open debates, we argue that it is only a matter of time before one can observe their transition from the Arria discussions to resolution voting and adopting processes. When regional and small powers host Arria meetings as non-permanent Council members, this reveals a consensus on the seriousness of these threats and consequently an enhancement of their international credibility. Mexican Diplomat Olabuenaga refers to a quantitative factor to indicate the credibility of the topic raised by its delegation:

> My view of the relation of time to the number of delegations is, to the contrary, that to have this three-hours-long 'Arria-formula' discussion is a confirmation of interest, especially when many 'Arria-formula' meetings are over in around an hour and a half or maybe two hours, and normally include many more briefers. (Modirzadeh and Olabuenaga, 2021, 320)

Considering the qualitative element of the Arria meetings, the booming interventions of non-UN attendees shed light on the legitimacy of the conveners' message. Elected members have also emphasised the usefulness of building support for initiatives from non-Council members (Ossoff et al. 2022, 33). The fundamental role is portrayed by an illustrative case of Switzerland and other non-Council members in the establishment of the 1267 Ombudsperson (Ossoff et al. 2022). The Office of the Ombudsperson is an institution introduced by Resolution 1904 (S/RES/1904 2009) mandated to assist the Committee of Sanctions when considering delisting Al-Qaida and the Taliban and associated individuals and entities (Huber and Rodiles 2012).

Diverse sources of input from multi-stakeholders with scientific and technical expertise may ameliorate the quality of the initiatives. The possible increased credibility of elected members might be achieved by building closer linkages with members of the New York media outlets and UN-focused NGOs (Ossoff et al. 2022).

Addressing non-traditional threats in this informal debate space allows to engage essential international actors such as NGOs which due to their grass-rooted and field-working nature are directly exposured to the manifestations of these threats. In the building up (Hill et al. 2003) of Resolution 1325 on Women, Peace, and Security, women civil society members and international non-governmental organisations took the floor in an Arria meeting to target the Council with reflections of war experiences, just like in the first ever encounter with the Venezuelan Ambassador, where a Croatian priest expressed his people's sufferings.

By integrating these applications of the Arria formula, other roles for the elected members emerge. Non-permanent members may become threat identifiers and subsequent debate conveners. However, most importantly, they can develop innovative debate spheres to keep the multilateralism flame alive.

6 Conclusion

Small and regional powers have an essential role to play in shaping the discussions on non-traditional threats at the UNSC, despite facing multiple challenges in terms of influencing a decision's outcomes. The E10 has managed to bypass these difficulties by employing, or even creating, like Venezuela has done with Arria meetings, a variety of informal tools to influence decision-making and acting as power brokers.

Through their strategic political use of tools like Arria-formula meetings and coalition-building, they can set the UNSC agenda and continue negotiations on topics that are not formally addressed in the Security Council, circumventing disputes between permanent members, putting forward their arguments and specific interests in the discussions. Small and regional powers' ability to bring to the table a broadening of perspectives on threats through soft diplomacy demonstrates the evolution of the E10's ability to influence decision-making and agenda-setting in the UNSC and to face current challenges to multilateralism.

In this regard, the creation of these informal mechanisms and spaces of diplomatic exchange and negotiation was vital to rebalancing power distributions within the Council. These tools help the elected members to shape the UNSC's views on non-traditional threats. This chapter has extensively focused on the role of Arria meetings, one of the informal mechanisms which established not only a space for long-term threat identification but also a space for the E10 to use and engage with as a means to instrumentalise political responses to contemporary challenges to multilateralism. The evolution of working methods at the UNSC has enhanced the E10's influence and has also led to the inclusion of a wider range of actors, such as civil society and NGOs, which are essential for incorporating field and scientific data into decision-making processes.

Broadening the security agenda beyond the state-centred view in the UNSC is more than crucial for addressing the issues that lie ahead for the international community. Climate change, as well as facets of cyberattacks, are two examples of threats that destabilise countries and regions, making the escalation of conflicts inevitable if they aren't properly addressed on an international level. Based on this rationale, this chapter chose to address these two pressing challenges. This focalisation on non-traditional threats, especially through a preventive perspective, has been considered to be crucial for many states because delaying action only magnifies the threats' impact. Such progress in the decision-making process through soft influence can also be considered to be an attempt to avoid situations like the blockages the international community witnessed during the COVID-19 pandemic, rendering the UNSC ineffective in tackling the crisis. Consequently, this highlights the evolution of the UNSC's practices towards enhancing the institution's capacity for proactive threat identification, rather than being frequently reduced to the role of crisis management.

Just as the Roman military writer wrote "*si vis pacem, para bellum*" (if you want peace, prepare for war) regarding traditional threats, nowadays one can say that the UNSC's adage for facing these new challenges is henceforth "*Qui pacem desiderat, inopinato paratur*" (he who longs for peace is prepared for the unexpected).

However, the power in UNSC's decision-making resides ultimately in the compliance of the permanent members. This practical reality, due to veto power, underscores the continuous structural imbalance in the UNSC. This consequently confines small and regional powers to rely on informal tools and mechanisms as the formal ones are subjected to division and blockage by the P5. It is a long and hard process, as non-traditional threats, because of their non-attributable or intricate components, can be interpreted very differently depending on states' interests and how they are impacted, including for the cases of small and regional powers. The E10, and more generally small and regional powers, are not a homogeneous group, as shown through diverse open debates on climate change. This heterogeneity underlines the further complexity and difficulty for addressing non-traditional threats at the UNSC. Nonetheless, such issues are gradually being covered in official spaces and related documents. "Between 2001 and 2020, documents mentioning climate and related topics grew from 0.19 to 9.01 per cent of the total" (Scartozzi 2022, 296), showing the increased consideration of such threats in the UNSC.

Further research is necessary to fully comprehend the role of small and regional powers in the UNSC. Understanding the E10's new role as debate conveners, as well as their agency role, can shed light on the power dynamics occurring during negotiations in the context of informal mechanisms. Additional analysis of informal organisational trends, such as Arria-formula meetings as a soft public diplomacy tool, is necessary to completely grasp the differences in power dynamics when compared to formal meetings. To date, no research has adequately explored this theme. Moreover, as put forward by many researchers, the literature on the topic of cybersecurity at the UN, and more broadly in international relations, particularly from the perspective of international peace and security, remains insufficient (Tikk and Schia 2020). It is imperative to conduct more research on this issue to fully understand its evolution. The events regarding cybersecurity during the year of the writing of this chapter, such as the Arria meeting on the topic on April 2024, suggest that negotiations related to further implications of the UNSC's actions in the area of cybersecurity will pave the way for future research on the topic, and illustrate whether cybersecurity will be treated differently compared to other non-traditional threats.

Appendix

Subsidiary Organs and Chair Positions African Group (1999–2024)

Subsidiary organs	Chairs	Year
Security Council Committee established pursuant to resolution 1373 (2001) concerning counter-terrorism	Algeria	2024
Security Council Committee established pursuant to resolution 2127 (2013) concerning the Central African Republic	Algeria	2024
Working Group established pursuant to resolution 1566 (2004)	Algeria	2024
Ad Hoc Working Group on Conflict Prevention and Resolution in Africa	Mozambique	2024
Informal Working Group on International Tribunals	Sierra Leone	2024
Security Council Committee established pursuant to resolution 1533 (2004) concerning the Democratic Republic of the Congo	Sierra Leone	2024
Security Council Committee established pursuant to resolution 2206 (2015) concerning South Sudan	Sierra Leone	2024
Informal Working Group on International Tribunals	Gabon	2023
Security Council Committee established pursuant to resolution 1533 (2004) concerning the Democratic Republic of the Congo	Gabon	2023
Security Council Committee established pursuant to resolution 2206 (2015) concerning South Sudan	Gabon	2023
Security Council Committee established pursuant to resolution 2653 (2022) concerning Haiti	Gabon	2023
Security Council Committee established	Ghana	2023

Subsidiary Organs and Chair Positions Asia-Pacific Group (1999–2024)

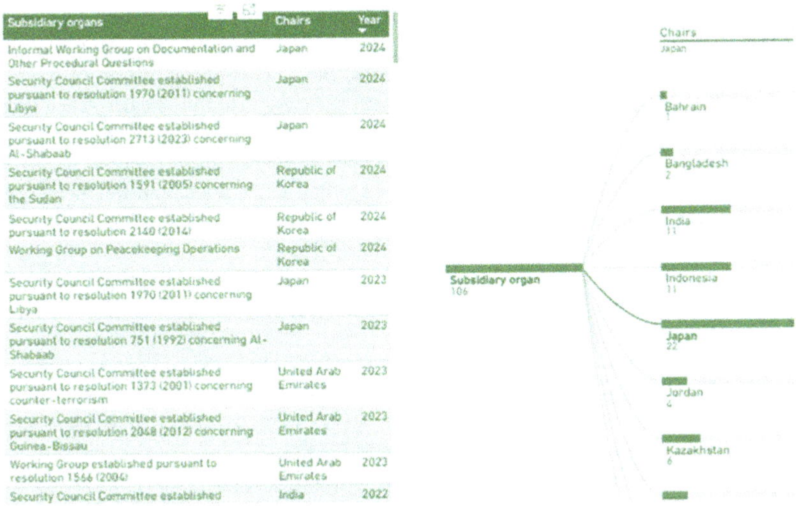

Source Extracted from UNSC Repertoire (2024) Subsidiary Organs Chairs and Vice-Chairs Dashboard

References

Boutellis, Arthur. "Lessons from E10 Engagement on the Security Council." *International Peace Institute*, 2022. https://www.ipinst.org/2022/11/lessons-from-e10-engagement-on-the-security-counci.

Briggs, Chad. Climate Security at the UN and in the United States, 2007–2020: The Contradictory Leadership and Silence of the US. In *Climate security in the anthropocene: Exploring the approaches of United Nations Security Council Member-States* (2023): pp. 319–345. Cham: Springer International Publishing.

Brosig, Malte, and Michal Lecki. "Regional Powers at the UN Security Council: More Mainstream Than Upstream?" *International Spectator* 58, no. 4 (2023): 149–168. https://doi.org/10.1080/03932729.2023.2226521.

Buzan, Barry, Ole Wæver, and Jaap de Wilde. *Security: A New Framework for Analysis.* Lynne Rienner, 1998.

Caballero-Anthony, Mely, ed. *An Introduction to Non-Traditional Security Studies*. SAGE Publications Ltd, 2016. https://doi.org/10.4135/9781473972308.

Cai, Congyan, Larissa van den Herik, and Tiyanjana Maluwa. "The UN Security Council: Between Centralism and Regionalism." In *The UN Security Council and the Maintenance of Peace in a Changing World*, 186277. Cambridge University Press, 2024. https://www.cambridge.org/core/product/BE3BDE7E862B11EF9CBE07B0874657F.

Carnegie Endowment for International Peace. *UN Security Council Reform: What the World Thinks*. Edited by Stewart Patrick. Carnegieendowment.org, June 28, 2023. https://carnegieendowment.org/research/2023/06/un-security-council-reform-what-the-world-thinks?lang=en.

Charbonneau, Bruno. "The COVID-19 Test of the United Nations Security Council." *International Journal: Canada's Journal of Global Policy Analysis* 76, no. 1 (2021): 6–16. https://doi.org/10.1177/0020702020986897.

Department of Public Information. "Security Council, in Statement, Says 'Contextual Information' on Possible Security Implications of Climate Change Important When Climate Impacts Drive Conflict." *UN Press*, July 20, 2011. https://press.un.org/en/2011/sc10332.doc.htm.

Department of Public Information of the United Nations. *UN Yearbook of the United Nations 1992*. Vol. 46. United Nations, 1992. https://www.unmultimedia.org/searchers/yearbook/page.jsp?volume=1992&bookpage=34.

Efremova, Ksenia. "Small States in Great Power Politics: Understanding the 'Buffer Effect.'" *Central European Journal of International and Security Studies* 13, no. 1 (2019): 100–121. https://doi.org/10.51870/cejiss.a130102.

Eriksen, Christine, Andrin Hauri, Joane Holliger, Simon J. A. Mason, Fabian Merz, and Benno Zogg. "L'Interface Entre Sécurité et Changement Climatique." *Politique de Sécurité: Analyses du CSS* 315 (2022). https://doi.org/10.3929/ethz-b-000584942.

Gailišs, Eduards. "Small Powers as Non-Permanent Members of the United Nations Security Council: A Case Study of the Baltic States." *Security and Defence Quarterly* 45 (2024). https://doi.org/10.35467/sdq/172983.

Gonsalves, Ralph. *Address to the Nations on St. Vincent and the Grenadines' Election to the United Nations Security Council*. Office of the Prime Minister St. Vincent and the Grenadines, June 13, 2019. https://pmoffice.gov.vc/pmoffice/images/stories/Speeches/ADDRESS-TO-THE-NATION-ON-SVGS-ELECTION-TO-THE-UNSC.pdf.

Goodwin, Louice. "The UN Security Council and Non-Traditional Security Threats: Why the Failures of the Council's Covid-19 Response Dampen Hopes for Council Action on Climate Change." *Victoria University of Wellington Law Review* 53, no. 2 (2022): 251–280. https://doi.org/10.26686/vuwlr.v53i2.7743.

Gordanić, Jelica. "NGOs and the UN Security Council: Between Informal Reality and Possibilities of Formal Interaction." *The Review of International Affairs* 72, no. 1182 (2021): 47–65. https://doi.org/10.18485/iipe_ria.2021.72.1182.3.

Haass, Richard. "The UN's Unhappy Birthday." *Project Syndicate*, September 10, 2020. https://www.project-syndicate.org/commentary/united-nations-75th-anniversary-little-to-celebrate-by-richard-haass-2020-09.

Hardt, Judith Nora. *Environmental Security in the Anthropocene: Assessing Theory and Practice.* 1st ed. (2017): 256 pp. London: Routledge. https://doi.org/10.4324/9781315202471

Hardt, Judith Nora, Cameron Harrington, Franziskus von Lucke, Adrien Estève, and Nicholas Simpson, eds. *Climate Security in the Anthropocene*. The Anthropocene: Politik—Economics—Society—Science 33, (2023): (pp. 400). Cham: Springer International Publishing. https://doi.org/10.1007/978-3-031-260 14-8

Huber, K., and A. Rodiles. An ombudsperson in the United Nations Security Council: A paradigm shift? *Anuario Mexicano de Derecho Internacional*, (2012): 107–142. https://doi.org/10.1016/j.anui.2012.07.005

Hill, Felicity, Mikele Aboitiz, and Sara Poehlman-Doumbouya. "Nongovernmental Organizations' Role in the Buildup and Implementation of Security Council Resolution 1325." *Signs: Journal of Women in Culture and Society* 28, no. 4 (2003): 1255–1269. https://doi.org/10.1086/368321.

Hulme, M. *Why We Disagree About Climate Change: Understanding Controversy, Inaction and Opportunity.* Cambridge University Press, 2009.

Intergovernmental Panel on Climate Change (IPCC). *AR5 Climate Change 2014: Impacts, Adaptation, and Vulnerability.* IPCC, 2014. https://www.ipcc.ch/report/ar5/wg2/.

Intergovernmental Panel on Climate Change (IPCC). Climate Change: Synthesis Report. Contribution of Working Groups I, II and III to the Sixth Assessment Report of the Intergovernmental Panel on Climate Change (2023): pp. 35–115. Edited by Core Writing Team, Hoesung Lee, and J. Romero. Geneva: IPCC. https://doi.org/10.59327/IPCC/AR6-9789291691647

Jones, B. D., C. Pascual, and S. J. Stedman. *Power and Responsibility: Building International Order in an Era of Transnational Threats.* Rowman & Littlefield, 2009.

Laux, Thomas. "What Makes a Global Movement? Analyzing the Conditions for Strong Participation in the Climate Strike." *Social Science Information* 60, no. 3 (2021). 413–435. https://doi.org/10.1177/05390184211022251.

Loik, Ramon, and Evelin Jürgenson. "Securitisation of Climate Change in Estonia: Widening Security Concepts in National Strategies and Foreign Policy Activities." *Climate Security in the Anthropocene*, vol. 33, 85–112. Springer Nature, 2023. https://doi.org/10.1007/978-3-031-26014-8_5.

Long, Tom. "Small States, Great Power? Gaining Influence Through Intrinsic, Derivative, and Collective Power." *International Studies Review* 19, no. 2 (2017): 185–205. http://www.jstor.org/stable/26407895.

Maertens, Lucile. "Le Changement Climatique en Débat au Conseil de Sécurité de l'ONU." *Revue Internationale et Stratégique* no. 109, no. 1 (2018): 105–114. https://doi.org/10.3917/ris.109.0105.

Maertens, Lucile. "Climatizing the UN Security Council." *International Politics* 58, no. 4 (2021): 640–660. https://doi.org/10.1057/s41311-021-00281-9.

Martin, Ian. "Elected Members Today: Overcoming the Handicaps." In *Elected Members of the Security Council: Lame Ducks or Key Players?*, 42–55. Brill | Nijhoff, 2020. https://doi.org/10.1163/9789004425392.

Modirzadeh, Naz K., and Pablo Arrocha Olabuenaga. "A Conversation Between Pablo Arrocha Olabuenaga and Naz Khatoon Modirzadeh on the Origins, Objectives, and Context of the 24 February 2021 'Arria-Formula' Meeting Convened by Mexico." *Journal on the Use of Force and International Law* 8, no. 2 (2021): 291–342. https://doi.org/10.1080/20531702.2021.1997514.

Natalucci, Fabio, M. S. Qureshi, and Felix Suntheim. "Rising Cyber Threats Pose Serious Concerns for Financial Stability." International Monetary Fund, April 9, 2024. https://www.imf.org/en/Blogs/Articles/2024/04/09/rising-cyber-threats-pose-serious-concerns-for-financial-stability.

Nick Pay, Vahid, and Przemsław Postolski. "Power and Diplomacy in the United Nations Security Council: The Influence of Elected Members." *The International Spectator* 57, no. 2 (2021): 1–17. https://doi.org/10.1080/03932729.2021.1966192.

Nolte, D., and L. L. Schenoni. "To Lead or Not to Lead: Regional Powers and Regional Leadership." *International Politics* 61, no. 1 (2021): 40–59. https://doi.org/10.1057/s41311-021-00355-8.

Oksamytna, Kseniya. Civil Society and the UN Security Council: Advocacy on the Rwandan Genocide. In *Partnerships in International Policymaking: Civil Society and Public Institutions in European and Global Affairs*, edited by Raffaele Marchetti, 131–145. Palgrave Macmillan UK, 2017. https://doi.org/10.1057/9781349949380_7.

Ossoff, William, Naz Modirzadeh, and Dustin Lewis. *Preparing for a Twenty-Four-Month Sprint: A Primer for Prospective and New Elected Members of the United Nations Security Council.* Harvard Law School Program on International Law and Armed Conflict (HLS PILAC), 2022. https://dash.harvard.edu/handle/1/37367713.

Permanent Mission of France to the United Nations in New York. *Joint Initiative to Address Climate-Related Security Risks.* France ONU, 2020. https://onu.delegfrance.org/Joint-initiative-to-address-climate-related-security-risks.

Pobjie, Erin. "COVID-19 and the Scope of the UN Security Council's Mandate to Address Non-Traditional Threats to International Peace and Security." November 5, 2020. https://papers.ssrn.com/sol3/papers.cfm?abstract_id=3725850.

Putin, Vladimir. Speech at the International Artic Forum. President of Russia (2017). http://en.kremlin.ru/events/president/news/54149

Reire, Gunda. "Small States in the United Nations Security Council: Legal and Conceptual Aspects Versus Practical Perspective." *Socrates* 3, no. 21 (2021): 90–104. https://doi.org/10.25143/socr.21.2021.3.090-104.

Rogers, James. "Threats to International Peace and Security Caused by Transnational Activities of Terrorist Groups: Address to UN Security Council Arria-Formula." *University of Southern Denmark*, October 1, 2022. https://portal.findresearcher.sdu.dk/en/publications/threats-to-international-peace-and-security-caused-by-transnation.

Rychnovská, D. "Transnational Threats and Reformulating Security in the UN." *Central European Journal of International and Security Studies* 9, no. 2 (2015).

Scartozzi, Cesare M. "Climate Change in the UN Security Council: An Analysis of Discourses and Organizational Trends." *International Studies Perspectives* 23, no. 3 (2022): 290–312. https://doi.org/10.1093/isp/ekac003.

Security Council Affairs Division. *Arria-Formula Meetings Dashboard*. United Nations Security Council. Accessed June 27, 2024. https://main.un.org/securitycouncil/en/content/repertoire/research-tools/Arria-formul.

Selby, Jan. "The Trump Presidency, Climate Change, and the Prospect of a Disorderly Energy Transition." *Review of International Studies* 45, no. 3 (2019): 471–490. https://doi.org/10.1017/S0260210518000165.

Stepanov, Igor. Climate Change in Security Perceptions and Practices in Russia. In *Climate Security in the Anthropocene: Exploring the Approaches of United Nations Security Council Member-States* (2023): pp. 209–230. Cham: Springer International Publishing.

Tikk, E., & Schia, N. N. (2020). The role of the UN Security Council in cybersecurity. In E. Tikk & M. Kerttunen (Eds.), International peace and security in the digital age (Chapter 30). Routledge. https://library.oapen.org/bitstream/handle/20.500.12657/43219/9781351038904_oachapter30.pdf

UNIDIR. UN Security Council Arria Meeting on Cybersecurity. UNIDIR → Building a More Secure World, (2024, April 5). https://unidir.org/un-security-council-arria-meeting-on-cybersecurity/

United Nations (UN). "Five Ways the Climate Crisis Impacts Human Security." United Nations. Accessed June 27, 2024. https://www.un.org/en/climatechange/science/climate-issues/human-security#:~:text=Yemen%2C%20Mali%2C%20Afghanistan%2C%20Democratic.

United Nations (UN). *United Nations Charter.* United Nations, 1945. https://www.un.org/en/about-us/un-charter/full-text.

United Nations (UN). "Security Council, in Statement, Says 'Contextual Information' on Possible Security Implications of Climate Change Important When Climate Impacts Drive Conflict." *United Nations Press Release*, July 20, 2011. https://press.un.org/en/2011/sc10332.doc.htm.

United Nations (UN). "We Must Not Sleepwalk into War, Secretary-General Warns in General Assembly, Citing Nuclear Peril, Terrorism, Inequality among Most Severe Global Threats." *United Nations Press Release*, September 19, 2019a. https://press.un.org/en/2017/sgsm18693.doc.htm.

United Nations. "St. Vincent and the Grenadines Breaks a Record, as Smallest Ever Security Council Seat Holder." *UN News*, June 7, 2019b. https://news.un.org/en/story/2019/06/1040071.

United Nations. "Security Council Fails to Adopt Resolution Integrating Climate-Related Security Risk into Conflict-Prevention Strategies." *United Nations Press Release*, December 13, 2021. https://press.un.org/en/2021/sc14732.doc.htm.

United Nations Security Council. Provisional rules of procedure of the Security Council. (Chapter 4, Rule 18), (2023). https://main.un.org/securitycouncil/en/content/provisional-rules-procedure-0

United Nations Security Council (UNSC). *Formats of Meetings Related to the Security Council: Names of Meetings Participation of Non-Council Members in the Discussion.* Accessed June 27, 2024. https://www.un.org/securitycouncil/sites/www.un.org.securitycouncil/files/meetings.pdf.

United Nations Security Council (UNSC). *S/23500: Note by the President of the Security Council.* January 31, 1992. https://www.securitycouncilreport.org/atf/cf/%7B65BFCF9B-6D27-4E9C-8CD3-CF6E4FF96FF9%7D/PKO%20S%2023500.pdf.

United Nations Security Council (UNSC). *Subsidiary Organs Chairs and Vice-Chairs Dashboard.* United Nations Security Council, January 2, 2024. https://www.un.org/securitycouncil/content/repertoire/research-tools/chairs.

Vihma, Antto, Mulugetta, Yacob, and Karlsson-Vinkhuyzen, Sylvia. Negotiating Solidarity? The G77 through the Prism of Climate Change Negotiations. *Global Change, Peace & Security* 23, no. 3 (2011): 315–334. https://doi.org/10.1080/14781158.2011.601853

Vuori, J. A. Climate security in China: An issue for humanity rather than the nation. *Climate security in the Anthropocene: Exploring the approaches of United Nations Security Council member-states* (2023): (pp. 45–63). Springer International Publishing.

Wellens, Karel. "The UN Security Council and New Threats to the Peace: Back to the Future." *Journal of Conflict and Security Law* 8, no. 1 (2003): 15–70. https://doi.org/10.1093/jcsl/8.1.15.

World Meteorological Organization (WMO). "Rate and Impact of Climate Change Surges Dramatically in 2011–2020." *World Meteorological Organization*, December 5, 2023. https://wmo.int/news/media-centre/rate-and-impact-of-climate-change-surges-dramatically-2011-2020.

World Nuclear Association (WNA). "Security of Nuclear Facilities and Material." *World Nuclear Association*, April 12, 2022. https://world-nuclear.org/information-library/safety-and-security/security/security-of-nuclear-facilities-and-material.

CHAPTER 7

Small and Emerging Powers in UNSC Decision-Making

Binghua Lu, Sahib Rasulov, and Umang Sodhi

1 Introduction

In the complex global governance architecture, the United Nations Security Council (from here on UNSC) emerges as a pivotal linchpin institution in constructing and maintaining international peace and security. The UNSC is a stage where the narratives of power, influence, and diplomacy intertwine, and within this milieu, the roles of small and emerging powers (S&E) have become increasingly salient. This book chapter embarks on an academic inquiry into the influence of these nations on the UNSC's decision-making processes over the past two decades, revealing a multifaceted and dynamic engagement that challenges the traditional hegemony of great powers and reshapes our understanding of multilateral governance.

The significance of this research is manifold, as it seeks to elucidate the mechanisms through which S&E nations navigate the corridors of power within the UNSC. In an era characterised by intensifying great power

B. Lu (✉) · S. Rasulov · U. Sodhi
Leiden University, Leiden, The Netherlands
e-mail: ChristineJi1997@hotmail.com

M. O. Hosli et al. (eds.), *Multilateralism and the United Nations Security Council*, https://doi.org/10.1007/978-3-031-85320-3_7

competition, the study of S&E influence on UNSC decision-making is not just relevant but imperative for comprehending the evolving dynamics of international relations. By dissecting the motivations, strategies, and outcomes associated with the active participation of S&E nations in the UNSC, this chapter offers a nuanced perspective on their role in the contemporary global order.

In terms of structure, this chapter tries to address a series of interrelated sub-questions that collectively form a comprehensive inquiry into the role of S&E in the UNSC. These sub-questions are designed to explore the underlying reasons for S&E aspirations for UNSC membership, the methodologies and strategies they employ to influence decisions, and the tangible impacts of their engagement on the UNSC's decision-making landscape.

The overarching research question frames this investigation: In the contemporary context of Great Power competition, what are the dynamics and dimensions of Small and Emerging Powers' influence on UNSC decision-making? To propose an answer, the chapter will delve into the following sub-questions through the analysis of various cases:

I. What are the motivations for small and emerging powers to seek membership in the UNSC, and what electoral strategies do they deploy to secure a seat?
II. As members of the UNSC, how do these powers exert influence over the decision-making process, and what unique contributions do they make to the council's deliberations?
III. What are the measurable outcomes of their participation in the UNSC, and how do these outcomes reflect on their influence and the broader UNSC decision-making landscape?

The main argument of this research posits that small and emerging powers, despite their relative lack of material capabilities compared to the P5 members, wield significant influence in the UNSC through strategic engagement, diplomatic understanding, and the advocacy of issue-specific expertise. This influence is not only manifested in their ability to shape discourse and policy but also in their capacity to act as catalysts for change within the council, pushing for more inclusive and representative decision-making processes.

Four cases will be studied in this chapter. Türkiye, Singapore, India, and UAE are representative in terms of understanding S&E in the UNSC in the past decade. These cases represent how emerging (otherwise called Middle) powers—Türkiye and India—differ from great powers. Specifically, we will demonstrate how similarly labelled powers vary not only in their conduct of election campaigns for a seat at the UNSC but also in their performance once elected and their overall perspective of the Security Council as the institution of global governance. The selection of these two countries is also justified by their record of winning and losing seats in the UNSC. Meanwhile, our choice of UAE and Singapore equally shows how small powers navigate themselves to the UNSC and highlight their differences. For example, the UAE, as a representative of the Arab States, demonstrates how Arab countries coordinate with each other in order to promote one candidate to the UNSC, thus concentrating their election campaign on non-Arab states to get necessary votes.

In each case, the aforementioned three sub-questions will be answered respectively. In the first sections of each case, we will explore the motivations of the selected countries and the electoral strategies that have led to their successful accession. The second section will delve into these nations' impact on UNSC decisions, analysing their methods and strategies and their unique contributions to the UNSC's deliberations. Finally, the third section will assess their membership outcomes, evaluating their progress and the broader implications for the UNSC and global governance. As we conclude this chapter, we will reflect on the broader implications of small and emerging powers' influence on the UNSC, considering the potential for reform, the challenges they face, and the future trajectory of their role in this critical arena of international relations.

2 Methods and Approaches

For the purpose of our analyses, the chapter aims to employ a robust methodological approach, including concept analysis to clarify the theoretical underpinnings of "small" and "emerging" powers, case studies to provide empirical evidence of their influence, and a thorough review of data and sources to help ensure academic rigour.

The concept of "small power" remains elusive and is often criticised for its lack of a precise definition or identifiable characteristics. This ambiguity becomes particularly problematic when attempting to contrast it with the notion of an "emerging power". The question arises: How do we discern that Country A is an emerging power? Traditionally, power has been measured through material indicators such as military capabilities and the extent of diplomatic representation (Baldacchino 2023, 21; Maass 2017, 220).

However, power can also be assessed comparatively, either within the same region or across different regions, highlighting the importance of recognising the asymmetrical relationships between states. While some countries exhibit clear dominance, others may possess high military and economic levels yet still be categorised differently.

This chapter proposes adopting the updated typology of state power by Neal G. Jesse and John R. Dreyer, which refines the original framework introduced by Anders Wivel and Kajsa Ji Noe Oest (Wivel and Oest 2010). According to this typology:

(1) A **Superpower** is a state that consistently maintains strength in its interactions with all other states at the global, regional, or sub-regional levels.
(2) A **Great state** is one that, while not as powerful as a superpower globally, surpasses non-great states at the global, regional, or sub-regional levels.
(3) A **Middle state** is consistently weaker at the global level but can be stronger than other states at the regional or sub-regional levels.
(4) A **Small state** is typically weaker at both the global and regional levels but may hold strength at the sub-regional level.
(5) A **Microstate** is generally weak at all levels, with the exception of interactions with other microstates.

This typology is advantageous as it facilitates the comparison of states of the same category across various regions, thereby illustrating the relativity of "smallness" to a state's geographical and political context (Jesse and Dreyer 2016, 13). Moreover, this typology is not static; it can evolve in accordance with a country's shifting regional and global political status.

The relevance of this typology to the UNSC is worth exploring, especially considering its egalitarian treatment of elected members (otherwise called E10). Despite their diverse regional and global standings, countries like Switzerland, the Republic of Korea, and Sierra Leone are treated equally within the UNSC. By correctly categorising countries according to this typology, we can highlight the distinct motivations and capacities of small and emerging powers—classified here as middle states—for their election to the Security Council and their potential to influence global governance within a limited timeframe.

Understanding the differences among small and emerging powers within the UNSC membership context is essential for grasping the dynamics of the elected members of the Council. This understanding, in turn, contributes to the broader behavioural dynamics within the UNSC, where even the P5—comprising France, the United Kingdom, the United States (P3), and the Russian Federation and People's Republic of China (P2)—display internal subgroupings. This dynamic enables the elected (non-permanent) 10 members to act, albeit not always, as a collective group or as an object of bargaining among the P5 to gain the necessary amount of votes (Martin 2019, 54).

As the subsequent sections will reveal, the crucial factor lies in the differing perceptions of small and emerging powers regarding their UNSC membership and their subsequent performance.

3 Literature Review

This literature review will highlight the evolution of S&E roles in the UNSC and identify gaps in current understanding. The academic literature has historically given short shrift to small states, with mainstream International Relations (IR) theories, particularly realists, largely maintaining the argument that small states are irrelevant due to their smallness (Maass 2017, 221). For this reason, the literature heavily emphasised that a small state's survival can only be guaranteed through strategic hedging and/or allying with a greater power (Thorhallsson et al. 2018, 15). Not surprising that only with the introduction of new theories and approaches—as a challenge to realism—was the literature able to expand analysis on small states' behaviour and especially its role in the UNSC.

However, with the end of the Cold War, more opportunities arose. The UNSC was no longer hampered by a bipolar world order characterised by great power rivalry, as was the case throughout the Cold War (Tyler and Pahlow 2014, 97). In post-Cold War international politics, small states gained more opportunities to assert their interests, specifically due to the larger space for geopolitical maneuverability. Active diplomacy, especially in coalition-building efforts both in the regional and international institutions, enabled small states to contribute meaningfully to global peace and security discussions, advocate for issues pertinent to their regions, and leverage their positions to gain international recognition and influence.

Similarly, a change occurred within the academic literature. Increased criticism of mainstream IR theories, particularly structural realism, enabled scholars to go beyond the narrative of small-state survival and systematic analyses of their interactions. During the Cold War, the majority of the IR literature was heavily influenced by structural realist arguments about an anarchical environment and military capability as the measurement of a state's true power. As Kenneth Waltz argued himself, "[I]t would be... ridiculous to construct a theory of international politics on Malaysia and Costa Rica" (Waltz 1979, 72–73). This, as Tom Long argues, "led to important errors of analysis and prediction" and caused a period of "biased case selection where systemic theories were developed with reference to a handful of largely European states and then presumed to be applicable to all" (Long 2022, 18). In short, small states were seen through the prism of great powers as countries that lacked the necessary means to sustain their security, let alone national interests. This led to the dominant view that smaller powers are either reduced to the role of spectators—thus largely irrelevant—or altogether reduced to the role of buffer state (Maass 2020, 23–24; Pedi 2020, 170–171).

Reevaluating the role of small states led to the advancement of a new understanding of small-power politics. International organisations emerged as mechanisms for advancing national and regional interests by small states, specifically through an emphasis on international norms. This, in turn, contributed to the expanding literature on the role of E10 at the UNSC. The accumulated literature demonstrated a unique ability of smaller powers to impact global governance, whether by utilising their flexible diplomatic corps organisation structure, expertise on one of several issues, or their international reputation, especially as successful mediators (for literature review see Thorhallsson 2018, 21). Yet, the post-Cold War literature tends to focus more on smaller powers, mainly from the West (Ekengren and Möller 2023; Schrijver and Blokker 2020).

It gets even more problematic when we look at emerging powers. The term smaller powers means weaker and smaller countries (in terms of power projection) than great powers. Thus, emerging powers such as Germany, Japan, India, Türkiye, Brazil, and South Africa are relatively weak to the P5, but on regional and sub-regional levels, they act as great powers with the aspiration to impact neighbouring regions and global politics (Brosig and Lecki 2023, 150; Patrick 2023, 3; Sever and Gök

2016, 1152). For these powers, membership in the UNSC is a delicate issue. These powers share a common belief that the UNSC's composition needs reform to address current and emerging issues—hence, increasing the effectiveness of the Council in addressing international security—reflect the current balance of power, and limit the P5 hegemony (Hosli and Dorfler 2019, 36). Yet, they significantly differ in terms of the scope of the reform. While Türkiye, as a member of the Uniting for Consensus (UfC) group, advocates for increasing the number of non-permanent seats and eliminiting veto powers (Yinanç 2023, 56), India, a member of G4, emphasises increasing the number of permanent members with veto rights (for a more detailed discussion, see Schaefer 2017, 74–76; Binder and Heupel 2020, 98; Hosli and Dörfler 2019).

It is here that understanding the role of emerging powers in the UNSC evolves into the issue of reforming the UNSC; in other words, adjusting the functions and responsibilities of the Security Council to the current regional and global dynamics and needs (see Brosig and Lecki 2023, 150). While it is true that emerging powers are at the centre of the UNSC reform, significant differences exist between them. As Yolanda Spies (2024) argues, the stark difference between the middle powers of the past and today is the emphasis on the hard power in their respective regions and increasing assertiveness when it comes to the seat at the UNSC. More specifically, while traditional middle powers such as Canada, Netherlands, and Sweden limited themselves to be actively elected as non-permanent members of the council, new emerging powers such as India, Türkiye, Japan, Germany, and South Africa focus more on reforming the UNSC, sometimes aiming at becoming permanent members (Spies 2024, 10; 13; 15).

3.1 *Case studies: Türkiye, Singapore, India, UAE*

Türkiye

I. *Rationality of Membership*

Republic of Türkiye's bid for a non permanent seat represents a long and complex process. With a series of military conflicts taking place around Türkiye in a period of five years—the 2003 US invasion of Iraq, the Second Lebanon War in 2006, and the Georgia-Russia war in 2008—as well as prospects for a potential military solution to Iran's nuclear file and the threat of terrorism, Türkiye found itself in an unpleasant security environment. Additionally, domestic political developments, such as the de-securitisation of its foreign policy and the implementation of democratisation packages as a part of the EU accession process, made it even more complicated for Türkiye to win the elections.

What perhaps made it more complex was the shadow of the past: Türkiye had been elected to the Council three times (1951–1952; 1954–1955; and in 1961), with unsuccessful attempts made in 1946, 1948, the 1970s, and 1990s (Balcı and Duman 2021; Kirecci 2009, 3). The membership at the Council coincided with the early period of the Cold War, when much of the UNSC dynamic was conditioned by the geopolitical rivalry between the United States and the Soviet Union and their allies. Balci and Hazar argue that Türkiye's membership was largely a product of the US efforts to sustain a pro-Western composition of the Security Council, as evident in Türkiye's reluctance to run the campaign during the 1953 and 1959 elections (Balci and Hazar 2021, 282). Furthermore, Ankara utilised its membership in the Council to "prove its loyalty to the Western alliance", as evident in the minimal independent initiative, thus assuming the role of supporter of matters brought by NATO allies (Balci and Hazar 2021, 283; 286; Balcı and Duman 2021, 291). Yet, as will be discussed below, the end of the Cold War, with global and regional shifting dynamics and domestic political developments, enabled Turkish policymakers to shift the foreign policy towards a more active and independent policy, transforming Türkiye into one of the central players of global governance.

Campaign for a Seat

Membership in the UNSC is seen as a way of bringing largely ignored regional matters to the Council, thus emphasising more fair and just representation in addressing often neglected issues (NEL and NOLTE 2010, 877). This argument is also linked to the overall shift of power and efficiency of the UNSC as the main body responsible for global stability and security (Hosli and Dörfler 2019, 35–36). Another practical reason, as demonstrated by several studies, is that elected members tend to receive more foreign aid, specifically from the United States, the United Nations (UN), and institutions such as the World Bank and the International

Monetary Fund (IMF) (Kuziemko and Werker 2006, 923–924; Mesquita and Smith 2010, 682).

For Türkiye, a seat at the UNSC would demonstrate the international community's recognition of its role as one of the centres of international relations, owing to its geostrategic location, historical ties to multiple surrounding regions, and capacity to level up its politics to the highest levels of global governance (Gül 2008, 14; Ilgit and Ozkececi-Taner 2014, 184). Guided by Ahmet Davudoğlu's "strategic depth" doctrine,[1] Türkiye's new government, led by the Justice & Development Party (JDP) since 2002, set elections for a seat in the Council as one of its immediate goals. An extensive multi-dimensional campaign, a novelty for the country's foreign policy, was implemented almost immediately after the JDP formed a new government. Not only has Türkiye expanded its diplomatic presence in multiple regions, but it has also organised and hosted various international summits focused on key issues and needs of those regions (Kirecci 2009, 4). For example, in 2008 alone, Türkiye hosted a summit for countries of the Caribbean Community and "The First Africa-Turkiye Cooperation Summit" (Kirecci 2009, 4). Similarly, Türkiye reached out to various regional and international institutions, such as the Arab League and the Organisation of Islamic Cooperation (Balci and Duman 2022, 377). In other words, by actively engaging on bilateral and multilateral levels, Türkiye constructed the image of a candidate who, once elected, will bring relevant issues to the agenda of the UNSC.

On a bilateral level, the period between 2002 and 2008 stands out as an exceptional time for Türkiye's diplomacy. Specifically, Turkish diplomacy achieved an improvement of bilateral relations with Greece and Armenia—traditionally unstable relations—while actively endorsing UN General Secretary Kofi Annan's plan to reunify Cyprus (Ilgit and Ozkececi-Taner 2014, 186–187). These processes went along with other initiatives, such as a series of op-eds by high-ranking officials and

[1] The doctrine envisioned a more central role for Türkiye in regional and global politics of the post-Cold War era. Specifically, the doctrine put emphasis on historical past and linkages (soft power) of Türkiye—together with material capabilities—as means of assuming leadership in the Middle East and acting as a strategic actor between East and West. With such a vision, Turkish Foreign Policy was based on five key principles: "(1) balance between security and democracy, (2) zero problems with neighbors, (3) proactive and pre-emptive peace diplomacy, (4) multi-dimensional foreign policy, and (5) rhythmic diplomacy" (Ozkececi-Taner, p. 204).

humanitarian assistance directly or via Non-Governmental Organisations (NGOs). Overall, Türkiye's campaign heavily focused on specific accomplishments such as contributing to peacekeeping missions, assuming roles of mediator, especially in the Middle East, and distributing humanitarian assistance (Aral 2009, 153–154).

Türkiye's campaign illustrates a more complex and multifaceted strategy. Diplomats and high-ranking officials have not only emphasised various accomplishments, but they have also contextualised them within historical, cultural, religious, and political ties to countries of neighbouring regions—Caucasus, Middle East, Balkans—and as an actor willing to bring issues of African, Caribbean, and even Pacific states to the UNSC's attention. One scholar argued that winning the seat is not about the power but rather what a candidate country brings to the Council (see Malone 2000). Yet, Türkiye's opponents for a seat at the UNSC—Austria and Iceland—equally invested energy and resources into their campaigns. While there are no common criteria for election success—perhaps with the exception of the country's contribution to maintaining international peace and security and other UN purposes as outlined by Article 23 of the UN Charter—the UN tends to favour a "turn-taking" system, which, in theory, grants preference to a country that never occupied a seat in the Council (Thorhallsson 2017, 48). Yet, as Balci and Duman (2022) argued, 2008s financial crisis significantly hampered Iceland's campaign, which was already disadvantaged due to the country's very low profile status within the United Nations (Balci and Duman 2022, 337; Thorhallsson et al. 2022, 86). Self-perception equally played a key role in the election outcome. While Iceland's campaign witnessed domestic criticism, the Turkish government and the general population were convinced that Türkiye deserved a seat in the Council (Jenkins, n.d.; Thorhallsson et al. 2022, 87).

II. *At the Council Table*

During its term at the UNSC (2009–2010), Türkiye played an active "agenda setter" role. Throughout its term, most diplomatic work within the Council focused on addressing security dynamics in the Middle East. Having served twice as a president of the Council, it resided over the formal meetings titled "Situation in the Middle East including the Palestinian Problem during June 2009 period" and "Ensuring the Security

Council's effective role in maintaining international peace and security" (Sever and Gök 2016, 1163). Among the issues brought to the Council was the conflict in Gaza, especially after the Mavi Marmara incident.[2] As Ilgit and Özkeçeci-Taner (2014) argue, "Türkiye's active stance within the UN platform on the Palestinian issue reached its peak at the end of May and the beginning of June 2010 when Israeli military forces boarded an international flotilla that was carrying civilian people and humanitarian assistance to the Gaza Strip in international waters off the coast of Gaza, where nine Turkish civilian passengers were killed" (Ilgit and Ozkececi-Taner 2014, 190). In the aftermath of the incident, Türkiye not only called for an emergency meeting of the Security Council but also called for extraordinary meetings of the North Atalantic Treaty Organisation (NATO) and Organisation of Islamic Cooperation (OIC) (Ilgit and Ozkececi-Taner 2014, 190). This was perhaps the first time Turkish diplomacy witnessed high activity in international and regional organisations simultaneously. Türkiye successfully pushed for the UNSC to adopt the presidential statement, which condemned the attack on the ships and called for an impartial investigation (UN News). Although several investigations took place, the report by the Panel of Inquiry, known as the Palmer Report, created more controversy. First, the report was leaked to the public. Second, the report "accuses[d] Israel of resorting to excessive use of violence that led to the death of nine Turkish citizens and demanded that Israel pay compensation" (Ilgit and Ozkececi-Taner 2014, 190). Dissatisfied with the report, Türkiye now capitalised on its seat at the Security Council to impose diplomatic pressure on Israel. This is evident in how the regional entities such as the Arab League (AL) and OIC, as well as participants of the Conference on Interaction and Confidence-Building Measures in Asia (CICA), condemned Israel's attack on the flotilla (Ilgit and Ozkececi-Taner 2014, 191). Least is known about Türkiye's attempts to reach out to the members of the UNSC, with the exception of Brazil—which adopted Türkiye's discourse—and perhaps Lebanon, a member of the AL and OIC ((Ilgit and Ozkececi-Taner

[2] Also known as the Gaza Flotilla Raid was an incident at the international waters of the Mediterranean Sea that occurred when a flotilla of six ships—organised by pro Palestinian NGOs—attempted to break Israel's naval blockade of the Gaza Strip—imposed as a result of its military operations. On May 31st, 2010, Israel's Navy attempt to stop the flotilla, led to civilian casualties on the board of Mavi Marmara—mostly Turkish citizens—thus emerging as the first most severe diplomatic crisis between Türkiye and Israel.

2014, 191). Although the UNSC Presidential Statement did not meet all conditions set by Türkiye—the statement did not mention an official apology and end of the Gaza blockade—Ankara managed to persuade Washington to meet two conditions: "immediate release of civilians and ships that were held by Israel and an international investigation" (Ilgit and Ozkececi-Taner 2014, 192).

The second issue brought by Türkiye to the UNSC was Iran's nuclear program. Unlike the Mavi Marmara and Gaza blockade incident, the issue of Iran's nuclear program represents a failed attempt to convince members of the UNSC and other regional entities to adopt a different approach as opposed to imposing the fourth set of sanctions. Türkiye's official position was clear: every country has the right to pursue a nuclear program for peaceful purposes only. In light of conflicts in the Middle East and economic sanctions—particularly against Iraq until the 2003 invasion—Türkiye attempted to mediate the issue and propose a confidence-building mechanism. Together with Brazil, after intensive rounds of negotiations, the parties issued a "Joint Declaration by Iran, Türkiye, and Brazil". The declaration envisioned the Islamic Republic's readiness to "deposit, while still having the ownership of, 1200 kg Low-enriched uranium (LEU) in Türkiye, which might be observed by the IAEA" (Ilgit and Ozkececi-Taner 2014, 195). However, despite their efforts, neither Türküye nor Brazil was able to gain needed support even among the elected members. Ultimately, the UNSC adopted the P3's draft resolution with 2 "against" (Türkiye, Brazil) and 1 abstention (Lebanon) (Ilgit and Ozkececi-Taner 2014, 195).

III. *End of the Term and Prospects for the Future*

Türkiye's term at the Security Council coincided with the larger dynamics in the Middle East. While Ankara attempted to address issues of neglected regions, it had to throw its entire diplomatic capabilities into addressing the issue of the Gaza blockade and Iran's nuclear program, issues that directly impacted it. The cross-organisational and bilateral support that Türkiye managed to generate in light of the Mavi Marmara incident, as well as the efforts along with Brazil to act as mediators between Iran, the

United States, and other members of the Vienna Group[3] (Russia, France, and the International Atomic Energy Agency [IAEA]), demonstrates the country's growing diplomatic profile and prestige. The joint effort with Brazil represents the ability of both countries to address global issues despite their differences in the future of the Security Council reform.[4]

However, some negative implications are visible. Although Türkiye's leading role in the UN in advocating the rights of Palestinians increased the country's prestige, the spillover effects of the Arab Spring and abandonment of "zero problems with neighbours" foreign policy in favour of more assertive actions across the Middle East significantly damaged the country's reputation. This is best evident in Türkiye's second campaign for a seat in 2014: as Aysegul Sever and Gonca Oguz Gok argue, Saudi Arabia and Egypt campaigned intensively against Türkiye's candidacy (Yinanç 2023, 1180). By the end of the elections, Türkiye scored only 60 votes compared to 151 in 2008.

Singapore

I. *Rationality of Membership*

Singapore is a somewhat unconventional case study. Its aspirations are to influence the UNSC's financial/sanctions policies, climate change capacity, and operations rather than gain a permanent seat, unlike the ambitions of other cases, such as India.

Singapore's desire to be part of the UNSC is driven by a combination of factors. Firstly, it seeks to fulfil its international obligations as a state that respects international law and multilateralism and maintains its status as a global city by actively participating in global governance forums (Storey 2014). Secondly, it aims at addressing climate change for small island states and securing economic opportunities, particularly in the Arctic region due to large untapped reserves of oil (Storey 2014). Thirdly,

[3] The Vienna Group is an informal name for a group of six + one (China, France, Germany, Russia, UK, and United States + International Atomic Energy Agency) to negotiate with Iran over its nuclear program. The main goal of the group was to resurrect 2015 agreement on ensuring that Iran's civilian nuclear prorgam could not enrich uranium for the development of the nuclear weapon (Vox).

[4] More specifically, Brazil—a member of the G4 group—advocates for expanding the UNSC and veto powers (Yinanç 2023, 56).

Singapore's interest in the South China Sea, where it plays the role of an effective coordinator and honest broker, is a crucial factor in its desire to be on and influence the agenda setting of the UNSC (Chan 2016, 42). Singapore's need to navigate its relationship with China, particularly in light of the South China Sea disputes, is another important consideration (Tan 2017).

Singapore's relevance in international relations is interesting when considered in the context of its growing status as a city-state of economic growth and perhaps, less positively, as a hub of tax-avoidant individuals from Western countries (Nee 2016). Thus, its role also applies to accepting and implementing UNSC resolutions on sanctions on a national level to demonstrate compliance.

Singapore's approach to its involvement in the UNSC can be described in a two-pronged manner taking into account its geographical location and its economic performance. Singapore's status as a small state in Southeast Asia has resulted in much importance being placed on climate-related agenda items in the UNSC. According to statements made by Gafoor, Ambassador of Singapore to the United Nations, the small state is vulnerable to temperature changes that threaten the livelihoods and environmental safety of its citizens (United Nations 2023). In relation to this, Singapore's vital interest is that the primary objective of the UNSC to maintain international peace and security should be fulfilled by recognising the threat that climate change-related events pose to society.

In light of these examples, the argument can be made that Singapore's aspirations for the UNSC are not necessarily to gain a permanent seat at the table, as can be said for countries like India, but rather to advocate for reforms for non-permanent members. This is significant, as it highlights the underlying modalities through which Singapore wishes to reform and put forth its interests and significantly deviates from the strategies of other countries who more actively demand permanent representation at the UNSC.

II. *At the Council Table: The Impact and Bargains of Singapore in UNSC Decisions*

Singapore's approach to influencing decision-making at the UNSC can be seen during its tenure as a non-permanent member of the Council from 2001 to 2002. UNSC documents (S/2002/519) and (S/2002/

685) provide an overview of Singapore's efforts at the UNSC. Topical analysis of the approach of Singapore's presidency reveals a strong focus on the views of developing countries, particularly those from Africa and Asia and small island states, whose views have not been fully accommodated at this point. Status reports on topics show a heavy commitment towards holding permanent members of the UNSC more accountable towards countries that do not have a seat at the UNSC (United Nations Security Council 2002).

For example, Singapore's tenure in 2001–2002 specifically focused on enlarging G20, something which has strategic value for the future. This was reflected in 2009 when Singapore formed an informal grouping system to promote transparency and accountability among all emerging and developed economies towards developing and underdeveloped countries (Ministry of Foreign Affairs Singapore, n.d.). This group, called the Global Governance Group, consists of 30 countries as member states, mostly small and emerging economies, as an effort to solidify the concerns of these countries at a multilateral level.

Singapore's unique engagement and spheres of influence in the UNSC and beyond are its strongest tools in its arsenal. Most innovatively, Singapore also recognises that it is unnecessary to be a part of the UNSC to influence its decision-making. This strategy hinges on utilising other platforms to ramp up pressure on the UNSC to consider climate change-related items and form advocacy and topic-based groups.

Singapore's involvement in the formation of the informal and non-ideological Forum of Small States in 1992 serves as a platform to discuss common problems of small states and informally influence the agenda setting of UN organs not limited to the UNSC to include grievances of small states (Ministry of Foreign Affairs Singapore, n.d(a)). This group has grown in membership and seeks to create more pressure to increase the accountability of G20 members towards non-G20 members.

More actively, Singapore plays an important role in pushing the agenda for reform on the contentious veto model in the UNSC for permanent members. In April 2022, Singapore co-sponsored a resolution supported by 83 other countries to table a discussion on methods to reform the veto (*The Straits Times* 2022). This is in line with Singapore's push to reform the UNSC by either expanding the veto to more members of the UNSC or limiting the instances in which the veto can be used by permanent members.

III. *End of the Term and Prospects for the Future*

Singapore, by its involvement in open-ended working groups on Security Council reform and informal groups, including the Security Council Retreat, sought to pose questions to the permanent members of the UNSC regarding their performance and commitment to principles of justice, protection of women and children in particular, and development objectives. It sought to influence the agenda by routinely tabling discussions on contentious armed conflict-related issues in Asia (such as the East Timor Independence issue) and Africa (for instance, in Sierra Leone, the Great Lakes Region, and the Democratic Republic of Congo).

In its Presidency of the UNSC during its term as a non-permanent member from 2001 to 2002, Singapore demonstrated a commitment towards creating transparency of agenda items for both the wider population of countries outside the UNSC and the wider public whose interest in the UNSC as a highly exclusive organ of the UN was increasing (Ministry of Foreign Affairs Singapore, n.d.).

Its impact, measurable directly through its presidency during 2001–2002, is evident by its presidency, where it published regular reports, particularly focusing on peacekeeping budgets and focus on African states. More informally, its drive to influence UNSC decision-making by pressuring the UNSC to consider specific items for its agenda stems from its lobbying and forming a forum of small states is considerable as well.

Such efforts seek to drive wider needs from developing and non-permanent member countries for the UNSC towards reform and maintain informal networks to influence the UNSC by creating common agendas and rallying a large group of small states with similar concerns.

India

I. *Rationality of Membership*

India's pursuit of a permanent seat on the UNSC is driven by a combination of factors. As a strategic rising power, India's involvement in the UNSC is directly related to its desire to secure a permanent seat at the UNSC. India's bid for a permanent seat has been supported by France, the United Kingdom (UK), Russia, and the United States (Chitre 2022). The absence of China's support is a symptom of strained relations between the two countries and explains why India seeks to balance the scales of power regionally. India's historic cross-border terrorism is a huge motivation for pursuing an aggressive campaign to gain permanent representation and a stake in existential discussions of security issues in the South Asian region. In this endeavour, gaining an equal voice in the UNSC is imperative.

India sees its status as an important rising power as a testament to its growing relevance in geopolitics. Murthy (2011) highlights India's desire to play a leadership role in addressing global challenges, such as terrorism and economic inequities. India's security interests and the strategic and geographic considerations (neighbouring countries of China and Pakistan, both nuclear powers) with a security threat make it an important aspirant for a permanent UNSC seat. Murthy's (2011) assertion is that the opportunity of India's tenure in 2011–2012 was not just a significant win in terms of geopolitical rivalry, but also a potential avenue for multilateral cooperation from regional rivals (Pakistan and China) as both had tacit support for India's tenure as a non-permanent member at the UNSC. This could be a huge motivation for India to pursue a foreign policy that is more inclusive of regional preferences, rather than just national ones.

Historically, India's role as a founding member of the Non-Alignment Movement has played a significant role in carving out a unique foreign policy, coming at a time when the Cold War divided countries into two camps. Therefore, the campaign for the Security Council is rooted in India's desire for a balanced and independent foreign policy. India has refrained several times from voting on certain resolutions and agenda points, especially those perceived to be a result of aggression by other countries (Dutta & Bhowmik 2022). India's push for a permanent seat at the UNSC is also grounded in its image as a representative of Global South concerns. For instance, according to Hazra (2024), the most recent influential act of New Delhi came under its G20 Presidency, when it lobbied and facilitated the inclusion of the African Union as a full-time member. This argument has been used as evidence of India's growing sphere of influence and role in bringing forth Global South concerns on a global level.

Domestically, such stances are used by governments and political parties to highlight the work done on foreign affairs. The topic of a permanent seat garners much attention, as it is often framed as a "competition" of sorts between China, Pakistan, and India. For instance, the use of a push for a permanent seat at the UNSC by the ruling Bharatiya

Janata Party (BJP) in its election manifesto in 2024 as a major campaign promise (*The Hindu* 2024).

The promise of the Security Council seat remains in domestic election rhetoric, a coveted prize at the international level that finds popular support among the general population. The issue specification of India's pursuit at the domestic level has intensified the national push from all parties, not just the ruling party, for a permanent seat at the UNSC.

This has international implications as the push for a permanent seat for India at the UNSC also reflects a reputational challenge for India, and its desire to be counted among geopolitical spheres of influence. India's view on the UNSC, therefore, reflects a motivation to join the UNSC as a permanent member, and also advocate for reform so that non-permanent members are also well represented.

II. *At the Council Table: The Impact and Bargains of India in UNSC Decisions*

India's main source of influence over decision-making in the UNSC stems from its heavy involvement as a non-permanent member. According to Mukherjee and Malone (2013), India's performance in the UNSC is heavily influenced by its efforts to set agendas on some points that find wide support among the public and other countries: first, increasing the accountability of the UNSC at the world stage, enlarging the UNSC permanent membership model, reforming working methods, and protecting the integrity of nation states especially when it comes to military interventions by the UNSC (Mukherjee and Malone 2013, 112).

Such analysis corroborates the argument that India's role in the UNSC is a systems-influencing state (Hazra 2024). India's policy of multi-alignment, or alignment with different powers on certain issues (such as Russia on terrorism, oil exports) and with the United States (on South Asian security and countering China's dominance), is therefore a big part of India's bargaining power in terms of getting support at the UNSC. Its strategic involvement with China (as a regional neighbour), Russia (as an international economic partner), and the United States (as a long-term partner for cooperation by countering China's influence) makes India's non-permanent membership an interesting case to follow.

India has acted on its security interests in the past and sought to influence the UNSC by participating actively in peacekeeping missions in

Iraq, Kuwait, Lebanon, and Gaza in the past (Mishra 2006). India's most significant method of influencing is the sheer dependence of peacekeeping forces on Indian soldiers. It has committed 3000 soldiers in Sierra Leone, the largest contribution in a single conflict from any country (Mishra 2006, 352).

India's efforts to utilise the emerging powers bloc (consisting of Brazil, Germany, and Japan) to encourage reform at the UNSC are characteristic of small and emerging states rallying together. The G4 Bloc agreed not to undercut each other's claims for permanent representation at the UNSC. India's alliance with these countries gave it significant backing from other countries as it lobbied for support for several agenda items, such as counter-terrorism initiatives and peacekeeping (Nafey 2005, 5). Therefore, India's use of diplomatic strategies has increased its influence in the UNSC in recent years.

III. *End of Term and Prospects for the Future*

India's outcomes at the UNSC are closely connected with its focus on regional geopolitics. Tumultuous political situations in the region, for instance, in Afghanistan and Pakistan, imply that India has a stake in the discussions on topics such as counter-terrorism and cross-border aggression.

According to the Indian Council of World Affairs (n.d.), in 2021, given the turmoil in Afghanistan, India's presence and push for a resolution to not tolerate any form of terrorism bases in Afghanistan was exceptionally important. India's focus on the region was expanded when operational reforms gave non-permanent members like India to relook and restructure the United Nations Mission in Afghanistan to reach the humanitarian aid goals provided through this mission (Indian Council of World Affairs, n.d.).

India's diplomatic prowess in the past, particularly in the years 2006–2007, resulted in uniting the African Union to collectively give support for India's bid for a permanent seat (Nafey 2005, 32). In this context, India's status as a strong contender for a permanent seat at the UNSC is solidified due to the international support it enjoys from other emerging powers.

India has sought to address existing issues in peacekeeping, proposing a four-point agenda for reform in UN peacekeeping forces by accommodating new technologies to make peacekeeping missions environmentally friendly and cost-effective (Kumar 2022). India is also one of the largest contributors to the UN peacekeeping forces in terms of personnel. Its impact through diplomatic channels, and proactively voting positively on most UNSC resolutions, shows that it is willing to play the long game by influencing the main decision-takers and gathering support from more emerging centres of influence such as Africa.

UAE

I. *Rationality of Membership: UAE Winning Seat at the UNSC*

The United Arab Emirates (UAE) is a new yet competitive figure in UNSC non-permanent members. The 75th election for the UNSC non-permanent members took place during the General Assembly session in June 2021 (UN News 2021). The UAE needed a two-thirds majority of votes cast by General Assembly members present and voting. With 179 votes, the UAE's overwhelming support in the election reflected the effectiveness of its diplomatic campaign and broad-based endorsements (UN News 2021). This successful bid marked a recognition of the UAE's proactive engagement in international affairs and its significant contributions to global peace and security.

The UAE has been strategically positioned as a regional and global pivotal player, especially in recent years. Its aspirations to secure a non-permanent seat on the UNSC stem from a blend of economic, political, and strategic motivations. The 2022–2023 term of the UNSC non-permanent member witnessed the very first participation of the UAE, which campaigned by emphasising its contributions to global peace, security, and development, receiving the recognition of regional cooperators and international ones. Highlighting its achievements and aspirations in international peacekeeping, humanitarian aid, climate action, and gender equality, the UAE successfully garnered significant support from various regions during its tenure, leveraging its economic strength, regional influence, and strong multilateral relations.

Key supporters of UAE becoming a UNSC non-permanent member included the Arab League member states, Gulf Cooperation Council (GCC) countries, African nations, and influential global powers from both the West and non-Western camps (GCC Studies Unit 2023). The Arab League member states informally designated the UAE as their representative, a decision that, although lacking formal recognition, carries significant weight in regional politics. Differing from the standard election process of a regional representative as a member of the UNSC, the UAE's reception of this representative role reflects the general will of the Arab states. The UAE's economic diplomacy, characterised by substantial investments and aid programs, played a pivotal role in garnering support for its candidacy. Furthermore, the UAE's proactive engagement in regional organisations and alignment with Western security and economic policies further solidified its position. Despite widespread backing, the UAE encountered opposition and obstacles from countries influenced by political rivalries, particularly within the Middle East, as well as concerns regarding its human rights record. Some Western nations and human rights advocacy groups raised concerns about freedom of expression and political dissent within the UAE (Human Rights Watch 2022). Geopolitical considerations also influenced the stance of certain countries aligned with rival blocs.

The UAE's economic strength and its role as a regional power hub are central to its bid for a UNSC seat. The nation's robust economic framework in recent years, underscored by its top ranking in the Arab Economic Competitiveness Index, showcases its superior investment climate and economic stability (Saleh et al. 2023). Furthermore, the UAE's high standing in the Global Soft Power Index—17th globally and 1st in the Middle East—demonstrates its influential position on the world stage (Saleh 2024). These factors collectively enhance the UAE's appeal as a candidate for the UNSC, presenting it as a nation capable of contributing meaningfully to global governance.

The UAE's level of global integration solidifies its suitability for the position. Being one of the most globally connected countries in the Middle East, the UAE's role as a trading hub and recipient of significant foreign investment has propelled it to become the second-largest economy in the Arab world (*The National* 2021). This extensive global interconnectedness allows the UAE to offer a distinctive viewpoint within the UNSC, advocating for policies that prioritise economic integration and collaboration.

One more notable factor adding to the UAE's ambition of securing a place in the UNSC is its highly developed infrastructure. This is of crucial relevance to the fulfilment of the duty as an E10 member, namely the ability of one country to practice its proposals. Without a solid infrastructure foundation which ensures an efficient toolbox for problem-solving, the significance of the security and peace-related proposals would be hindered. The UAE tops various infrastructure indices, including those of mobile phone usage and access to electricity. It is also 14th in the world for goods trade exports (Emirates News Agency 2022)—achievements that demonstrate the UAE's ability to partake in large international undertakings aiming at global development goals. In addition, being a global technology and innovation hub places the UAE squarely in line with UNSC objectives on sustainable development plus addressing global challenges through technological means (WIPO 2023). The nation's advanced infrastructure underscores its vision of using technology—such as peacekeeping tech or humanitarian aid tech—as a tool for ensuring security while also implying a promising adoption for future initiatives aimed at these noble causes.

The UAE's attainment of non-permanent membership in the UNSC is part of its efforts to enrich its leadership and international status resources, which comes with increased honour. This has been achieved through proactive diplomacy that has seen the nation enter into multilateral partnerships in both aid and security. These partnerships are meant to strategically bring economic benefits to the UAE—at the same time, placing the nation favourably in its region to solidify support for its bid for a UNSC seat. The high premium placed on conflict prevention underscores UAE's suitability as a member of the UNSC, demonstrated by active involvement in UN peacekeeping missions plus the promotion of inclusive transitional processes. On top of this, cybersecurity promotes women as well as climate change: these are all areas supported by the Women, Peace and Security (WPS) agenda, an area advocated by the UAE, thus demonstrating how well-aligned their priorities would be if allowed on board to influence UNSC agenda items effectively for global peace and security.

II. *At the Council Table: UAE Influences the UNSC Decision-Making Process*

The UAE, as a non-permanent member of the UNSC, uses different strategies to influence the decision-making process. These strategies are based on the UAE's diplomatic strategy and its role in international organisations; also they depend on how much the UAE is committed to these global challenges.

When it comes to diplomacy, the UAE has put forward its preference for restraint plus dialogue as the means to address regional tensions. Its advocacy for diplomatic solutions and its call for maximum restraint in times of crisis speak volumes of its dedication to resolving conflicts peacefully. Among the proposals that the UAE has floated, covering climate change, humanitarian assistance, peace and security, as well as tolerance—include Draft Resolution No. 2720 on humanitarian assistance to Gaza through which it aims at enhancing global security efforts. The proactive approach demonstrated by these initiatives illustrates how the UAE takes up its UNSC membership responsibly (Permanent Mission of the United Arab Emirates to the United Nations 2022; UN Meetings Coverage and Press Releases 2023). This method of diplomacy not only works towards stabilising the region, but it also helps to boost the UAE's standing as a responsible global player.

The UAE's "diversified balance" strategy involves leveraging its regional leadership and using both military hard power and economic aid to influence political situations. This approach allows the UAE to navigate complex regional threats and maintain flexibility in its responses, which influence is further amplified by its involvement in international organisations. As a dialogue partner in the Shanghai Cooperation Organisation (SCO), the UAE contributes to global political stability and economic prosperity (United Arab Emirates Ministry of Foreign Affairs 2023). This engagement demonstrates the UAE's commitment to multilateralism and its ability to collaborate with various international actors.

By establishing cooperation with different countries and regions, the UAE is able to mitigate risks and, at the same time, widen its diplomatic reach. The countries' strategic alliances, such as their normalisation of relations with Israel, exemplify their hedging strategy (Uppal and Barrington 2023). This not only boosts its geopolitical influence but places it as a primary intermediary in the Arab world, fostering wider alliances and collaborations. On an international level: Abu Dhabi's commitment to the "One China" policy forms a basis for stable and supportive relations with China. China, as one of the P5 members, becomes one major resource of support when the UAE seeks opportunities during the initiative for non-permanent membership. On March 17, 2022, briefing co-organised by UAE during the first presidency term meeting on 2022–2023, activities between the UN and the League of

Arab States (LAS) took place. The UAE takes it as a priority to foster a new international order with the Arabic world more engaged and presented (*Security Council Report* 2023). Domestically, political stability is achieved through solid policies and dealing with threats that could destabilise politics in the country. The effort of not supporting political Islamism is part of efforts to keep the political environment stable and hence supportive of the UAE's international aspirations that would require a reliable base from global engagements.

The UAE's commitment to global agendas, particularly in climate change and Women, Peace, and Security (WPS), impacts the UNSC's decision-making. The UAE's climate initiatives, such as the National Climate Change Strategy and its pledge to reduce greenhouse gas emissions, set a precedent for international climate action (UAE UNSC Candidate 2021b). The efforts made by the country in expanding coverage plus enhancing coastal resilience speak volumes of proactive measures taken by them on board against climate change even at high costs. In the area of WPS, the GCC saw the launch of the WPS National Action Plan by the UAE, which was the first of its kind. This plan, along with being part of the WPS Chiefs of Defence Network, demonstrates their commitment towards gender equality and women's empowerment (The Official Portal of the UAE Government 2024). The importance placed by the UAE on policy coordination as well as multi-sectoral cooperation does not go unnoticed: it reinforces these spheres' influence while also gaining international recognition supported through various means.

III. *From Participation to Progress: The Fruits of UAE Membership in the UNSC*

The UAE's tenure (2022.01–2023.12) as a non-permanent member of the UNSC has yielded several notable outcomes, reflecting its ability to influence international policies and contribute to global stability.

The UAE's voting behaviour and priorities within the UNSC have shaped the agenda of the Security Council. As discussed above, during its presidency, the UAE prioritised the WPS agenda, climate security, and cooperation with the Arab League. These priorities not only advanced specific issues but also highlighted the UAE's leadership in addressing global challenges. The UAE's proactive stance on climate change has led to the adoption of new approaches within the UNSC. By advocating for the integration of climate-related security risks into the council's agenda, the UAE has enhanced the UNSC's capacity to address environmental challenges (Massoud 2023). The country's successful hosting of the 28th Conference of the Parties (COP28) to the United Nations Framework Convention on Climate Change (UNFCCC) further underscores its influence on global climate governance (UN MPTF Office 2024; UNFCCC 2023).

Notwithstanding its economic and soft power strengths, the UAE encounters challenges in reconciling varied international interests. The convoluted political landscape calls for a keen awareness of the dual internal and external pressures. Managing to advance its interests is an indication of diplomatic finesse and strategic vision, which helped the UAE secure landmark resolutions. Such initiatives highlight UAE's approach to using UNSC as a tool for bringing tangible changes, while, at the same time, not jeopardising the complex relations it holds with the United States and Western allies on different fronts.

The UAE's UNSC engagement significantly enhanced regional and international peace. It has received appreciation for its peacekeeping efforts that focus on inclusive transitional processes. (Massoud 2023) The UAE's support for multilateralism—as seen in its backing of India for a UNSC seat reform—underscores its quest for a collaborative world order where all major stakeholders have a say. This has helped the UAE stake a solid place among key players in both regional and global spheres. The proactive involvement of the UAE in addressing humanitarian crises in various instances, along with fostering international cooperation, has helped build these profiles: a responsible member state interested in global issues and an influential actor whose actions matter on the world stage.

4 Conclusion

This chapter embarked on an intellectual odyssey to unravel the multifaceted roles of small and emerging powers (S&E) within the United Nations Security Council (UNSC). Through a detailed exploration of their motivations, strategies, and outcomes, we have sought to shed light on the intricate dynamics of S&E influence in the contemporary context of great power competition. As we reflect on the journey traversed, several key insights emerge, painting a comprehensive picture of the evolving landscape of UNSC decision-making.

Firstly, the UNSC aspirations of states in S&E, such as Türkiye, Singapore, India, and the UAE, are multifaceted. They go beyond strategic and political considerations to also include moral dimensions. Their quest for a place at the high table is an ambition to increase their standing on the world stage and use the platform to bring attention to regional issues that are important to them with hopes of finding sustainable international peace and security. Their electoral tactics in some cases reflect their diplomatic sophistication, consisting of manifold approaches involving more than one party, be it bilateral or multilateral engagement plus issue advocacy, which might lead to the formation of strategic alliances. Most crucially, these states represent existing diversity among emerging and small powers. It shows that while these countries are interested in better reflection of the balance of power, they present different ideas and visions of how to reflect this balance of power within the institutional structure of the UNSC.

Secondly, S&Es have transformed their role within the UNSC, transitioning from passive to active participants. They've become vital agenda setters and mediators, deftly using diplomacy to steer discussions on critical global issues. This shift exemplifies their ability to navigate and influence the UNSC's complex political landscape, showcasing a strategic and informed approach to global governance.

Thirdly, the tangible outcomes of S&E membership in the UNSC are evident in the visible progress they have made in shaping the council's agenda and influencing its decisions. Their contributions to global governance, while varied in scope and impact, have collectively enriched the council's deliberations and enhanced its capacity to address emerging threats and challenges. From advocating for climate security to promoting gender equality and advancing regional stability, the imprint of S&E powers is indelible in the UNSC's evolving narrative.

It should be stated however that our arguments must be evaluated by looking at other smaller and emerging powers. Cases such as Singapore and UAE better reflect current trends of how smaller powers navigate themselves through great power rivalry. This was done in parallel with our analysis of Türkiye and India. While the literature on these state actors and their aspirations for the UNSC is rich, revisiting the topics helps to put into perspective the past and current trends. For a better understanding of how S&E powers influence the UNSC, we need to expand and cross-compare between them in the context of their present political activism to become influential members of the UNSC.

To conclude this chapter, it is imperative to acknowledge the broader implications of S&E's influence on the UNSC. Their active engagement challenges the prevailing power structures and advocates for a more inclusive and representative decision-making process. It underscores the potential for reform within the council, pushing for a reconfiguration that reflects the changing global realities and the rising influence of non-traditional powers. Moreover, the chapter's findings prompt a critical reflection on the future trajectory of S&E roles in the UNSC. As the global power dynamics continue to shift, the strategic positioning of these nations will be pivotal in shaping the council's response to emerging challenges. Their ability to adapt, forge alliances, and leverage their unique strengths will determine their continued influence in the council's deliberative landscape.

References

Aral, Berdal. "Turkey in the UN Security Council: Its Election and Performance." *Insight Turkey* 11, no. 4 (2009): 151–168.

Balci, Ali, and Ahmet Hazar. "Turkey in the UN Security Council During the Cold War: Elections, Voting Motivations and Alliance Commitments." *Middle Eastern Studies* 57, no. 2 (2021): 279–291. https://doi.org/10.1080/00263206.2020.1842369.

Balcı, Ali, and Timur İ. Duman. "Turkey's Candidature to the UN Security Council Seat in 1948: Why the West's 'Favorite' Candidate Lost." *Turkish Historical Review* 11, no. 2–3 (2021): 284–302. https://doi.org/10.1163/18775462-bja10017.

Balci, Ali, and Timur İ. Duman. "Muslim Solidarity in the UN General Assembly: Evidence from Elections of Rotating Members to the Security Council." *Global Governance: A Review of Multilateralism and International Organizations* 28, no. 3 (2022): 330–354. https://doi.org/10.1163/19426720-02803001.

Baldacchino, Godfrey. "Reproposing the Small State." In *The Success of Small States in International Relations: Mice That Roar?* 1st ed., 17–26. Routledge, 2023. https://doi.org/10.4324/9781003314745.

Binder, Martin, and Monika Heupel. "Rising Powers, UN Security Council Reform, and the Failure of Rhetorical Coercion." *Global Policy* 11, no. S3 (2020): 93–103.

Brosig, Malte, and Magdalena Lecki. "Regional Powers at the UN Security Council: More Mainstream Than Upstream?" *The International Spectator* 58, no. 4 (2023): 149–168. https://doi.org/10.1080/03932729.2023.2226521.

Chan, Jane. "Singapore and the South China Sea: Being an Effective Coordinator and Honest Broker." *Asia Policy* 21 (2016): 41–46. https://doi.org/10.1353/asp.2016.0017.

Chitre, M. "List of Countries Backing India's Bid for Permanent Seat at UN Security Council." *Hindustan Times*, 2022, December 15. https://www.hindustantimes.com/india-news/list-of-countries-backing-india-s-bid-for-permanent-seat-at-un-security-council-101671078247949.html.

Dutta, M., and Bhowmik, K. "India's Legacy of Non-alignment." *Asia Times*, 2022, March 22. https://asiatimes.com/2022/03/indias-legacy-of-non-alignment/.

Ekengren, Ann-Marie, and Ulrika Möller. *The Quest for Power in the UNSC: The Campaigns and Selection of Non-permanent Members*. Brill | Nijhoff, 2023. https://doi.org/10.1163/9789004687110.

Emirates News Agency. "UAE Ranked Among Leading Countries on Digital Lifestyle Indexes: TDRA." *Emirates News Agency*, 2022. https://www.wam.ae/en/details/1395303078941.

Global Strategies Unit. "The UAE's UNSC Membership Furthered Multilateral Action in a Polarized World." December 2023. https://www.epc.ae/en/details/brief/the-uae-s-unsc-membership-furthered-multilateral-action-in-a-polarized-environment.

Gül, Abdullah. "Why Is a Permanent Seat for Turkey at the UNSC Important for Herself, Her Region, and the World?" *Transatlantic Policy Quarterly* 6, no. 4 (2008): 13–16.

Hazra, Aniket. "Great Power Ambitions: India's Aim at the UN Security Council." *The Interpreter*, 2024. https://www.lowyinstitute.org/the-interpreter/great-power-ambitions-india-s-aim-un-security-council.

Hindustan Times. "List of Countries Backing India's Bid for Permanent Seat at UN Security Council." *Hindustan Times*, December 15, 2022. https://www.hindustantimes.com/india-news/list-of-countries-backing-india-s-bid-for-permanent-seat-at-un-security-council-101671078247949.html.

Hosli, Madeleine O., and Thomas Dörfler. "Why Is Change So Slow? Assessing Prospects for United Nations Security Council Reform." *Journal of Economic Policy Reform* 22, no. 1 (2019): 35–50. https://doi.org/10.1080/17487870.2017.1305903.

Human Rights Watch. "United Arab Emirates: Events of 2021." In *World Report 2022*. 2022. https://www.hrw.org/world-report/2022/country-chapters/united-arab-emirates.

Ilgit, Asli, and Binnur Ozkececi-Taner. "Turkey at the United Nations Security Council: 'Rhythmic Diplomacy' and a Quest for Global Influence." *Mediterranean Politics* 19, no. 2 (2014): 183–202. https://doi.org/10.1080/13629395.2013.829329.

Indian Council for World Affairs. "India in the UN Security Council: Monthly Recap for August 2021: Focus on India's Priority Areas in the UNSC, Afghanistan by Ambassador Asoke Kumar Mukerji, Former Permanent Representative of India to the United Nations." Accessed 2021. https://icwa.in/show_content.php?lang=1&level=1&ls_id=6380&lid=4393.

International Trade Administration of the U.S. "United Arab Emirates—Market Overview." November 2023. https://www.trade.gov/knowledge-product/united-arab-emirates-market-overview.

Jenkins, Gareth. "Turkey's Security Council Seat Promises Challenges as Well as Kudos." Accessed July 12, 2024. https://jamestown.org/program/turkeys-security-council-seat-promises-challenges-as-well-as-kudos/.

Jesse, Neal G., and John R. Dreyer. "Small States as Distinct Units of Analysis and as Different than Large and Middle Powers." In *Small States in the International System: At Peace and at War*, 3–19. Lexington Books, 2016. https://login.ezproxy.leidenuniv.nl:2443/login?URL=https://search.ebscohost.com/login.aspx?direct=true&db=e000xww&AN=1241833&site=ehost-live.

Kirecci, Ahmet. *Turkey in the United Nations Security Council.* SETA (Foundation for Political Economic and Social Research), 2009. https://setadc.org/turkey-united-nations-security-council/.

Krzymowski, Adam. "The European Union and the United Arab Emirates as Civilian and Soft Powers Engaged in Sustainable Development Goals." *Journal of International Studies* 13, no. 3 (2020): 41–58. https://doi.org/10.14254/2071-8330.2020/13-3/3.

Kumar, Rajesh. "India at the United Nations Security Council." *Manohar Parrikar Institute for Defense Studies and Analyses*, 2022. https://idsa.in/idsacomments/India-in-the-United-Nations-Security-Council-rkumar-031022.

Kuziemko, Ilyana, and Eric Werker. "How Much Is a Seat on the Security Council Worth? Foreign Aid and Bribery at the United Nations." *Journal of Political Economy* 114, no. 5 (2006): 905–930. https://doi.org/10.1086/507155.

Long, Tom. *A Small State's Guide to Influence in World Politics.* Oxford University Press, 2022. https://doi.org/10.1093/oso/9780190926205.001.0001.

Maass, Matthias. "The Story of Small State Survival: Past, Present, and Future." In *Small States in World Politics: The Story of Small State Survival, 1648–2016,* edited by Matthias Maass, 220–235. Manchester University Press, 2017. https://doi.org/10.7228/manchester/9780719082733.003.0006.

Maass, Matthias. "Small States: Surviving, Perishing and Proliferating Through History." In *Handbook on the Politics of Small States*, 20–37. Edward Elgar Publishing, 2020. https://doi.org/10.4337/9781788112932.00008.

Malone, David M. "Eyes on the Prize: The Quest for Nonpermanent Seats on the UN Security Council." *Global Governance: A Review of Multilateralism and International Organizations* 6, no. 1 (2000): 3–23.

Martin, Ian. "Elected Members Today: Overcoming the Handicaps." In *Elected Members of the Security Council: Lame Ducks or Key Players?* Vol. 99, 42–55. Brill | Nijhoff, 2019. https://doi.org/10.1163/9789004425392_004.

Massoud, Ahmed. "What the UAE Has Achieved in Its Two-Year Term on the UN Security Council." *The National*, December 2023. https://www.thenationalnews.com/weekend/2023/12/22/what-the-uae-has-achieved-in-its-two-year-term-on-the-un-security-council/.

Mesquita, Bruce Bueno de, and Alastair Smith. "The Pernicious Consequences of UN Security Council Membership." *Journal of Conflict Resolution* 54, no. 5 (2010): 667–686. https://doi.org/10.1177/0022002710371670.

Mishra, Manoj Kumar. "India's Permanent Membership of the U.N. Security Council: Changing Power Realities and Notions of Security." *The Indian Journal of Political Science* 67, no. 2 (2006): 343–354. http://www.jstor.org/stable/41856221.

Mukherjee, Rohan, and David M. Malone. "India and the UN Security Council: An Ambiguous Tale." *Economic and Political Weekly* 48, no. 29 (2013): 110–117.

Murthy, C. "India as a Non-permanent Member of the UN Security Council in 2011–12." Accessed 2011. https://library.fes.de/pdf-files/iez/08143.pdf.

Nafey, Abdul. "Permanent Membership in the UN Security Council: India's Diplomatic Initiatives and Strategies." *India Quarterly* 61, no. 4 (2005): 1–38. http://www.jstor.org/stable/45073359.

Nee, L. Y. "Singapore Fifth Worst Tax Haven in the World: Oxfam." *TODAY*, 2016, December 12. https://www.todayonline.com/business/singapore-fifth-worst-tax-haven-world-oxfam.

Nel, Philip, and Detlef Nolte. "Introduction: Special Section on Regional Powers in a Changing Global Order." *Review of International Studies* 36, no. 4 (2010): 877–879. https://doi.org/10.1017/S0260210510001348.

Ozkececi-Taner, Binnur. "Disintegration of the 'Strategic Depth' Doctrine and Turkey's Troubles in the Middle East." *Contemporary Islam* 11, no. 2 (2017): 201–214. https://doi.org/10.1007/s11562-017-0387-5.

Patrick, Stewart. *UN Security Council Reform: What the World Thinks*. Carnegie's Global Order and Institutions Program, 2023. https://carnegieendowment.org/research/2023/06/un-security-council-reform-what-the-world-thinks?lang=en.

Pedi, Ruxandra. "Small States in Europe as a Buffer Between East and West." In *Handbook on the Politics of Small States*, 168–188. Edward Elgar Publishing, 2020. https://doi.org/10.4337/9781788112932.00018.

Permanent Mission of the United Arab Emirates to the United Nations. "UNSC Campaign Archive." Accessed June 29, 2024. https://uaeun.org/unsc-campaign-archive/.

Permanent Mission of the United Arab Emirates to the United Nations. "UAE Statement at the UN General Assembly Debate Following A Veto Cast in the UN Security Council." 2022. https://uaeun.org/statement/uae-unga-unscveto-9jan/.

Permanent Representative of Singapore to the United Nations. "Letter Dated 20 June 2002 from the Permanent Representative of Singapore to the United Nations Addressed to the President of the Security Council (Letter S/2002/685)." *UNSC*, 2002. http://www.mfa.gov.sg/SINGAPORES-FOREIGN-POLICY/International-Issues/Small-States.

Ross, Karen. "Power in Numbers." *The World Today* 57, no. 5 (2001): 23–24.

Saleh, A. "UAE Holds Firm at 10th Place Globally in Brand Finance Soft Power Index 2024." *Emirates News Agency*. https://wam.ae/en/article/b1wprhv-uae-holds-firm-10th-place-globally-brand-financ.

Saleh, A., R. AlGhoul, and M. Aamir. "UAE Ranks First Among Arab Economies in Competitiveness." *Emirates News Agency*, 2023. https://wam.ae/article/aq9klgm-uae-ranks-first-among-arab-economies.

Schaefer, Karl. "Reforming the United Nations Security Council: Feasibility or Utopia?" *International Negotiation* 22, no. 1 (2017): 62–91.

Schrijver, Nico J., and Niels M. Blokker. *Elected Members of the Security Council: Lame Ducks or Key Players?* Brill | Nijhoff, 2020. https://doi.org/10.1163/9789004425392.

Security Council Report. "Cooperation Between the UN and the League of Arab States, June 2023 Monthly Forecast: Security Council Report." *Security Council Report*, May 2023. https://www.securitycouncilreport.org/monthly-forecast/2023-06/cooperation-between-the-un-and-the-league-of-arab-states-4.php.

Sever, Ayşegül, and Gözde O. Gök. "The UN Factor in the 'Regional Power Role' and the Turkish Case in the 2000s." *Cambridge Review of International Affairs* 29, no. 3 (2016): 1150–1185. https://doi.org/10.1080/09557571.2016.1230731.

"Singapore Fifth Worst Tax Haven in the World: Oxfam." *Today Online*. Accessed July 13, 2024. https://www.todayonline.com/business/singapore-fifth-worst-tax-haven-world-oxfam.

Spies, Yolanda. "Middle Power Diplomacy." In *The SAGE Handbook of Diplomacy*, edited by Costas M. Constantinou, Pauline Kerr, and Paul Sharp, 281–293. SAGE Publications Ltd., 2024. https://sk.sagepub.com/reference/the-sage-handbook-of-diplomacy.

Storey, Ian. "Disputes in the South China Sea: Southeast Asia's Troubled Waters." *Politique étrangère*, 2014. Accessed from: https://www.ifri.org/sites/default/files/atoms/files/05_storey_en_0.pdf.

Tan, Andrew T. H. "Singapore's Survival and Its China Challenge." *Security Challenges* 13, no. 2 (2017): 11–31. http://www.jstor.org/stable/26457716.

The Government of the United Arab Emirates. "The UAE NAP for the Implementation of UN SCR 1325 on Women, Peace and Security." Accessed 2024. https://u.ae/en/about-the-uae/strategies-initiatives-and-awards/strategies-plans-and-visions/social-affairs/national-action-plan-on-women-peace-and-security.

The Hindu. "India Will Get Permanent UNSC Seat, but It Will Have to Work Harder This Time: EAM Jaishankar." 2024. Accessed from: https://www.news18.com/elections/bjp-2024-lok-sabha-election-manifesto-man-on-moon-space-permanent-seat-un-security-council-india-8851062.html.

The National. "UAE Is Middle East's Most Globalised Country, Report Finds." *The National*, 2021. https://www.thenationalnews.com/business/2021/12/22/uae-is-middle-easts-most-globalised-country-report-finds/.

The Straits Times. "Singapore Welcomes UN Move to Debate Vetos Used by Security Council Permanent Members." 2022. Accessed from: https://www.straitstimes.com/singapore/singapore-welcomes-un-move-to-debate-vetos-used-by-security-council-permanent-members.

Thorhallsson, Baldur. "Small States in the UN Security Council: Means of Influence?" 2012. https://doi.org/10.1163/187119112X628454.

Thorhallsson, Baldur. "Small States in the UNSC and the EU: Structural Weaknesses and Ability to Influence." In *Small States in a Legal World*, 35–64. Springer International Publishing AG, 2017.

Thorhallsson, Baldur. "Studying Small States: A Review." *Small States & Territories* 1, no. 1 (2018): 17–34.

Thorhallsson, Baldur, Sverrir Steinsson, and Thorsteinn Kristinsson. "The Small State in International Relations." In *Small States and Shelter Theory*, 1st Edition, 13–23. Routledge, 2018.

Thorhallsson, Baldur, Jóhanna Steinunn Elínardóttir, and Anna Maria Eggertsdóttir. "A Small State's Campaign to Get Elected to the UNSC: Iceland's Ambitious Failed Attempt." *The Hague Journal of Diplomacy* 18, no. 1 (2022): 64–94.

Tyler, Michael C., and Emma Pahlow. "Australia on the UN Security Council 2013–14: A Voice for Small and Medium Countries?" *The Round Table* 103, no. 1 (2014): 95–108. https://doi.org/10.1080/00358533.2013.874168.

"UN Chief Receives Report of Panel of Inquiry into Gaza Flotilla Incident." *UN News*, September 2, 2011. https://news.un.org/en/story/2011/09/385572.

UNFCCC. “UN Climate Change Conference—United Arab Emirates.” 2023. https://unfccc.int/cop28.

United Arab Emirates. “UAE Campaign Infographic.” Accessed June 2021. https://uaeun.org/app/uploads/2021/06/UAE_Campaign_Infographic_Vertical.pdf.

United Arab Emirates. “UAE UNSC Campaign Fact Sheet.” Accessed September 2020. https://uaeun.org/app/uploads/2020/09/UAE-UNSC-campaign-Fact-Sheet.pdf.

United Arab Emirates Ministry of Foreign Affairs. “UAE Partners with UN Climate Security Mechanism to Advance the Climate, Peace and Security Agenda.” 2024. http://mptf.undp.org/news/uae-partners-un-climate-security-mechanism-advance-climate-peace-and-security-agenda.

United Arab Emirates Ministry of Foreign Affairs. “UAE Granted Dialogue Partner Status in Shanghai Cooperation Organization.” Accessed May 6, 2023. https://www.mofa.gov.ae/en/mediahub/news/2023/5/6/06-05-2023-uae.

United Nations Media and Communication Releases. “Unanimously Adopting Resolution 2628 (2022), Security Council Endorses Decision to Reconfigure Existing Entity into African Union Transition Mission in Somalia.” 2022. https://press.un.org/en/2022/sc14847.doc.htm.

United Nations News. “UN Elects Five New Members to Serve on the Security Council.” *UN News*, June 2021. https://news.un.org/en/story/2021/06/1093882.

United States Mission to the United Nations. “Explanation of Vote on a United Arab Emirates-Drafted UN Security Council Resolution on the Situation in the Middle East.” *United States Mission to the United Nations*, December 2023. https://usun.usmission.gov/explanation-of-vote-on-a-united-arab-emirates-drafted-un-security-council-resolution-on-the-situation-in-the-middle-east/.

Uppal, Rajesh, and Lisa Barrington. “UAE Plans Long-Term Economic Ties with Israel Despite Political Strains.” *Reuters*, April 3, 2023. https://www.reuters.com/world/middle-east/uae-plans-long-term-economic-ties-with-israel-despite-political-strains-2023-04-03/.

Waltz, K. N. *Theory of International Politics*. McGraw-Hill, 1979.

“With Climate Crisis Generating Growing Threats to Global Peace, Security Council Must Ramp Up Efforts, Lessen Risk of Conflicts, Speakers Stress in Open Debate.” *Meetings Coverage and Press Releases*. Accessed July 13, 2023. https://press.un.org/en/2023/sc15318.doc.htm.

Wivel, Anders, and Kjell Engelbrekt Oest. “Security, Profit, or Shadow of the Past? Explaining the Security Strategies of Microstates.” *Cambridge Review of International Affairs* 23, no. 3 (2010): 429–453. https://doi.org/10.1080/09557571.2016.1230731.

World Intellectual Property Organization. *Global Innovation Index 2023*. World Intellectual Property Organization, 2023. https://www.wipo.int/edocs/pubdocs/en/wipo-pub-2000-2023/ae.pdf.

Yinanç, Barçın. "UN Security Council Reform: What the World Thinks." Carnegie's Global Order and Institutions Program, 2023. https://carnegieendowment.org/research/2023/06/un-security-council-reform-what-the-world-thinks?lang=en.

Young, Karen E. "New Perspectives on UAE Foreign Policy." *Journal of Arabian Studies* 7, no. 1 (2017): 81–82. https://doi.org/10.1080/21534764.2017.1316045.

CHAPTER 8

Multilateralism in Action: The European Union's Engagement in the United Nations Security Council

Viraj Balutkar and Anri Stepanian

1 Introduction

Over the years, the European Union (EU) has become a significant actor in the global multilateral system. Its actions have reaffirmed its aim to foster agreeable relations with other regional and global powers based on the principles of equal rights and cooperation. Similarly, its presence in International Organisations (IOs) is justifiable from a legal perspective, as the EU's treaties established a division of competencies between the EU and its Member States that makes its participation in many institutions logical (Wessel and Odermatt 2019, 6). An important legal development related to this is the adoption of the Treaty of the European Union (TEU), the formal legal name of the Maastricht Treaty, and later the enforcement of the Lisbon Treaty, making the EU a more visible and effective player in global governance (Wessel and Odermatt 2019, 6).

V. Balutkar (✉) · A. Stepanian
Leiden University, The Hague, The Netherlands
e-mail: cviraj7.balutkar08@gmail.com

M. O. Hosli et al. (eds.), *Multilateralism and the United Nations Security Council*, https://doi.org/10.1007/978-3-031-85320-3_8

The TEU reflects the EU's ambitious goals in multilateralism and global governance, as stated in Articles 3[5] and 21, respectively: the "Union shall uphold and promote its values in relations with the wider world and shall contribute to peace, security, the sustainable development of the Earth…." and "the Union's actions on the international scene[...] seeks to advance in the wider world: democracy, the rule of law, the universality and indivisibly of human rights…"(European Union 2012, 17–28). The EU's active participation on the global stage, especially in the issues of international security and global governance, has been easily discernible in its political statements, objectives, and goals. More specifically, the EU's presence in the United Nations Security Council (UNSC) through its member states serves as a manifestation of the principles mentioned above. Indeed, effective multilateralism is a central element of the EU's external policy as, to respond successfully to global crises, threats, and challenges, the EU believes that the international community benefits from a multilateral system built on universal rules and values (Delegation of the European Union to the UN and other international organisations in Geneva 2021). Subsequently, to further advocate for this system, the EU's involvement within the UNSC reflects a convergence of complementary strengths: the EU's capacity to coordinate collective action and provide substantial economic and developmental resources, paired with the UNSC's authority to enforce binding decisions in the areas of international peace and security.

This chapter aims to examine the EU's endeavours as a multilateral actor and the EU's engagement in the UNSC. Firstly, it addresses the historic origins of the EU's multilateral actions and its efforts to legitimise itself alongside the United Nations (UN). To explain the EU's rise as an institution and its efforts in achieving effective multilateralism on the global governance stage, we refer to the approaches of institutionalism and principal-agent theory. Secondly, the EU's commitment to multilateralism and steps taken to cement a legitimate position on the global stage are discussed. Thirdly, it delves into the EU's involvement with the UNSC through its member states engaging it in multilateralism on the global stage. Finally, Brexit's impact on the EU's insertion in the UNSC and the UNSCs' calls for reform are analysed. Accordingly, our objective is to summarise the EU's presence in multilateral settings, with a particular focus on EU-UN and EU-UNSC relations.

2 EU and the Rise of Multilateralism

The current age of globalisation has led to the expansion and deepening of interdependence between states, underlying the importance of common action in tackling global problems related to economy, poverty, the environment, energy, and security. For European nations, a strong call for collective action after the Second World War was a cornerstone for prosperity, with European leaders adopting policies aimed at fostering peace and accelerating European economic development (Regelsberger et al. 1997, 1). The European Political Cooperation's (EPC) birth in the 1970s was a response to the need for greater coordination among the members of the European Community (EC) for the pursuit of common regional and global goals, and from which each member state would gain a steady and concrete standing in regional political and economic affairs (Regelsberger et al. 1997, 4). Jean Monnet, one of the founding fathers of the European Union, recognised that the continued rising tensions between European countries in the aftermath of the Second World War and the need for economic growth were issues that could not be tackled by a single sovereign state (Watts 2008, x). Thus, the construction of the European Community (EC), the EPC, and later the EU, illustrates that there was a growing awareness within European states that important issues, such as economy, trade, defence, security, or foreign policy, should also follow a common stance on the part of its member states. Indeed, the economic union later progressed to a political and foreign policy one, as it will be discussed below.

In the later years of the twentieth century, European states recognised the need for political and foreign policy unanimity, resulting in the signing of the Maastricht Treaty in 1992, paving the way for the Common Foreign and Security Policy (CFSP) contemplated in the TEU (Regelsberger et al. 1997, 7). The CFSP called upon EU members to not only support and protect the common interests and independence of the union, but also to strengthen the security of the Union and its member states (Regelsberger et al. 1997, 1). As the EU developed its own network of institutions to facilitate multilateral action within the continent, it sought to apply similar strategies on the global stage.

Parallel to the EU, the emergence of the United Nations (UN) was based on similar multilateral and cooperative principles. According to Article 1 of the UN Charter, "nations will take effective measures for the prevention of and removal of threats" and further states that there is a need for achieving "international cooperation in solving international problems" and "to develop friendly relations among nations" (United Nations, n.d.). With similar ideologies, the EU's presence in the United Nations General Assembly (UNGA) and the United Nations Security Council (UNSC) is, then, not surprising. The EU's strategic objective is also to build its presence on the global governance stage based on stable and effective multilateralism (de Vasconcelos 2010; Jokela 2011, 56). Accordingly, there are multiple parallels between the activities of the EU and the UN. For example, both actively enforce economic sanctions on human rights violators through their institutions—the European Council for the EU and the UNSC for the UN. Apart from human rights, the EU and UN advocate for other important policy goals such as the reduction of poverty, tackling climate change and peaceful resolution of conflicts (Hosli 2022, 68).

The EU's influence in international affairs is often regarded as directly proportional to the strength of its CFSP, and if the reasoning goes that the EU's international legitimacy is based on its reliance on international norms and the UN system, then the EU cannot augment its role without primarily supporting and promoting the role and authority of the UN (Ojanen 2006, 8). For example, while the UN prioritizes peaceful resolution of conflicts, its capacity is limited, as it relies on the acceptance of national members to provide practical support in resolving armed conflict. The EU faces similar challenges, depending on its member states for action. However, with the EU and the UNSC's intertwined efforts and resources, their collective influence can provide a rather powerful and coordinated response, strengthening patterns of global governance. The EU considers itself an indispensable partner of the UN, motivated by the desire to have a real influence within the UN system and with this, on the world stage. The EU's increasing share of contributions to the UN budget since the early 2000s is a prominent example of continuous efforts to strengthen its role on the international stage (Hosli 2022). By contributing to the strength of the UN, the EU aims for multilateralism to survive on the global stage, under the assumption that mutual knowledge and backing would allow for more global challenges to be tackled and with this, enhance the effectiveness of IOs (Ojanen 2006, 39).

The EU's engagement with the UNSC derives from a logical rationale based on a perceived progressive success of the UNSC. The UNSC has, over the decades (and notably after the end of the Cold War), become more of an executive body with the potential capacity of mitigating world crises. In what might have been its most successful year, 2016, the UNSC adopted 72 resolutions in 457 meetings and only 3 resolutions were vetoed. The percentage of vetoes as a portion of the total of resolutions also dropped significantly, from 85% during the active years of the Cold War to 15% starting from the 1990s (Trent and Schnurr 2018, 59–60). The UNSC as a platform for global crisis mitigation and cooperation, in spite of international frictions, has fostered a space where institutional agreements can be reached and where leading states can help guide other states, involved in unconstitutional behaviours, towards more humanitarian approaches, showing that Council members can work harmoniously towards the stability of the international order when conditions allow for this (Trent and Schnurr 2018, 58). The UNSC has, for instance, demonstrated the ability to invoke the Responsability to Protect (R2P) to facilitate discussion, coordination, applied diplomacy, and the deployment of peace operations also under adverse circumstances. Moreover, it has shown willingness to initiate peacekeeping mechanisms and provide aid in times of crisis.

In the face of global instability, such as marked by the war in Ukraine, the Israel-Palestine conflict, and the presidential elections in America, with policies initiated after the return of Donald Trump for a second mandate, the global political stage can be seen as being in turmoil. The ongoing Russian aggression against Ukraine, the US destabilising foundational elements of global governance, and the increasing competition between the USA and China created an environment where the EU picks up the torch for multilateral action—a position that has become vital. The UN's significance over the years made it the prime partner for the EU in its efforts for multilateral action and global governance based on a rules-based order. Given the shared mission, it no mystery why the EU has been pro-actively advocating to be more involved within the UN and, in particular, within the UNSC, even though not being a member of the Security Council as a regional entity.

The post-Cold War role of the Security Council has been highlighted several times for its influence and transformative impact, particularly through its more assertive interventions in internal conflicts that involved severe human rights violations (Trent and Schnurr 2018, 58). The Council's multilateral approach, closely aligned with the EU's principles in terms of security and defence, emphasises the role of multilateralism, the rule of law, and the promotion of human rights, forming a strong foundation for collaborative efforts. Additionally, the EU has played a significant role in the UN by presenting a united front in advocating for its positions and priorities on multiple issues in areas such as international security and human rights. This was particularly evident at the end of the Cold War, when overall support for the UN grew, also within the EU. Western European countries demonstrated a significant role in the renewed prominence of peacekeeping activities, which became a UN flagship in the early 1990s (Keatinge 1997, 280). In 1993, the combined share of twelve EU member states and four at the time EU candidate countries (Austria, Sweden, Finland, and Norway) comprised approximately 40% of all UN peacekeeping personnel (Keatinge 1997, 280). Moreover, the EU's role in the UN was considerably strengthened by the CFSP, which allowed the EU to address a wide range of issues related to foreign strategy, security, crisis management, and defence policies while more effectively coordinating its representation in both the UNGA and the UNSC (Marchesi 2010)—although the United Kingdom (UK)'s departure from the EU left France as the only EU member state represented in the UNSC's permanent membership (Gifkins et al. 2019, 1349).

Furthermore, coordination was seen in a series of formal and informal mechanisms designed to increase both internal effectiveness—the capacity of the EU to reach a common position through a single voice within the UN—and external effectiveness—the capacity of the EU to successfully promote its position in the UN (Marchesi 2010). The EU-UN cooperation was mutually beneficial as the EU could enhance its capability of acting independently in the international sphere, while the UN needed to leverage the EU's power to counterweight traditional great powers and rising nation-states after the Cold War in terms of developing the international system as a part of global development (Ojanen 2006). Heinikainen's chapter in this volume has already discussed the kind of power struggles that often ensue between such older as well as new powers. Still, the international balance of power is ever-evolving and, currently, there are other small and emerging powers that matter in the face of waning US hegemony (see Lu et al. and Luers and Galy-Jammou-Préfontaine, this volume). Here, the EU's position as a counterweight can be relevant.

3 Situating the EU Within UN Structures

The mutual interest of both the UN and the EU in maintaining international peace and security, foster deeper cooperation and shape a common ambition is to offer effective multilateral institutions on the global stage (Tardy 2007, 193). Both institutionalism and principal-agent (PA) theory can offer valuable frameworks for understanding the EU's engagement in the UNSC based on this rationale. Firstly, from an institutionalist perspective, the interdependence of international society matters, and international cooperation is possible as institutions provide a cooperating mechanism to aid states in capturing the maximum gains from combatting transborder challenges (Keohane and Martin 1995, 44; Whyte 2012, 2). To solve the dilemma of global anarchy and related challenges, states are prone to choose cooperation, to which international rules and institutions can provide effective solutions (Axelrod and Keohane 1985, 247). In addition, PA theory can provide a framework for understanding the delegation of power from principals to agents, also in the context of global institutions.

Institutionalism has long been used to explain the formation of the EU and its subsequent endeavors. Institutionalist approaches suggest that the EU is more likely to succeed in coping with crises as regional integration strengthens, which can occur through the accumulation of cooperative and formalised practices. This follows the logic of path dependency and rule-following (Olsen 2009, 9; Rieker and Giske 2024, 19) implying that decisions made in the past shape future policy decisions, often reinforcing previously applied cooperation patterns, while rule-following reinforces stability over time. Institutions are further characterised by their ability to improve and adapt the existing methods of handling varying crises and then employ them in a renewed and effective manner (Ansell et al. 2016, 43; Rieker and Giske 2024, 19). Institutionalism, which emphasises the role of regional integration, leads nations to interact despite the significance of national borders, thereby enabling the development of a strong network of functionality with a spillover effect across various sectors of cooperation, ultimately culminating in the creation of a (strong) supranational entity. This has been observed for the case of the the European Union (Lopez-Claros et al. 2020, 73). Within the broad spectrum of institutionalist approaches, liberal institutions are characterised by: a) multiple channels of interaction between actors; b) equal attention to all issues; c) the pursuit of maximum absolute joint gains through cooperation rather than zero-sum outcomes (Devitt 2011, 2). This is again in line with EU-UN principles as they not only recognise the sovereignty of multiple states that remain being their member nations, but also, through the varying institutions associated with the EU and the UN, the organisations facilitate cooperation in adverse circumstances and peaceful resolution of varying challenges including those related to climate change, poverty, disrespect for human rights, armed conflict, and disasters. Following institutionalism, the EU and UN while adhering to founding principles, can help induce more prosperous socio-economic and politically based growth on the global stage. Although a critical assessment of this process can reveal the challenge of gridlock and inability to function as member states constitute these IOs, pursuing their own agendas and interests, undermining the capacity for institutions to act multilaterally. Still, institutionalism has shown important consequences of multilateralism and explained the formation of many multilateral forums. In turn, such forums have increased the agenda-setting and convening power of states, incorporating an international legitimacy which might not have been enjoyed through other means (Ruggie 1992, 584).

In addition to institutionalist approaches, principal-agent theory is widely used in explaining why states confer power and crucial tasks of global governance to IOs (Hawkins et al. 2006, 4). PA theory explains acts of delegation between the principal and the agent where the relationship between the two is guided by a formal or informal contract (Drieskens 2008, 602). This approach also addresses how states ensure surveillance and control of IOs' behaviours once the authority is delegated and how international organisations solve global issues while maintaining the state interests (Hawkins et al. 2006, 4–5). The EU's engagement in the UNSC can be regarded as a good example of principal-agent theoretical predictions if EU member states are seen as the "principal" and the EU as the "agent". In this instance, the EU may manage to overcome dilemmas of collective action, by reducing the transaction costs of cooperation with other countries, and improve decision-making efficiency through (global) agenda-setting on peace and security issues. Additionally, there is a delegating pattern, where member states collectively hand over power to the EU to deliver policies for common action. While contrary to basic tenets of PA theory, there are multiple principles within the EU, i.e. the member states; another somewhat paradoxical characteristic of applying PA theory to the EU and its member states is that a double role is being embodied. In the UNSC, the EU has no formal representation and thus relies on its member states to represent its views and policies, making member states its agents in this situation (Drieskens 2008, 599; Orban 2021, 70). So, with a role reversal at the UNSC, the EU countries, per the articles of the TEU, ensure the defence of the EU's position and interests, theoretically in turn improving the impact of the EU on the global governance stage (Drieskens 2008, 603).

The EU's commitment to upholding international peace and security is mirrored in its member states' significant contributions to UN peacekeeping operations and to development cooperation. In 2003, all member states of the EU together were contributing approximately 38% to the UN's budget (European Commission 2004, 7) and, by 2022, this has gone up to 43% (EEAS 2023), with the EU being the largest donor of development aid to developing countries; this helps support the UN's development goals. The EU is also deeply committed to the United Nations Sustainable Development Goals (UNSDGs) and has policies oriented in this direction. Levorato et al. (this volume) discuss these policies and their impact in more detail. Moreover, the EU's diplomatic efforts, including its coordinated approach to foreign policy, can help to build consensus among UN member states on key issues, including those related to peace and security. Furthermore, the EU is involved in the coordination of UN resolutions in the UNSC. One such example is the Libyan crisis which emerged as a result of actions by Muammar Gaddafi (the former dictator of Libya) in terms of the violent crackdown against protestors in parts of Libya. The situation escalated into a broader conflict and, ultimately, became one of the key moments within the Arab Spring revolutions. In spite of divisions amongst its member states on the subject, the EU showed an active involvement in devising frameworks for the de-escalation of the situation. Faced with an intensifying conflict, the EU acted from two perspectives: on the one hand, by issuing joint statements to the establishment of a common position; on the other hand, by adopting military action under the framework of UNSC (Blavoukos and Bourantonis 2011). With the adoption of Resolutions 1970 and 1973 by the UNSC, a comprehensive arms embargo on Libya was conducted, the assets of main Libyan leaders frozen, and interventions with the aim of protecting human rights and responsibility to protect specified (United Nations 2011, 4). Before Resolution 1973, the EU held a European Council meeting and adopted the declaration that reflected the EU's willingness to support the UN in its actions in Libya (Blavoukos and Bourantonis 2011, 735). The EU further took the responsibility to protect civilians seriously and supported activities including military actions towards Libya (Lindström and Zetterlund 2012). This resolution reflected the will of the EU as an entity to comply with the UNSC approach to de-escalate the conflict in Libya. While these measures applied and supported by the EU aimed to stabilize the region, Libya's post-Gaddafi challenges highlight the complexities of international intervention and, at the same time, reveal the need for a multi-laterally governed global order based on shared responsibility for conflict-resolution.

The EU is the first supranational organisation to maintain a continuous presence in the UNSC as an entity through its member states, and its participation in the UNSC remains an essential component of its efforts to promote global peace, security, and stability (Helou 2019, 1). The member states that represent the EU can be both permanent members of the UNSC (France, and the UK until leaving the EU, represented the Union's visions as permanent members) and non-permanent members (European Commission 2004, 8). The EU member states have successfully supported multilateral UNSC-centred activities in accordance with the European Security Strategy's (ESS) objectives and international development aims, both individually and collectively (Blavoukos and Bourantonis 2011). The EU's commitment to effective multilateralism, in this sense, has strengthened the UN's role as the cornerstone of global governance. EU support on issues such as climate change, human rights, and sustainable development has helped to ensure that the UN remains central to global efforts to address such challenges. The EU representation in the UNSC can be understood through the four pillars of its CFSP mechanism: a) external objectives (foreign policy actions towards any specific issue); b) inter-relational objectives (increasing cooperation with other members); c) integration objectives (promoting European integration); and d) identity objectives (asserting a European identity) (Keukeleire and Macnaughtan 2008, 12–13; Marchesi 2010, 8). As such, the EU will likely continue to work closely with the UNSC and the UN more generally, as well as other international organisations to promote its vision for strategies enhancing prospects for a more peaceful, secure, and prosperous world. EU-UN coordination, as well as the EU's delegations operating around the world, have enhanced the EU's influence in the UN system of agencies, programmes, and related organisations (European Parliamentary Research Services 2020). The following section touches upon the mechanism set in place by the EU to increase coherence and with this, gain legitimacy on the world stage.

4 Mechanisms of EU Engagement in UNSC

As stated earlier, the EU is the only supranational organisation present permanently in the UNSC through its members France and the UK (pre-Brexit) (Helou 2019). Increasing EU-UN engagement can be explained by their core shared values and objectives, and by the EU's formal and informal institutional mechanisms for participation within the UNSC. Furthermore, the EU has also enhanced the applicability of its common foreign and security policy through the creation of the European External Action Service (EEAS), and the Political and Security Committee (PSC). Moreover, the Lisbon Treaty reinforced the role of the High Representative (HR) (Blavoukos and Bourantonis 2011). In the context of the EU since then HR refers to the High Representative of the Union for Foreign Affairs and Security Policy. The HR plays a significant role in representing the EU's common foreign and security policy, notably in relations with the UNSC. Within the UNSC this is mainly related to the coordination and representation of the EU's foreign policy. The HR works in close coordination with the EU member states and the EU delegation to the UN in New York to ensure that the EU's positions and perspectives are expressed effectively in this multilateral setting. The role of the High Representative of the European Union is necessary when diverging political aspirations arise in place of a uniform EU approach (Blavoukos and Bourantonis 2011). Furthermore, setting up the ESS was also a strong indicator of what the EU aimed to achieve on the international stage with the UN through strategies emphasising the global multilateral order and reinforcing the commitment to international cooperation (Ojanen 2006). The importance of the ESS lies in its foundational nature, which has shaped the EU's approach to security and defence in the early twenty-first century. It established a framework for addressing global security challenges and also laid the groundwork for the EU's role as a security actor on the international stage.

Article 19 of the Treaty of the European Union (TEU) focuses on the equal implementation of EU laws in all of the member states and has fostered a strong coordination among them. As a result, it comes as no surprise that issues raised in the UNSC for international peace and security, are often already prepared and discussed in unison by members of the EU. The meetings of the UNSC are often coupled with weekly meetings of the heads of the EU member states' representations in New York. Further, monthly meetings are conducted by permanent representatives and UNSC coordinators of the EU members sitting in the UNSC, with additonal targeted meetings in the EU capitals by EU countries with a seat in the Security Council (Pirozzi 2010, 3). Yet, certain proceedings of the UNSC, which allow for discussions of urgent and unpredictable issues, do not provide the EU with sufficient time to act correspondingly. Thus, to resolve this challenge, the EU has been developing a systemic coordination mechanism, aligning with its representative member states in the Security Council, to facilitate information sharing and coordination. Article 220(1) of the Treaty of the Functioning of the European Union (TFEU) requires an appropriate level of cooperation with the organs of the UN and its agencies; Article 24(3) of the TEU enunciates that members ought to defend the position and interests of the EU within the UNSC, while Article 34 of the TEU mandates EU members present in the Council to "concert and keep other member states and HR fully informed" (Erlbacher 2019; European Union 2012). These articles had entrusted the UK and France—pre-Brexit and now only applicable to France— with the responsibility of representing and defending the actions and positions of the Union (Pirozzi 2010). The European Union's ability to benefit from its members holding permanent seats and veto powers in the Council has strenghtened its potential influence within the UNSC. While this situation has changed due to Brexit, the UK still very much functions as an ally in the UNSC.

Such formal mechanisms, as discussed above, include all EU member states and consist of debriefings that are given by the "briefer of the month" and weekly meetings focusing on the development of dynamics within the UNSC (Paasivirta and Ramopoulos 2019). All member states have access to documents and information regarding the current and ongoing activities of the UNSC (Paasivirta and Ramopoulos 2019). In addition, regular meetings in which counsellors of states in UNSC and EU delegations discuss the programmes of work and possible actions, are held monthly (Paasivirta and Ramopoulos 2019). Making use of both formal institutions and informal mechanisms to exchange information has proved successful for the EU's approach concerning the issues at stake in the UNSC (Bailey and Daws 1998). The PSC has also regularised discussions of UNSC's agendas, and debates are being conducted once a month in Brussels (Pirozzi 2010). Agora—a data-sharing platform adopted by the EU and member states—is used for the sharing of data and information among the Commission and member states. Along with these formal mechanisms, there are certain informal ways through which the member states communicate among themselves and with the Commission about the proceedings of the UNSC. EU delegations share briefing documents with member states, adding remarks and comments to provide a European viewpoint on any topic. Additionally, they hold regular meetings to identify and discuss areas on which they can work together (Paasivirta and Ramopoulos 2019).

To ensure geographical representation, the UN has established five regional groups from which member states are elected. These groups are active within themselves to varying degrees, facilitating the exchange of information, views, and coordination of positions (Dee and Smith 2017). Among these, the EU has leveraged its participation through the Western European and Others Group (WEOG), which holds two rotating seats, and the Eastern European Group (EEG), which has one seat. As a result, the EU consistently has a minimum of three of its member states represented in the UNSC at any given time. Any UNSC member can propose and submit draft resolutions, which are universally binding if adopted. This presence has provided the EU with a degree of influence in the UNSC. However, the EU has acknowledged the reduction in the number of its member states on the UNSC as a challenge, citing the need for improved communication and coordination across policies as a key area for enhancing its effectiveness within the UNSC (Gailišs 2024).

The joint communication to the European Parliament (EP) and the Council of the EU (2021) reiterated that "the EU must develop a more stringent and strategic approach to its multilateral engagement and contribute to effective reform of the multilateral institutions" (European Commission 2021). The document further states that "the EU has a strong interest in ensuring that the UN Security Council can fulfil its role in the face of increasing geopolitical tension and rivalries paralysing its work and preventing it from fulfilling its responsibilities (European Commission 2021). In this sense, the EU also aims to continue imposing autonomous sanctions wherever necessary and will continue to report regularly to the UNSC about the wide-ranging EU-UN cooperation on international peace and security and thus remains a vital partner to the UNSC (European Commission 2021).

Still, it is important to acknowledge that the United Kingdom's (UK) departure from the EU has significantly altered existing political structures and enacted a new panorama of EU-UN relations; in particular the EU's role in the UNSC was affected (Gowan 2018). The UK was a key player in the EU, particularly influential in the development of the EU single market. Although the UK supported EU economic integration, its role in the EU's CSDP was less central compared to its involvement in economic matters. This all changed with the UK's departure from the EU based on the Brexit refereundum. Its implications are discussed in the next section.

5 EU-UN Trends Post-Brexit

The UK has been widely viewed as a rather influential member of the UN. Most importantly, its position on the world stage has been characterised by its permanent seat in the UNSC. Its membership, though, has been boosted by the fact that the UK has been a long-standing member of the EU, which is a rather well-organised and well-resourced group at the UN. This status matters because of the high importance that groups have and the significant role they play in the UN and in the UNSC (Dee and Smith 2017). However, the UK's decision to leave the EU after a referendum on the 23rd of June 2016 was a political trembler, setting in motion a series of political processes and implications which would have far-reaching ramifications (Patrick 2023).

As a permanent member of the UNSC, the UK enjoys prerogatives such as veto power, selecting the United Nations Secretary General, influencing peacekeeping mission's formation and deployment, etc. However, Brexit has arguably weakened the UK's networks and diplomatic influence, thereby reducing its power in the UNSC and damaging its reputation (Gifkins et al. 2019). Yet, it is important to acknowledge that perspectives on the negative impact of Brexit may diverge. Some proponents argue that potential long-term benefits or opportunities may arise from the UK's departure from the EU (Chen et al. 2018). Consequently, assessing the overall impact of Brexit remains a multifaceted task, with its consequences poised to evolve over the forthcoming years. The UK's decision to leave the EU has encouraged nationalist and anti-EU movements in other member states, leading to concerns about the stability and unity of the EU (Chen et al. 2018). The EU has been addressing these concerns, however, through increased investments in social programmes and the promotion of greater political unity and cooperation among all member states (Hix 2018).

The UK's departure from the EU has also significantly impacted the EU's security dimensions. The UK has a significant military power with both nuclear and conventional weapons (UK Government 2025; UK Parliament and Mills 2024). Although a degree of partnership remains, the EU will now be more limited in its ability to indirectly influence military decisions of both the North Atlantic Treaty Organisation (NATO) and the UN (Oleksiejuk 2020). After the Brexit referendum, the EU's High Representative acted quickly to provide reassurance on the the global stage - aiming at dispelling uncertainties - by emphasizing the priority of fostering a shared vision and a common action on the political arena (European External Action Service 2016).

The institutional challenges of Brexit are also a noteworthy concern for the EU. The EU had to adjust its decision-making structures to account for the loss of the UK's voice in discussions and negotiations in a variety of processes both internally and externally (Hix 2018). There are also concerns that the UK's departure might lead to a power imbalance within the EU. Although Brexit has created some challenges for the EU, these are largely temporary compared to the significant global shifts it has caused, specifically in the UNSC, where Brexit has altered the balance of power from the EU's standpoint. The instability that has accompanied Brexit has underscored the necessity for both the UK and the EU to navigate a complex landscape of economic, security, and political challenges. Brexit has triggered significant disruptions, including economic volatility due to new trade barriers, regulatory divergences, and shifts in investment patterns, as well as alterations in security and defense collaborations. These changes have impacted the UK's influence on the EU and recalibrated its global role. Nevertheless, there exists an opportunity for the UK and the EU to negotiate new agreements that could stabilise their economic relations, enhance security cooperation, and realign political dynamics in response to their mutual interests. Concurrently, the EU's advocacy for reforming the UNSC reflects a strategic desire to adapt the Council's composition to the modern geopolitical context and might serve the UK's interests. The proposed expansion of the UNSC, which involves increasing both permanent and non-permanent seats, seeks to better represent the evolving global political landscape. This reform aims to address long-standing criticisms of the UNSC's representation, which is perceived as anachronistic given the current international situation. By broadening the Council's membership, the EU seeks to ensure a more inclusive and representative decision-making process, thereby enhancing the Council's legitimacy and effectiveness (Press and Information Team of the Delegation to the UN in New York 2025). However, such reforms are intricately complex and require extensive negotiation, particularly given the entrenched interests of the P5 members, who hold veto power and influence over the Council's operations. Balancing the need for greater representation with the imperative of maintaining the UNSC's operational efficiency remains a central challenge in these discussions. A UNSC reform would be dually beneficial for both actors, as the EU would reaffirm its presence on the global stage, while the UK would remain involved politically and organisationally without having its authority undermined. Mutually benefiting security policies seem to be key for the creation of a straightforward relationship where diplomatic benefits are aligned with both the EU's external policies and the UK's own needs (Whitman 2016).

6 Calls for Reform

The UNSC resolves disputes under the guidelines from Chapter VI of the UN Charter, which authorises the Security Council to call on parties to seek solutions. Chapter VII of the UN Charter also gives the UNSC the authority to take assertive actions. Peacekeeping missions have been one of the most evident work of the Security Council and, as of 2023, it oversaw 12 operations involving nearly 88 000 personnel (*The UN Security Council*, n.d.).

The UNSC's membership has not been changed since 1965, when the original membership of 11 countries was increased to 15 by giving space for the addition of four non-permanent members. The permanent membership dominated by the West has, in recent years, probably damaged the legitimacy of the UNSC (CFR 2024). The veto power of the P5 further complicates the situation. Russia's blocking of any condemnation of its invasion of Ukraine and its veto along with that of China against the new sanctions related to North Korean ballistic missiles, is fundamentally hampering the primary UN body responsible for international peace and security (Cameron 2022).

The Security Council, as believed by former Secretary-General Kofi Annan, is the UN body with the greatest capacity to organise action and respond rapidly (Genser 2022). Yet, the power of the P5 to keep critical issues at bay has undermined the UNSC's work and forced the Secretary-General to "hold out a begging bowl to implement decisions" (*General Assembly Fifty-Ninth Session* 2004). Annan based on expert reports proposed two reform models. The first model entails the creation of six new permanent seats without the veto power as enjoyed by the P5 and two new non-permanent seats based on regional representation. The second model envisionates an entirely new category of non-permanent seats elected for four years and one additional elected for a two-year term.

Building on Kofi Annan's views on UNSC reform, "The Group of Four" (G4) and the "Uniting for Consensus" groups proposed similar reforms, but in opposition to each other. On the one hand, the "Group of Four" is composed of Japan, Germany, India, and Brazil, countries which have expressed ambitions of becoming permanent members of the Security Council (Chakraborti 2021). The G4 proposes a 25-member Security Council, with an additional four non-permanent seats and six permanent seats. The new permanent seats would be allocated as follows: two for Asia, two for Africa, one for Europe, and one for America (Niklas Rolf, Juval Janssen and Liedtke 2021). On the other hand, the Uniting for Consensus group consists of 40 countries, most of which oppose the G4 proposal. Some members' specific objections concern blocking Brazil and India from obtaining permanent seats. However, for the entire group of Uniting for Consensus, regional representation in the UNSC is the crucial focus. A proposition of allocating six seats for Africa, four for Latin America and the Caribbean, five for Asia, and three for Western Europe has been put on the table with the aim of improving regional representation and bringing more transparency to the UNSC methods (Chakraborti 2021).

The reform of the UNSC has also thrown limelight on the divide within the European continent (Patrick 2023). Over the years, the cohesion of the EU has been extensively debated among scholars. The UK's vote to leave has intensified this debate, as Brexit has significantly diminished the EU's collective diplomatic power. In 2018, France rejected Germany's unofficial proposal suggesting to transform the French permanent seat on the UNSC into a shared EU permanent seat (Hosli 2022). Instead, France argues for the enlargement of the UNSC by increasing the number of permanent seats. In the same token, the EU argues that an expanded UNSC would better reflect the current global political landscape and make the UNSC more representative of the international community.

The EU has actively proposed several reforms to the UNSC, reflecting its commitment to enhancing the Council's effectiveness and representativeness. Over recent years, the EU's influence within the UNSC has grown, partly due to its strategic alignment with the Council on various global issues. This alignment has been facilitated by the EU's enhanced institutional mechanisms, which enable more effective coordination with the UNSC. The Lisbon Treaty significantly bolstered the EU's role on the global stage by granting it legal personality, thereby formalising its ability to engage in international relations and strengthening its participation in global governance. The EU's proactive stance on UNSC reform and its strengthened presence underscores its role in shaping and participating in this evolving global order, aiming to contribute to more effective and inclusive international decision-making processes (Schrijver 2020).

Since the creation of the UNSC, the world has undergone significant changes, and the global power structure has shifted. A key reason behind the EU's push for UNSC expansion is its belief that a more representative Council would be better equipped to address global challenges (EEAS, n.d.). The UNSC will serve as an effective platform for EU foreign policy and will help the EU strenghten its role as a global actor in promoting human and social causes and protection of fundamental rights, independence, and legitimacy through its core values (Schrijver 2020). This provides the EU enough reason to stay committed to the UNSC reform in the hopes of securing adequate allocated seatings in the future.

7 Conclusion

The European Union's involvement in the United Nations Security Council is a significant aspect of its efforts to foster global peace, security, and stability. The EU's engagement in the UNSC stems from its shared commitment to effective multilateralism and to the promotion of human rights. Through its CFSP, the EU strives to advance its external relations, contributing to a cohesive and unified EU presence in the UNSC. Various institutional mechanisms, such as the European External Action Service (EEAS) the Political and Security Committee, and the role of the High Representative of the Union for Foreign Affairs and Security Policy, facilitate coordination and representation of the EU's foreign policy in the UNSC. The EU member states also effectively support the multilateral UN-centred efforts in line with the ESS strategic objectives. This has created positive connotations for the EU as a whole (Blavoukos and Bourantonis 2011).

The EU's presence in the UNSC extends beyond mere formal representation and encompasses contributions to UN peacekeeping operations, development aid, and diplomatic efforts. By supporting UN resolutions and initiatives, the EU strengthens its role in maintaining international peace and security. The EU's coordinated approach to foreign policy helps build consensus among UN member states on crucial issues, thereby reinforcing the UN's role as the foundation of global governance. The EU remains the single largest financial contributor to the UN system, with its countries funding 43% of the UN's regular budget, more than two-fifths of UN peacekeeping operations, and about one-half of all UN Member States' contributions to UN funds and programmes. More than USD 1.35 billion is contributed to the UN external assistance programmes by the European Commission, and EU institutions provide 56% of the global aid to development (EEAS 2021).

Looking ahead, the EU is expected to continue its close collaboration with the UN and other international organisations to advance its vision of a more peaceful and prosperous world. Even though it might be more challenging, since France is now the only permanent seat representative of the EU in the UNSC, the EU's commitment to multilateralism and to the pursuit of its common foreign and security policy objectives will guide its engagement in the UNSC. By leveraging its collective strength, coordinating positions, and contributing to global peacekeeping efforts and development initiatives, the EU will strive to play an influential role in shaping the decisions and actions of the UNSC.

To sum up, the EU's prospects and opportunities in the UNSC are firmly grounded in its shared values, dedication to multilateralism, and ability to effectively coordinate and represent the interests of its member states. The EU's engagement in the UNSC exemplifies its unwavering commitment to promoting global peace, security, and stability through collaborative and diplomatic means. Moreover, it displays the EU's efforts in engaging with current and future geopolitical realities, and its belief that it is possible to achieve greater success through effective global multilateralism.

References

Ansell, Christopher K., David Levi-Faur, and Jarle Trondal. "An Organizational–Institutional Approach to Governance." In *Governance in Turbulent Times*, edited by Christopher K. Ansell, Jarle Trondal, and Morten Øgård, 27–54. Oxford University Press, 2016. https://doi.org/10.1093/acprof:oso/9780198739517.003.0002.

Axelrod, Robert, and Robert O. Keohane. "Achieving Cooperation Under Anarchy: Strategies and Institutions." *World Politics* 38, no. 1 (1985): 226–254. https://doi.org/10.2307/2010357.

Bailey, Sydney D., and Sam Daws. "The Council Convenes." In *The Procedure of the UN Security Council*, edited by Sydney D. Bailey and Sam Daws, 193, 235. Oxford University Press, 1998. https://doi.org/10.1093/0198280734.003.0002.

Blavoukos, Spyros, and Dimitris Bourantonis. "The EU's Performance in the United Nations Security Council." *European Integration* 33 (2011): 731–742. https://doi.org/10.1080/07036337.2011.606697.

Cameron, Ian. 2022. 'Reforming the UN Security Council: Analyzing Obstacles to Reform'. American Security Project. September 29, 2022. https://www.americansecurityproject.org/reforming-the-un-security-council-analyzingobstacles-toreform/.

CFR. "The UN Security Council | Council on Foreign Relations." *Council on Foreign Relations*, 2024. Accessed August 16, 2024. https://www.cfr.org/backgrounder/un-security-council.

Chakraborti, Tribid. 2021. 'United Nations Security Council Reform: A Shattered Illusion'. *Politico,* 13(1): 106–127. https://politicosse.in/uploads/101.pdf.

Chen, Jiaqian, Christian Ebeke, Li Lin, Haonan Qu, and Jesse Siminitz. 2018. 'The Long-Term Impact of Brexit on the European Union.' IMF Blogs. 2018. https://www.imf.org/en/Blogs/Articles/2018/08/10/blog-the-long-term-impact-ofbrexit-on-the-eu.

Conant, Lisa. "Compliance and What EU Member States Make of It." In *Compliance and the Enforcement of EU Law*, edited by Marise Cremona, 1–30. Oxford University Press, 2012. https://doi.org/10.1093/acprof:oso/9780199644735.003.0001.

de Vasconcelos, Álvaro. "A Strategy for EU Foreign Policy." *European Union Institute for Security Studies (EUISS)*, 2010. Accessed August 16, 2024. https://eulacfoundation.org/system/files/digital_library/2023-07/giving_substance_to_the_strategic_partnerships.pdf.

Dee, Megan, and Karen E. Smith. 2017. 'UK diplomacy at the UN after Brexit: Challenges and Opportunities'. *The British Journal of Politics and International Relations,* 19(3): 527–542. https://doi.org/10.1177/1369148117710208.

Delegation of the European Union to the UN and other international organisations in Geneva. 2021. 'The European Union and the United Nations'. Delegation of the European Union to the UN and other international organisations in Geneva. 2021. https://www.eeas.europa.eu/un-geneva/european-union-and-united-nations_en?s=62#top.

Devitt, Rebecca. "Liberal Institutionalism: An Alternative IR Theory or Just Maintaining the Status Quo?" *E-International Relations*, September 2011. Accessed December 19, 2024. https://www.e-ir.info/pdf/13482.

Drieskens, Edith. "EU Actorness at the UN Security Council: A Principal-Agent Comparison of the Legal Situation Before and After Lisbon." *European Journal of Law Reform* X, no. 4 (2008): 599–619.

Erlbacher, Friedrich. "Article 220 TFEU." In *The EU Treaties and the Charter of Fundamental Rights: A Commentary*, edited by Manuel Kellerbauer, Marcus Klamert, and Jonathan Tomkin, 1676–1686. Oxford University Press, 2019. https://doi.org/10.1093/oso/9780198759393.003.351.

European Commission (with Directorate-General for External Relations). "The Enlarging European Union at the United Nations—Making Multilateralism Matter." *Publications Office*, 2004.

European Commission. 2021. 'Joint Communication to the European Parliament and the Council on strengthening the EU's contribution to rules-based multilateralism'. European Commission, 17 February 2021.

European External Action Service. 2016. 'Shared vision, common action—A stronger Europe—A global strategy for the European Union's foreign and security policy'. European External Action Service. 2016. https://doi.org/10.2871/9875, https://op.europa.eu/en/publication-detail/-/publication/3eaae2cf-9ac5-11e6-868c-01aa75ed71a1.

European Parliamentary Research Services. (2020). 'European Union involvement in the United Nations system: Broad partnership based on shared commitment to multilateralism: in depth analysis'. Publications Office. https://data.europa.eu/doi/10.2861/009144

European Union. "Consolidated Version of The Treaty on the Functioning of the European Union." *Official Journal of the European Union*, October 26, 2012. Accessed August 16, 2024. https://eur-lex.europa.eu/LexUriServ/LexUriServ.do?uri=CELEX:12012E/TXT:en:PDF.

Gailišs, Eduards. 2024 "Small Powers as Non-Permanent Members of the United Nations Security Council: A Case Study of the Baltic States." *Security and Defence Quarterly* 45, no. 1 (2024): 33–54. https://doi.org/10.35467/sdq/172983.

Genser, Jared. "The United Nations Security Council's Implementation of the Responsibility to Protect: A Review of Past Interventions and Recommendations for Improvement." *Chicago Journal of International Law*, 2022. https://cjil.uchicago.edu/print-archive/united-nations-security-councils-implementation-responsibility-protect-review-past.

Gifkins, Jess, Samuel Jarvis, and Jason Ralph. "Brexit and the UN Security Council: Declining British Influence?" *International Affairs* 95, no. 6 (2019): 1349–1368. https://doi.org/10.1093/ia/iiz205.

Gowan, Richard. "Separation Anxiety: European Influence at the UN After Brexit." *ECFR*, May 8, 2018. Accessed September 12, 2024. https://ecfr.eu/publication/separation_anxiety_european_influence_at_the_un_after_brexit/.

Hawkins, Darren, David A. Lake, Daniel L. Nielson, and Michael J. Tierney. *Delegation and Agency in International Organizations*. Cambridge University Press, 2006. https://login.ezproxy.leidenuniv.nl:2443/login?URL=https://search.ebscohost.com/login.aspx?direct=true&db=e000xww&AN=179800&site=ehost-live.

Helou, Tareq Yacoub. "The EU in the United Nations Security Council: Trends from the United Kingdom and France." *Policy Brief 7*, UNU-CRIS, Bruges, 2019.

Hix, Simon. 2018. 'Brexit: Where is the EU–UK Relationship Heading?' *Journal of Common Market Studies* 56, (S1): 11–27. https://doi.org/10.1111/jcms.12766.

Hosli, Madeleine O. *The European Union and the United Nations in Global Governance*. Bristol, UK: Bristol University Press, 2022.

Jain, Gautam. "What Trump Can Do to Reverse US Climate Policy—And What He Probably Can't Change." *The Conversation*, November 7, 2024. Accessed December 12, 2024. http://theconversation.com/what-trump-can-do-to-reverse-us-climate-policy-and-what-he-probably-cant-change-243129.

Joint Communication to the European Parliament and the Council on Strengthening the EU's Contribution to Rules-Based Multilateralism (2021). Accessed December 19, 2024. https://eur-lex.europa.eu/legal-content/en/ALL/?uri=CELEX%3A52021JC0003.

Jokela, Juha. "'Global Governance and Effective Multilateralism' THE G-20: A Pathway to Effective Multilateralism?" *European Union Institute for Security Studies (EUISS)*, 2011. Accessed August 16, 2024. https://www.iss.europa.eu/sites/default/files/EUISSFiles/The_G20_-_a_pathway_to_effective_multilateralism.pdf.

Keatinge, Patrick. "The Twelve, the United Nations, and Somalia: The Mirage of Global Intervention." In *Foreign Policy of the European Union*, edited by Elfriede Regelsberger, Philippe de Schoutheete de Tervarent, and Wolfgang Wessels, 275–296. Lynne Rienner Publishers, 1997. https://doi.org/10.1515/9781685856137-017.

Keohane, Robert O., and Lisa L. Martin. "The Promise of Institutionalist Theory." *International Security* 20, no. 1 (1995): 39–51. https://doi.org/10.2307/2539214.

Keukeleire, Stephan, and Jennifer Macnaughtan. *The Foreign Policy of the European Union*, 2008. https://api.semanticscholar.org/CorpusID:154096513.

Lindström, Madeleine, and Kristina Zetterlund. 2012. 'Setting the Stage for the Military Intervention in Libya—Decisions made and their implications for the

EU and NATO'. Swedish Defence Research Agency. https://www.foi.se/rest-api/report/FOI-R--3498--SE.

Lopez-Claros, Augusto, Arthur L. Dahl, and Maja Groff. "European Integration: Building Supranational Institutions." In *Global Governance and the Emergence of Global Institutions for the 21st Century*, edited by Augusto Lopez-Claros, Arthur L. Dahl, and Maja Groff, 65–78. Cambridge University Press, 2020. https://www.cambridge.org/core/product/7C3571057963 4D19969FC44B8D40BD3C.

Marchesi, Daniele. "The EU Common Foreign and Security Policy in the UN Security Council: Between Representation and Coordination." *European Foreign Affairs Review* 15, no. 1 (2010): 30. https://doi.org/10.54648/EERR2010006.

Niklas Rolf, Jan, Niall Juval Janssen and Max Liedtke. 2021. 'Projecting General Assembly Voting Records onto an Enlarged Security Council: An Analysis of the G4 Reform Proposal'. *Global Policy* 12, (3): 313–324.

Ojanen, Hanna. "The EU and the UN: A Shared Future." *Ulkopoliittinen Instituutti Utrikespolitiska Institutet The Finnish Institute of International Affairs*, 2006. August 16, 2024. https://www.fiia.fi/wp-content/uploads/2017/01/neteu-yk.pdf.

Oleksiejuk, Michal. 2020. 'The Impacts of Brexit on the Security and the Defence Industry in the European Union and the United Kingdom'. Warsaw Institute. April 20, 2020. https://warsawinstitute.org/wp-content/uploads/2020/04/RS_15-04-2020_EN-3.pdf.

Olsen, Johan P. "Change and Continuity: An Institutional Approach to Institutions of Democratic Government." *European Political Science Review* 1, no. 1 (2009): 3–32. https://doi.org/10.1017/S1755773909000022.

Orban, Endre. "The EU-Member State Relationship as a Principal-Agent Problem." *SSRN*, November 5, 2021. Accessed September 12, 2024. https://papers.ssrn.com/abstract=3957501.

Paasivirta, Esa, and Thomas Ramopoulos. 2019. 'UN General Assembly, UN Security Council, and UN Human Rights Council: The EU in State-Centred Multilateral Frameworks'. In *Research Handbook on the European Union and International Organizations*, edited by Ramses A. Wessel and Jed Odermatt, 58–81. Edward Elgar. https://doi.org/10.4337/9781786438935.00010.

Patrick, Stewart. "UN Security Council Reform: What the World Thinks." *Carnegie Endowment for International Peace*, 2023. Accessed September 12, 2024. https://carnegieendowment.orgundefined?lang=en.

Pirozzi, Nicoletta. "The EU's Contribution to the Effectiveness of the UN Security Council: Representation, Coordination and Outreach." *Istituto Affari Internazionali*, July 2010. Accessed August 16, 2024. https://www.iai.it/sites/default/files/iai1014.pdf.

Press and information team of the Delegation to the UN in New York. 2025. "EU Statement—UN Security Council Open Debate: Practicing Multilateralism, Reforming and Improving Global Governance." EEAS. February 2025. https://www.eeas.europa.eu/delegations/un-new-york/eu-statement-un-security-council-open-debate-practicing-multilateralism-reforming-and-improving_en#:~:text=The%20EU%20supports%20comprehensive%20reform,of%20underrepresented%20regions%2C%20especially%20Africa.

Regelsberger, Elfriede, Philippe de Schoutheete de Tervarent, and Wolfgang Wessels. "From EPC to CFSP: Does Maastricht Push the EU Toward a Role as a Global Power?" In *Foreign Policy of the European Union*, edited by Elfriede Regelsberger, Philippe de Schoutheete de Tervarent, and Wolfgang Wessels, 1–18. Lynne Rienner Publishers, 1997. https://doi.org/10.1515/9781685856137-017.

Rieker, Pernille, and Mathilde T. E. Giske. "Conceptualising the Multi-actorness of EU(ropean) Foreign and Security Policy." In *European Actorness in a Shifting Geopolitical Order: European Strategic Autonomy Through Differentiated Integration*, edited by Pernille Rieker and Mathilde T. E. Giske, 15–42. Springer Nature Switzerland, 2024. https://doi.org/10.1007/978-3-031-44546-0_2.

Ruggie, John Gerard. "Multilateralism: The Anatomy of an Institution." *International Organization* 46, no. 3 (1992): 561–598.

Schrijver, Nico. "Strengthening the EU's Role in the UN Security Council Today." *Foundation for European Progressive Studies*, September 8, 2020. Accessed August 10, 2024. https://feps-europe.eu/strengthening-the-eus-role-in-the-un-security-council-today/.

Tardy, Thierry. "The European Union and the United Nations: Global Versus Regional Multilateralism." *Studia Diplomatica* 60, no. 1 (2007): 191–209.

Trent, John, and Laura Schnurr "Chapter 2—Peace and Security: Fixing the Security Council." In *A United Nations Renaissance: What the UN Is, and What It Could Be*, 56–71. Barbara Budrich Publishers, 2018. Accessed August 16, 2024. https://www.ssoar.info/ssoar/bitstream/handle/document/66518/ssoar-2018-trent_et_al-A_United_Nations_Renaissance_What.pdf?sequence=1&isAllowed=y&lnkname=ssoar-2018-trent_et_al-A_United_Nations_Renaissance_What.pdf.

UK Government. 2025. "Quarterly Service Personnel Statistics: 1 January 2025." GOV.UK. February 20, 2025. https://www.gov.uk/government/statistics/quarterly-service-personnel-statistics-2025/quarterly-service-personnel-statistics-1-january-2025#:~:text=UK%20Service%20Personnel%20are%20the,cent%20of%20UK%20Service%20Personnel.

UK Parliament, and Claire Mills. 2024. "Nuclear Weapons at a Glance: United Kingdom." House of Commons Library. August 1, 2024. https://commonslibrary.parliament.uk/research-briefings/cbp-9077/.

United Nations. "The United Nations Charter: Chapter I: Purposes and Principles (Articles 1–2)." *United Nations*. Retrieved August 16, 2024. Accessed December 19, 2024. https://www.un.org/en/about-us/un-charter/chapter-1.

United Nations. "Resolution 1970 (2011) | United Nations Security Council | S/RES/1970 (2011)." *United Nations*, 2011. Accessed December 19, 2024. https://documents.un.org/doc/undoc/gen/n11/245/58/pdf/n1124558.pdf.

Watts, Duncan. *The European Union*. Edinburgh University Press, 2008. https://doi.org/10.1515/9780748632251-004.

Wessel, and Jed Odermatt. "Chapter 1 The European Union's Engagement with Other International Institutions." In *Research Handbook on the European Union and International Organizations*, edited by Ramses A. Wessel and Jed Odermatt, 2–24. Edward Elgar Publishing, 2019. https://doi.org/10.4337/9781786438935.

Whitman, Richard G. 2016. 'The UK and EU Foreign, Security and Defence Policy after Brexit: Integrated, Associated or Detached?' *National Institute Economic Review, 238*(1): R43–R50. https://doi.org/10.1177/002795011623800114.

Whyte, Alexander. "Neorealism and Neoliberal Institutionalism: Born of the Same Approach?" *International Relations* 7 (2012).

Wouters, Jan, and Alex Andrione-Moylan. "Chapter 3: The Changing International Cooperation Network of the EU." In *Research Handbook on the European Union and International Organizations*, edited by Ramses A. Wessel and Jed Odermatt, 2–24. Edward Elgar Publishing, 2019. https://doi.org/10.4337/9781786438935.

CHAPTER 9

EU Member States in the Elected 10: Voting and Co-sponsorship in the UNSC

Barney Jansen and Koen van Schijndel

1 Introduction

As the terms of several United Nations Security Council (hereafter UNSC) members came to an end in June 2024, new elections for non-permanent members have recently taken place. The ascension of new members (also known as the elected 10 or E10) is expected to generate a new batch of literature covering topics relating to the UNSC. Historically, this literature and non-academic focus tend to focus on the inefficiencies and gridlock within the UNSC or how one new member can position itself as a champion of certain issues.

This chapter aims to pinpoint how (if at all) different European Union (EU) member states display similar or diverging sponsorship and voting

B. Jansen (✉) · K. van Schijndel
Leiden University, The Hague, The Netherlands
e-mail: barneyjansen1997@hotmail.com

K. van Schijndel
e-mail: k.van.schijndel@umail.leidenuniv.nl

M. O. Hosli et al. (eds.), *Multilateralism and the United Nations Security Council*, https://doi.org/10.1007/978-3-031-85320-3_9

behaviours regarding different resolutions, specifically looking at sanctions and peacekeeping topics within the UNSC. Therefore, the central research question of this chapter is the following: How do non-permanent EU member states of the UNSC differ in their sponsorship and voting behaviour? This allows for the discernment of present (or absent) patterns in voting behaviour regarding these two types of resolutions, besides revealing whether EU member states tend to cooperate or not as non-permanent members within the UNSC. In order to answer this, this chapter analyses the dynamics of sponsorship and voting behaviours of a big EU country (Germany), a middle-sized member state (Portugal), and a small EU state (Luxembourg), within and across the realms of sanctions and peacekeeping resolutions in the UNSC from 2011 until 2020.

In terms of scientific relevance, this chapter aims to provide new insights and conclusions regarding the sponsorship and voting behaviours of EU member states that hold non-permanent seats within the UNSC. It is important to note that this chapter only analyses votes taken within the UNSC concerning peacekeeping and sanctions resolutions. To date, the bulk of academic literature has focused primarily on the inefficiencies and gridlock within the body, discussing possible reforms to make the UNSC more efficient and/or democratic. Furthermore, the topic of how non-permanent members can position themselves as champions on certain issues or become a voice for smaller states also seems to have been analysed often (Conley Tyler and Pahlow 2014, 95–96). However, scholars have dedicated considerably less attention to the aforementioned topic of voting behaviour among non-permanent states. This chapter seeks to modestly address this existing gap in the literature, as much more research is needed in order to create a better understanding on the subject.

The choice to focus on EU member states serving as non-permanent members of the UNSC between 2011 and 2020 stems from several reasons. During this period, the EU countries that served as non-permanent members were Germany, Luxembourg, Poland, Portugal, Spain, and Sweden.

This chapter examines three specific countries—Germany, Luxembourg, and Portugal—selected for their contrasting profiles in terms of economic influence, colonial legacies, and strategic interests. Portugal was chosen due to its historical ties to colonies in Africa and Latin America, which continue to shape its foreign policy priorities and alignments. Luxembourg, by contrast, does not have a colonial history; its inclusion represents smaller EU states with distinct economic and geopolitical dynamics. This allows us to contrast the behaviours of states with and without colonial ties, exploring how factors like size and economic priorities alone influence UNSC strategies.

Germany serves as a distinct case of a large, economically powerful EU member with significant regional influence. Its inclusion enables an analysis of whether economic strength correlates with active engagement in the UNSC—an assumption that our findings challenge. Germany's two terms as a non-permanent member during this period also provide more data for analysis, enriching the comparative perspective of this study.

Some countries, such as Italy and the Netherlands, were excluded because they served split terms outside this timeframe, limiting the availability of comprehensive data. Poland, Spain, and Sweden were not included in our analysis. While Spain had colonies it also has important industry and is therefore a more complicated case. Sweden too does not fall nicely into one bucket. It has a population of roughly 10 million people and a relatively large land mass. It, thus, is not a small state but also can hardly be described as a large state in the same way Germany can and therefore too is excluded. Poland carries this same problem, in terms of definitely not being a small state but compared to Germany or Italy not containing large industries.

As far as societal relevance is concerned, determining the sponsorship and voting behaviours of these different EU member states within the UNSC might not only prove beneficial for each of those countries separately if no patterns of cooperation can be found, but also for the overall transparency of the UNSC towards the global community. Perhaps even the EU (or other entities) could benefit from such knowledge in order to put in place more efficient strategies in the future. Moreover, this research contributes to better understanding of the internal and external workings of the UNSC and to help improve its efficiency.

Our expectations are that the three countries will prove to have acted differently regarding peacekeeping and sanctions resolutions. On the one hand, Germany, as a large state with many export goods, has many economic incentives to prevent anything that upsets markets and economies (Chiaka 2016). Therefore, since some decisions taken in the UNSC could negatively impact its exports, we believe it may display different sponsorship and voting behaviour than the other two countries. Portugal, on the other hand, has several former colonies with which it remains closely involved through the Portuguese-Speaking

Language Community (CPLP), working together on cultural, military, and economic issues (Chiaka 2016). Therefore, it is expected that Portugal will be more likely to sponsor sanctions or peacekeeping resolutions since it also wishes to realise CPLP's priorities. In other words, we deem it probable that the country displays similar voting behaviour to France, which sponsors a lot of resolutions concerning former colonies. Lastly, we expect Luxembourg to be more reluctant in sponsorship and related voting patterns compared to the larger states. As a small state without colonies or major exports to drive its sponsorship, we anticipate other factors to explain its voting behaviour, such as maintaining good relations with other states. Moreover, Luxembourg is dependent on trade relations with other countries and does not possess the economic or military might to pressure other states. Thus, it is our expectation that the country would rather strive to maintain the best possible relations with other nations and in doing so, not support any deal unless it can count on broad international support.

This chapter will proceed as follows: firstly, it will start with a literature review, covering the sponsorship and voting behaviours of non-permanent members within the UNSC, in particular the positions and voting behaviours regarding peacekeeping and sanctions of Germany, Portugal, and Luxembourg. Secondly, we will do a comparative analysis between the mentioned countries within the same class of resolutions, as well as across the two types of resolutions, covering the topics of sanctions and peacekeeping for all three countries. Finally, the last section lays out the main findings and provides an answer to the general research question.

2 Sponsorship & Voting Behaviour of Non-Permanent Members in the UNSC

Before discussing the analytical section of the chapter, it is important to contextualise this study. To this end, this section will critically reflect on the existing literature. This encompasses five important topics, namely coalition building and voting behaviour, China and the UNSC, small and medium-sized states, regional groupings and expertise, and voting patterns.

The first topic concerns coalition building and voting behaviour in general. One prominent author who discusses these topics in her work is Monteleone (2015), focusing on successful coalition building in the past and analysing how these beat out weaker coalitions from the UNSC. In order to do so, the article examines the existence, formation, and transformation of coalitions in the international system by analysing variations in the behaviour of the UNSC members from 1993 to 2012 (Monteleone 2015). She finds that the "creation and evolution of coalitions in the international system are influenced by alterations in their bargaining power and bargaining environment, linked to the global leadership cycle, as well as by long-term changes in the international political system" (Monteleone 2015, 64). Furthermore, Monteleone (2015) argues that it is more useful to examine sponsoring behaviour rather than voting behaviour, and highlights two notable facts, namely that on emerging issues, coalitions are relatively unstable, while with longstanding issues, coalitions have solidified. In addition, coalition building is less attractive for the five permanent members than it is for the non-permanent members, as a result of their absolute veto power (Monteleone 2015).

Another prominent author who touches upon coalition building and voting power in the UNSC is O'Neill (1996). Although this author focused on voting behaviour during the Cold War, his findings remain relevant to date. O'Neill (1996) argues that coalitions can be formed by forging trust among states. This is reflected in the voting behaviour of states when they choose to vote alike, even when that means suppressing their own interests at times, in exchange for solidarity and long-term influence. This applies even if a country is only in the UNSC for a limited amount of time (O'Neill 1996, 235–236). An example of such a coalition given by the author is the Non-Aligned Movement (hereafter NAM) during the Cold War. However, these alliances face the real danger of losing members due to P-5 lobbying or threats, which make coalitions without P-5 members relatively weak (O'Neill 1996, 235–236). Moreover, greater coalitions do not necessarily ensure a greater chance of success, nor does a greater coalition mean that member states lose or gain power when a new member joins (O'Neill 1996, 235–236). Therefore, coalitions without P-5 members have a relatively low chance of succeeding, since they have to convince all the P-5 of the importance of the resolution. When this is the case, countries with a veto gain relative power, as they can sink any proposal (O'Neill 1996, 235–236).

Several authors align with these points of view such as Dong-Ryul (2007) and Junbo and Zhimin (2016). All three use China's voting behaviour as an example to illustrate how this P-5 member differs from non-permanent EU states and how it has influenced the voting behaviour of the latter countries within the UNSC. On the one hand, Dong-Ryul

(2007) argues that China's voting behaviour in the UNSC is shaped by a complex set of factors including its domestic politics, its relationships with other major powers, and its strategic priorities on the global stage. As a result, even though China has become more active in the United Nations (UN) system in recent years, it continues to prioritise its national interests above all else, often voting against resolutions that are detrimental to these interests (Dong-Ryul 2007). This, in turn, has a great impact on the voting behaviour of non-permanent EU states as O'Neill (1996) and Monteleone (2015) highlighted. On the other hand, Junbo and Zhimin (2016) also concur with O'Neill (1996) and Monteleone (2015) on the fact that there exists considerable competition between China and the EU member states, although all authors agree that these differences are not irreconcilable. Therefore, they advocate for increased cooperation between the UNSC permanent members and the non-permanent countries that belong to the EU in the future, as this would be beneficial to all parties (Junbo and Zhimin 2016, 91).

Another topic to be discussed is that of countries falling under the small/medium state categories. Thorhallsson (2012) is one of the authors who has chosen to analyse these types of countries in the UNSC. In his article, he examines the factors that contribute to small states' ability to have an impact in the UNSC, arguing that smaller states often have a harder time being elected into the UNSC. In his article, Thorhallsson (2012) posits that there are two main categories of qualitative factors that determine the capacity of small states to shape the decisions of the UNSC. The first category pertains to administrative competence encompassing knowledge, initiative, and diplomatic, coalition-building, and leadership skills (Thorhallsson 2012, 159–160). The second category focuses on the state's image within the international system, specifically its perceived neutrality and reputation as a norm entrepreneur in specific policy domains (Thorhallsson 2012, 159–160). By leveraging these categories, small states can transcend the role of passive recipients of UN membership action and assume an active role in international affairs (Thorhallsson 2012, 159–160). Furthermore, it is important to acknowledge that not all small states within the EU possess equal capabilities. Variances in material resources such as wealth and the capacity of alliance formation, alongside soft power assets, contribute to disparities among small states.

An interesting addition to this literature review section is the contribution of Conley Tyler and Pahlow (2014). In their article, they discuss how

Australia has acted as a voice for both small and mid-sized countries in the UNSC, and how the country emphasises the importance of coalitions within the body. Again, these authors also comply with points previously made by O'Neill (1996). Being seen as a reliable coalition partner also increases the confidence of states having such a potential partner. Thus, without trust, others might not wish to align themselves with the given state since they might end up on the wrong side of a vote, isolating them and creating tensions between them and other UNSC members. Yet, the article of Conley Tyler and Pahlow (2014) points out that the UNSC tenures of non-permanent members are short, and building trust between parties in a period of only two years is hard, which an important aspect to consider (Conley Tyler and Pahlow 2014, 106–107).

Other authors present additional relevant findings. For instance, Nortvedt (2019) highlights that, despite the asymmetrical power structure of the UNSC, small and mid-sized countries are able to substantially influence and achieve leverage through based on the institutional arrangements of the UNSC, as well as their own states' identities. In order to do so, the author examined the cases of Luxembourg, New Zealand, and Sweden, concluding that they all achieved leverage in the UNSC regarding the case of Syria between 2013 and 2018 (Nortvedt 2019). Therefore, the author claims that the UNSC is not solely governed by the P-5, but the impact derived from small non-permanent states is noticeable. In the cases the author examined, all three countries established themselves as leaders of humanitarian issues regarding Syria and developed a number of important resolutions (Nortvedt 2019). This is in line with the argument put forth above by Thorhallsson (2012).

The argument is further backed up in a report generated by Haugevik et al. (2021) who delved deeper into the cases of Estonia and Norway as elected members of the UNSC. The authors underscore that the opportunities presented to the E10 to truly impact the UNSC agenda are limited for a number of reasons, including power struggles, complex subject matters, and inefficient working strategies and methods (Haugevik et al. 2021, iv). Nevertheless, the authors also emphasise the achievements of both countries in their role as members of the UNSC. Diplomatic experience and reputation-building seem to be the two most important aspects for elected members (Haugevik et al. 2021, iv). "Knowing how to play the game", in the words of the author, is identified as the key ability for countries to punch above their weight (Haugevik et al. 2021, iv). Thus, it becomes clear that the bulk of academic literature that examines elected small and mid-size states that participate in the UNSC tends to highlight how these countries are indeed capable of exerting a limited amount of power. In the end, there are ways in which this can be done that are both inherent to the UNSC's institutional arrangements and other factors over which they have partial influence as mentioned above.

The fourth topic relates to regional groupings and expertise. Wouters and Pineau (2019) examine the role of non-permanent EU members in the UNSC. They question whether these non-permanent members possess power without responsibility or responsibility without power, considering their perceived inferior status compared to the permanent five (P-5) members who possess veto power. The authors analyse Belgium's terms in the UNSC from 2007 to 2008 and then upcoming term from 2019 to 2020 to shed light on this issue (Wouters and Pineau 2019). The authors find that the penholder system—an informal practice in the UNSC where one or more members, typically permanent members, take the lead in drafting resolutions and coordinating negotiations—has widened the negotiation and consultation gap between permanent and non-permanent members (Wouters and Pineau 2019, 135). Non-permanent members are discouraged from making significant alterations to carefully negotiated drafts among the diverging coalitions within the P-5.

However, the authors argue that non-permanent members can still contribute effectively when they possess specific expertise, such as on a particular region. Belgium, for example, can offer valuable input on resolutions concerning its former colonies due to its recognised expertise in these areas (Wouters and Pineau 2019, 134–135). Nonetheless, the authors conclude that non-permanent members have limited influence in shaping resolutions when they lack expertise in a given subject. This is particularly evident for contentious issues like sanctions, which can stir political tensions among the P-5. Consequently, the authors anticipate that countries with ties to former colonies will play a more active role in sponsoring resolutions related to their former colonies (Wouters and Pineau 2019, 134–135). These countries maintain strong connections with their former colonies and are recognised by the P-5 as experts in related matters, granting them meaningful opportunities to contribute (Wouters and Pineau 2019, 152). Applying this insight to our research, this can be the case for Portugal.

Another finding relevant to this theme is covered by Lai and Lefler (2017). Their article draws on literature from legislative politics and regional similarities to link classic notions of representation—descriptive representation, where members physically resemble or share characteristics with the populations they represent, and substantive representation, where members advocate for the interests and policies preferred by their constituents—to the geographic representation of UN members in the UNSC. Yet, the argument put forth is that the election process for the UNSC leads to the selection of states that are unlikely to represent their regions (Lai and Lefler 2017, 585). By using United Nations General Assembly's (UNGA) voting patterns as a proxy for preferences, two sets of analyses were conducted to test whether states within the same region generally have higher levels of General Assembly voting similarity, and if members display similar voting patterns with states in their region (Lai and Lefler 2017, 585). The findings revealed that, although regional groupings tend to have higher patterns of vote similarity, this effect is not present when comparing the states voted into the UNSC with states in their region (Lai and Lefler 2017, 607–610).

The last topic concerns voting patterns in the UNSC. Romita (2018) argues that, although the Cold War era is often characterised as a struggle between the East and the West, voting patterns in the UNSC reveal a more complex picture (Romita 2018, iv–v). Despite being members of the North America Treaty Organisation (NATO) alliance and three of the UNSC's 5 permanent members (known as the permanent three or P3), "France, the United Kingdom (UK), and the United States of America (USA) frequently voted differently on council resolutions during the Cold War era, particularly on issues related to colonialism and Israel/Palestine" (Romita 2018, iv–v). This article suggests that the divisions among the P3 were partly due to the UNSC's underdeveloped negotiating processes and the tendency of assertive UNSC members from the NAM to propose politically charged resolutions that were unlikely to be adopted (Romita 2018, iv–v). However, as the Cold War ended, the P-5 recognised the potential of a UNSC unhindered by significant East-West tensions, and sought to consolidate their control of the UNSC's work, achieving nearly 92% voting unanimity on adopted resolutions since 1992 (Romita 2018, iv–v). The article argues that the NAM has "lost its unity and political influence in the post-Cold War era, as its members are less likely to propose resolutions that will be vetoed" (Romita 2018, iv–v). Nonetheless, the elected members of the UNSC (known as the elected ten or E10) have played a constructive role in bridging divisions among the permanent members, despite their differing views (Romita 2018, iv–v).

The last two authors in this debate are Renard and Hooijmaaijers (2011), who mention that "relations between the EU and the strategic partners in the UNSC suggest that cooperation is still limited", and that "partnership between the EU and the third country does not seem yet to have an impact on bilateral cooperation within the UN system" (Renard and Hooijmaaijers 2011, 6). According to them, on certain issues, cooperation tends to be even harder as new emerging powers are willing to and capable of shaping the UN agenda. Yet, it remains unclear whether these patterns "will become the rule or the exception" (Renard and Hooijmaaijers 2011, 6). Therefore, these authors advocate for strategic partnerships and argue that they should become the tool to ensure a more cooperative future (Renard and Hooijmaaijers 2011, 6).

3 Comparative Analysis

3.1 Expectations

Based on the discussed literature, this chapter posits different expectations for the way each state will operate within the UNSC regarding sponsorship. As pointed out by Thorhallsson (2012), there needs to be a willingness to take a leadership role. There is evidence that Germany does not have this willingness, due to its role during the Second World War (Barber 2019). Hence, we do not predict Germany to take an active role in sponsoring resolutions. Expectations for Portugal are slightly different. Because of its enduring close relations with former colonies, we foresee that the country will take an active role in sponsoring resolutions concerning its former colonies. As it can be observed in states like France and Belgium, we expect Portugal to not only take an active role, but also to be granted it by the UNSC (Wellings and Mycock 2019, 63), as it can provide valuable input on issues regarding these states and be perceived as an expert (Wouters and Pineau 2019, 149). When it comes to Luxembourg, it is expected that the country in general will prefer broad coalitions and cooperation (Conley Tyler and Pahlow 2014, 106). It can take specific topics that it would like to focus on like humanitarian issues, as it did in the past, but these are outside the scope of this research (Nortvedt 2019).

There is a common theme that ties the three countries analysed in this research which is the EU and NATO membership. They are also relatively close to each other geographically in the same region, Western Europe.

Therefore, one might assume that these countries vote and sponsor similar resolutions, as this happens in the UNGA (Lai and Lefler 2017, 607). Yet, as pointed out, cooperation and coordination between EU members in the UNSC remain limited (Renard and Hooijmaaijers 2011, 6). It is still forecasted that these states will act differently despite their proximity and memberships of both the EU and NATO.

This research will contribute to create a better understanding of non-permanent EU states' behaviour in the UNSC, which, up until this point, has not been directly addressed in the literature. In the analysis, we will first discuss sponsorship of resolutions concerning sanctions and peacekeeping to then lay out our expectations per state.

3.2 Sanctions

Sanctions are a tool for the UNSC to seek changes in the behaviour of states and individuals in a conflict. Examples of sanctions can be arms embargoes, travel bans, or restrictions of commodities or goods. Each sanctions regime has different goals such as cessation of hostilities or of nuclear proliferation. These goals are stated in the UNSC resolution and also include criteria that have to be met for sanctions to be lifted.

One would expect Germany, Portugal, and Luxembourg to have different positions in the topic of sanctions. We anticipate Germany to act in a way that would prevent any negative impacts on said exports, as a large share of its GDP comes from exports. Examples of these exports include vehicles, pharmaceutical products, and machinery components. In total, exports of all goods and services make up more than 50% of the German GDP (World Bank 2023). While a lot of exports go to its neighbours in the EU, and to allies like the US and Japan; Germany also trades extensively with the Global South. This makes Germany very dependent on its access to foreign markets. An active sanctions regime could hurt relations and potentially limit access to foreign markets, negatively affecting the overall economy (Klobucista and Ferragamo 2023).

Germany has also been hesitant to take centre on the world stage (Cunha 2021, 2). Keenly aware of its history, the country has tried not to be seen as aggressive. Receiving the nickname "reluctant hegemon" gives away the position Germany has had when it comes to leadership (Barber 2019). While Germany has taken a leadership role in the European Union during several crises in the past, this does not automatically translate into active sponsorship of sanctions. While Chancellor Scholtz spoke of a "Zeitenwende" after the Russian Ukraine invasion, he has been hesitant to actually fulfil the expectations placed on Germany. It has not taken the lead in a strong EU defence policy, while also alienating the country from its EU and Western allies (Puglierin 2024).

All in all, we believe that these two factors will translate into a more reluctant sanctions sponsorship. Sanctions, after all, are not only hurting exports, but are also inherently political and can be portrayed as economic aggression towards other states. Because of this, our prediction is that Germany will not sponsor large numbers of sanction resolutions as they do not wish to damage relations and limit market access.

On the contrary, we expect Portugal to behave differently from Germany. Portugal does not have an economy focused on exports, being less influenced by economic incentives. Thus, it is not as concerned with maintaining market access nor is it influenced by a similar historical burden. Another factor that might result in different behaviour is that Portugal has several former colonies with which it remains closely involved through the Portuguese Speaking Language Community (CPLP), where these countries work together on culture, military and economic issues (Chiaka 2016). We foresee this to translate into Portugal being more likely to sponsor sanctions resolutions as they aim at resolving instability which could threaten these interests. In this way, its behaviour is similar to countries like France and England, which are still deeply rooted in the Francosphere and Anglosphere, respectively, and actively involve themselves in matters concerning former colonies (Wellings and Mycock 2019, 64).

Lastly, we assume Luxembourg to be more reluctant in sanction sponsorship when compared to larger states. As a small state, it possesses neither an export-based economy like Germany, nor former colonies to which it could have had ties like Portugal. Expectations are that the country will attempt to bolster its image and try to seek a reputable status, as other small states have done in the past (Thorhallsson and Eggertsdóttir 2020, 55). We expect that Luxembourg will strive to maintain the best possible relations with other nations and that it will only support a deal on these issues if it gathers broad international support. Where Portugal might be willing to be a sole supporter of a sanctions regime due to close ties with former colonies, we do not expect Luxembourg to act similarly. This way, we expect Luxembourg and Germany to act in similar ways, although the underlying motivations differ.

3.2.1 German Sanctions Sponsorship

The available data used by this chapter range from 2011 to 2020. They contain all voting behaviour in the UNSC in this timeframe. During this time period, Germany has been elected as non-permanent UNSC member twice, serving terms in 2011–2012 and 2019–2020. Throughout its UNSC tenure, Germany (co-)sponsored 79 resolutions, with eight of these being sanctions-related. Six of these sponsorships took place in 2011–2012, while it sponsored only two sanctions resolutions in 2019–2020.

The German-sponsored sanctions resolutions were all related to either Al-Qaida, Afghanistan, Iran, or Libya. The resolution to sanction Al-Qaida was only sponsored by Western countries, including France, the UK, Portugal, and the USA, as well as Togo. German-sponsored sanctions against Afghanistan were related to freezing the assets of Taliban members and affiliated organisations (UNSC Sponsorship Data 2023). Resolutions regarding Libya in 2011 and 2012 intended to prevent further human rights abuses, given that Libya was undergoing a civil war, and were supported by a large group of states including China, the US, India, Morocco, and Pakistan. The resolution regarding sanctions on Iran extended the term of the panel of experts who supported the Iran Sanctions Committee (United Nations Security Council 2012b).

An overall assessment of German-sponsored resolutions leads to the conclusion that its approach was one of relative caution. In comparison with permanent UNSC members, the country sponsored few sanctions resolutions (UNSC Sponsorship Data 2023). The ones it did sponsor were either with broad international support, such as the Libyan sanctions or the sanctions regarding the expert panel on the Iran sanction regime, or targeted at individuals that were part of terrorist organisations. It did not sponsor sanctions on North Korea or other states or entities that were seen as worth sanctioning by its allies like France or the USA. This illustrates Germany's reluctance in sponsoring sanctions, being in line with German behaviour outside the UNSC, where it is often cautious about directly involving itself in a potential conflict. Even in cases in which it has little to lose economically or politically, like in the case of actions on North Korea, Germany is not keen to sponsor sanctions. Historic conscience makes Germany desperately not wanting to be seen as an aggressor or in any way fanning the flames of the conflict (Fix 2022).

3.2.2 *Portuguese Sanctions Sponsorship*

Portugal was a member of the UNSC in the 2011–2012 period (UN Media 2010). During this time, it sponsored sanctions seven times, with five of these sanctions concerning Libya, one concerning terrorist organisations, and one concerning Guinea-Bissau. The sanctions on Libya were tied to the first Libyan civil war. Like a large group of nations, such as Pakistan, Morocco, South Africa, and Togo, Portugal sponsored several sanctions against the country to prevent the violation of human rights (UNSC Sponsorship Data 2023). Like Germany, it supported sanctions against terrorist groups like Al-Qaida and the Taliban.

Yet, this chapter identifies that the most notable sponsorship was that of sanctions on Guinea-Bissau as Portugal was the only country to sponsor this resolution (United Nations Security Council, n.d.). Up until 1973, Guinea-Bissau was a Portuguese colony (MacQueen 2003, 1). The two countries have maintained relatively good relations after independence was recognised by the Portuguese in 1974 (MacQueen 2003, 2). In April of 2012, a military coup took place in Guinea-Bissau as a result of unease in military leadership with the way the country's President had handled tensions with neighbouring Angola (Dabo 2012). The CPLP came together, denounced the coup d'état and called for the international community to work towards restoring constitutional order in the country. It later called for military intervention by the UN (MacQueen 2003, 6). In May 2012, Portugal introduced its sanctions resolution in the UNSC, which passed unanimously (United Nations Security Council 2012c). The UNSC later condemned the coup in Guinea-Bissau.

Portugal acted on its own in this case, not seeking any support from potential allies to sponsor this resolution. It was treated not just as a former coloniser but rather as an expert on the country and its situation, which can create consensus with both non-permanent and permanent members of the UNSC. It seems Portugal had special interests in Guinea-Bissau as it did not introduce similar sanction resolutions when coups in other African countries, like Mali, Sudan, or the Ivory Coast, took place during its tenure at the UNSC. This shows that Portugal did take special interest in its former colony, which aligns with our initial expectations.

3.2.3 *Luxembourgian Sanctions Sponsorship*

Luxembourg was a UNSC non-permanent member in 2013–2014. During its tenure, it sponsored only three of the 15 resolutions related to sanctions (UNSC Sponsorship Data 2023). The first sanction-related resolutions pertained to the importance of an already existing framework regarding arms supplies and funds into Libya after the outbreak of the second civil war in the country; the second reaffirmed assets freezes, travel bans, and arms embargoes for all individuals on the UNSC's Al-Qaida Committee Sanctions lists; and the third focused on extending the UN mission in Somalia and renewing and broadening the mandate for already existing sanctions on Somalia (United Nations Security Council 2013).

Luxembourg only sponsored sanctions where fellow Western countries, such as France, Spain, and the US, were co-sponsors. This does not mean that every sanctions-related resolution with Western support was (co-) sponsored by Luxembourg. It did not sponsor several sanctions resolutions where some, all, or most Western allies were sponsors, as in the cases of Yemen or North Korea. In the end, Luxembourg voted for some of these but chose not to sponsor them, giving no direct reason why it opted to do so. Luxembourg never supported any broad new sanctions regime to be put in place. This does not mean that the country took a backseat to sponsoring the UNSC in terms of resolutions overall. In fact, it sponsored a total of 56 resolutions during its tenure.

This overall Luxembourgian reluctance to sponsor a sanctions-related resolution matches our expectations. As a small nation reliant on trade with other countries, it wishes to stay away from statements that might anger potential partners. Sanctions can become fraught political matters where a potential stance might result in retaliation or damage to its reputation or image. Luxembourg only seems to have chosen to act in cases where sanction regimes were merely expanded. Thus, the cost of expanding already existing sanctions seems lower, as the actors in question have already been deemed worthy of sanctions by the UNSC. Creating new sanction regimes, however, would first require a consensus among the permanent members that the actor in question was deserving of sanctioning in the first place. This can hurt relations and could damage either the image or reputation as states might not agree on which actors require sanctions.

3.3 *Peacekeeping*

Peacekeeping has been one of the most important tools the UN has to resolve conflicts and restore stability. While the effectiveness of the missions is widely debated, they can achieve their goals at much lower costs than counterinsurgency campaigns (Walter et al. 2021). Peacekeeping missions have not been without their incidents. Mismanagement, failure to act to protect civilians, and preventing war crimes have occurred during missions (Klobucista and Ferragamo 2021). UNSC intervention through peacekeeping operations requires consensus among the permanent members. This means that interventions by the UNSC are inherently political as a permanent member almost never allows intervention in cases concerning their own interests (Sorenson and Wood 2005, 3).

This chapter anticipates that German, Portuguese, and Luxembourgian behaviour in peacekeeping is more ambiguous in comparison to sanctions. Overall, the assumption is that countries are less hesitant to support peacekeeping missions. While sanctions have been used to incentivise or change behaviour by international actors, peacekeeping operations are used to prevent a full-scale breakdown of order, uphold stability, and prevent large humanitarian disasters in the region (Klobucista and Ferragamo 2021). Since peacekeeping operations require consent from the host government, they are less politically divisive in the UNSC.

Despite this, we assume there will be differences in the behaviour of the three countries. We still expect Germany to be more hesitant—sending troops, even under the umbrella of the UN, to other states, is something that Germany tends to avoid. Evidently, Germany's role in the Second World War still influences its behaviour on the world stage (Cunha 2021). We envisage Portugal to take a more active role in peacekeeping, especially concerning missions in its former colonies and surrounding regions as it has a direct interest in maintaining stability in these areas (Duarte et al. 2023, 493). Since we presume that Portugal is also positive towards the achievement of CPLP ambitions, we believe the country will be more supportive of peacekeeping operations. For Luxembourg, our expectation is that the country, like in the case of sanctions sponsorship, will only sponsor resolutions that are based on broad international support. As its image and good relations are paramount to Luxembourg, it does not suit the country to ruffle any feathers in the UNSC.

3.3.1 German Peacekeeping Sponsorship

During Germany's two terms at the UNSC (2011–2012 and 2019–2020), a total of 97 peacekeeping resolutions were proposed—41 in the first term and 56 in the second. Of these, Germany sponsored 21, reflecting a general hesitance to take an active role in initiating peacekeeping measures. Most of the resolutions it supported concerned extending existing missions, such as those in Bosnia-Herzegovina (UNSC Sponsorship Data 2023), which typically enjoyed broad external support. Germany avoided sponsoring resolutions where it was the sole or one of only a few sponsors, with the notable exception of Resolution 1974 in 2011, which extended the mandate of a UN mission in Afghanistan.

Significantly, Germany did not sponsor any new mandates for peacekeeping missions during either term. This cautious approach underscores its preference for upholding the status quo rather than engaging in unilateral action. Extending mandates for existing missions carries less political risk, as these actions build on previously established consensus and are less likely to provoke scrutiny. This behaviour aligns with the broader pattern of Germany's restrained engagement at the UNSC, favouring continuity over intervention.

Germany has sponsored more peacekeeping resolutions than sanctions resolutions, which leads us to conclude that Germany takes a more active role when it comes to peacekeeping compared to sanctions. Yet, before making such claims, we ought to remember that simply comparing the total number of resolutions sponsored does not show the full picture. The overall number of peacekeeping resolutions vastly outnumbered those focused on sanctions, with 97 peacekeeping and 40 sanctions resolutions during Germany's tenure. Germany sponsored roughly one in five peacekeeping resolutions (21 in total). When it comes to sanctions, it also sponsored one in five of the resolutions, 8 in total. Germany sponsored around 21% of the peacekeeping resolutions and 20% of the resolutions concerning sanctions. This shows not so much a difference in behaviour, but rather a consistent behaviour regardless of the subject of the resolution.

3.3.2 *Portuguese Peacekeeping Sponsorship*

Portugal sponsored 8 out of a total of 41 peacekeeping resolutions during its tenure at the UNSC. Most of Portugal's sponsored resolutions had extensive backing in the UNSC with many states as sponsors. There were two exceptions to this: the sponsorship in 2011 of an extension of a peacekeeping mission in Guinea-Bissau; and the sponsorship of an extension of a peacekeeping mission in Timor-Leste, also a former colony, in 2012. In the first case, Portugal, Brazil, and Nigeria were the only three resolution sponsors (United Nations Security Council 2011; UNSC Sponsorship Data 2023). The second one was only sponsored by the

US, UK, France, Guatemala, and South Africa (United Nations Security Council 2012a; UNSC Sponsorship Data 2023).

Portugal, like Germany, only sponsored resolutions that would extend mandates of pre-existing peacekeeping missions. Of the eight resolutions it sponsored in its tenure at the UNSC, three concerned former colonies and CPLP members. In these cases, Portugal championed resolutions even in the absence of other sponsoring states. In all three cases, it was either the sole sponsor or one of two, the other being Australia which supported the extension of peacekeeping missions in Timor-Leste (which neighbours Australia). All of the resolutions regarding Portugal's former colonies passed. The reason for these resolutions passing without many co-sponsors is Portugal was seen as an expert of the state it concerned largely due to its colonial history (Wouters and Pineau 2019, 149).

Portugal sponsored about as many peacekeeping resolutions as it did sponsor sanctions resolutions, despite the fact that there were more than double the number of peacekeeping resolutions (UNSC Sponsorship Data 2023). All resolutions concerning former colonies and CPLP were (co-)sponsored by Portugal, whether sanctions or peacekeeping-related. When looking at the broader picture, Portugal was less active, however, when it came to sponsoring peacekeeping missions than sponsoring sanctions. This shows that factors that might drive Portugal to take an active role in the area of sanctions, such as economic interests, may not motivate it to take a similar active role in peacekeeping endeavours. Furthermore, although Portugal takes an active stance when it comes to former colonies, this apparently does not mean it acts similarly in other cases. This shows that, while Portugal is not a country that rushes to support peacekeeping resolutions, it will act in cases where a former colony is concerned.

3.3.3 *Luxembourgian Peacekeeping Sponsorship*

During Luxembourgian tenure, a total of 65 peacekeeping resolutions were voted on in the UNSC. Luxembourg sponsored a total of 30 of these resolutions. About half of these had broad support in the UNSC and were related to extending existing peacekeeping mandates. The other half of the resolutions sponsored by Luxembourg had about five other sponsors. Most of the time, these were fellow Western countries, such as France, the UK, and the US, but Luxembourg also found partners in Morocco, South Korea, and Togo. With them, Luxembourg mainly focused on sponsoring peacekeeping missions in Africa, like in Sierra

Leona or the Central African Republic. However, this always meant extending already existing mandates (UNSC Sponsorship Data 2023).

Similar to sanctions sponsorship, Luxembourg always ensured that it would not be the only sponsor. Instead, its sponsored resolutions always had at least four other sponsors, with most exceeding that number (UNSC Sponsorship Data 2023). Yet, it took a much more active role when it came to peacekeeping resolutions compared to its sanction sponsorship. The country sponsored one in five resolutions in this area; yet when it came to peacekeeping, it sponsored nearly half of the resolutions. This is in line with our expectation that Luxembourg would sponsor those resolutions with broad support, striving to be seen as an actor for peace and stability on the world stage. As peacekeeping missions, especially already existing ones, can be seen as a force for positive change, it is not surprising that Luxembourg takes a more active role in sponsoring peacekeeping resolutions. Sponsoring already existing missions also comes at little risk since they have received UNSC mandates before, demonstrating the urgency to act in the first place. This allows the country to sponsor peacekeeping missions freely without the fear of being perceived as aggressive or hurting its image in any way. Peacekeeping missions are simply not as divisive compared to sanctions, with a true aim to change behaviour.

4 Conclusion

This chapter started with the assumption that EU countries act differently in the UNSC when it comes to resolution sponsorship. Based on the literature we assumed German reluctance to take an active role in sponsorship as it did not wish to take centre stage. We presumed Portugal to be active when resolutions concerned former colonies while we expected Luxembourg to sponsor only in cases of broad UNSC support. Our analysis shows that Germany, Portugal, and Luxemburg each take different approaches when it comes to sponsoring both sanctions and peacekeeping-related resolutions. When looking at sponsoring resolutions on sanctions, Germany only went for resolutions with broad support in the council. This fit earlier analyses of Germany as a reluctant hegemon. Portugal was more active in sponsoring sanctions, supporting more resolutions in two years than Germany did in four. As the country is deeply rooted in the community of Portuguese speaking countries, it was seen as an expert on matters concerning these countries. This expertise gave

Portugal the legitimacy to take an active role as P-5 members viewed its contributions as valuable. We can clearly see this in Portugal's sponsorship being related to former colonies. Lastly, Luxembourgian behaviour was also as expected. It only sponsored resolutions which had broad support. In this way, it ensured its image as an actor for positive change on the world stage. Active sanctioning policy, however, would not have fit this label.

On the other hand, when looking at sponsorship of peacekeeping missions, different patterns of behaviour emerged. As peacekeeping is not as direct a threat nor as potentially politically divisive, countries sponsored more resolutions in this area compared to those focused on sanction regimes. The exception to this might be Germany which, although sponsoring more peacekeeping resolutions than sanctions-related ones in terms of absolute numbers, percentage-wise has sponsored about as many sanctions as peacekeeping-related resolutions: Germany sponsored nearly 21% of the peacekeeping resolutions and 20% of those focused on sanctions. This seems to match previous descriptions of the German position on the world stage, as an actor reluctant to take centre stage despite its extensive industrial capabilities. When looking at Portuguese sponsorship behaviour, a different picture emerges. While Portugal sponsored all measures regarding its former colonies, it took a backseat on most other peacekeeping resolutions. A definitive conclusion on what caused this is not presented in this chapter, but the trend shows that factors driving Portuguese assertiveness on the sanctions front are not also driving its peacekeeping sponsorship. Lastly, Luxembourgian sponsorship of peacekeeping resolutions outnumbers both Portuguese and German resolution sponsorship combined. This shows the importance these resolutions have for Luxembourg, as they display to the world how the country is an actor for positive change, by supporting resolutions that aim to ensure peace and stability. As Luxembourg sponsors such resolutions, it arguably attempts to strengthen its image on the world stage and with this, enhance its soft power.

While these findings are insightful, it is important to acknowledge limitations of this research. The scope of the chapter only allowed for the comparison of three non-permanent EU member states in the UNSC. We selected three different countries in terms of size, economic interests, and colonial past in order to highlight differences between the three types of states, as well as (though to a lesser extent) differences compared to the permanent EU member states. Naturally, this is not representative for all the EU member states that are also non-permanent members within the UNSC. The findings and comparisons of Germany, Portugal, and Luxembourg are but a small part of a bigger picture. In order to fully understand the voting patterns and behaviour of all the non-permanent EU countries in the UNSC, one would need to critically analyse and compare all E10 member states. Moreover, the focus of this study is on the topics of peacekeeping and sanctions, while the UNSC also discusses other issues such as counterterrorism. In the end, we chose two topics, sanctions and peacekeeping, to ensure feasibility of the comparisons and to prevent drawing conclusions that are too broad. In addition, in order to gain a full understanding of the sponsorship and voting behaviour of the non-permanent EU member states, it is crucial to also consider external factors and actors such as China or the USA. Lastly, it might also prove relevant to not only offer comparisons across the different types of countries, as we did in the analytical part of this chapter, but to also present comparisons within each type, to uncover differences between countries belonging to the same category. Further research could look into such topics and thereby shed further light on the sponsorship and voting behaviour of both permanent and non-permanent members within the UNSC in more general terms.

References

Barber, Tony. "Germany and the European Union: Europe's Reluctant Hegemon?" *Financial Times*, March 11, 2019. Accessed September 3, 2024. https://www.ft.com/content/a1f327ba-4193-11e9-b896-fe36ec32aece.

Chiaka, Olga Wumbi. "Twenty Years of the Community of Portuguese Speaking Countries (CPLP): Results and Prospects." *Vestnik Rossiĭskogo Universiteta Druzhby Narodov. Seriia Mezhdunarodnye Otnosheniia* 16, no. 2 (2016): 246–254.

Conley Tyler, Melissa, and Eleanor Pahlow. "Australia on the UN Security Council 2013–14: A Voice for Small and Medium Countries?" *Round Table* 103, no. 1 (2014): 95–108. https://doi.org/10.1080/00358533.2013.874168.

Cunha, Alberto. "Europe's Hegemon? The Nature of German Power During Europe's Crisis Decade." *E-International Relations*, August 23, 2021. Acessed August 3, 2024. https://www.e-ir.info/2021/08/23/europes-hegemon-the-nature-of-german-power-during-europes-crisis-decade/.

Dong-Ryul, Lee. "China's Diplomatic Behavior in the United Nations: Voting Behavior in the UNSC." *Korea and World Politics* 23, no. 3 (2007): 95–128.

Duarte, Paulo Afonso B., Rui Albuquerque, and António Manuel Lopes Tavares. *Portugal and the Lusophone World: Law, Geopolitics and Institutional Cooperation*. 1st ed. Springer Singapore Pte. Limited, 2023. https://doi.org/10.1007/978-981-99-0455-6.

Dabo, A. Bissau army hold president, former premier in coup, 2012. https://web.archive.org/web/20160304053223/http://af.reuters.com/article/worldNews/idAFBRE83D00S20120414

Fix, Liana. "On the Ukraine War, Germany Has a Leadership Problem. Here's Why." *Council on Foreign Relations*, 2022. Accessed August 27, 2024. https://www.cfr.org/in-brief/ukraine-war-germany-has-leadership-problem-heres-why.

Haugevik, Kristin M., Piret Kuusik, Kristi Raik, and Niels Nagelhus Schia. "Small States, Different Approaches: Estonia and Norway on the UN Security Council." *Norwegian Institute of International Affairs,* 2021. Accessed September 3, 2024. https://nupi.brage.unit.no/nupi-xmlui/handle/11250/2832241?locale-attribute=en.

Junbo, Jian, and Chen Zhimin. "China and the EU in the UN." In *China, the European Union, and the International Politics of Global Governance*, 75–93. London: Palgrave Macmillan, 2016. https://doi.org/10.1057/9781137514004_5.

Klobucista, Claire, and Danielle Renwick. The Role of Peacekeeping in Africa. Council on Foreign Relations, 2021. https://www.cfr.org/backgrounder/role-peacekeeping-africa

Klobucista, Claire, and Mariel Ferragamo "The Role of Peacekeeping in Africa." *Council on Foreign Relations*, 2023. Accessed September 3, 2024. https://www.cfr.org/backgrounder/role-peacekeeping-africa.

Lai, Brian, and Vanessa. A. Lefler. "Examining the Role of Region and Elections on Representation in the UN Security Council." *The Review of International Organizations* 12, no. 4 (2017): 585–611. https://doi.org/10.1007/s11558-016-9254-z.

MacQueen, Norrie. "A Community of Illusions? Portugal, the CPLP and Peacemaking in Guiné-Bissau." *International Peacekeeping* 10, no. 2 (2003): 1–26.

Monteleone, Carla. "Coalition Building in the UN Security Council." *International Relations* 29, no. 1 (2015): 45–68. https://doi.org/10.1177/0047117814552140.

Nortvedt, Jenny Therese Gregersen. ""Punching Above Their Weight": An Analysis of Small States' Leverage in the Case of Syria in the UN Security Council." *Master Thesis*, University of Oslo, 2019. Accessed December 19, 2024. https://www.duo.uio.no/handle/10852/69745.

O'Neill, Barry. "Power and Satisfaction in the United Nations Security Council." *Journal of Conflict Resolution* 40, no. 2 (1996): 219–237. https://doi.org/10.1177/0022002796040002001.

Puglierin, Jana. Turning point or turning back: German defence policy after Zeitenwende, March 19, 2024. https://ecfr.eu/article/turning-point-or-turning-back-german-defence-policy-after-zeitenwende/

Renard, Thomas, and Bas Hooijmaaijers. "Assessing the EU's Strategic Partnerships in the UN System." *Egmont Institute*, 2011. Accessed August 27, 2024. https://www.jstor.org/stable/resrep06588.

Romita, Paul M. "(Dis)unity in the UN Security Council: Voting Patterns in the UN's Peace and Security Organ." *CUNY Academic Works*, 2018. Accessed August 29, 2024. https://academicworks.cuny.edu/gc_etds/2684/.

Sorenson, David S., and Wood, Pia Christina. *The Politics of Peacekeeping in the Post-Cold War Era*. F. Cass, 2005.

The Observatory of Economic Complexity. "Germany (DEU) and Brazil (BRA) Trade." *The Observatory of Economic Complexity*, 2023. Accessed August 29, 2024. https://oec.world/en/profile/bilateral-country/deu/partner/bra.

Thorhallsson, Baldur. "Small States in the UN Security Council: Means of Influence." *Hague Journal of Diplomacy* 7, no. 2 (2012): 135–160.

Thorhallsson, Baldur, and Anna Margrét Eggertsdóttir. "Small States in the UN Security Council: Austria's Quest to Maintain Status." 2020. https://doi.org/10.1163/1871191X-BJA10017.

United Nations Security Council. "Resolution 2030." 2011.

United Nations Security Council. "Resolution 2037 (2012)." 2012a. Accessed August 27, 2024. https://documents.un.org/doc/undoc/gen/n12/240/01/pdf/n1224001.pdf.

United Nations Security Council. "Security Council 1737 Committee Adds New Entries to Consolidated List of Individuals and Entities | Meetings Coverage and Press Releases." *United Nations Press*, 2012b. Accessed August 27, 2024. https://press.un.org/en/2012/sc10871.doc.htm.

United Nations Security Council. Resolution 2048. 2012c. https://documents.un.org/doc/undoc/gen/n12/346/47/pdf/n1234647.pdf

United Nations Security Council. "Resolution 2060 (2013)." 2013.

UN Media. "Assembly Elects Five New Non-Permanent Members of Security Council." *UN Media*, October 12, 2010. Accessed August 29, 2024. https://media.un.org/photo/en/asset/oun7/oun7417159.

UNSC Sponsorship Data. "[Dataset]." 2023.

Walter, Barbara F., Lise Morjé Howard, and V. Page Fortna. "The Astonishing Success of Peacekeeping." *Foreign Affairs*, November 29, 2021. Accessed September 4, 2024. https://www.foreignaffairs.com/articles/world/2021-11-29/astonishing-success-peacekeeping.

Wellings, Ben, and Andrew Mycock. *The Anglosphere: Continuity, Dissonance and Location*. 1st ed. Published for the British Academy by Oxford University Press, 2019.

World Bank. World Bank Open Data "[Dataset]", 2023. https://data.worldbank.org/indicator/NE.EXP.GNFS.ZS?locations=DE

Wouters, Jan, and Nina Pineau. "Belgium in the UN Security Council: Responsibility Without Power?" In *Elected Members of the Security Council: Lame Ducks or Key Players?*, 133–152. Leiden: Brill Nijhoff, 2019. https://doi.org/10.1163/9789004425392_010.

CHAPTER 10

NextGenerationEU and the UN Sustainable Development Goals

Beatrice Levorato, Guilherme Pucarinho Soares de Oliveira, and Madeleine O. Hosli

1 Introduction

This chapter investigates how the alignment of the European Union (EU) and United Nations (UN) environmental agendas has influenced EU fiscal governance, with a focus on the integration of the United Nations' Sustainable Development Goals (UNSDGs) into the EU's NextGenerationEU (NGEU) initiative. This focus complements the analyses of other chapters in this book focusing notably on the UNSC and on EU actorness within the UN. Situating our discussion within the broader

B. Levorato (✉) · G. Pucarinho Soares de Oliveira · M. O. Hosli
Leiden University, The Hague, The Netherlands
e-mail: s2525208@vuw.leidenuniv.nl; levoratobarsotti@gmail.com

G. Pucarinho Soares de Oliveira
e-mail: guilhermeps.oliveira@gmail.com

M. O. Hosli
e-mail: m.o.hosli@fgga.leidenuniv.nl

M. O. Hosli et al. (eds.), *Multilateralism and the United Nations Security Council*, https://doi.org/10.1007/978-3-031-85320-3_10

discourse on multilateralism and global governance, our chapter examines how this alignment exemplifies the EU and UN's complementary roles in strengthening the multilateral system and collaboration between regional and global governance institutions. The dynamic partnership explored addresses not only the shared challenges posed by climate governance but also compensates for the inherent limitations of each actor (on the regional and global level, respectively), thereby strengthening global governance (Tallberg et al. 2023).

Our chapter argues that the EU-UN alignment advances multilateralism by leveraging the strengths of both actors to address global governance deficiencies, not least in the areas explored here. Through its capacity to implement sustainability goals and harmonise fiscal governance with environmental objectives, a regional organisation such as the EU can strengthen the UN's ability to achieve the UNSDGs, while the UN provides the overarching legitimacy and normative coherence needed to unify regional efforts. This synergy not only underscores the importance of multilateralism in addressing transboundary challenges like climate change but also highlights the transformative potential of partnerships between global and regional actors. The UN is based on the core principle of 'one member one vote', notably as regards representation in the UNGA. However, regional organisations can play a core role in the UN framework, not least in terms of implementation of actions decided upon at the UN level. This includes collaboration on peace missions and activities such as implementation of the SDGs into national-level and regional systems. This synergy's longevity is also established in programmes that deepen integration not just with external parties like the UN, but also within the EU via the mechanisms found in the European Semester and NextGenerationEU.

This research focus is very relevant because it allows us to examine the intersection of sustainability and economic policy at a time when global challenges demand cohesive and unified responses, often complementing activities stuck by global geopolitical power rivalries. Understanding how such agendas influence governance structures is crucial for assessing the effectiveness of international collaboration in driving sustainable development. The UN arguably is a primary global actor in the context of global climate governance as it is the only organisation that enjoys almost universal membership (United Nations 2022). Within this context, the EU is a leading regional power that arguably engages most with climate-related issues.

Joint EU-UN efforts to tackle climate change can be traced back to the early 1990s (Oberthür and Dupont 2021, 1095). This collaboration intends to uphold sustainability as a core value of the international multilateral system, in close alignment with the attainment of the SDGs. Generally, both actors have committed to jointly address global crises, threats, and challenges in pursuit of a peaceful, just, and sustainable world (European External Action Service 2024). In this regard, the EU has embraced the UN Agenda 2030 as a 'blueprint' for its push for sustainable development, defining its strategic priorities and key challenges based on the UNSDGs (Silander 2020). Therefore, a significant aspect of this cooperation is the harmonisation of the environmental agendas, which is crucial for advancing sustainability goals and multilateralism and complements activities defined by institutions such as the UNGA.

Indeed, a new pattern of harmonisation has emerged to face the challenge of climate change, as evident in the incorporation of the UNSDGs into the NGEU. The latter was created as the main EU response to the COVID-19 crisis, encompassing financial support of around 750 billion euros (European Commission, n.d). This EU-UN alignment not only strengthens the collaborative framework between the two entities, but also promotes multilateralism. The UNSDGs, besides setting sustainability as a universal value, function as a guiding framework for countries, emphasising the importance of global cooperation in achieving these goals (Tallberg et al. 2023). This aligns with the perspective that global international actors like the UN play a crucial role in establishing ethical frameworks and values (Tallberg et al. 2023, 11), with their ideological influence surpassing that of regional actors such as the EU. Arguably, this also affects much of the work of the UNSC and resolutions passed by this institution (Helou et al., this volume; Bueno et al., this volume).

Our chapter explores the implications of harmonising the environmental agendas of the UN and the EU, focusing on the consequences that it entails for EU fiscal and economic governance, as well as in terms of both EU and global integration. With this, the chapter contributes to the analysis of the evolving relationship between regional actors and international institutions, while briefly addressing the broader multilateral implications via spillover effects of the EU's NGEU. Furthermore, the chapter aims to fill a gap in the existing literature by exploring the ramifications of this harmonisation and patterns from the perspective of sustainability and global climate governance, paralleling efforts taken on the international level. While much of the existing research focuses on the NGEU's impact on European governance and its borrowing mechanisms, there is limited analysis of this process in terms of sustainability and alignment with priorities defined at the UN level. By examining how the integration of UNSDGs within the NGEU framework and the European Semester reshapes EU policy coordination, the chapter also seeks to contribute to an understanding of the transformative potential of aligning the UN and EU sustainability agendas.

The first section of this chapter outlines the mixed theoretical approach and the rationale behind that choice. The second section examines the incorporation of the UNSDGs in the European Semester (ES) through country reports and the Recovery and Resilience Facility (RRF)—the latter largely being a repercussion of the economic effects of the COVID-19 pandemic. The characteristics of the ES are analysed first, then expounding on how and why the ES became the policy framework of the NGEU project, highlighting its flexibility and versatility as a policy tool. The third section of our chapter delves into the NGEU project itself, outlining its novelty in manifold aspects, considering the incorporation of the UNSDGs in its structure, and assessing how it supports their implementation. This part also addresses the broader implications of undertaking such a bold and arguably risky policy, especially when considering the swift approval of the project in the COVID-19 era. The fourth section delineates the ramifications of the harmonisation of EU-UN agendas in three areas: the economic and fiscal policy of the Union, the solidarity level among member states, and the overall effects on EU integration. It also explores further challenges in the implementation of the UNSDGs and in combining EU-UN agendas. The fifth section of our chapter considers the external implications of the NGEU and its supported programs, more specifically, on external partners and investment projects, primarily focusing on the green transition of the Belt and Road Initiative (BRI) and its competing initiatives, including the links with the private sector. Finally, our chapter concludes by overviewing the NGEU project and data presented and making a final claim on the effects of the resulting socio-economic shift. Moreover, these conclusions explore the relationship between the UN and EU in light of the projects and consider the impact of changes in the push for sustainability on a global scale.

2 Theoretical Framework

Our chapter adopts a mixed theoretical approach, notably encompassing neofunctionalism and historical institutionalism, to analyse and interpret figures and information obtained. The overall discussion is reconducted on the underpinnings of international cooperation, as the research focus is relevant to the dynamics and challenges of global climate governance.

Through the application of neofunctionalism, our research focus argues that EU's adoption of UN Agenda 2030 initiated a process of deeper integration in terms of economic and fiscal governance, particularly after the COVID-19 crisis. As asserted by Haas, integration in one sector leads to spillovers in others (Haas 2006). Scholarly work has already used this approach to analyse the conditions in which a crisis can lead to greater integration (Brooks et al. 2023; Nicoli 2020; Niemann and Ioannou 2015). Hence, this chapter contends that the alignment of EU policies with the UNSDGs represents more than a commitment to global sustainability; it propels further integration and a shift towards transnational governance.

Unlike the sovereign debt crisis, which led to fragmented national responses, the pandemic prompted a collective European reaction. The incorporation of the UNSDGs into the European Semester and the launch of the NGEU illustrate this shift. By embedding sustainability goals within economic and fiscal policy coordination and linking substantial funding mechanisms to UNSDG-aligned reforms, the EU has fostered closer cooperation and solidarity among member states, thereby aligning with neofunctionalist theory. Overall, this integration highlights the EU's role in leading global climate initiatives and reinforces the interconnected nature of sustainability governance, further promoting harmonisation and cooperation between the EU as a regional organisation and the UN.

Historical Institutionalism further enriches this framework by examining how past institutional developments shape current and future policy paths. In brief, this approach underscores the relevance of critical junctures, such as the COVID-19 pandemic, in leading to novel institutional choices (Verdun and Zeitlin 2017, 2018; D'Erman and Verdun 2021; Vanhercke and Verdun 2022; Pan et al. 2023). The embedding of the UNSDGs into the European Semester and the establishment of the NGEU itself represent such critical junctures, locking in new patterns of governance and financial cooperation within the EU. Moreover, as shaping a sustainable future continues at the forefront of transnational governance, it is not unlikely that other projects will arise. For instance, when adopting a historical institutionalist lens, we expect that once the UNSDGs conclude in 2030, the European Semester will most likely become vital to future partnerships.

3 The European Semester and UNSDGs

The ES encompasses a wide range of EU political, legal, and fiscal instruments (Verdun and Zeitlin 2017, 1). Created in 2010, following the financial and sovereign debt crises, the ES has been periodically renamed, most significantly by the Juncker Commission in 2015 (Verdun and Zeitlin 2017, 1). The ES is a framework that guides and monitors the economic policies of EU member states, ensuring convergence and stability within the EU. Its procedures build on the EU's pre-existing processes of fiscal, economic, employment, and social policy coordination, including the Stability and Growth Pact (SGP), the Broad Economic Policy Guidelines (BEPGs), the European Employment Strategy, the Lisbon Strategy, and the Social Open Method of Coordination (Verdun and Zeitlin 2017, 1–2). Overall, it brings together a variety of EU governance instruments with different legal bases, where the European Commission and the Council and the European Council work in tandem to set priorities for the Union, review national performance, budgets, and reform programmes, and issue Country-Specific Recommendations (CSRs), in some cases backed up with financial sanctions (EC 2024, 11). The CSRs are at the heart of the SDGs integration into the European policy and economic framework (EC 2024, 11).

Initially introduced as part of far-reaching measures to reinforce EU economic governance in response to the Euro crisis, as the 'Six-Pack', 'Two-Pack', and 'Fiscal Compact' (Verdun and Zeitlin 2017, 2), the ES has been central for scholars given its implications for EU political and economic governance. It became even more important after the incorporation of the SDGs set by the UN Agenda 2030 (D'Erman and Verdun 2021; Fabbrini 2021). Many scholars have noted the significant changes in European governance resulting from the ES and subsequent developments. They identify the period following the sovereign debt crisis as the initial incorporation of sustainable measures, posing a pivotal turning point (D'Erman and Verdun 2021; Fabbrini 2021; Petmesidou et al. 2023). Furthermore, this integration of sustainability considerations into the ES has yielded substantial consequences for EU financial and economic governance. Therefore, the incorporation of the UN's SDGs into the ES is significant not only because it demonstrates the EU's commitment to the UN's Agenda 2030 and the alignment of its policies with the UN agenda, but also because it signifies a shift in patterns of EU socio-economic governance.

The first integration of the SDGs in the ES was led by the Juncker Commission, in the Commission's broader efforts to align EU policies with the objectives outlined in the UN Agenda 2030 (Verdun and Zeitlin 2017, 1–3). The specific process of SDGs' integration began around 2017, following the 2015 adoption of the Agenda 2030 (Verdun and Zeitlin 2017, 2). The Commission worked to ensure that the SDGs were reflected in the annual cycle of ES economic policy coordination. This involved revising the framework to include indicators and assessments related to the SDGs, as well as encouraging member states to align their national policies and priorities with the SDGs' objectives. The aim was to mainstream sustainability considerations into EU economic governance and policy-making processes (Eurostat 2020, 1–34); Verdun and Zeitlin 2017).

The next significant step towards SDGs' incorporation occurred in December 2019 with the Autumn Package, which refocused the ES on 'competitive sustainability' terms ((Eurostat 2020, 1–34), aligning it with the objectives set by the European Green Deal (EGD). In addition, the European Semester's Winter Package of February 2020 marked the first step where country reports identified not only SDG-relevant policies and challenges, but also the member state's performance on the SDGs and their trend over the past 5 years, as incorporated in an additional Annex. The progress report is based on the SDGs' indicators as compiled by Eurostat (Eurostat 2020, 1–34). Hereof, these reports contribute to the monitoring of progress towards the SDGs by assessing national policies in areas that overlap with SDG objectives, such as economic growth (SDG 8), reduced inequalities (SDG 10), and quality education (SDG 4). The advantage of this approach is that the CSRs can guide member states in aligning their policies with the SDGs, ensuring a more holistic sustainable development strategy.

Finally, the incorporation of the SDGs into the ES is bolstered by the latter's central role as the primary institutional vehicle for implementing the RRF, the main funding instrument of the NGEU project operating by borrowing on global capital markets (EC 2024). This fund is the main element of the NGEU budget, comprising around 90% of the total available, wherein 20% of expenditure must be related to digital transitions and 37% to the climate transition (EC 2024). Considering the large percentages and the post-pandemic economic insecurity involved, Koundouri and Sachs (2021) explain how investments must work with established projects and strategies, namely the EGD, the Just Transition Mechanism, Industrial Strategy, and 'Farm to Fork' approaches. Crucially, these are established policies 'with the potential for new ways of participating in capitalism, for new routes to economic growth, and a new prioritization of citizens in the post-COVID society' (Koundouri and Sachs 2021, 79). Other initiatives, such as the 'New European Bauhaus', launched in 2021, present a green culture-focused program seeking to intertwine the world of science and technology with art and culture. Every year it has given monetary prizes to projects, usually from representatives of the civil society, promoting green projects and ideas from the ground up (European Commission 2023c). This engagement with civil society can also help member states promote the SDGs in society itself and enhance attention by the public sector (Koundouri and Sachs 2021).

Scholars have debated whether using the ES to address the COVID-19 pandemic's consequences signifies a continuation or a departure from previous crisis management strategies. D'Erman and Verdun (2021) argue that it is a significant departure from the previous crisis management strategies, noting that the rationale behind the choice was the proven efficiency of the ES as a policy tool, mainly the methods of incorporation utilised at both domestic and EU levels (D'Erman and Verdun 2021, 5). Vanhercke and Verdun (2021) identify the flexible nature of the ES as the main reason for its incorporation in the response to COVID-19 (Vanhercke and Verdun 2021, 216). Indeed, the ES is a flexible tool that strongly influences member states' economic policies without directly transferring any sovereignty from the domestic to the supranational level. The fundamental rationale for ES surveillance remains to limit negative spillover effects in the single market between different national EU member state economies (D'Erman and Verdun 2021, 8).

The European Commission's mid-term report of February 2024 showed that 225 billion euros were disbursed and approximately 75% of 2023 targets were considered satisfactory or had been reported as completed by EU member states (European Commission 2024, 1). The report also underscores that RRF worked in tandem with the Just Transition Mechanism and European Social Fund Plus to 'make the green transition fair' (European Commission 2024, 6). Moreover, it confirms that all EU member states have exceeded the 37% expenditure goal with an average of 40%, with some member states even committing over 50% of their total plan to climate objectives (European Commission 2024, 6). This suggests that working with pre-existing policies has fostered further investment, indicating that the solid sustainability basis built throughout the ES likely benefited future policies, namely the NGEU, in terms of further integration of the SDGs. Furthermore, there is potential to capitalise on strengths as the NGEU is allowed to borrow on capital markets, which provides the package with considerable financial power.

Vanhercke and Verdun (2021) uphold that governance of the RRF allows member states to implement their preferred domestic policies while providing sufficient constraints (Vanhercke and Verdun 2021, 11). Building on the previous argument about intertwining with existing policies to offer potentially lower-risk investments, EU member states have allocated considerable portions of their budgets to other sustainable areas not mandated by the NGEU fund, with the largest allocation going to social policy investments (European Commission 2024, 14). In its assessment of the Recovery Plans, the European Commission determined that around 30% were in alignment with several of the SDGs (European Commission 2024). From a historical institutionalist perspective, this can be an important development in terms of upholding a 'soft' governance approach (Knodt et al., 2020). In fact, the ability of EU member states to integrate UNSDGs into their national plans while adhering to the RRF's framework illustrates how the NGEU fund facilitates a more adaptable (and arguably inclusive) form of governance. This integration reflects a broader trend in which institutional frameworks allow for greater flexibility and responsiveness to national priorities, while still aligning with overarching EU objectives. Such an approach represents a notable development in how the EU and its member states manage and promote sustainable development within a complex governance landscape.

Overall, the integration of the UNSDGs into the ES represents an important evolution in EU governance, strengthening the coordination of economic, social, and environmental policies. As Verdun and Zeitlin (2017) state, the ES has effectively assimilated economic and social objectives, providing a framework that accommodates sustainable development without compromising in terms of fiscal consolidation and competitiveness (Verdun and Zeitlin 2017). This integration also induces enhanced cooperation between supranational and intergovernmental actors, blurring the boundaries between EU institutions and member states, which is crucial for achieving the comprehensive and collaborative efforts required and mandated by the UNSDGs. Despite critiques of technocratic governance (Verdun and Zeitlin 2017), which emphasise the potential for policy decisions to be driven by technical expertise at the expense of democratic engagement, the ES arguably fosters an interactive cycle of deliberation, involving expert peer reviews that inform sustainable development policies, thereby also enhancing democratic debate and public engagement. This dynamic process not only challenges traditional theoretical frameworks of EU governance, but also helps ensure that economic growth is inclusive, equitable, and environmentally sustainable. Ultimately, embedding the UNSDGs into the ES reshapes modes of EU policy coordination, promoting a more holistic and adaptive approach to governance that aligns with the broader objectives of sustainable development and the UN agenda.

4 NextGenerationEU (NGEU)

In the aftermath of the 2008–2009 financial crisis, the EU had been practising an austerity-dominated fiscal approach. However, the NGEU has caused a certain transition of this policy. The NGEU's inception came as a rapid response, agreed by the European Council in July 2020, to the challenges created by COVID-19. Its comprehensive framework aims at revitalising the EU's economic and social fabric, as reflected in the RRF accounting for 90% of its budget (European Commission 2024). The NGEU is expected to amount to €712 billion by 2026 while having an initial budget of €750 billion–€360 billion in loans and €390 billion in grants (European Commission, n.d).

The European Court of Auditors, which does not have any legislative powers, but whose purpose is to advise and regulate the European Commission's budget, has committed itself to creating several reports on the sustainability initiatives of the NGEU as part of its latest work programme update. This includes initiatives that are not mentioned or incorporated into the NGEU plan but overlap with the UNSDGs, such as the UN's Spotlight Initiative (European Court of Auditors 2023; chapter 3 of Hosli (2022). These documents have highlighted interesting developments and information. For instance, in 2021, 45 out of 60 programmes (75%) contributed towards one or more of the UNSDGs;

each UNSDG had at least five programs contributing to its completion, with the average being around 13 programs for each goal; and SDG 8—'Decent Work and Economic Growth'—had 24 programs dedicated to it (European Parliament 2021). In 2022, 44 out of 48 EU programs with financial backing (92%) contributed towards at least one UNSDG, reflecting an increase of 17% (European Commission, n.d). In the period 2021–2022, every UNSDG, with the exception of SDG 17 (Partnerships for the goals specified), gained contributing programs, indicating that NGEU's implementation of sustainable projects fostered further investment and presented less financial scepticism from the actors involved in the NGEU-related borrowing mechanisms included the never-before-used EU Bills Program for short-term borrowing (European Commission 2023a). Alongside this, the NGEU is seeking to raise 30% of NGEU funds via the NGEU green bonds aimed at financing green policies (European Commission 2023b). Table 1 provides an overview of NGEU initiatives per SDG.

Table 1 shows the distribution of NGEU initiatives per SDG. Although some initiatives may affect different SDGs (as the SDGs themselves

Table 1 Number of NGEU Initiatives per SDG

SDGs		*Number of Initiatives*
1	No Poverty	15
2	Zero Hunger	13
3	Good Health and Well-Being	22
4	Quality Education	20
5	Gender Equality	22
6	Clean Water and Sanitation	15
7	Affordable and Clean Energy	20
8	Decent Work and Economic Growth	25
9	Industry, Innovation, and Infrastructure	24
10	Reduced Inequalities	18
11	Sustainable Cities and Communities	21
12	Responsible Consumption and Production	18
13	Climate Action	25
14	Life Below Water	13
15	Life on Land	17
16	Peace, Justice, and Strong Institutions	18
17	Partnerships for the Goals	10

Source Adapted from European Commission (n.d.)

are partially interrelated), a simple quantitative assessment demonstrates that the mean of this distribution is 18.6 initiatives, the median 18 and the mode also 18, which indicates an almost perfect symmetrical distribution across the SDGa, as most values are in and around the mean mark. All SDGs are represented in similar ways with only a few outliers, namely Partnerships for the Goals (SDG 17), with 10 initiatives, and Decent Work and Economic Growth (SDG 8), with a total of 25 initiatives. Considering that the NGEU is, above all, a response to a (health-related and economic) crisis, the stronger focus on financial and infrastructure recovery makes sense, including elements present in SDG 8, and SDG 7 (Affordable and Clean Energy). This latter SDG is another outlier, yielding 24 initiatives that pertain to industry, innovation, and infrastructure considerations. SDG 17, promoting partnerships, is the least represented and could be strengthened in view of multilateral collaboration. Regardless, times of crisis cannot be representative of 'normal' phases, and thus, as the NGEU was drafted via national plans to recover (economically) from the COVID-19 pandemic, it is not unlikely that SDG 17 will see more participation in the future, especially if the multilateral promises of EU-UN integration of ambitions continue to develop.

Given NGEU's relative economic success so far, some authors have advocated for making the NGEU a permanent EU-wide scheme. They argue that its innovative RRF and borrowing mechanisms could enable the EU to allocate a portion of the (common) wealth derived from substantial private profits of the internal market, all while promoting sustainable projects (Allemand et al. 2023). While the same authors argue it is too early to reach such conclusions, the quick reaction by European institutions to COVID-19, novel ideas implemented, and rapid growth in programmes from 2021 to the present have been well received by most EU member states, and critics alike (Allemand et al. 2023). Conversely, as previously noted, the entities funding these projects will develop and consequently contribute more green competition and alternatives to the multilateral investment projects emerging. Such initiatives also align goals defined at the UN level with those pertaining to the EU as a regional integration scheme representing its member states' interests.

5 The Belt and Road Initiative (BRI) and External Engagement

The NGEU arguably yielded strong consequences for the EU's external engagement, as it was used in the European integration context to combat economic effects the COVID-19 pandemic had generated. It can be argued that this framework further connected the EU to goals specified at UN level (notably by alignment with green and digital transitions), but may also have diminished connectedness with other (regional) organisations or actors. NGEU likely caused spillover effects affecting the influence of competing initiatives on the global level, such as China's Belt and Road Initiative (BRI), aiming to bring the EU's agenda closer to the developmental and environmental priorities that are a primary concern for UN activities (Brautigam 2020). The BRI—coined as a substantial Chinese foreign infrastructure investment dubbed 'the New Silk Road'—and of high economic importance in China's neighbourhood, likely has considerable soft power implications. However, due to initiatives such as the NGEU, it has arguably lost ground in Europe, losing partnerships in key countries such as Italy (Casarini 2024). To fully grasp the scope of BRI, a World Bank report outlined that just the transport projects (as of 2018) would 'reduce travel times along economic corridors by 12 percent, increase trade between 2.7 percent and 9.7 percent, increase income by up to 3.4 percent, and lift 7.6 million people from extreme poverty' (World Bank 2018); in this way, there are clear links to the SDGs. The BRI, however, has been criticised before for ignoring human rights violations and for disregarding environmental considerations (Brautigam 2020, 4)—characteristics that stand in contrast to goals contained in the SDGs. In terms of alignment with the SDGs, NGEU's impact, as has been argued in a European Economic and Social Committee (EESC) 2023 brief, has strengthened and is likely to continue strengthening economic and political ties with the EU's partner countries. It does so by enabling the EU to compete effectively on a global level in the provision of infrastructure while aiming to defend democratic and social principles (EESC 2023); in this sense, the NGEU aligns with P3 priorities more generally (see Bueno et al., this volume).

While other factors, such as the BRI's overall success, may have undermined the project's reach, the NGEUs commitments to the SDGs are likely a factor contributing to the very challenges facing the BRI project in recent years (Brautigam 2020): It offers a competing initiative and linkages between the promotion of EU values and sustainability arguably complicate the coexistence of the BRI and NGEU. Although the BRI and the NGEU—and consequently the Global Gateway—are not entirely mutually exclusive, there is evidence of some potential (transnational) spillover effects between the projects.

For example, in 2018, fossil fuels made up 80% of Chinese overseas energy investments based on the BRI (Sims Gallagher 2018). By 2023, the Chinese government had announced green initiatives with firm commitments by 2025 and 2030 pledging to support the Paris Climate Agreement and immediately cease production of new coal power plants (De Boer et al. 2023). However, it is difficult to measure the scale of the projected Chinese green action accurately; while the EU created its own alternative, so did the US (De Boer et al. 2023; Nedopil 2023). New transnational projects include the Blue Dot Network (2019) and the India-Middle East-Europe Economic Corridor (2023). Such initiatives develop in parallel to geopolitical rivalries as very much seen, for example, in the context of the UNSC (Helou et al., this volume; Bueno et al., this volume). However, such new projects and initiatives have been criticised for focusing on economic aid and initiatives rather than mere cooperation and with this, tend to undermine the (global) collaborative nature of SDG goals (Nedopil 2023). Regardless, the pressure of competing green initiatives has arguably been recognised as a vital factor in the green 'U-turn' undertaken by the BRI (Nedopil 2023); in this sense, economic pressures may enhance norm adaptation at the global level and induce green transitions by rival geopolitical entities.

Simultaneously, there might also be avenues for cooperation and coordination in areas such as infrastructure development, connection initiatives, and sustainable investment practices between the two major projects. Although EU-China approaches may differ and both powers articulate different priorities, there could be common areas of interest where such collaboration can be mutually beneficial, such as supporting sustainability objectives, dealing with climate change, and advancing digital connectivity; such initiatives would arguably align with the SDG agenda. Moreover, the shift towards sustainability as encompassed in the ES and the NGEU project will not necessarily diminish the prospects for collaboration of the EU with China.

Yet, originally, the BRI approach largely stood in contrast to NGEU-supported projects, as principles in BRI investments did not generally incorporate aspects such as transparency, environmental sustainability, and social inclusion. However, such principles also influence the broader discourse around global infrastructure investments, which include NGEU-backed projects under the Global Gateway scheme. In this sense, emphasis on high standards and values could create contrasts between BRI-related projects and those supported by EU (NGEU) funding, thereby potentially altering the attitudes of the recipient and host countries, together with perceptions in the global community about them. While the BRI arguably constitutes a large economic success, such clashes in perspectives can transmit back into global governance discourses, in turn affecting the standing of global powers such as China (or the EU) in the multilateral context. Furthermore, such competing (economic) initiatives emerge with multiple states providing aid or direct involvement in terms of nurturing the private sector to further grow economically while developing 'green,' but arguably, the BRI predominantly leverages national public companies to fund projects (Sial and Sol 2022). For example, Huawei, a public entity, has built around 70% of the 4G network in Africa, but as of 2022, private sector companies led the BRI funding (Sial and Sol 2022; Nedopil 2023). As privatisation increases, global competition does too and while this may not affect core aspects of the BRI, it will likely support shifts towards global 'green' production and quality.

6 Domestic and Multilateral Implications and Challenges of EU-UN Alignment

The relevance of the NGEU arguably extends beyond its immediate economic impact. It encompasses significant implications for European fiscal and economic governance, demonstrating a given shift towards greater solidarity among member states and greener production, as reflected in the principles underpinning the program (Lentschig et al. 2022). This section discusses the consequences of the NGEU as a representation of harmonisation efforts between EU-UN agendas along different thematic lines. While the NGEU generates ramifications for EU economic and fiscal governance as well as a solidarity dimension as reflected in initiatives such as the European Social Union (ESU)—and on European governance overall—it is of interest to explore what these steps might imply in terms of further European integration and federalisation. In this context, it is relevant to see how the NGEU contributes to the achievement of the UNSDGs and to identify main implementation challenges. Such processes, in turn, have implications for the alignment of EU-UN agendas, such as in terms of digitalisation efforts and global climate governance perspectives.

Arguably, from an economic and fiscal angle, considerable implications arise from the novel borrowing mechanism incorporated into the NGEU, notably the RRF. Unlike previous instances, such as the sovereign debt crisis, the allocation of funds and loans under the NGEU marks the first time the EU's social and solidarity dimensions are very much incorporated in a financial recovery package. However, long-term effects (and risks) of the approach are not entirely known yet. Nonetheless, the initiative supports respect for the rule of law, as well as a commitment to the green and digital transitions, as elements of conditionality rather than being based solely on fiscal considerations (Buti and Fabbrini 2023; Fabbrini 2023; Fernández 2021; Schramm et al. 2022). Furthermore, the novelty of the approach also lies in the 'unprecedented' amount of financial space generated (Hodson and Howarth 2023). In this sense, the new framework moves the EU closer to constituting an actual fiscal union.

The spending targets indicate that the RRF is designed as a long-term initiative rather than merely constituting a short-term recovery plan from the COVID-19 pandemic (Schramm et al. 2022). This perspective is reflected in the provisions outlined in Articles 3 and 4 of Regulation 2021/2411, which delineate the six pillars governing the scope of application of the RRF, emphasising its commitment to 'contributing to the implementation of the European Pillar of Social Rights' and supporting the green transition. Moreover, the scheme encompasses alignment with the EU's 2030 climate targets and the objective of EU climate neutrality by 2050, in addition to promoting the digital transition (REG 2021/2411).

Additionally, the NGEU initiative has profound constitutional repercussions for the EU, as it has arguably increased fiscal alignment (and solidarity) among EU member states, while marking a pivotal step towards strengthening the Economic and Monetary Union (EMU) (Fabbrini 2021; Patrin 2023; Woźniakowski 2023). Moreover, it has enhanced the role of EU supranational institutions (notably the European Commission) in fiscal governance not just of EMU, but also of EU member states, creating a step towards EU fiscal union. With this, unlike the responses to the Euro crisis that aimed at maintaining fiscal stability in the EU by strictly monitoring national-level fiscal policies, the NGEU transcends mere fiscal surveillance to embrace a trend towards fiscal federalism (chapter 3 of Hosli 2022). Such a move constitutes an overhaul of the EU's economic governance architecture (Fabbrini 2021). This transformation is notably underscored by the endowment of the European Commission with enhanced authority and means to steer the EU economy via the RRF scheme. It also constitutes a scheme encompassing all of the EU, not just the Eurozone.

Moreover, it can be asserted that the NGEU advances EU's federalisation processes by conferring it with a fiscal capacity, alongside existing tools of fiscal regulation mainly available for the Eurozone (next to the EU-wide ES as a monitoring mechanism). In a nutshell, fiscal federalism refers to the division of responsibilities and financial resources between central and subnational government levels within a federal system (Oates 1999). In this regard, as an answer to the COVID-19 crisis, the NGEU constitutes a rather creative scheme enhancing fiscal authority at the EU's (supranational) level, despite traditional national-level resistance to such efforts. Hence, according to Woźniakowski (2023), this framework makes the EU resemble more mature (fiscal) regimes worldwide, by having established features in the EU akin to those of fiscal unions; the author draws on federalist theories to compare US's and EU's fiscal federalisation processes, underlining how the former originated in response to an internal threat, and that a similar dynamic might be observed in the latter following the COVID-19-induced crisis.

Therefore, the NGEU arguably has the potential to represent an important step towards this trajectory. Fabbrini (2021) builds on this argument, contending that the COVID-19 crisis acted as the necessary catalyst for the EU to gradually progress towards fiscal union. By enabling the EU to finance itself through the issuance of common debt on global financial markets, this project overcomes longstanding challenges associated with the EU budget and shifts the focus away from member states' (fiscal) contributions. This contrasts with an earlier logic characterising previous budget negotiations, even though arguably, the long-term borrowing generates some future challenges in terms of the repayments of the (collective) debt. Finally, from a legal and institutional standpoint, the NGEU strengthens the Commission's authority to steer European economic policy and solidifies its role as the core of an 'EU Treasury department in the making', consolidating its position as a key actor in EU economic governance. In this sense, in a neo-functionalist logic, the NGEU might well shift the balance from intergovernmental decision-making in fiscal policy domains to more supranationalism, which in turn may make the position of the EU in international institutions more cohesive.

The elements examined above have clear repercussions on European integration and in the light of related governance theories, scholars have explored the role and importance Ladiof the NGEU for European integration (Ladi and Wolff 2021; Schramm et al. 2022); some authors even argue that the project represents a step towards EU federalisation (Bongardt and Torres 2021; Fabbrini 2021). In terms of revitalising EU integration, the European Commission had already mentioned sustainable development as a potential driving force and solution in the European Agenda 2020 framework (Silander 2020), showcasing the interconnections between the two overarching initiatives. Furthermore, Boni and Zevi's (2021) focus on the roles of cities in implementing the NGEU, defining the project as a 'pan-European process', emphasises the idea that the NGEU is more than a mere financial recovery tool. As the NGEU has its roots in the Agenda 2030 while incorporating the SDGs, it arguably is the first time that a joint UN-EU effort has shaped an EU project with such extensive repercussions on the EU's own integration process.

Global challenges like climate change expose weaknesses in both global and regional governance systems. For example, the UN Framework Convention on Climate Change (UNFCCC), as the principal forum for international climate cooperation, faces significant constraints in terms of material and institutional power. It relies heavily on ideational authority—shaping global norms and inspiring voluntary action—but lacks the enforcement mechanisms and resource capabilities necessary for effective implementation (Tallberg et al. 2023, 11). In contrast, the EU, while regionally limited in scope, possesses stronger institutional capacity, binding legislation and financial mechanisms (Tallberg et al. 2023) as evidenced by its ambitious climate laws and major initiatives like the NGEU. However, such differences can support synergies: the UN's universal legitimacy aspirations and agenda-setting role complement the EU's capacity for implementation and enforcement, demonstrating how regional and global actors can mutually reinforce each other within the international multilateral system. The integration of UNSDGs within the NGEU exemplifies such interactions, illustrating how the EU operationalises UN norms and approaches into concrete policy and funding mechanisms. By embedding such global goals into its fiscal governance through the ES mechanisms, the EU addresses governance gaps in sustainability while advancing the universal objectives of Agenda 2030. This collaboration showcases how the EU, as a regional organisation, can act as a critical intermediary within the multilateral institutional architecture, translating the UN's (collective) ideational power into actionable policies at the regional level.

Arguments regarding how the NGEU contributes to advancing European integration are bolstered by its recognised importance to the EGD. In this sense, it can be asserted that the Agenda 2030 and the SDGs serve as a catalyst for further European integration, since they have led to the approval of measures such as the EGD and, subsequently, the NGEU, which in turn have significantly impacted the role of European institutions (and patterns of transnational solidarity). The EGD itself has been defined as a break from past patterns of EU climate governance (Dupont et al. 2023), as it adds a foundational element to the European economic model, alongside the single market and EMU for the Eurozone, therefore transcending other initiatives for green growth. According to Bongardt and Torres (2021), the COVID-19 crisis provided a crucial link between the EGD's long-term objectives and the implementation of short-term policies. In this sense, the EGD emerged as a kind of third pillar shaping the European economic model, alongside the single market and EMU, and a major crisis had to be addressed within its framework. Interestingly, COVID-19 played a dual role in this context: On one hand, it impeded progress on sustainability goals (see Brzyska and Szmarej-Baran 2023; Fetting 2020; Wang and Huang 2021). On the other hand, it acted as a catalyst to create a stronger framework for policy implementation, arguably serving as a bridge to long-term objectives and, hence, acting as a missing link between EGD long-term objectives and the adoption of short-term policies (European Commission 2020).

The NGEU has extensive consequences for power-sharing mechanisms among EU institutions and member states. It strengthens what can be called 'coordinative Europeanization' (Ladi and Wolff 2021), by involving member states in consultations and fostering collaboration between the EU and national arenas in terms of the development and implementation of policy solutions (which contrasts with more coercive, top-down approaches). Europeanisation refers to the close involvement of member states in EU policy-making while simultaneously, the term implies a fusion of tasks and responsibilities (Wessel 2016) applicable to both the vertical dimension (between the EU and member states) and the interaction of EU-level actors. On the theoretical level, according to Schramm et al. (2022), the novelty of these developments is that they go 'beyond classical theories of European integration' (Schramm et al. 2022, 9), notably in the framework of an analysis of whether a policy leads to 'more' or 'less' integration following the shift of policy competences from the national to the EU level, or vice versa. Accordingly, the RFF is seen as leading to 'more Europe'. It does not, however, take the form of a clear strengthening of supranational actors, but rather of joint tasks and procedures, and related pressures to succeed, or fail, collectively.

Moreover, Schramm et al. (2022) discuss the increasing requests to either turn the NGEU into a permanent EU-level instrument or to adopt another NGEU to cope with the costs of climate change mitigation and adaptation in the future, particularly in times of geopolitical uncertainty and related costs due to ongoing conflicts (such as the war against Ukraine), potentially as a tool to face ongoing challenges to multilateralism. This showcases the importance of the RFF for the EU to 'become more "sovereign" and develop towards a fiscal and political union', which has clear political repercussions. Still, the authors discuss trade-offs of the recovery plan—while the bottom-up approach and national ownership secure the broad involvement of domestic actors and can lead to increased legitimacy and efficiency of aimed-for investments and reforms, the national plans necessarily fall short of a broader European perspective.

The NGEU is indeed an ambitious project, yet it is not without its challenges. The first noticeable challenge arises from financial concerns. Although the loans and funds are being used to implement projects in line with the green and digital transitions, there are concerns in terms of the capacity to reabsorb the debt, starting in 2058 at the latest. Obstacles in repaying the debt, in turn, might represent a hurdle to the achievement of the SDGs and related initiatives in the future. Most of the NGEU projects have long-term objectives, and need constant funding, making financial security and consistency paramount for the project's overall success.

In addition, even though the loan receipts in EU member states depend on the approval of RFF plans, successful implementation of the project ultimately hinges on national governance patterns. Current or future member states at risk of mismanaging European funds due to aspects such as corruption or inefficiency, in this sense, can pose a risk to the success of the initiatives entailed in the project, making transparency and accountability vital to avoiding pitfalls. Monitoring and evaluation mechanisms to track the progress of funded projects can help mitigate risks of mismanagement. For instance, European Court of Auditors' reports on EU fund utilisation can provide empirical data on (past) challenges encountered and improvements needed.

The important trade-offs in terms of power, effectiveness, and legitimacy in global climate governance, stemming from the differences of being a regional organisation like the EU and a global institution like the UN, underscore the importance of a greater collaboration between the two levels of governance. In fact, within the international governance discourse, deficiencies in power, effectiveness, and legitimacy are seen as critical axes determining the relative success of global institutions such as the UN in terms of tracking and governing transboundary challenges such as climate change (Dupont and Moore 2019; Tallberg et al. 2023). As is the case for regional organisations such as the EU, scholars have highlighted several deficiencies in the UN's capacity to comprehensively address urgent global issues. These include governance gaps in crucial policy areas, a lack of the necessary legal authority to develop adequate global solutions, and institutional means that are not optimised for effective global cooperation (Tallberg et al. 2023). The latter includes institutional hurdles such as those related to the operation of the UNSC (Bueno et al., and Helou et al., this volume). Such limitations only emphasise the importance of multilateralism as a process in the context of the current conflictual geopolitical landscape. Although the UN holds relevant 'ideational power', it is necessary for audiences reflecting both state and society in its member states to engage and listen (Tallberg et al. 2023).

The EU, on the other hand, although partially better equipped institutionally and economically, cannot by any means replace global action, since it is mainly focused on Europe. The benefits of EU-UN collaboration are evident in their comparative effectiveness in combating climate change (similar to what AU-UN collaboration can imply in terms of conflict resolution and peace missions). The EU's ambitions in implementing the Agenda 2030 are positive from a global perspective and may largely exceed efforts by several UN member states (Tallberg et al. 2023; European Commission 2023a), yet regional collaboration remains essential to such aims. As the EU only accounts for about 10% of current total world greenhouse gas emissions, however, its efforts on the regional level are insufficient to achieve global climate goals (Tallberg et al. 2023). Similar reflections refer to the implementation of SDGs more generally.

Consequently, a greater alignment of EU and UN agendas related to SDG implementation, and collaboration between regional and global levels in such areas, can foster green and digital transitions, needed to create more coordinated and impactful approaches in addressing climate change goals (and achieving the SDGs more generally). This is not least of crucial importance due to the setbacks generated for the 2030 Agenda and the SDGs by the various repercussions of the COVID-19 pandemic in terms of aspects such as inequalities, access to education, gender balance, and even reaching climate goals (Protopsalti 2021; O'Malley 2022 or Orlassino 2022).

7 Conclusions

The NGEU project features two key elements that differentiate it from earlier EU-level (or Eurozone) financial rescue mechanisms and packages: it links economic recovery with investments into sustainability goals. The NGEU, in this sense, has created synergies between sustainability and investment aims, while enhancing EU-UN alignment on the SDGs that was already initiated in the ES context.

Our chapter draws on insights from neofunctionalism and historical institutionalism to interpret developments concerning the integration of the SDGs into the ES and the contours of the NGEU initiative. By exploring implications through a neofunctionalist lens, we argue that the adoption of Agenda 2030 on the EU level has spurred deeper EU integration, particularly in terms of economic and fiscal governance patterns resulting from the COVID-19 crisis. Integration in these areas encompasses the entire EU rather than just the Eurozone, in contrast to earlier phases and schemes created, such as the European Stability Mechanism (ESM) established for the Eurozone (Pan et al. 2023). In this sense, integration has been facilitated by the alignment of EU policies with the SDGs, serving as a catalyst for further cooperation and 'solidarity' mechanisms among member states, largely induced by spillover effects (particularly in response to a crisis), in agreement with neofunctionalist predictions.

In addition, insights based on historical institutionalism can show how past institutional developments, such as the incorporation of the SDGs into the ES, have shaped ensuing policy paths. Following this line of reasoning, our chapter shows that embedding of sustainability goals into EU economic and fiscal governance schemes reflects a critical juncture that has led to strengthened patterns of integration. The evolution also underscores the EU's commitment to Agenda 2030 and a shift in terms of patterns of EU socio-economic governance, while emphasising aspects such as the green and digital transitions.

The ES as a central component of EU fiscal governance has been instrumental in terms of integrating the SDGs into EU policy action, by providing a monitoring framework and guiding member states' economic policy approaches. The NGEU initiative, with its emphasis on green and digital transitions, paralleled by innovative borrowing mechanisms, arguably represents a landmark endeavour affecting EU economic and fiscal governance patterns post-pandemic. By aligning with the UNSDGs and promoting (regional and global) sustainability, the project has arguably strengthened economic and political monitoring mechanisms within the EU, while enhancing the role of supranational actors, and with this, integration. Simultaneously, the green and digital transition goals incorporated into the NGEU project may have affected the relative influence of competing initiatives, such as the BRI. This matters in terms of global contrasting narratives on the relative merits of such schemes and their embedding into global (climate) ambitions.

The NGEU's effects may also contain challenges, however, as financial concerns for the future and the need for transparent and accountable governance at national levels will matter to the initiative's relative success. Moreover, the EU's ambitions in terms of the green transition, and the incorporation of the SDGs into its major policy aims and initiatives, cannot suffice to address global climate challenges. Accordingly, regional organisations need to be aligned with actions taken at the level of international institutions, such as the UN, with goals formulated based on (global) multilateral negotiation and agreement. Thus, while alignment of EU-UN agendas and collaboration between regional and international levels are important to creating coordinated and impactful approaches to transnational challenges such as climate change, regional action in itself does not suffice.

A departure from the primarily bilateral agreements established in the early BRI phase demonstrates new opportunities arising, not least in terms of green transitions. Alternatives to the BRI—including the Global Gateway, Blue Dot Network, or India-Middle East-Europe Economic Corridor—also crucially involve private actors. The NGEU incorporates several initiatives related to specific SDGs, such as SDG 7 and 8, which are linked to economic and industrial development. Compared to BRI's primary reliance on national public companies, however, the NGEU and other (multilateral) initiatives involve multiple states and the private sector in initiatives related to green development, arguably strengthening efforts to incorporate similar elements in BRI projects. In this sense, (regional) spillover effects demonstrate how an initiative such as the NGEU, agreed upon based on regional-level intergovernmental negotiations, can affect not only internal economic recovery prospects, but also global approaches and those of other major powers in terms of infrastructure development and sustainability initiatives. In a medium-term perspective, such economic initiatives and frameworks are likely to also affect global power balances.

By analysing alignment between the NGEU and the SDGs, moreover, our chapter underscores the relevance and far-reaching implications of EU-UN collaboration in terms of norm development and patterns of multilateralism. In an era where global challenges such as climate change necessitate global multilateral action, while opposition to current features of the multilateral institutional system exists and maybe even continue to grow, the alignment of agendas between regional and global organisations emerges as a crucial requirement. The incorporation of the SDGs into the ES provides an example of how collaboration on the regional and international levels can streamline efforts defined internationally, enhance their effectiveness, and ensure a more coordinated (multilateral) approach to address pressing global challenges. Such alignment not only strengthens the global multilateral system but also highlights potentials for synergies, including those among geopolitical rivals, reinforcing collective capacities to address transnational challenges and sustainable development globally. A project such as the NGEU, established as a response to a crisis, arguably enhances integration and with this, affects the role of a regional actor such as the EU in the context of geopolitical rivalries, including those reflected in international institutions such as the UN (and the UNSC).

References

Allemand, Frédéric, Jérôme Creel, Nicolas Leron, Sandrine Levasseur and Francesco Saraceno. "Making Next Generation EU a Permanent Tool." *The Foundation for European Progressive Studies (FEPS)*, Policy Study, March 2023. Accessed October 10, 2024. https://feps-europe.eu/wp-content/uploads/2023/03/Making-Next-Generation-EU-a-permanent-tool.pdf.

Bongardt, Annette, and Torres, Francisco. The European Green Deal: More Than an Exit Strategy to the Pandemic Crisis, a Building Block of a Sustainable European Economic Model. JCMS: *Journal of Common Market Studies* 60, no. 1 (2021): 170–185. https://doi.org/10.1111/jcms.13264.

Boni, Anna Lisa, and Andrea Tobia Zevi. "Next Generation EU Cities: Local Communities in a Post-Pandemic Future." *Torrossa*, 2021. Accessed September 12, 2024. https://www.torrossa.com/it/resources/an/5157020.

Brautigam, Deborah. "A Critical Look at Chinese 'Debt-Trap Diplomacy': The Rise of a Meme." *Area Development and Policy* 5, no. 1 (2020): 1–14. https://doi.org/10.1080/23792949.2019.1689828.

Brooks, Eleanor, Anniek de Ruijter, Scott L. Greer, and Matthias, Wismar. EU Health Policy in the Aftermath of COVID-19: Neofunctionalism and Crisis-Driven Integration. *Journal of European Public Policy* 30, no. 4 (2023): 721–739. https://doi.org/10.1080/13501763.2022.2141301.

Brzyska, Joanna, and Izabela Szmarej-Baran. "The Covid-19 Pandemic and the Implementation of the Sustainable Development Goals: The EU Perspective." *Sustainability* (2023). https://www.mdpi.com/2071-1050/15/18/13503.

Buti, Marco and Sergio Fabbrini. The Political Determinants of Fiscal Governance in the EU: Towards a New Equilibrium, *Politics and Governance* 11, no. 4 (2023). https://doi.org/10.17645/pag.v11i4.7248.

Casarini, Nicola. "The Future of the Belt and Road in Europe: How China's Connectivity Project Is Being Reconfigured across the Old Continent—And What It Means for the Euro-Atlantic Alliance." *Istituto Affari Internazionali*, 2024. Accessed August 16, 2024. https://www.iai.it/sites/default/files/iai p2402.pdf.

De Boer, Dimitri, Christoph Nedopil, and Danting Fan. "China Clarifies Its Vision for a Green Belt and Road Initiative." *Client Earth; ClientEarth*, March 7, 2023. Accessed August 16, 2024. https://www.clientearth.asia/latest/news/china-clarifies-its-vision-for-a-green-belt-and-road-initiative/.

D'Erman, Valerie, and Amy Verdun. "An Introduction: Macroeconomic Policy Coordination and Domestic Politics: Policy Coordination in the EU from the European Semester to the Covid-19." *JCMS: Journal of Common Market Studies* 60, no. 1 (2021): 3–20. https://doi.org/10.1111/jcms.13276.

Dupont, Claire, and Brendan Moore. "Brexit and the EU in Global Climate Governance." *Politics and Governance* (2019). https://doi.org/10.17645/pag.v7i3.2137.

Dupont, Claire, Brendan Moore, Elin Lerum Boasson, Viviane Gravey, Andrew Jordan, Paula Kivimaa, Kati Kulovesi, Caroline Kuzemko, Sebastian Oberthür, Dmytro Panchuk, Jeffrey Rosamond, Diarmuid Torney, Jale Tosun, Ingmar von Homeyer. "Three Decades of EU Climate Policy: Racing Toward Climate Neutrality?" *WIREs Climate Change* 15, no. 1 (October 15, 2023). https://doi.org/10.1002/wcc.863.

Eurostat. Sustainable development in the European Union, Monitoring report on progress towards the SDGs in an EU context. In Eurostat (4th ed., pp. 1–34). 2020. The Publications Office of the European Union. https://ec.europa.eu/eurostat/documents/15234730/15241679/KS-02-20-202-EN-N.pdf/d3ee9cc0-1cb4-a27f-4358-ab468ac03633?t=1667386824396.

European Court of Auditors. The Spotlight Initiative to end violence against women and girls. In European Court of Auditors (pp. 1–24). 2023. https://www.eca.europa.eu/ECAPublications/SR-2023-21/SR-2023-21_EN.pdf.

European Commission. "Strategic Plan 2020–2024: DG Environment." September 18, 2020. https://commission.europa.eu/system/files/2020-10/env_sp_2020_2024_en.pdf.

European Commission. "The EU Budget and the Sustainable Development Goals." *Commission.europa.eu; The Publications Office of the European Union.* Accessed September 10, 2024. https://commission.europa.eu/strategy-and-policy/eu-budget/performance-and-reporting/horizontal-priorities/eu-budget-and-sustainable-development-goals_en.

European Commission. "Funding Instruments." *Commission Europa*, 2023a. Accessed September 10, 2024. https://commission.europa.eu/strategy-and-policy/eu-budget/eu-borrower-investor-relations/funding-instruments_en#nextgenerationeu-green-bonds.

European Commission. "Press Corner." *European Commission—European Commission*, The Publications Office of the European Union, June 22, 2023b. Accessed September 11, 2024. https://ec.europa.eu/commission/presscorner/detail/en/ip_23_3451.

European Commission. "Sustainable Development in the European Union: Monitoring Report on Progress Towards the SDGs in an EU Context." June 2023c. Accessed September 11, 2024. https://commission.europa.eu/system/files/2023-06/SDG-Report-WEB.pdf.

European Commission. "Strengthening the EU through Ambitious Reforms and Investments." *European Commission*, Brussels: The Publications Office of the European Union, 2024. Accessed September 11, 2024. https://commission.europa.eu/document/download/f953f881-5a01-4040-804c-16be479ed3c4_en?filename=COM_2024_82_1_EN_ACT_part1_v5.pdf.

European Committee of the Regions (ECON). "Multi-Level Governance of Sustainability Transition in the EU." 2022. Accessed December 19, 2024.

European External Action Service. The EU and the UN: A partnership that delivers. European Union External Action; EEAS Press. September 20, 2024. https://www.eeas.europa.eu/eeas/eu-and-un-partnership-delivers_en.

European Economic and Social Committee. "Global Battle of Offers—From the Chinese Belt and Road Initiative to the EU Global Gateway: The Vision of European Organised Civil Society." *European Economic and Social Committee.* The Publications Office of the European Union, January 25,

2023. Accessed December 19, 2024. https://www.eesc.europa.eu/en/our-work/opinions-information-reports/opinions/global-battle-offers-chinese-belt-and-road-initiative-eu-global-gateway-vision-european-organised-civil-society.

European Parliament. The Sustainable Development Goals in the EU budget . In European Parliament (pp. 1–10). 2021. Publication Office of the European Union. https://www.europarl.europa.eu/RegData/etudes/BRIE/2021/696211/IPOL_BRI(2021)696211_EN.pdf.

European Union. *Regulation (EU) 2020/2094 Establishing a European Union Recovery Instrument to Support the Recovery in the Aftermath of the COVID-19 Crisis.* Official Journal of the European Union L 433I, December 22, 2020.

Fabbrini, Federico. "The Legal Architecture of the Economic Responses to COVID-19: EMU Beyond the Pandemic." *JCMS: Journal of Common Market Studies* 60 (2021): 186–203.

Fabbrini, Federico. "Next Generation EU and the Future of Economic Governance: Towards a Paradigm Change or Just a Big One-Off?" *Journal of European Public Policy* 30, no. 4 (2023): 676–695.

Fernández, Echebarria J. (2021). Critical analysis on the European Union's measures to overcome the economic impact of the COVID-19 pandemic. *European Papers,* 5(3), 1399–1423. https://doi.org/10.15166/2499-8249/437.

Fetting, Constanze. "Impacts of the Covid-19 Pandemic on Sustainable Development and the SDGs in Europe." *ESDN Report*, 2020. Accessed August 16, 2024. https://www.esdn.eu/fileadmin/ESDN_Reports/ESDN_Report_July_2020.pdf.

Haas, Ernst B. "The Uniting of Europe: Political, Social and Economic Forces 1950–1957." In *Debates on European Integration*, 105–16. 2006. https://doi.org/10.1007/978-0-230-20933-6_5.

Hodson, Dermot, and David Howarth. "The EU's Recovery and Resilience Facility: An Exceptional Borrowing Instrument?" *Journal of European Integration* 46, no. 1 (2023): 69–87. https://doi.org/10.1080/07036337.2023.2243378.

Hosli, Madeleine O. *The European Union and the United Nations in Global Governance*. Bristol, UK: Bristol University Press, 2022. https://doi.org/10.51952/9781529217575

Hosli, Madeleine O. (with Hannah Lentschig and Carolina d'Ambrosio). "Crises, Integration and the EU as an External Actor", chapter 3 in *The European Union and the United Nations in Global Governance,* (2022): 29–56. Bristol: Bristol University Press. https://doi.org/10.51952/9781529217575.ch003

Knodt, Michèle, Marc Ringel, and Rainer Müller. "'Harder' Soft Governance in the European Energy Union." *Journal of Environmental Policy & Planning*

22, no. 6 (2020): 787–800. https://doi.org/10.1080/1523908X.2020.1781604.

Koundouri, Phoebe, and Jeffrey Sachs. *Transformations for the Joint Implementation of Agenda 2030 for Sustainable Development and the European Green Deal: A Green and Digital, Job-Based and Inclusive Recovery from the COVID-19 Pandemic.* Sustainable Development Solutions Network, 2021.

Ladi, Stella, and Wolff, Sarah. The EU Institutional Architecture in the Covid-19 Response: Coordinative Europeanization in Times of Permanent Emergency. JCMS: *Journal of Common Market Studies* 59, (2021): 32–43. https://doi.org/10.1111/jcms.13254.

Nedopil, Christoph. "Ten Years of China's Belt and Road Initiative (BRI): Evolution and the Road Ahead." *Green Finance & Development Center; Fudan University Press*, October 12, 2023. Accessed September 12, 2024. https://greenfdc.org/ten-years-of-chinas-belt-and-road-initiative-bri-evolution-and-the-road-ahead/.

Nicoli, Francesco. Neofunctionalism Revisited: Integration Theory and Varieties of Outcomes in the Eurocrisis. *Journal of European Integration* 42, no. 7 (2020): 897–916. https://doi.org/10.1080/07036337.2019.1670658.

Niemann, Arne, & Ioannou, Demosthenes. European Economic Integration in Times of Crisis: A Case of Neofunctionalism? *Journal of European Public Policy* 22, no. 2 (2015): 196–218. https://doi.org/10.1080/13501763.2014.994021.

Oates, Wallace E. "An Essay on Fiscal Federalism." *Journal of Economic Literature* 37, no. 3 (1999): 1120–1149.

Oberthür, Sebastian, and Claire Dupont. "The European Union's International Climate Leadership: Towards a Grand Climate Strategy?" *Journal of European Public Policy* 28, no. 7 (2021): 1095–1114. https://doi.org/10.1080/13501763.2021.1918218.

O'Malley, Alanna. "School's Out Forever? 'The Effect of COVID-19 on Educational Opportunities for Women and Girls in the Global South'." In *The Global, Regional and Local Politics of Institutional Responses to COVID-19: Implications for Women and Children*, edited by Madeleine O. Hosli, Amy Blessing, and Irini Iacovidou. 179–195. Palgrave Macmillan, 2022.

Orlassino, Chiara. "Preventing a Knock-on Pandemic: How the World's Biggest Children's Charity Responded to the Virus that Doesn't Make Children Sick." In *The Global, Regional and Local Politics of Institutional Responses to COVID-19: Implications for Women and Children*, edited by Madeleine O. Hosli, Amy Blessing, and Irini Iacovidou, 89–109. Palgrave Macmillan, 2022.

Pan, Wen, Madeleine O. Hosli, and Michaël Lantmeeters. Historical Institutionalism and Policy Coordination: Origins of the European Semester. *Evolutionary and Institutional Economics Review*, 20 (2023): 41–167. https://doi.org/10.1007/s40844-023-00253-z.

Patrin, Maria. Governance by Funding: NGEU, Solidarity and the EU Institutional Balance. SSRN *Electronic Journal*. (2023). https://doi.org/10.2139/ssrn.4361461.

Petmesidou, Maria, Rui Branco, Emmanuele Pavolini, Sergio González Begega, and Ana Marta Guillén. "The EPSR and the Next Generation EU: Heralding a Reconfiguration of Social Protection in South Europe?" *Social Policy & Administration* 57, no. 4 (2023): 497–512.

Protopsalti, Dimitra. "UNICEF & UN WOMEN in the Post-COVID-19 Era: How the Pandemic Is Expected to Reshape the Humanitarian Agenda." In *The Future of Multilateralism: Global Cooperation and International Organizations*, edited by Madeleine O. Hosli, Taylor Garrett, Sonja Niedecken, and Nicholas Verbeek, 19–38. Rowman and Littlefield, 2021.

Schramm, Lucas, Ulrich Krotz, and Bruno De Witte. "Building 'Next Generation' After the Pandemic: The Implementation and Implications of the EU Covid Recovery Plan." *JCMS: Journal of Common Market Studies* 60, no. S1 (2022): 114–124. https://doi.org/10.1111/jcms.13375.

Sial, Farwa, and Xavier Sol. "The Emperor's New Clothes: What's New About the EU's Global Gateway?" *Eurodad*. Brussels: Eurodad, 2022. Accessed October 10, 2024. https://counter-balance.org/uploads/files/EU-global-gateway-report-FINAL.pdf.

Silander, Daniel. "The EU and Agenda 2030." In *Implementing Sustainable Development Goals in Europe*, edited by Charlie Karlsson and Daniel Silander, 1–13. Edward Elgar Publishing, 2020. https://doi.org/10.4337/9781789909975.00005

Sims Gallagher, Kelly. "China's Belt and Road Is Conduit for Polluting Investments." *Financial Times*, August 9, 2018. Accessed September 12, 2024. https://www.ft.com/content/f965fa22-9be4-11e8-9702-5946bae86e6d.

Tallberg, Jonas, Karin Bäckstrand, Jan Aart Scholte and Thomas Sommerer. *Global Governance: Fit for Purpose?* SNS Democracy Council, 2023. Accessed October 10, 2024. https://www.sns.se/en/articles/sns-democracy-council-2023-global-governance-fit-for-purpose/.

United Nations. "The Role of the United Nations in Addressing Global Climate Change." *United Nations*, 2022. Accessed October 10, 2024. https://www.un.org/en/climatechange/un-climate-change-activities.

Vanhercke, Bart, and Amy Verdun. "From the European Semester to the Recovery and Resilience Facility: Some Social Actors Are (Not) Resurfacing." *SSRN Electronic Journal* (2022). https://doi.org/10.2139/ssrn.4013325.

Vanhercke, Bart, and Amy Verdun. "The European Semester as Goldilocks: Macroeconomic Policy Coordination and the Recovery and Resilience Facility." *JCMS: Journal of Common Market Studies* 60, no. 1 (2021): 204–223. https://doi.org/10.1111/jcms.13267.

Verdun, Amy, and Jonathan Zeitlin. "Introduction: The European Semester as a New Architecture of EU Socioeconomic Governance in Theory and Practice." In *EU Socio-Economic Governance Since the Crisis*, 1–12. 2017. https://doi.org/10.4324/9781351025621-1.

Verdun, Amy, and Jonathan Zeitlin. Introduction: The European Semester as a new architecture of EU socioeconomic governance in theory and practice. *EU Socio-Economic Governance since the Crisis: The European Semester in Theory and Practice* (2018): 1–12. https://doi.org/10.4324/9781351025621-1.

Wang, Qiang, and Rui Huang. "Impact of the Covid-19 Pandemic on Sustainable Development Goals—A Survey." *Environmental Research* 202 (2021): 111637. https://doi.org/10.1016/j.envres.2021.111637.

Wessel, Ramses A. "Lex Imperfecta: Law and Integration in European Foreign and Security Policy." *European Papers 1*, no. 2 (2016): 439–468. https://doi.org/10.15166/2499-8249/52.

World Bank. "Belt and Road Initiative." *World Bank; The World Bank Group*, March 29, 2018. Accessed September 12, 2024. https://www.worldbank.org/en/topic/regional-integration/brief/belt-and-road-initiative.

Woźniakowski, Tomasz P. "No Borrowing Without Taxing? Fiscal Solidarity of Next Generation EU in Light of the American Experience." *Politics and Governance* 11, no. 4 (2023): 73–81. https://doi.org/10.17645/pag.v11i4.7233.

CHAPTER 11

Conclusion: The UNSC, Multilateralism, and Patterns of Global Governance

Katyayni Champawat, Sofia Pires Lopes, Gabriela M. G. Bueno, and Madeleine O. Hosli

The contributions to this book project delve into the United Nations and Multilateralism in a two-fold way: by addressing both the voting, co-sponsorship, and coalition patterns in the United Nations Security Council (UNSC), and by exploring how international organisations and regional powers act in the UNSC. This book offers a novel overview of voting patterns in areas such as peacekeeping and veto usage, coalition formation, co-sponsorship, and great power rivalry within the UNSC. It also focuses on small, emerging, and regional powers' efforts in leaving their mark throughout their tenure in the UNSC while also devoting attention to the special role of the European Union (EU) in the UNSC, given its unique nature as a highly integrated regional bloc. Each chapter

Present Address:
K. Champawat (✉) · S. P. Lopes · G. M. G. Bueno · M. O. Hosli
Leiden University, The Hague, The Netherlands

M. O. Hosli
e-mail: m.o.hosli@fgga.leidenuniv.nl

M. O. Hosli et al. (eds.), *Multilateralism and the United Nations Security Council*, https://doi.org/10.1007/978-3-031-85320-3_11

of this project contributes with unique arguments that answer several research gaps in analyses focused on Multilateralism, the United Nations, and other regional organisations.

The book's chapter one introduces the reader to the core concepts of this book, namely, multilateralism and the UNSC. It situates the United Nations (UN) in the broader framework of multilateralism, highlighting its central role in global governance. The UN system is intricate, encompassing numerous agencies, funds, and programs that actively collaborate with regional and local actors as well as other intergovernmental and non-governmental organisations. These partnerships include close synergies with regional and global entities. Some of these organisations also participate as Permanent Observers in UN General Assembly sessions and other UN offices and have direct influence on the discussions.

The chapter then narrows its focus to examine the structure and procedures of the UNSC, highlighting the UN's composition of 193 member states which includes both democratic and autocratic regimes. This diversity creates challenges in its decision-making processes. Rivalries among member states and global power politics heavily influence the UN's operations, reflecting the complex dynamics of contemporary international relations. The following chapters of the book unpack these complex dynamics as reflected in, arguably, the UN's most contentious organ, the Security Council.

Building on the foundational knowledge of chapter one, the second chapter, by Bueno et. al., titled "Coalitions, Peace Missions and UNSC Decision-Making", examines the tensions surrounding peace missions in the UNSC. Stemming from a novel data collection on UNSC resolutions and voting patterns, this chapter explores how the UNSC's permanent and non-permanent members assess peace operations, either passing or blocking decisions on peacekeeping and peacebuilding missions and how coalition patterns are formed. The authors offer an encompassing approach to the topic by addressing peace operations from January 1948 to April 2024, presenting a dataset that yields large academic and practical potential.

The authors begin by discussing coalition formation theories, which are crucial for this chapter's purposes as they intend to predict behaviour through a combination of actor preferences and institutional constraints (Bueno et al., this volume). Actors can aim at collecting the most individual gains as possible, which entails joining a coalition with as few members as possible to curb division and the need to make compromises

(Bueno et al., this volume). Yet, in the context of the UNSC's power disparities, these coalitions necessarily need the P5 members. Actors can also form coalitions based on members' similar perspectives on different issues at stake. Coalitions often encapsulate members with similar policy and ideological views (Bueno et al., this volume).

Despite the importance of these perspectives, Bueno et. al. present a novel understanding of coalition formation in the UNSC, arguing that within International Organisations (IOs), traditional knowledge of coalition formation might not suffice. They bring to the table factors such as policy legitimacy, member states' disparate interests, or IO's cohesion, which influence coalition formation. In the context of the UNSC, coalitions ought to include as many members as possible to foster legitimacy and to take into consideration member states' individual interests. This latter element is fundamental, as member states may oppose a proposal if they consider their national interests and "good standing" within the organisation to be jeopardised by it (Bueno et al., this volume). These considerations comprise the three Tiers introduced by the authors—Tier I encompasses countries' national interests, Tier II member states' influence within the organisation, and Tier III includes securing the standing of the organisation itself (Bueno et al., this volume).

After drawing an adapted theoretical approach to coalition formation in the UNSC, the authors assess how member states form coalitions in the UNSC through its contested votes, including abstentions and negative votes. This is particularly interesting as the theoretical framework points out that the "default" option in the UNSC is unanimity. Thus, understanding why and in which circumstances countries join dissenting coalitions or resolutions that are halted or not approved is fundamental, constituting the main aim of this chapter and its key contribution to academic research in the field. The authors use a mixed-methods approach, choosing peace missions that caused several abstentions or negative votes and then resorting to qualitative materials like meeting records, public statements, and other documents to unveil the reasons behind such choices.

In connection to peace operations, there have been 23 vetoes or "no" votes since 1946, a small portion of the 242 vetoes overall. In addition, only one of these vetoes has resulted in the termination of a peace operation—the 2009 Russian veto of the two-week United Nations Observer Mission in Georgia (UNOMIG). The authors argue that this veto corresponds to Tier I of this chapter's theoretical framework, as Russia vetoed this resolution because it considered that the resolution was compromised owing to Western interference and that it ran against Russian national interests (Bueno et al., this volume). Abstention patterns also comprise Tier I considerations, as member states join a dissenting coalition by abstaining if they consider a draft resolution to jeopardise their interests (Bueno et al., this volume). This was the case, for example, for the 2016 UNSC vote on the United Nations Mission for the Referendum in Western Sahara (MINURSO) peace mission.

In regard to Tier II, the authors contend that P5 members abstaining from Resolutions based on this tier is more significant than is the case for non-permanent members, as their abstention does not mean that the Resolution was blocked. Indeed, we see a high pattern of abstention on the part of UNSC permanent members. In the period under analysis, there have been 88 abstentions by P5 members on peace missions initiations and extensions. China is the P5 member who has abstained the most, followed by Russia and the former USSR (Bueno et al., this volume). China also accounts for the P5 member with the most abstentions alongside another UNSC member (Bueno et al., this volume). Tier II considerations make sense as these countries abstain in order to maintain a "good standing" within the UNSC.

Notwithstanding the importance of Tier I and II, Tier III is crucial to analyse as it directly concerns the organisation itself. As maintained by the authors, "(…) a more cohesive voting pattern within the UNSC is likely to enhance the legitimacy of the organisation's decisions, especially when its reputation is under public scrutiny." (Bueno et al., this volume). The authors have unveiled that Tier III is widely used by both default and dissenting coalitions, which is an interesting observation. Oftentimes, coalitions resort to the UN Charter, UN principles, and other elements to defend their positions in regard to a Resolution and the decision of voting in favour, abstaining, or voting against (Bueno et al., this volume). This might be a justification for the high rates of abstentions yielded by some peace missions.

Another fascinating element uncovered by this chapter is that permanent and non-permanent UNSC members are equally part of dissenting coalitions. Even though Western powers do not frequently go against the default, the U.S., as a P5 member, has vetoed 11 Resolutions on the extension of peace operations (Bueno et al., this volume). P5 members arrange themselves in coalitions according to the issues at stake, and the same is the case for non-permanent members (Bueno et al., this volume).

Still, China and Russia are the P5 members which must go against the *status quo* (Bueno et al., this volume), and they may then lead their own respective coalitions. While characterised by high tensions, the UNSC is still a venue that formally brings together the P5 members to deal with topics related to international security.

This chapter concludes by reinforcing the idea that challenging the default coalitions is a rare occasion as consensus and unanimity usually reign in an international setting like the UNSC. The objective, as argued by the authors, is unanimity, confirming Tier III considerations. However, dissenting perspectives might also occur. In this case, the authors have established that dissenting coalitions mostly take place owing to differences in underlying policy preferences. As stated before, vetoes are very rare, and abstentions are usually the way through which member states show their discontentment (Bueno et al., this volume). Yet, both abstentions and vetoes are the minority in terms of vote choices on UNSC Resolutions. These results yield much academic potential, underlining "(…) the complex dynamics underlying coalition formation and decision-making in international institutions such as the UNSC (Bueno et al., this volume).

The third chapter, titled "Coalition Formation and Co-Sponsorship in the United Nations Security Council", authored by Helou et al., provides an extensive overview of coalition formation and co-sponsorship in the UNSC and addresses whether such patterns are also observable in the United Nations General Assembly (UNGA), a comparison that has been rarely touched upon. While the second chapter introduces the existence, formation, and influence of coalitions in the UNSC, Helou et al. focus on investigating if coalition-formation influences agenda-setting through an analysis of co-sponsorship of resolutions. They do so by using a novel dataset with trends from 2011 to 2023 and by observing patterns in it to illustrate motives behind members' decision to sponsor or co-sponsor, as "introducing a draft also allows the sponsor to shape the context in which the issue is debated" (Helou et al., this volume).

With a focus on the P3—France, UK, and the USA.—the authors' findings corroborate other literature, showing a tendency towards more independence in authorship of draft resolutions, led by different national interests and government compositions, while China and Russia tend to gather more alignment in authorship and veto in the UNSC (Helou et al., this volume). Later in their examination, the authors posit whether these member states follow the same behaviour in the UNGA, as to understand if their coalition and voting patterns are specific to a UN body structure or are more crucial to members' overall beliefs. They notice a significant decrease in P3 co-sponsorship in the UNSC, except in the case of the UK and France (Helou et al., this volume). In addition, in UNGA, the three countries show less politically significant sponsorship. This is not the case for the P2, as the authors attest that China and Russia have intensified collaboration in both UN bodies (Helou et al., this volume). However, more individualised sponsorship patterns are closely related to the practice of "penholdership", often attributed to P3 member states.

This chapter also delves into the study of the UNSC dynamics in agenda-setting. They find that P5 focus resides on peacekeeping, although China shares the lowest number in their data (32%), compared to its own total sponsorships rates; sanctions, human rights, and internal security also show a lower trend in agenda-setting (Helou et al., this volume). Seeing that, they observe member state behaviour in the UNSC by analysing their veto data, noticing that Russia often paralyses the UNSC using its veto to block drafts, and China maintains cooperation among members. While the P3 remain powerhorses—also showing a greater number of agenda-setting and authorship initiatives—countries try to avoid isolation in the UNSC (Helou et al., this volume). Hence, with this chapter, this book can confirm that there are "patterns of coalition formation among the P5 through actual voting on UNSC resolutions, affirming P3 and P2 adhesion when focusing on veto use", further providing crucial information on processes and dynamics in the UNSC (Helou et al., this volume).

Hitherto, chapters two and three of this book focused on the general pattern of coalition formation and sponsorship within the UNSC. Chapter four narrows the focus to the three great powers within the UNSC. The chapter, titled "Multilateral Cooperation and Great Power Rivalry in the UNSC", analyses the rhetoric in the UNSC discussions between the USA., Russia, and China on the Syrian Civil War in 2011, 2016, and 2021. Heinikainen (this volume) finds evidence of heightened tensions between these countries, especially the USA. and Russia. Interestingly, China appeared to be the most neutral among the three on this theme.

This analysis is not only relevant but also timely. It was assumed that the post-Cold War era of U.S. hegemony would moderate the power struggles, which for some time was indeed true. This is reflected in the fact that the P5 did not need to use the veto as much as during the Cold War. However, as the author posits, by 2007, China and Russia's aspirations to oppose U.S. hegemony had become visible (Heinikainen, this volume). By 2010, the rivalries became revived and the tensions further grew as Russia invaded Ukraine in 2022, alongside the situation which unfolded in Gaza in 2023 (Heinikainen, this volume). Building on Von Einsiedel, Malone, and Stagno Ugarte's (2015) observation that the shifting balance of power within the permanent members of the UNSC will come to pose significant challenges to the effectiveness and relevance of UNSC, the chapter endeavours to uncover the rhetoric of these countries.

The author examines the UNSC discussions on Syria in 2011, 2016, and 2021. The case of Syria is famously considered a prime example of great power rivalries leading to UNSC paralysis. The analysis looks at the minutes from eight meetings that took place across the years mentioned above. Employing a rhetoric analysis, the author engages with recurring stylistic choices and tone, exploring the arguments that the three states make regarding their relations with each other and how they seek to persuade others to support their narratives. The analysed texts are situated within the realities on the ground, which were likely to influence the speeches analysed, aiming at looking past the diplomatic niceties to determine what each representative implied about their rivals. (Heinikainen, this volume).

The analysis reveals the heightened tensions between the great powers, especially between Russia and the U.S. Indeed, Russia openly challenged the U.S. and its Western allies in 2016. Generally, the Russian narrative challenged Western hegemony, acusing the U.S. and its allies of having interventionist motives that could lead to regime changes in foreign countries serving Western interests. Russia also brought up the growing anti-Russian sentiment allegedly under force by the U.S., which was claimed to hinder collective action. Overall, the tone Russia adopted was negative. Similarly, the U.S. also enforced a negative tone, accusing Russia, and sometimes China, of causing the deaths of civilians and of supporting the Al-Assad regime. Interestingly, however, both countries adopted a more neutral tone in what were unanimous meetings. Contrastingly, China had a more diplomatic and neutral tone during such discussions. It brought the themes of sovereignty into them and supported collective peaceful resolution through the UN. Its challenges to the U.S. were scarce, indirect, and more implicit.

In this sense, the chapter posits that, while both China and Russia posed challenges for the U.S., Russia was a much more aggressive rival than China. More importantly, the author concludes that, although the great power rivalries pose serious challenges in UNSC decision-making, they have not paralysed the UNSC completely. In this, the chapter presents an alternate view to popular understandings of this issue. This is not to say that the rivalries with the attached vetoes did not offer serious challenges; nevertheless, despite these hardships, multilateralism as a governance principle survived and there is hope for continued multilateral cooperation. The second part of the book focuses even more explicitly on this expectation, highlighting how even the non-permanent UNSC members, from the Global South and North, are focused on reforming the system instead of abandoning it.

In the fifth chapter of this book, "A Crystal Ball for Great Power Plays? Predicting Security Council Vetoes Through Machine Learning", Cross dives into the veto mechanism in the UNSC's P5 by creating a prediction model tailored for Russia and the U.S., two of the most divergent members of the UNSC. Both member states hold significant power within and outside of the UNSC which they often use against each other. Such aggregation of power and the related rivalries have been heavily criticised, yet there has been no significant reform. In this context, a predictive mechanism for veto in the UNSC can prove to be a powerful tool. Therefore, the author has taken this context into account while creating a prediction model conceptualising what is national interest and linking it to the position of Russia and the U.S. Her methodology consists of the investigation of 2800 draft resolutions from January 1960 until December 2023, invoking an impressive 4,448 "internal" and "external" predictors (Cross, this volume).

In the analysis, Cross confirms that there is a divide between the "Western Powers" (France, UK, U.S) and "Non-Western Powers" (China and Russia) within the P5 configuration; however, although there is "disagreement among the P5, the veto has been used sparingly" (Cross, this volume). The data presented show that there is a veto prevalence greater in the ongoing decade than in earlier years, illustrating a noticeable growing division over recent issues and ideological approaches between Russia and the U.S. in the UNSC (Cross, this volume). Furthermore, Cross uncovers that the U.S will not avoid the usage of the veto regardless of their ideology, politics, and cultural alliances, while Russia has vetoed zero resolutions authored by China, but cast it primarily against Western Power authorship. In addition, the statistical results generated by the analysis show that there is a clear divergence between the U.S and

Russia in terms of veto usage, showing that their subjective interpretation of an issue discussed is what mostly leads to their casting of a veto. This also entails a complete "absence of common ground between two of the largest power players in the international arena," thus, establishing two distinct patterns to predict the veto for P5 members (Cross, this volume). For the U.S., resolution authorship is a strong indicator, just as the text words relating to Israel strongly predict a resolution "block"; while for Russia, authorship is not an indicator, but the words "intervention", "Ukraine", "Syria", "Energy", and "Land Area" are indicators that Russia will block a resolution by casting a veto (Cross, this volume). Significantly, Cross' examination demonstrates how the "P5 consistently utilise the veto in disproportionate amounts in relation to resolutions where they are the subject of the resolution".

Moreover, the study reveals that Russia's decision-making process in using its veto is not as obvious as its considerations based on political, economic, and political interests, which invites further investigation on what drives a key actor in the P5 to use veto (Cross, this volume). Most importantly, the investigation shows that there is an abuse of the veto mechanism by the P5, especially the U.S. and Russia, supporting the critics asking for reform. Moreover, it shows that attempting to reform the UNSC will imply that members can and will abuse their veto privileges. Thus, this increases demands for a reform of the influence of the veto and not of expanding its use—perhaps member diversification is not the main issue but rather the power of the mechanism itself (Cross, this volume).

These five chapters comprise the first half of this book. They arguably provide novel and important insights into the voting patterns, coalition-building mechanisms, sponsorship, veto predictions, and great power rivalry in the UNSC. The second half of this book takes a narrower approach and focuses on regional actors and their roles within the UN (and the UNSC). This more concise angle is important to unveil concrete policies and actions taken by regional organisations in upholding multilateralism. Special attention is given to the EU, countries of the Global South, and to non-traditional threats to security and multilateralism. The first two chapters (Chapters 6 and 7) aim to place the "small and emerging" (S&E) powers and their role within the UNSC context. Their bid for a seat at the table, along with their multifaceted and increasingly non-traditional concerns, is explored. Herein, "small and emerging powers" are not bound by strict criteria; however, countries are referred to that have seen extensive economic growth and increasing political influence. They mostly belong to the Global South and have only recently emerged as active and influential players within the multilateral system. These countries also often but not always play the role of a "regional" power. The last three chapters (Chapters 8–10) scrutinise the various synergies that exist between the EU member states and the UNSC. In this regard, the chapters explore EU voting and co-sponsorship patterns related to resolutions dealing with sanctions, the significance of the EU bloc within the UNSC, and the degree of synergy between EU policies and the UN agenda. Thus, part two of the book provides an opening for further research with an eye on the developing global context.

The sixth chapter of this book, "The Small and Regional Powers Claim for Agency: A Strategic Usage of Non-Traditional Threats Through Arria Meetings", delves into this emerging trend. To this end, Leurs and Galy-Jammou-Préfontaine (this volume) analyse the role of small and emerging countries in terms of influencing agenda-setting and decision-making within the UNSC, in attempts to address emerging "non-traditional" threats, such as climate change and (lacking) security in cyberspace. They find that Arria formula meetings and coalition building are some of the useful tools employed by members to build a degree of mutual understanding and consensus on such topics.

Arguably, the structure of the UNSC and its veto processes poses a grave challenge to the decision-making capacity of the UNSC. For instance, the P5 have opposing views on the challenge of climate change: While France and the UK push for greater climate change mitigation policies, China prioritises its economic development, and the U.S. advocates a position highly dependent on its domestic politics. Power rivalries among the P5, as discussed in Chapters 3 and 4, can lead to paralysis in UNSC. Meanwhile, the countries that suffer the most because of these non-traditional threats do not have the capacity to fight against them on their own. Thus, their only possibility is to influence agenda-setting processes in their favour and put pressure on the more powerful states. In this sense, the Arria formula meetings have served as a strategic tool. The concept of Arria meetings was first conceived in 1992 (United Nations 2002) with the aim of providing a safe, informal, and confidential space to such member states. This, in turn, allows member states to engage with each other without the pressure of being watched, creating a more fluid discussion. These meetings also have space to include state or non-state parties deemed relevant for a particular concern, widening the scope of engagement and discussion. Both climate change and cyber security have increasingly become themes addressed in such meetings. The authors analyse the meetings organised by UNSC members and find a wide diversity of sub-issues brought to the table. They predict that the upcoming years will see a transition of discussion on these topics towards more formal settings, including the UNSC meetings.

In essence, such informal meetings allow small and emerging non-permanent UNSC members to circumvent disputes between the great powers, aligning with the Global South's commitment to non-alignment and providing them with a way to consolidate their resources and political might, which can then be leveraged in face of the unequal global hierarchical order. Still, in the current global order, the agency of such states is limited, notably by the permanent member's veto power. Hence, reform of and within the UNSC is becoming one of the principal demands of small and emerging states. The following chapter focuses on the position in the UNSC of some of the countries in this group of member states.

In the seventh chapter, "Small and Emerging Powers in UNSC Decision-Making", Lu et al. analyse the situation of four selected countries: Turkiye, India, Singapore, and the United Arab Emirates (UAE). These nations represent some diversity within the broad category of "small and emerging powers". While India is a large and rapidly growing member state, Turkiye is a middle power that plays a crucial role as a bridge between the East and the West. In contrast, UAE and Singapore both represent smaller states and can be considered to be regional powers, but differ largely in terms of their social, political, cultural, and economic dimensions. The authors explore the motivations and aspirations behind these countries' bid for UNSC seats; the methods with which they influence UNSC decision-making; their unique contribution to the discussions; and the overall outcome of this in the UNSC. Despite the relative lack of resources and capacities of these states compared to the P5 members, the small and emerging powers exercise significant influence based on strategic and diplomatic engagement, leveraging their issue-specific expertise. More importantly, these countries have consistently been pushing for reform and advocating for a more inclusive and representative decision-making process.

This chapter is a welcome addition to the literature on the UNSC, not least as small states' survival is often directly tied to their alliance with the great power and their independent influence has been ignored. However, since the post-Cold War era, small states have arguably had an impact on global governance through strategic diplomacy. The analysis of this chapter reveals that the aspirations of India, Singapore, Türkiye, and UAE go beyond purely political considerations and include moral dimensions. These states have utilised their regional and/or issue-specific expertise to raise their global status. As they have taken on a gradually more active role, they have become agenda-setters and mediators by themselves. Today, these small and middle-power countries are not only trying to get elected to the UNSC, but actively working on reforming the UNSC from within. Their impact on the activities of the UNSC is increasingly apparent, even when the scope differs compared to other members. Importantly, the small and emerging states are bringing to the fore some novel "non-traditional" threats to their security, including climate change and cyber security, as discussed in Chapter 6. Overall, what emerges in these two chapters is the growing significance of these countries within the UNSC setting. Their active engagement is a testament to changing power dynamics within the global hierarchies, by pushing for a more representative multilateral system. Listening to these voices will be imperative to determining the evolving landscape.

While these "blocs" and uneasy cooperations between the small and emerging states are increasingly visible in the UNSC, traditional and often more powerful blocs already exist. The EU is one such bloc. It is unique in its highly unified position and also has the advantage of having one (two pre-Brexit) of its members within the P5. Given this, an inquiry into EU-UN and, more specifically, EU-UNSC relations is a worthwhile endeavour, as it offers important lessons for other emerging blocs.

To this end, Balutkar and Stepanian (this volume) provide a historical contextualisation of the EU's growing multilateral role and how it co-exists with the UN, more specifically the UNSC, in their chapter titled "Multilateralism in Action: The European Union's Engagement in the United Nations Security Council". The chapter offers an overview of EU-UN relations, and sets the stage for further inquiry in the following two chapters.

The authors describe the EU's growing presence in international affairs in parallel with the UN agenda. The 1992 Maastricht Treaty inaugurated the EU's presence in the UNSC and the UNGA alongside also institutionalising the Common Foreign and Security Policy (CFSP), closely connecting EU policy instruments to UN universal priorities like conflict prevention and management (Balutkar and Stepanian, this volume). The authors argue that, from this moment onwards, the EU strived to tie its foreign action to the UN agenda, also aiming at increasing its influence in this international organization and in the international stage overall.

After contextualising the EU's first important steps in the multilateral stage, Balutkar and Stepanian (this volume) delve into theoretical perspectives that can account for the EU's engagement in the UNSC. The EU does not hold a seat in the UNSC, as this is reserved for nation-states, but it is represented by its member states, making it the only supranational organisation that enjoys such privileges (Balutkar and Stepanian, this volume). Therefore, it is vital to understand how such engagement unveils in practice.

The EU's common position in foreign affairs should be coordinated by an effective and cooperative foreign policy that promotes the European integration process and EU identity. The EU has worked towards facilitating information sharing and coordination between its member states to ease the construction of a common stance in foreign affairs. Applying these principles to the UNSC means that the EU expects that its member states represented in this institution follow the EU's commitment to multilateralism and to upholding international peace and security. Besides France's permanent seat in the UNSC, which gives the EU a permanent representation in this setting, the EU is represented in the Western Europe and Others Group (WEOG) and the Eastern European Group (EEG). The EU employs formal and informal mechanisms to leverage its action. An example of such principles applied to a practical situation is the EU's continuous support to UN peacekeeping and development endeavours and the EU's coordinator role in UN Resolutions (Balutkar and Stepanian, this volume).

Discussing the EU's engagement in the UNSC brings to the table the departure of the UK from the EU. This topic has significant importance as, with Brexit, the EU lost one of its dual representatives in the permanent seat of the UNSC. More than discussing the implications for the UK, the authors focus on the ramifications of Brexit for the EU's defence of multilateralism and international peace and security. It is asserted that the EU not only inevitably loses power in the UNSC owing to Brexit, as it lost a member state that had veto power in this setting, but also the UK's material capabilities in terms of peace and security. Yet, Brexit was also a wake-up call to EU decision-makers, and the EU's High Representative at the time, Federica Mogherini, assured that "(...) the need of the hour is a shared vision and common action" (Balutkar and Stepanian, this volume). The authors take this argument a step further and contend that Brexit has led the EU to call for UNSC reform in order to reaffirm its presence on the global stage and its relevance for upholding multilateralism, peace, and security. This is not a novel topic in the UNSC—its membership has not changed since 1965, which has led to various calls for change, as its current composition is said to ineffectively and inadequately reflect world power balances.

The chapter makes it apparent that the EU and its member states have great aspirations within the multilateral system. Their commitment to global peace, security, and stability is clearly reflected in their efforts to coordinate a common position. How this is done in practice is further studied in Chapter 9 by van Schijndel and Jansen. The EU's continued will to participate in and strengthen its role within the UNSC through reform portrays the continued relevance of the institution, despite challenges faced.

The ninth contribution to the book, brought forward by van Schijndel and Jansen, is titled "EU Member States in the Elected 10: Voting and Co-Sponsorship in the UNSC". It discusses the sponsorship and voting behaviours of EU member states that hold non-permanent seats in the UNSC. This chapter unveils the degree to which the EU member state's position in the UNSC is influenced by virtue of them being a member of the EU. This assessment is very relevant as the EU strives to achieve a unison voice in Foreign Affairs and other related topics, while voting behaviour among EU member states is understudied (van Schijndel and Jansen, this volume).

The authors have selected three EU member states' tenure in the UNSC—Germany, Portugal, and Luxembourg—to analyse their sponsorship and voting behaviours on the topics of sanctions and peace operations. Such an analysis presumes a theoretical backing focused on not only coalition-building and voting behaviour in the UNSC—in line with other contributions in this book—but also on how regional groups can leave their mark during their two-year UNSC mandate.

The authors of this chapter recur to the literature on coalition formation and voting behaviour and present a similar assessment as made by Bueno et. al.: Member states often leave aside their national interests to support survival of the institution (in this case, the UN) and to uphold the principle of solidarity. In addition, coalitions in which P5 country or countries are represented yield a better chance of succeeding.

Yet, the the interesting approach presented by the authors resides in their discussion of small and medium state categories, a particularly important dichotomy when addressing the EU member states mandate in the UNSC. Drawing on the insights provided by Thorhallson (2012), Nortvedt (2019), and others, it is stated that small and medium countries might have more difficulties in accessing the UNSC non-permanent seats, but that does not make that mission impossible (van Schijndel and Jansen, this volume). More specifically, small states have at their disposal an array of instruments that can bolster their UNSC influence—diplomatic tactics, leadership skills, and, of course, coalition-building techniques (van Schijndel and Jansen, this volume). Countries can also leverage UNSC's institutional arrangements, a topic also examined by the contribution of Luers and Galy-Jammou-Préfontaine (this volume).

In their discussion of regional groupings in the UNSC, van Schijndel and Jansen depart from the interesting observation of Wouters and Pineau (2019): Do EU member states in the UNSC "(…) possess power without responsibility or responsibility without power"? (van Schijndel and Jansen, this volume). It is concluded that the penholder system is the element that separates non-permanent from permanent members in the UNSC, as the former are discouraged from drastically changing draft resolutions. Yet, this does not preclude non-permanent states from having something to offer in their tenure, and this usually takes the shape of regional expertise.

In their comparative analysis of sanctions, the authors assert that the three countries act differently. The authors argue that Germany's heavy reliance on external economic markets, as well as its "reluctant hegemony" position, made the country very hesitant to sponsor sanctions (van Schijndel and Jansen, this volume). In its two tenures, Germany sponsored eight sanctions-related Resolutions (out of 79 in total), proceeding with extreme caution (van Schijndel and Jansen, this volume). Portugal followed Germany's example and sponsored seven Resolutions against terrorist groups. Nevertheless, the authors underscore that Portugal was the only country to sponsor a Resolution on sanctions on Guinea-Bissau after a coup d'état in the country, a Resolution which passed unanimously. The justification behind Portugal's rationale—sponsoring a Resolution without any support from its allies—is that the country has vested interests in the country as it is a former colony now part of the Community of Portuguese Language Countries (CPLP). Portugal seems to want to be the spokesperson for the interests of its former colonies in the UNSC (van Schijndel and Jansen, this volume). In the case of Luxembourg, the authors claim that the country only sponsored sanctions-related Resolutions that its Western neighbours also sponsored, to avoid conflict with its partners (van Schijndel and Jansen, this volume). Even so, Luxembourg was the country of the three that most sponsored Resolutions on sanctions during its tenure (56 in total).

Regarding peacekeeping-related Resolutions, the authors foresee the three countries to be more proactive in terms of sponsorship endeavours, given that it is through these missions that the UNSC upholds international peace and security, and they are arguably less contentious issues than sanctions (van Schijndel and Jansen, this volume). During their mandates, Germany, Portugal, and Luxembourg have sponsored, respectively, 21, 8, and 30 Resolutions on peace operations. Nonetheless, there are several elements to take into consideration when interpreting these results. Germany has supported Resolutions that yielded vast international support and that extended peace operations already on the group, but it has not supported any Resolution that started a new peacekeeping mission (van Schijndel and Jansen, this volume). Portugal followed Germany's pattern of only sponsoring Resolutions that extended missions already existing, yet it has not hesitated in being the only sponsor, or the only one of a few sponsors, on Resolutions on CPLP member states (van Schijndel and Jansen, this volume). Luxembourg has also only supported Resolutions that enjoyed a broad international backing as it favours its image of an actor that strives for peace and security (van Schijndel and Jansen, this volume).

This analysis brings an important understanding of EU member states' tenures as non-permanent members of the UNSC. It shows that although these countries are part of the same regional organisation, this does not preclude them from acting in different ways according to their national interests. Even though the analysis has limitations in terms of the scope of countries studied, this can be a first step towards a more encompassing analysis of EU-UNSC relations.

The tenth and final chapter of this book is titled "NextGenerationEU and the UN Sustainable Development Goals". In this contribution, Levorato et al. follow the example of the two previous contributions and explore EU-UN relations. The authors provide a new research angle by analysing a mutual harmonisation of the environmental agendas of both IOs and how that impacts European fiscal and economic governance. This chapter attributes special attention to mechanisms put in place by the EU to support a post-COVID-19 recovery, which is the case of the NextGenerationEU (NGEU) project that includes the Recovery and Resilience Facility (RRF).

Both the EU and the UN attribute great importance to environmental considerations, placing them as a priority in a long list of key challenges to be addressed based on multilateralism. In particular, the authors argue that the United Nations' Sustainable Development Goals (SDGs)—notably climate change-related goals, but also those addressing healthcare, economic situations, gender equality, and others—were incorporated in the EU's response to the economic effects of the COVID-19 pandemic. In the face of this health crisis, the EU interlaced its response to it with the UNSDGs (Levorato et al., this volume). In this sense, financial support for EU member states to address economic effects of the pandemic was interlinked with compliance with the SDGs, aiming at "a greener, more digital, and more resilient future" (Levorato et al., this volume).

The authors put forward a multilayered theoretical framework to explain their original supposition, using insights from Neofunctionalism, Historical Institutionalism, and Global Governance approaches. Neofunctionalism's conceptualisation of spillover effects is notably useful to understand how the harmonisation of EU policies with the UN agenda induces further integration and transnational governance (Levorato et al., this volume). Moreover, as argued by the authors, "by embedding sustainability goals within economic and fiscal policy coordination and linking substantial funding mechanisms to SDG-aligned reforms, the EU has fostered closer cooperation and solidarity among member states" (Levorato et al., this volume). Historical Institutionalism's cruciality lies in the idea that "past institutional developments shape current and future policy paths" (Levorato et al., this volume). Applying this idea to the present case, it means that the establishment of the NGEU based on UN considerations affected novel patterns of EU fiscal and economic governance.

As this chapter focuses on EU fiscal and economic governance, it is important to provide more institutional contextualisation on the policies and mechanisms behind it. The EU has very specific institutional instruments that are crucial to EU-UN relations. While the contribution by Balutkar and Stepanian presents a more general picture of EU-UN synergies in regard to multilateralism, and van Schijndel and Jansen discuss voting and sponsorship patterns of EU member states in the UNSC, the chapter by Levorato et. al. specifically addresses the EU's framework on fiscal and economic governance in relation to the UN Agenda 2030. The authors discuss the European Semester (ES), initiated after the

European sovereign debt crisis, as a policy framework "that guides and monitors the economic policies of member states, ensuring convergence and stability within the EU" (Levorato et al., this volume). This framework also encompasses the bulk of the SDGs' integration in EU policies. However, as the chapter demonstrates, the NGEU does not represent the first time that the SDGs are incorporated in EU guidelines, as the UN Agenda 2030 was integrated by the EU in 2015 and, starting from 2017, efforts were made to "(...) include indicators and assessments related to the SDGs" and to "encourage member states to align their national policies and priorities with the SDGs' objectives" (Levorato et al., this volume).

Given this, what is the novelty of the SDG's incorporation in the NGEU? In line with the literature, the authors contend that the EU's response to COVID-19 through the NGEU represents an evolution in EU governance, "enhancing the coordination of economic, social, and environmental policies" (Levorato et al., this volume). The NGEU budget is composed of several elements, one of which is the RRF "wherein 20 percent of expenditure must be related to digital transitions and 37 percent to the climate transition" (Levorato et al., this volume). Thus, the proposed projects and strategies for the post-pandemic recovery must obey green, digital, and sustainable considerations. According to this chapter, this is only possible because of the flexible and generally effective nature of the ES (Levorato et al., this volume).

The positive outcomes brought by NGEU have led to calls to make this a permanent EU mechanism (Levorato et al., this volume). Yet, it is important to understand some of the challenges associated with this project, which could impact the achievement of the SDGs and with this, EU-UN relations. Some of the obstacles entail the EU's capacity to absorb the financial debt caused by these multifaceted policies, the implementation of these projects being reliant on EU member states' national governments, and a given lack of monitoring and evaluation mechanisms to track the progress of funded projects (Levorato et al., this volume). In addition, the EU and the UN have different scopes of action, as one is a regional and the other a universal organisation. Yet, as pointed out by the authors, this brings to the table, once again, the importance of multilateral action and rules-based governance and prioritisation of multilateral approaches. In the end, as concluded by the authors,"he incorporation of the SDGs into the ES provides an example of how collaboration on the regional and international levels can streamline efforts defined internationally, enhance their effectiveness and ensure a more coordinated (multilateral) approach to address pressing global challenges". (Levorato et al., this volume).

Overall, this book aims to offer several new insights into the operation, composition, and patterns of decision-making of the UNSC, while situating it into a broader multilateral context. Unequal power structures entrenched within the UNSC are visible in coalition formation and sponsorship patterns of the institution. However, increasing power rivalries are not signalling an end to multilateralism as a global governance approach. Instead, there is evidence of political will to continue multilateral cooperation from several UN member states, also those represented in the UNSC. While the EU demonstrates continued commitment to UN principles and policies, as this book shows, even emerging countries in the Global South, while opposing the inequalities of global order, are pushing for "reform from within". Their emerging voices may be especially important to the ongoing evolution of multilateral institutions.

Future research can further explore such aspects, potentially using some of the information and data provided in this volume. Much more research can be conducted on the UNSC, its embedding into the UN and patterns of global governance, and its ways of operation in the context of a gradually changing global order. While there are clear challenges to multilateralism and the institutional structures underpinning it, as this book demonstrates, they are still of central importance to current patterns of international organisation and global affairs.

References

Coalitions, Peace Missions, and UNSC Decision-Making (Gabriela M. G. Bueno, Madeleine O. Hosli, Alexandra Hall).

Coalition Formation and Co-Sponsorship in the United Nations Security Council (Tareq Helou, Madeleine O. Hosli, Rennan Pastich Loureiro).

Multilateral Cooperation and Great Power Rivalry in the UNSC (Peppi Heinikainen).

A Crystal Ball for Great Power Plays? Predicting Council Vetoes Through Machine Learning (Breanna Cross).

The Small and Regional Powers Claim for Agency: A Strategic Usage of Non-Traditional Threats Through Arria Meetings (Natalia Luers, Elise Galy-Jammou-Préfontaine).

Small and Emerging Powers in UNSC Decision-Making (Binghua Lu, Sahib Rasulov and Umang Sodhi).
Multilateralism in Action: The European Union's Engagement in the United Nations Security Council (Viraj Balutkar, Anri Stepanian).
EU Member States in the Elected 10: Voting and Co-Sponsorship in the UNSC (Koen van Schijndel, Barney Jansen).
NextGenerationEU and the UN Sustainable Development Goals (Beatrice Levorato, Guilherme Oliveira, Madeleine O. Hosli).
Arria Meetings (United Nations 2002).

Index

M. O. Hosli et al. (eds.), *Multilateralism and the United Nations Security Council*, https://doi.org/10.1007/978-3-031-85320-3

V

W

GPSR Compliance
The European Union's (EU) General Product Safety Regulation (GPSR) is a set of rules that requires consumer products to be safe and our obligations to ensure this.

If you have any concerns about our products, you can contact us on

ProductSafety@springernature.com

In case Publisher is established outside the EU, the EU authorized representative is:

Springer Nature Customer Service Center GmbH
Europaplatz 3
69115 Heidelberg, Germany

www.ingramcontent.com/pod-product-compliance
Lightning Source LLC
Chambersburg PA
CBHW071711240925
33102CB00004B/188
* 9 7 8 3 0 3 1 8 5 3 1 9 7 *